The **Rough Guide** to

Miami
& South Florida

written and researched by

Mark Ellwood

ROUGH
GUIDES

NEW YORK • LONDON • DELHI

www.roughguides.com

Contents

Introduction to

Miami & South Florida

**For a place built on holidays and hype, Miami lives up to,
and revels in, every cliché: the people on the beach are
indeed as tan and toned as they are on TV; the weather
seldom dips below balmy; the cafés are full of aspiring
models; and the nightlife is pumping and hedonistic.
A gorgeous, gaudy city, resting on the edge of the
Caribbean, Miami abounds with lazy palm trees, and
its wide, golden beaches are spacious enough to seem
empty even on a sweltering Sunday in high season. The
city's not all beaches and beautiful people, though; what
few visitors anticipate is the city's diversity, exhibited
in its glorious tropical gardens and excellent modern
art museums, as well as its vibrant Cuban and Haitian
immigrant communities.**

Founded little more than a century ago, Miami
has grown up fast from its beginning as a humble
trading post, losing its backwater feel with the
arrival of Henry Flagler's railroad in 1896. In the
1920s, local businessmen aggressively capitalized
on the new vogue for vacations in the sun, and
a hotel building boom in Miami Beach ensued,
producing some of the greatest Art Deco masterpieces in the US. Aside
from a brief period during World War II, Miami remained a prime vacation
destination until the early 1960s, when the first wave of Cuban refugees
arrived, fleeing a newly installed Fidel Castro and his Communist regime.
This set the stage for a further flood of immigrants from Cuba and other
Latin American countries; indeed, more than half of Miami–Dade County's

▶ Townhouse hotel roof deck

current population was born overseas. Because of this, to many further north, Miami is seen as barely part of the US, a place tropically lawless and suspiciously bilingual. Yet at the heart of the city is a glorious contradiction: to Venezuelans, Peruvians, Nicaraguans, and other new Latin arrivals, it's a quintessentially American town: ordered, safe, and filled with opportunity.

In some ways, both sides are right. In addition to dealing with its transformation into a multiethnic metropolis over the course of a few furious decades, Miami endured violent, headline-grabbing race riots, an alarming murder rate (at one point the nation's highest), and a reputation as a prominent port-of-entry for the drug trade. However, by the 1990s the situation was improving, thanks to a stronger local economy and a number of city revitalization projects. Miami's makeover as a hip, hot city was cemented when South Beach was "discovered" by fashion photographers, bringing the glitterati, both models and visitors, in their wake. Some of that glamorous sheen has already, perhaps inevitably, worn off, but so have some of the more damaging parts of the city's reputation – making for a constant and welcome defying of expectations for the casual visitor.

> The city has emerged from its shadowy vice-lined past as a modern jetset playground, something of a cross between Cannes and Manhattan

Indeed, Miami's economy has never been stronger, its most notable boom being in luxury real estate; high-rise condo towers, packed with multimillion-dollar apartments, appear seemingly overnight across the city's skyline. Today, the city has emerged from a shadowy vice-lined past as a modern jetset playground (something of a cross between Cannes and Manhattan). Miami is a city in transformation – and a thrilling place to visit.

Bikini cuisine

Miami has developed a home-grown cooking style, ideal for anyone planning to spend hours sunning and posing on the beach. Known variously as **Floribbean**, **Nuevo Cubano**, or **Nuevo Latino**, it first emerged in the mid-1990s via a group of adventurous local chefs who ditched some of the less diet-friendly elements of Latino cuisine – a fondness for deep frying, few (if any) green vegetables – while retaining many of its tasty staples, like avocado and guava. They then added fresher, less fatty ingredients, including exotic fruits and fresh fish, and spiced

every dish delicately, often using capsicum peppers, citrus marinades, or honey-cinnamon glazes. The mouthwatering results can be savored in some of Miami's more inventive restaurants; for reviews, see Chapter 11.

Not all South Florida's food is fancy and (virtually) fat free, however. Traditionalists should drive down to the Keys, where almost every restaurant serves a custom version of **Key Lime Pie** and **conch fritters**. Sadly, though, these days it's a misnomer to call either dish a local staple. Thanks to overfishing most of the conch is farmed in the Caribbean and flown in for cooking; and as for so-called key limes – which actually look like small, hard lemons – they're native to Mexico.

What to see

Radiating out from the mouth of the Miami River and stretched along the sandbanks sheltering Biscayne Bay from the ocean, Miami is an enormous city. It's made up of two core areas, which are, technically, separate cities (although most of the amenities are shared): **mainland Miami** and the huge sandbar known as **Miami Beach**. In turn, each of these cities is made up of dozens of small, dense districts grouped together. While the central neighborhoods are just minutes' drive from each other, Greater Miami is a large city that's only getting larger: in fact, Metro-Dade County is the size of Rhode Island, and the sprawling suburbs in its western district are some of the fastest-growing in America.

Undeniably, the most famous of the city's dozens of districts is **South Beach**, where its trademark Art Deco buildings were erected in the Twenties and Thirties, and whose decadent lifestyle made headlines (and much money) for the city during the 1990s. This is still likely to be the place where you spend the most time: a huge number of the city's hotels are grouped together here, and the strip of Deco edifices along Ocean Drive is iconic Miami. The rest of **Miami Beach** is often ignored. So-called Middle Beach is condemned for its forest of monolithic condo buildings, though the *Fontainebleau Hilton* and adjoining *Edec Roc* hotel are emblematic examples of Miami's other signature style, known as MiMo. There are plenty more mid-century masterpieces in North Beach and Normandy Isle. Bal Harbour's synonymous with luxury shopping, thanks to its legendary mall, while the sandbar's northernmost reaches offer some of the best and widest beaches in the city, especially around Haulover Park and Sunny Isles Beach.

Across Biscayne Bay from Miami Beach lies the city's mainland hub. Thoroughly Latin **Downtown** bustles with Spanish-speaking businesses and small Cuban lunch counters; most major sights can be found along its central artery, Flagler Street, or Brickell Avenue, its gleaming new canyon of skyscrapers, and home to numerous international banks. Miami's surge of

The Cuban connection

Southern Florida's links to **Cuba** have always been strong – after all, Key West is closer to Havana than to the continental United States. Once Fidel Castro came to power in the early 1960s, Cubans began arriving en masse. Thousands of refugees, mostly middle-class professionals, fled their suddenly Communist homeland and settled in Miami, transforming the old Jewish neighborhood of Riverside into a Spanish-speaking enclave locals nicknamed **Little Havana** (see p.96). They planned to stay until Castro was ousted – forty years on, they're still here.

In fact, expat Cubans have become the most powerful minority in the city: it's almost impossible to win political office in Miami without ground-level support from the Cuban community (the current mayor was elected in the afterglow of his defending refugee Elián González's right to remain in America). Yet for the casual visitor, the refugees' legacy is much less politically charged: rather, there's a Latin flavor to almost every area in Miami, from the dozens of streetside cafés Downtown selling cheap thimblefuls of the sticky espresso known as **cafecito** to the raucous nightclubs in Little Havana and even the **mojitos** that pop up on swanky bar menus across South Beach.

▼ Ocean Drive, South Beach

urban renewal is most evident in the area just north of Downtown **along the Biscayne Corridor**. After several decades of decay, this district's buzzing: a massive Performing Arts Center is soon to open and bring Miami's cultural heart to the area, while its Design District and Wynwood are artsy enclaves, filled with showrooms, galleries, and witty modern architecture. The one largely unchanged area here is Little Haiti; despite its deep history and lively streetlife, it makes few concessions to outsiders.

Southwest of Downtown, just across the Miami River, lies **Little Havana**, a residential neighborhood of sherbert-colored houses that became the first home of Cuban refugees as they arrived in America. It's still the immigrant heart of the city, though with an increasingly diverse Latin population. Southeast from here, along the soaring Rickenbacker Causeway, lie almost-deserted **Virginia Key** and swanky **Key Biscayne**, the tony island on the bay whose smart central village is sandwiched between Miami's two best parks.

On the city's southern extreme stands **Coconut Grove**, the earliest settlement in the area and an artsier, more bohemian place than much of Miami. Though not the counterculture hotbed it once was, it is home to two of the city's most intriguing sights – the Barnacle and Villa Vizcaya. West from here, the city of **Coral Gables** – which technically isn't Miami at all, but yet another separate city – is a Spanish-inspired confection of Mediterranean Revival mansions and grand civic amenities. The brainchild of one man, George Merrick, it's an eccentric exercise in ego and enthusiasm. To the

> After the bustle of Miami, the Everglades' silent, sawgrass plains and vast emptiness are a refreshing surprise

south, as the suburb of **South Miami** blends with the outskirts of neighboring Homestead, there are several major gardens and animal parks amid the vast stretches of farmland.

8

Miami's Deco look

Miami Beach has the weather to thank for its signature **Art Deco** look – not the sun, though, but the destructive power of Florida's hurricanes. Just as the resort's popularity was peaking in the 1920s, a devastating storm leveled most of its hotels. The owners turned to the quickest and cheapest contemporary style to replace them: Art Deco.

The boxlike buildings, made from poured concrete, were a smart and stylish solution: architects added touches like reliefs of flamingos or tropical palms as a nod to Miami's climate. However, after World War II, both South Beach and its buildings fell out of fashion; the old hotels became low-rent rooming houses, while paint on apartment blocks blistered in the sun and concrete eroded from the sea air. By the 1970s, in an attempt to revive the area's future, plans were made to start demolishing these outmoded buildings, until conservationists protested and wangled to have the entire area landmarked. Such was their success that today, renovating a Deco hotel is a complex process, and there are strict guidelines as to what changes can be made to all exteriors. For more on Art Deco and its various styles, see box, p.64.

While Miami and its neighborhoods hold enough to engage a variety of itineraries, the city is also an ideal base for exploring the rest of South Florida. **Everglades National Park** fills up most of the rest of the state's southern tip: after the bustle of Miami, its silent, sawgrass plains and vast emptiness are a refreshing surprise. Come here to birdwatch, hike, or kayak through the backwaters – and expect to see plenty of alligators. Carry on past the Everglades to reach the strip of islands known as the **Florida Keys**, which trail like a broken necklace through the Caribbean. A single road threads through this isolated, rebellious backwater to reach **Key West**, the one-time counterculture hub whose historic buildings have seen rapid gentrification in recent years.

Much like Key West, **Fort Lauderdale**, Miami's northern neighbor, is rapidly upgrading. Just 40 minutes' drive from Downtown Miami, it has often been seen as a homely younger sister, the place where retirees lived year-round, their lives punctuated by raucous spring breakers. Today, as new residents have moved into its mid-century homes, it seems set to become a less attitude-packed answer to South Beach.

▼ Beachgoers

When to go

Miami's weather is tropically warm throughout the year: its tender winters have brought snowbirds down from the Northeast for more than a hundred years. **High season** is January through March, when the weather hovers around 80°F (27°C), while rainfall and humidity are low; it's also when crowd-pulling events like the Winter Music Conference and the Miami Film Festival are held.

Low season, June through August, is often unbearably hot, plus stiflingly humid, and hotel rates not surprisingly hit rock-bottom: expect sun most mornings, and tropical downpours come afternoon – you'll need to be an early riser if you want to work on your tan. The **hurricane season** is traditionally May through October, with the occasional flurry in November. Don't fret, though: warning systems are now sophisticated enough that even should a heavy storm roll in while you're there, you'll be alerted in ample time. The best times to visit may well be the **shoulder seasons** – April, May, October, and November; the weather's good, if not flawless, while the hotel bargains are still plentiful.

Miami climate

	Jan	Feb	Mar	Apr	May	Jun	Jul	Aug	Sep	Oct	Nov	Dec
Average daily temperature												
max (°F)	75	76	79	82	85	88	89	89	88	84	80	77
max (°C)	24	24	26	28	30	31	32	32	31	30	27	24
min (°F)	59	60	64	68	72	75	76	77	76	72	67	61
min (°C)	15	15	18	19	23	24	25	25	24	23	17	15
Average rainfall												
inches	2.0	2.1	2.4	2.8	6.2	9.3	5.7	7.6	7.6	5.6	2.7	1.8
mm	51	53	61	72	158	237	145	192	194	143	67	46

things not to miss

It's not possible to see everything that Miami and South Florida have to offer in one trip – and we don't suggest you try. What follows is a selective and subjective taste of the area's highlights, from its remarkable beaches and playful architecture to inventive food and vibrant nightlife. They're arranged in five color-coded categories to help you find the very best things to see, do, and experience. All entries have a page reference to take you straight into the text, where you can find out more.

01 **Villa Vizcaya** Page **120** • Opulent, excessive, and unmissable, Vizcaya is Coconut Grove's early wealth made manifest in one crazy, Baroque palace.

02 Sky Bar at the Shore Club Page **155** • Dress to impress and order a bottle if you want to lounge in a cabana at this beachfront bar, packed with see-and-be scenesters every night.

04 Bahama Village Page **245** • The one section of Key West's Old Town still resolutely ramshackle and largely untouched by tourist dollars, it gives a vivid impression of the town's past.

06 Coral Castle Page **204** • Hands down, the oddest attraction in South Florida, this coral-rock playland was built by an oddball Latvian immigrant as a tribute to his lost love.

03 The Living Room Building Page **89** • A new landmark for the city, this Design District project presents both an irresistible photo opportunity and a surreal visual farce.

05 Miami Art Museum Page **51** • Visit this outstanding Downtown modern collection, which showcases top-tier conceptual art that's intelligently but accessibly curated.

07 Seven AM on South Beach Page **62** • One of the few times you'll be able to enjoy the world-renowned beach in relative solitude is during the early-morning crystal-white light.

09 **The Bacardi Building**
Page **88** • A landmark along the Biscayne Corridor, the US headquarters of the rum company is celebrated for its astonishing exterior, covered in blue and white mosaics.

08 **Yambo Café** Page **148** • Take a jaunt to Nicaragua at *Yambo*, where the food is cheap and superb, little English is spoken, and the vibe is unmistakably Central American.

10 **Key Lime Pie and conch fritters** Page **248** • Two local staples of the Florida Keys that every visitor should try: a slice of the lemon-meringue-like Key Lime Pie and a handful of those chewy, deep-fried nuggets.

11 **The Holocaust Memorial** Page **68** • This masterful, sobering memorial is located in South Beach, home to one of the heaviest concentrations of Holocaust survivors in the US.

13 No Name Pub Page **236** • Almost impossible to find without directions, this bar's a legend for its bizarre decor – thousands of dollar bills are stapled to every surface.

12 Casa Casuarina Page **63** • Better known as the Versace mansion, this macabre landmark is now an ultra-exclusive members club.

14 The Deering Estate Page **201** • For some rare peace and nature only a short drive from the city, this is a serene counterpoint to the flashy opulence of its sibling estate at Vizcaya.

15 Stiltsville Page **126** • This village of seven ramshackle huts standing in the mudflats off Key Biscayne is charged with precious modern Miami history.

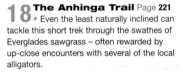

16 **The beaches of Fort Lauderdale** Page **212** • The sands here are just as wide, clean, and golden as their Miami counterparts, and the casual, laid-back vibe's a welcome relief to the catwalk-conscious scene further south.

18 **The Anhinga Trail** Page **221** • Even the least naturally inclined can tackle this short trek through the swathes of Everglades sawgrass – often rewarded by up-close encounters with several of the local alligators.

17 **The Venetian Pool** Page **109** • Coral Gables' civic amenities don't come better than this – a quarry turned lagoon that's both loungeworthy and historic.

20 **Cafecito at David's Café** Page **138** • Savor the thimblefuls of Cuban coffee that keep Miami going – there's nowhere better for a quick shot than at *David's* on the beach.

19 **Stranahan House** Page **212** • Pioneer life, Fort Lauderdale–style: this waterfront house is one of the most vivid evocations of early European settlement in South Florida.

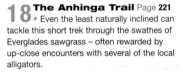

21 The Fontainebleau Hilton Page **78** • The Miami Modern gem that kickstarted the development of Central Miami Beach is still a swoopingly beautiful building.

23 Rascal House Page **146** • A throwback to Sunny Isles Beach's heyday in the 1950s – and that includes much of the diner's staff, too.

22 Fort Jefferson Page **247** • Stand at the edge of the world in the thrillingly isolated Dry Tortuga islands, the last of the Florida Keys.

24 The Rubell Collection Page **91** • Art mavens, hoteliers, and real estate developers, the Rubells have enough money and taste to buy the best contemporary art around; their enormous collection is ably displayed in this huge space in Wynwood.

25 Lincoln Road Page **67** • Whether you're posing, blading, or window-shopping, the best place to spend an afternoon is this pedestrianized outdoor mall in South Beach. Grab a coffee or a cocktail at one of the dozens of sidewalk cafés.

Basics

Basics

Getting there

Unless you are coming from close by in Florida, the quickest and easiest way of getting to Miami is to fly. Airfares to Miami and South Florida invariably depend on the **season**: international rates are often highest June through August – ironically, when Miami's weather is often at its most unpredictable – while domestic fares peak during the warm winter months when the weather's at its best. Both domestic and international travelers will find that prices drop during the "shoulder" seasons – March–May, September–October – which makes it an appealing time to visit. Remember, too, that fares during the Christmas and New Year's period will always be at a premium, and that flying on weekends ordinarily adds $40–50 to the fare for each leg; price ranges quoted below assume midweek travel.

You can often cut costs by going through a **specialist flight agent** – either a consolidator, who buys up blocks of tickets from the airlines and sells them at a discount, or a **discount agent**, who in addition to dealing with discounted flights may also offer special student and youth fares and a range of other travel-related services such as travel insurance, rail passes, car rentals, tours, and the like. Some agents specialize in **charter flights**, which may be cheaper than anything available on a scheduled flight, but again departure dates are fixed and withdrawal penalties are high. You may find it cheaper to pick up a bargain **package deal** (especially a fly-drive with inclusive car hire) from one of the tour operators listed below. A further possibility is to see if you can arrange a courier flight, although you'll need to have a flexible schedule, and preferably to be traveling alone with very little luggage. In return for shepherding a parcel through customs, you can expect to get a deeply discounted ticket. You'll probably also be restricted in the duration of your stay.

Booking flights online

Many airlines and discount travel websites offer you the opportunity to book your tickets online, cutting out the costs of agents and middlemen. Good deals can often be found through discount or auction sites, as well as through the airlines' own websites.

Online booking agents

ⓦ **www.cheapflights.co.uk** (in UK & Ireland), ⓦ **www.cheapflights.com** (in US), ⓦ **www.cheapflights.ca** (in Canada), ⓦ **www.cheapflights.com.au** (in Australia). Flight deals, travel agents, plus links to other travel sites.

ⓦ **www.cheaptickets.com** Discount flight specialists (US only). Also at ☏ 1-888/922-8849.

ⓦ **www.expedia.co.uk** (in UK), ⓦ **www.expedia.com** (in US), ⓦ **www.expedia.ca** (in Canada). Discount airfares, all-airline search engine, and daily deals.

ⓦ **www.flyaow.com** "Airlines of the Web" – online air travel info and reservations.

ⓦ **www.gaytravel.com** US gay travel agent, offering accommodation, cruises, tours, and more. Also at ☏ 1-800/GAY-TRAVEL.

ⓦ **www.hotwire.com** Bookings from the US only. Last-minute savings of up to forty percent on regular published fares; no refunds, transfers, or changes allowed.

ⓦ **www.lastminute.com** (in UK), ⓦ **www.lastminute.com.au** (in Australia), ⓦ **www.lastminute.co.nz** (in New Zealand), ⓦ **www.site59.com** (in US). Good last-minute holiday package and flight-only deals.

ⓦ **www.orbitz.com** Comprehensive Web travel source, with the usual flight, car hire, and hotel deals but also great follow-up customer service.

ⓦ **www.priceline.co.uk** (in UK), ⓦ **www.priceline.com** (in US). Name-your-own-price website that has deals at around forty percent off standard fares. Often the cheapest option.

ⓦ **www.travelocity.co.uk** (in UK), ⓦ **www.travelocity.com** (in US), ⓦ **www.travelocity.ca** (in Canada), ⓦ **www.zuji.com.au** (in Australia).

Destination guides, hot fares, and great deals for car rental, accommodation, and lodging.

ⓦ **www.travelshop.com.au** Australian site offering discounted flights, packages, insurance, and online bookings. Also at ☏ 1800/108 108.

ⓦ **travel.yahoo.com** Incorporates some Rough Guides material in its coverage of destination countries and cities across the world.

ⓦ **www.travelzoo.com** Great resource for news on the latest airline sales, cruise discounts, and hotel deals. Links bring you directly to the carrier's site.

From elsewhere in North America

From most places in North America, **flying** is the most convenient way to reach Miami and South Florida. It is, however, also very accessible by bus, train, or car.

By air

Most domestic flights touch down at **Miami International Airport** (MIA): carriers offering the most frequent services include American (Miami is its hub for frequent flights to the Caribbean), Delta, and Continental. Increasingly, more travelers are opting to fly to **Fort Lauderdale International Airport** (FLL), 40 minutes north of Miami: if you join them, expect bargain fares – most of the budget carriers like JetBlue, Song, and Spirit touch down here.

The usual off-season price range for flights **from the Northeast and Mid-Atlantic** (New York, Boston, and Washington, DC) is $200 although New York is often much cheaper, since the NY–Miami route is highly competitive; as budget carriers jostle for a share in this lucrative market, rates can drop to astonishingly low levels – even $50 each way. **From the West Coast**, expect non-stop fares to start at $300 while you'll pay from $200 or so to fly in from Chicago.

If you're traveling **from Canada**, Air Canada has direct flights to Miami from Toronto and Montréal (around Can$350 round-trip).

Airlines

Air Canada ☏ 1-888/247-2262, ⓦ www .aircanada.com.
Air Tran ☏ 1-800/247-8726 or 770/994-8258, ⓦ www.airtran.com.
American Airlines ☏ 1-800/433-7300, ⓦ www .aa.com.

Continental Airlines Domestic ☏ 1-800/523-FARE, International ☏ 1-800/231-0856, ⓦ www .continental.com.
Delta Domestic ☏ 1-800/221-1212, International ☏ 1-800/241-4141, ⓦ www.delta.com.
JetBlue ☏ 1-800/JET-BLUE, ⓦ www.jetblue.com.
Northwest/KLM Domestic ☏ 1-800/225-2525, International ☏ 1-800/447-4747, ⓦ www.nwa.com, ⓦ www.klm.com
Southwest Airlines ☏ 1-800/435-9792, ⓦ www .southwest.com.
United Airlines Domestic ☏ 1-800/241-6522, International ☏ 1-800/538-2929, ⓦ www.united .com.
US Airways Domestic ☏ 1-800/428-4322, International ☏ 1-800/622-1015, ⓦ www.usair.com.

Discount travel agents

Airtech ☏ 212/219-7000, ⓦ www.airtech.com. Standby seat broker; also deals in consolidator fares.
Flightcentre US ☏ 1-866/WORLD-51, ⓦ www .flightcentre.us, Canada ☏ 1-888/WORLD-55, ⓦ www.flightcentre.ca. Rock-bottom fares worldwide.
STA Travel US ☏ 1-800/329-9537, Canada ☏ 1-888/427-5639, ⓦ www.statravel.com. Worldwide specialists in independent travel; also student IDs, travel insurance, tours, packages, and more.
Worldtek Travel ☏ 1-800/243-1723, ⓦ www .worldtek.com. Discount travel agency for worldwide travel.

By train

The Amtrak **trains** (☏ 1-800/USA-RAIL, ⓦ www.amtrak.com) along the Eastern corridor (of which Miami is the southern hub) are arguably the best in the country – but that's not saying much. Even with Amtrak's much vaunted service improvements, traveling by train's a more picturesque than punctual option, and is best for either flying phobics or anyone looking for a leisurely alternative.

From New York, the **Silver Meteor** and **Silver Star** reach Miami via Orlando (daily service); the other option is the less-direct Palmetto, which zigzags across Florida, taking in Jacksonville and Tampa before finally hitting Miami. Expect to pay between $150 and $400 for a round-trip and for the journey to take anything between 26 and 29 hours, depending on highly likely delays. Check for offers on the Amtrak website – which also provides a booking service – or by phone. If Miami is part of a longer journey, Amtrak and VIA (Canada's national rail company ⓦwww.viarail.ca) offer a **North America Rail Pass**. It allows thirty days unlimited travel for $695 or Can$899 high season (June–mid-Oct) and $495/Can$637 low season (mid-Oct–May); there's a ten percent discount for seniors and students.

By bus

Bus is usually the cheapest option, but it takes forever and you'll have to try and sleep in those seats – think of it as an endurance test. **Greyhound** (☎1-800/231-2222, ⓦwww.greyhound.com) prices for a 7-day advance purchase on round-trip tickets should hover around $125 from New York (27 hours), $140 from Boston (1 1/2 days), $140 from Chicago (1 1/2 days), $150 from Los Angeles (2 1/2 days).

Greyhound Discover Passes buy unlimited travel on the entire Greyhound network, but are only really worthwhile for travelers including Miami as part of a longer itinerary, or for those coming from the West Coast. The **Domestic Ameripass**, for example, is valid across the entire country for periods of between seven days ($239) and sixty days ($669); there's a fifty percent discount for accompanying children, ten percent off for seniors and students. Passes for overseas visitors must be bought before leaving home: most travel agents can oblige, as can specialist agents like STA and Trailfinders.

By car

Florida **car rental** rates vary wildly, though in general you'll get better deals over the weekend than during the week. You can often realize significant savings by booking car rental in advance with a major firm that has representation in Miami or Fort Lauderdale – most agencies in the city have branches at both airports as well as Downtown Miami. When booking be sure to get free unlimited mileage and be aware that rates can go up by as much as $200 if you want to pick up the car in one location and leave it at another, although in South Florida there are often deals where this charge isn't applied. If you choose not to pay until you arrive, take a written confirmation of the price with you. Always read the small print carefully for

details on Collision Damage Waiver (sometimes called Liability Damage Waiver), a form of **insurance** that often isn't included in the initial rental charge but is well worth having. This specifically covers the car you are driving (you are in any case insured for damage to other vehicles). At $10–15 a day, the waiver can add substantially to the total rental cost, but without it you're liable to every scratch to the car, even those that aren't your fault. Then again, don't be suckered into insurance you already have – call your credit card company to see if they offer free insurance if you use your card to pay. If you are under 25 be prepared for hefty surcharges on top of the usual rates. The best loophole through such a problem is usually to arrange and pay for your rental back home and collect the car with a prepaid voucher: this means you should avoid underage-driver premiums. Check with the various companies for up-to-date information. As for **driving times**, expect to take approx. 20 hours to reach Miami from Chicago or New York; from LA, it's more like 45 hours behind the wheel.

Also worth considering are **fly-drive deals**, which give cut-rate (and sometimes free) car rental when buying your air ticket. They usually work out cheaper than renting on the spot and are especially good value if you intend to do a lot of driving.

Car rental agencies

Alamo US ☎1-800/522-9696, ⓦwww.alamo.com.
Avis US ☎1-800/331-1084, Canada ☎1-800/272-5871, ⓦwww.avis.com.
Budget US ☎1-800/527-0700, ⓦwww.budgetrentacar.com.
Dollar US ☎1-800/800-4000, ⓦwww.dollar.com.
Enterprise Rent-a-Car US ☎1-800/325-8007, ⓦwww.enterprise.com.
Hertz US ☎1-800/654-3001, Canada ☎1-800/263-0600, ⓦwww.hertz.com.
National ☎1-800/227-7368, ⓦwww.nationalcar.com.
Thrifty ☎1-800/367-2277, ⓦwww.thrifty.com.

Motoring organizations

In North America

American Automobile Association (AAA) Each state has its own club – check the phone book

for local address and phone number (or call ☎1-800/222-4357, ⊛www.aaa.com).
Canadian Automobile Association (CAA)
☎613/247-0117, ⊛www.caa.com. Each region has its own club – check the phone book for local address and phone number.

In the UK and Ireland

RAC UK ☎0800/550 055, ⊛www.rac.co.uk.
AA UK ☎0800/444 500, ⊛www.theaa.co.uk.
AA Travel Dublin ☎01/617 9988, ⊛www
.aaireland.ie.

In Australia and New Zealand

Australian Automobile Association
☎02/6247 7311.
New Zealand Automobile Association
☎09/377 4660.

Flights from the UK and Ireland

There are daily **nonstop flights** to Miami **from London Heathrow** with British Airways and Virgin Atlantic, plus regular service by Continental and American airlines. These flights take about 9 1/2 hours, though following winds ensure return flights are always an hour or so shorter than outward journeys. Flights out usually leave Britain mid-morning, while flights back from the US tend to arrive in Britain early in the morning. Most other airlines serving Miami, like Air France and KLM, fly from London via their respective European or American hubs. These flights take an extra two to five hours each way, depending on how long you have to wait for the connection.

Return **fares** to Miami run around £700 between June and August and at Christmas, though £500 is the more usual range. Prices in winter often fall to around £350. More flexible tickets to Miami, requiring less advance booking time or allowing changes or refunds, cost from £100 more whenever and from whomever you buy.

Aer Lingus offers direct service **from Dublin** to New York and Boston (around €400 off-peak round-trip), with connecting service on to Florida.

Airlines

Aer Lingus UK ☎0845/973 7747, Republic of Ireland ☎0818/365 000, ⊛www.aerlingus.ie.

Air France UK ☎0845/084 5111,
Republic of Ireland ☎01/605 0383, ⊛www
.airfrance.co.uk.
American Airlines UK ☎0845/778 9789 or 020/8572 5555, Republic of Ireland ☎01/602 0550, ⊛www.aa.com.
British Airways UK ☎0845/773 3377, Republic of Ireland ☎1800/626 747, ⊛www.britishairways
.com.
British Midland UK ☎0870/607 0555, Republic of Ireland ☎01/407 3036, ⊛www.flybmi.com.
Canadian Airlines UK ☎0870/5247 226, Republic of Ireland ☎01/679 3958, ⊛www
.cdnair.ca.
Continental UK ☎0800/776 464, Republic of Ireland ☎1890/925 252, ⊛www.flycontinental
.com.
Delta UK ☎0800/414 767, Republic of Ireland ☎01/407 3165, ⊛www.delta.com.
KLM UK ☎0870/507 4074, ⊛www.klmuk.com.
United Airlines UK ☎0845/8444 777, ⊛www
.ual.com.
Virgin Atlantic Airways UK ☎01293/747 747, ⊛www.virgin-atlantic.com.

Discount travel and flight agents

In Britain

Bridge the World UK ☎020/7911 0900, ⊛www
.bridgetheworld.com. Specializing in round-the-world tickets, with good deals aimed at the backpacker market.
Co-op Travel Care Belfast ☎028/9047 1717, ⊛www.travelcareonline.com. Flights and holidays around the world.
Destination Group UK ☎020/7400 7045, ⊛www.destination-group.com. Good discount airfares, as well as Far East and USA inclusive packages.
Flightbookers UK ☎0870/010 7000, ⊛www
.ebookers.com. Low fares on an extensive selection of scheduled flights.
North South Travel UK ☎&℗01245/608 291, ⊛www.northsouthtravel.co.uk. Friendly, competitive travel agency, offering discounted fares worldwide – profits are used to support projects in the developing world, especially the promotion of sustainable tourism.
Premier Travel Derry ☎028/7126 3333, ⊛www
.premiertravel.uk.com. Discount flight specialists.
Quest Travel UK ☎0870/442 2699 or 020/8547 3322, ⊛www.questtravel.com. Specialists in round-the-world discount fares.
STA Travel UK ☎0870/1600 599, ⊛www
.statravel.co.uk. Worldwide specialists in low-cost

flights and tours for students and under-26s, though other customers welcome.

Trailfinders UK ☎020/7628 7628, ⓦwww .trailfinders.com. One of the best-informed and most efficient agents for independent travelers; produce a very useful quarterly magazine worth scrutinizing for round-the-world routes.

Travel Bag UK ☎0870/900 1350, ⓦwww .travelbag.co.uk. Discount flights to USA; official Qantas agent.

Travel Cuts UK ☎020/7255 2082, ⓦwww .travelcuts.co.uk. Canadian company specializing in budget, student, and youth travel and round-the-world tickets. Amtrak passes available.

In Ireland

Apex Travel Dublin ☎01/241 8000, ⓦwww .apextravel.ie. Specialists in flights to US.

CIE Tours International Dublin ☎01/703 1888, ⓦwww.cietours.ie. General flight and tour agent.

Joe Walsh Tours Dublin ☎01/676 0991, ⓦwww .joewalshtours.ie. General budget fares agent.

Lee Travel Cork ☎021/277 111, ⓦwww.leetravel .ie. Flights and holidays worldwide.

Trailfinders Dublin ☎01/677 7888, ⓦwww .trailfinders.ie. One of the best-informed and most efficient agents for independent travelers; produce a very useful quarterly magazine worth scrutinizing for round-the-world routes.

usit NOW Dublin ☎01/602 1600, ⓦwww.usitnow .ie. Student and youth specialists for flights and trains.

Tour operators

Airtours UK ☎0870/238 7788, ⓦwww .uk.mytravel.com. Large tour company offering trips worldwide.

American Adventures UK ☎01892/512 700, ⓦwww.americanadventures.com. Small group camping adventure trips throughout the US and Canada, including in and around Miami.

British Airways Holidays ☎0870/242 4245, ⓦwww.baholidays.co.uk. Using British Airways and other quality international airlines, offers an exhaustive range of package and tailor-made holidays around the world.

Thomas Cook UK ☎0870/5666 222, ⓦwww .thomascook.co.uk. Long-established one-stop 24-hour travel agency for package holidays or scheduled flights, with bureau de change issuing Thomas Cook travelers' checks, travel insurance, and car rental.

Virgin Holidays ⓦwww.virginholidays.co.uk. Flights, fly-drive deals, tailor-mades, and packages to almost anywhere in and around Miami, including the Florida Keys.

Flights from Australia and New Zealand

Because of the enormous distance, there are no direct flights to Miami **from Australia and New Zealand**. Travelers should fly to Los Angeles or San Francisco – the main points of entry to the US – and make their way from there. Of the airlines, United Airlines, Air New Zealand, and Qantas are the best at arranging trouble-free connecting service through Miami.

A basic round-trip economy class ticket on these airlines out of Sydney or Melbourne will cost around Aus$1700 during low season and Aus$2800 high season, while from Auckland (to Los Angeles) budget NZ$2300/3000, with an additional NZ$100 for departures from Christchurch or Wellington. Once in the US, it will cost you around US$350 to connect to Miami – ask about various coupon deals that are often available with your main ticket.

If you intend to visit Miami as part of a world trip, a **round-the-world** (RTW) ticket offers the greatest flexibility. In recent years, many of the major international airlines have allied themselves with one of two globe-spanning networks: the "Star Alliance" includes Air New Zealand, United, Lufthansa, Thai, SAS, Varig, and Air Canada, while "One World" combines British Airways, Qantas, American Airlines, AerLingus, Cathay Pacific, Iberia, and LANChile. Both networks offer RTW deals with three stopovers in each continental sector you visit, with the option of adding additional sectors relatively cheaply. Fares depend on the number of sectors required, but start at around Aus$2200 (low season) for a US-Europe-Asia-and-home itinerary. If this is more flexibility than you need, you can save Aus$200–300 by going with an individual airline (in concert with code-sharing partners) and accepting fewer stops.

Air New Zealand Australia ☎13 24 76, ⓦwww .airnz.com.au, New Zealand ☎0800/737 000, ⓦwww.airnz.co.nz.

America West Airlines Australia ☎1300/364 757 or 02/9267 2138, New Zealand ☎0800/866 000, ⓦwww.americawest.com.

American Airlines Australia ☎1300/130 757, New Zealand ☎0800/887 997, ⓦwww.aa.com.

British Airways Australia ☎1300/767 177, New Zealand ☎0800/274 847 or 09/356 8690, ⓦwww .britishairways.com.

Continental Airlines Australia ☎1300/361 400, New Zealand ☎09/308 3350, ⓦwww.continental.com.

Delta Australia ☎02/9251 3211, New Zealand ☎09/379 3370, ⓦwww.delta.com.

Japan Airlines Australia ☎02/9272 1111, ⓦwww.au.jal.com/en, New Zealand ☎09/379 906, ⓦwww.nz.jal.com/en.

Korean Air Australia ☎02/9262 6000, New Zealand ☎09/914 2000, ⓦwww.koreanair.com.au

Lufthansa Australia ☎1300/655 727, New Zealand ☎0800/945 220, ⓦwww.lufthansa.com.

Qantas Australia ☎13 13 13, New Zealand ☎0800/808 767 or 09/357 8900, ⓦwww.qantas.com.

United Airlines Australia ☎13 17 77, ⓦwww.united.com.

Travel agents

Holiday Shoppe New Zealand ☎0800/808 480, ⓦwww.holidayshoppe.co.nz. Great deals on flights, hotels, and holidays.

STA Travel Australia ☎1300/733 035, New Zealand ☎0508/782 872, ⓦwww.statravel.com.

Specialists in low-cost flights and holiday deals. Good discounts for students and under-26s.

Trailfinders Australia ☎02/9247 7666, ⓦwww.trailfinders.com.au. One of the best-informed and most efficient agents for independent travelers; especially good airfare deals to Miami.

travel.com.au Australia ☎1300/130 482 or 02/9249 5444, ⓦwww.travel.com.au, New Zealand ☎0800/468 332, ⓦwww.travel.co.nz. Comprehensive online travel company, with discounted fares and packages to Miami.

Tour agents

Contiki Australia ☎02/9511 2200, New Zealand ☎09/309 8824, ⓦwww.contiki.com. Frenetic trips for 18-to-35-year-old party animals, including touristy Miami breaks.

USA Travel Australia ☎02/9250 9320, ⓦwww.usatravel.au. Good deals on flights, accommodation, city stays, car rental, and trip packages.

Viator ⓦwww.viator.com. Books piecemeal local tours and sightseeing trips within Miami.

Red tape and visas

Under the **Visa Waiver Scheme**, if you're a citizen of the UK, Ireland, Australia, New Zealand, or most Western European countries (check with your nearest US embassy or consulate) and visiting the United States for a period of less than ninety days, you only need an onward or return **ticket**, a full **passport**, and a **visa waiver form**. The latter (an I-94W) will be provided either by your travel agency or by the airline during check-in or on the plane, and must be presented to immigration on arrival. The same form covers entry across the land borders with Canada and Mexico.

For a brief excursion into the US, **Canadian citizens** do not necessarily need even a passport, just some form of ID, though for a longer trip you should carry a passport, and if you plan to stay for more than ninety days you need a visa, too. If you cross into the States by car, your vehicle is subject to spot searches by US Customs personnel.

Remember, too, that Canadians are legally barred from seeking gainful employment in the US.

Prospective visitors from other parts of the world not mentioned above require a valid passport and a non-immigrant visitor's visa for a maximum ninety-day stay. How you obtain a visa depends on what country

US embassies

For details of foreign embassies and consulates in Miami, see p.194, "Directory."

Australia Moonah Place, Yarralumba, Canberra, ACT 2600 ☏02/6214 5600, ⓦwww
.usembassy-australia.state.gov/embassy

Canada 490 Sussex Drive Ottawa ON K1P 5T1 ☏613/238-5335, ⓦwww
.usembassycanada.gov

Ireland 42 Elgin Road, Ballsbridge, Dublin 4 ☏01/668-7122, ⓦwww.usembassy.ie

New Zealand 29 Fitzherbert Terrace, Thorndon, Wellington ☏04/462-6000, ⓦwww
.usembassy.org.nz

UK 24 Grosvenor Square, London W1A 1AE ☏020/7499-9000, 24hr visa hotline
☏09068/200-290, ⓦwww.usembassy.org.uk

you're in and your status on application, so contact your nearest US embassy or consulate. Most travelers do not require inoculations to enter the US, though you may need **certificates of vaccination** if you're en route from cholera- or typhoid-infected areas in Asia or Africa – check with your doctor before you leave.

On arrival, the date stamped on your passport is the latest you're legally allowed to stay. Recently the INS has toughened its stance on anyone violating their visa status, so even overstaying by a few days can result in a protracted interrogation from officials. **Overstaying** may also cause you to be turned away next time you try to enter the US.

To get an extension before your time is up, apply at the nearest **US Immigration and Naturalization Service (INS)** office, whose address will be under the Federal Government Offices listings at the front of the phone book. In Miami, the office is at 7800 Biscayne Blvd, on the corner with the 79th Street Causeway (☏1-800/375-5283, ⓦwww.ins.gov). INS officials will assume that you're working in the US illegally, and it's up to you to convince them otherwise by providing evidence of ample finances. If you can, bring along an upstanding American citizen to vouch for you. You'll also have to explain why you didn't plan for the extra time initially.

Insurance

Even though EU health-care privileges apply in the US, residents of the UK would do well to take out an **insurance policy** before traveling to cover against theft, loss, illness, or injury. Before paying for a new policy, it's worth checking if you are already covered – some all-risks home insurance policies may cover your possessions when overseas, and many private medical schemes include cover when abroad. In Canada, provincial health plans usually provide partial cover for medical mishaps overseas, while holders of official student/teacher/youth cards in Canada and the US are entitled to meagre accident coverage and hospital in-patient benefits. Students will often find that their student health coverage extends during the vacations and for one term beyond the date of last enrolment.

After exhausting these possibilities, you might want to contact a specialist travel insurance company, or consider the travel insurance deal Rough Guides offers (see box below). A typical travel insurance policy usually provides cover for the loss of baggage, tickets, and – up to a certain limit – cash or checks, as well as cancellation or curtailment of your journey. Most of them exclude so-called dangerous sports unless an extra premium is paid: this can mean whitewater rafting and trekking, though probably not kayaking. Many policies can be chopped and changed to exclude coverage you don't need – for example, sickness and accident benefits can often be excluded or included at will. If you do take medical coverage, ascertain whether benefits will be paid as treatment proceeds or only after return home, and if there is a 24-hour medical emergency number. When securing baggage cover, make sure that the per-article limit – typically under £500 – will cover your most valuable possession. If you need to make a claim, you should keep receipts for medicines and medical treatment, and in the event you have anything stolen, you must obtain an official theft report from the police.

Rough Guides travel insurance

Rough Guides has teamed up with Columbus Direct to offer you travel insurance that can be tailored to suit your needs.

Readers can choose from many different travel insurance products, including a low-cost backpacker option for long stays; a short-break option for city getaways; a typical holiday package option; and many others. There are also annual multi-trip policies for those who travel regularly, with variable levels of cover available. Different sports and activities (such as trekking and skiing) can be covered if required on most policies.

Rough Guides travel insurance is available to the residents of 36 different countries with different language options to choose from via our website – ⓦwww .roughguidesinsurance.com – where you can also purchase the insurance.

Alternatively, UK residents should call ☎0800/083 9507; US citizens should call ☎1-800/749-4922; Australians should call ☎1300/669 999. All other nationalities should call ☎44 870 890 2843.

Health

Foreign travelers should be comforted that if you have a serious accident while you're in Miami, emergency services will get to you sooner and charge you later. For emergencies, dial toll-free ☏911 from any phone. If you have medical or dental problems that don't require an ambulance, most hospitals will have a walk-in emergency room: for your nearest hospital, check with your hotel or dial information at ☏411. The same applies for dental work.

Should you need to see a doctor, lists can be found in the *Yellow Pages* under "Clinics" or "Physicians and Surgeons." Be aware that even consultations are costly, usually around $75–100 each visit, payable in advance. Keep receipts for any part of your medical treatment, including prescriptions, so that you can claim against your insurance once you're home.

For minor ailments, stop by a local **pharmacy**, many of which are open 24 hours. Foreign visitors should note that many medicines available over the counter at home – codeine-based painkillers, for one – are prescription-only in the US. Bring additional supplies if you're particularly brand loyal.

By far the most common tourist illness in Miami is sunburn: year-round the summer sun can be fierce, so plenty of protective **sunscreen** (SPF 15 and above) is a must. Surfers and swimmers should also watch for **strong currents and undertows** at some beaches: we've noted in the text where the water can be especially treacherous. Note that despite the media's frenzied circling around the story of man-eating sharks, it's still a blip on beach safety compared with sunburn and swimming difficulties.

Travelers from Europe, Canada, and Australia do not require inoculations to enter the USA.

Arrival

Most visitors arrive in Miami via one of the two major regional **airports**, though the city's equally well-connected by Greyhound **buses** and Amtrak **trains**. Major **US interstates** shuttle drivers directly into Downtown Miami – and a great view of the Miami skyline can be seen from the approaching elevated highways.

By air

All flights arrive at **Miami International Airport** (☏305/876-7000, ⓦwww.miami -airport.com) only six miles west of Downtown. While the airport's well-connected to the rest of the city, be aware that there's limited signage at the airport itself. Its hub-and-spoke design makes the airport especially tricky to navigate, so allow plenty of extra

time for check-in or if you're there to meet and greet.

Once on the ground, most people opt to take a **taxi**. The rates have been simplified and standardized into seven flat-fare zones, so there's no risk of overcharging: a one-way trip to Downtown costs $19, to South Beach $28, and Key Biscayne $36 (for full fare information, see ⓦwww.miami-airport .com/html/taxi_and_shuttle_servic). A smart alternative for solo travelers is the **Super-Shuttle** minivan, which will deliver you to any address in Miami for $10–16 (☎305/871-2000, ⊚www.supershuttle.com) – if you want to book a trip back to the airport, call 24 hours in advance.

For the patient or budget conscious, there are also **public bus** connections from the airport to the main transit hubs: #7 goes Downtown, a trip of 30 minutes or so ($1.25, exact fare required; every 15–30min Mon–Fri 5.20am–8.50pm, every 20–40min Sat & Sun 6.20am–7.30pm), or the "J" Metrobus that trundles out to the beaches ($1.25 plus a 25¢ surcharge to South Beach; every 20min weekdays 4.40am–11.40pm, service varies Sat 6am–1am, Sun 5am–11pm). Don't worry if you arrive late at night: there's an **Airport Owl shuttle** that runs on an infrequent but reliable route looping through South Beach, Downtown, and back to the airport ($1.25; hourly, 11.20pm–7am). For additional schedule information, call ☎305/770-3131 (Mon–Fri 6am–10pm, Sat & Sun 9am–5pm).

Several domestic budget airlines, including Song, JetBlue, and Spirit, now use **Fort Lauderdale Hollywood International Airport** (☎954/359-1200, ⊚www.broward.org/airport/) as their South Florida hub. It's a perfectly viable alternative to the mess that is Miami airport, but make sure to factor into the cost any car rental – driving is effectively the only efficient way to shuttle from Fort Lauderdale down to Miami or Miami Beach, unless you're prepared to trundle to the Tri-Rail and shuttle down to Miami that way (see p.35).

By train and bus

Of the several **Greyhound** stations in Miami, the Miami West station at 4111 NW 27th St (☎305/871-1810 or 24-hour information line 1-800/229-9424, ⊚www.greyhound.com) is the busiest and just a short cab ride from the airport. If you're planning to connect to the beaches or coming to and from Key West, you're better aiming for the Downtown hub at 100 W 6th St (☎305/374-6160). Remember that the latter station's in Overtown, a less than salubrious part of the city especially by night, so take care when in transit here. Greyhound connects Miami directly with Key West, West Palm Beach, and Fort Myers, with ongoing service across the country.

Miami is on the **Amtrak** Silver Service route, linking South Florida with New York City via Washington, DC, and the Carolinas. The main station, at 8303 NW 37th Ave, is seven miles northwest of Downtown (☎305/835-1222 or 1-800/USA-RAIL, ⊚www.amtrak.com). The best way to connect with the rest of the city is to hop on Metrobus #L, which terminates in South Beach; en route, it connects with the Metrorail station (see "City transportation," p.34) eight blocks away, where you can hop a local commuter train to Downtown, Coconut Grove, or Coral Gables.

By car

Driving **from the north**, you're likely to approach Miami on I-95, the freeway that runs down the entire length of Florida's east coast and deposits you in Downtown Miami.

Road names and numbers

Numerous major thoroughfares in the city have nicknames alongside their official designations; the following should provide some quick reference if you're listening for traffic information on the radio or asking for directions.

Collins Avenue is Hwy-A1A

Dolphin Expressway is Route 839

Don Shula Expressway is Route 874

Florida's Turnpike (Homestead Extension) is Route 821

John F. Kennedy Causeway is Route 934

Julia Tuttle Causeway is I-195

LeJeune Road in Coral Gables is also SW 42nd Avenue

MacArthur Causeway is I-395

Palmetto Expressway is Route 826 (which is known as 163rd Street on its way to the beach)

South Dixie Highway is Hwy-1, south of the city

Tamiami Trail is Hwy-41 (and becomes **SW 8th Street** is also known as Calle Ocho)

From here, the MacArthur and Julia Tuttle causeways both lead to the beaches.

If you're coming up **from the Keys**, Hwy-1 leads north through Coconut Grove and Coral Gables to Downtown and beyond. However, it's a slower suburban route, with plenty of stoplights – you'd do better turning off onto the Palmetto Expressway, which skirts the western edge of Miami before turning east through its northern portion, or taking Florida's Turnpike from Hwy-1 and then the Don Shula Expressway (which connects to the Palmetto Expressway).

Coming into the city **from the west**, you're likely to be driving Hwy-41, or the Tamiami Trail – follow this until it becomes SW 8th Street, which slices its way into the center of the city.

Information, websites, and maps

Miami's **CVB** produces a comprehensive free visitors guide every year and you can contact them before you arrive to have information and brochures mailed to your home. Once in Miami, you can stop by its offices Downtown – though its out-of-the-way location means that you'll often be better relying on the **Miami Beach Chamber of Commerce** instead or on the **Miami Design Preservation League's Welcome Center** at 1001 Ocean Drive, whose staff is usually helpful and knowledgeable about all things South Beach.

We've listed below all the local chambers of commerce and tourist offices below, as well as online resources and suggestions for reliable maps. For transportation information head to the **Metro-Dade Center**, adjoining the Cultural Center Downtown. This high-rise (also called the **Government Center**) chiefly comprises county government offices, but useful bus and train timetables can be gathered from the **Transit Service Center** (daily 7am–6pm; ☎305/770-3131) by the Metrorail entrance at the eastern side of the building.

Tourist offices and information centers

Coconut Grove Chamber of Commerce Mon–Fri 9am–5pm, 2820 McFarlane Rd, Coconut Grove ☎305/4444-7270, ⓦwww.coconutgrove.com.
Coral Gables Chamber of Commerce Mon–Fri 9am–5pm, 360 Greco Ave, Suite 100, Coral Gables ☎305/446-1657, ⓦwww.coralgableschamber.org.
Downtown Miami Partnership Mon noon–6pm, Tues 10am–6pm, 25 SE 2nd Ave #1007, Downtown ☎305/379-7070, ⓦwww.downtownmiami.net.
Greater Miami Convention & Visitors Bureau Mon–Fri 8.30am–6pm, 701 Brickell Ave, Downtown

#2700 ☎305/539-3000 or 1-800/933-8448, ⓦwww.miamiandbeaches.com. Note that there's a satellite information center at the Miami airport on level 2, Concourse E, open daily 5am–10pm.
Key Biscayne Chamber of Commerce Mon–Fri 9am–5pm, 88 W McIntyre St, Suite 100, Key Biscayne ☎305/361-5207, ⓦwww .keybiscaynechamber.org.
Miami Beach Latin Chamber of Commerce Mon–Fri 9am–5.30pm, 1620 Drexel Ave, 1st floor (enter at 510 Lincoln Rd), South Beach ☎305/674-1414, ⓦwww.miamibeach.org.
Miami Beach Visitor Center Mon–Fri 9am–6pm, Sat & Sun 10am–4pm, 1920 Meridian Ave, Room 831, South Beach ☎305/672-1270, ⓦwww .miamibeachchamber.com.
North Beach Development Corporation Mon–Fri 9.30am–5.30pm, 210 71st St, North Beach ☎305/865-4147, ⓦwww.gonorthbeach.com.
Sunny Isles Beach Resort Association Mon–Fri 9am–2pm, 17070 Collins Ave, Sunny Isles Beach ☎305/947-5826, ⓦwww.sunnyislesfla.com.

Useful websites

Countless **websites** contain travel information about Miami; you may want to do some extra research before (or during) your trip. What follows is a short list of fun and informative sites that will help you find what's on around town. Be sure, too, to check out our own website at ⓦ www.roughguides.com.

ⓦ **www.cooljunkie.com** One of the best local sites for nightlife, this offers different channels for clubs, bars/lounges, galleries, and music, with spot-on reviews of each venue. There's also a day-by-day listings feature so you can check what's coming up next week.

ⓦ **www.digitalcity.com/southflorida** AOL's answer to Citysearch is often more comprehensive, if a little bland and less opinionated. Good for its regular highlights of local events, as well as restaurant listings.

ⓦ **www.miami.com** The online home of the *Miami Herald*, this is a comprehensive local site – unsurprisingly, strong on news and politics. It's rather let down by a messy search feature, though.

ⓦ **miami.citysearch.com** The local chapter of Microsoft's national listings website is sparky and plugged in – great for up-to-date information on the latest hot restaurants or club openings. The search facility's patchy, though.

ⓦ **miami.metroguide.com** The best listings resource for Miami on the Web, divided into channels: retail, event, dining, night, and hotel. It doesn't provide editorial reviews, but is thorough and reliable for phone numbers and addresses.

ⓦ **www.miamibeach411.com** This site does exactly what it says it will – comprehensively and accurately list hotels, restaurants, and other attractions in Miami Beach.

ⓦ **www.miamiboutiquehotels.com** Given Miami's reputation as a hotbed of haute hotels, the CVB has created a special website which lists all the trendy accommodations in every budget – there's also a hard-copy brochure available from the CVB's office or by mail.

ⓦ **www.oceandrive.com** The best place to check on anything relating to South Beach, it features a good archive of old features, and up-to-date listings of major events. It doesn't incorporate the exhaustive listings of bars and clubs in the print edition, though.

Maps

The **maps** in this book, along with the free city plans you can pick up from the Miami CVB in its *Visitors Planning Guide*, will be sufficient to help you find your way around. If you want something more comprehensive, the new Rough Guide *Map to Miami and the Keys* is unbeatable ($8.95, Can$13.50,

or £4.99) – the waterproof paper will last through even a torrential summer afternoon shower, and attractions, restaurants, and hotels we've listed are all marked. Otherwise, the *Streetwise Miami* map at $5.95 is dependable and durable (ⓦ www.street wisemaps.com).

If you're planning on traveling to the Everglades and down to the Keys, Rand McNally produces good commercial state maps for around $4. The American Automobile Association (ⓣ 1-800/222-4357, ⓦ www.aaa .com) provides free maps and assistance to its members, and to British members of the AA and RAC.

Map outlets

In the US and Canada

Book Passage 51 Tamal Vista Blvd, Corte Madera, CA 94925 ⓣ 1-800/999-7909 or 415/927-0960 or 1 Ferry Plaza #46, San Francisco ⓣ 415/835-1020, ⓦ www.bookpassage.com.

Distant Lands 56 S Raymond Ave, Pasadena, CA 91105 ⓣ 1-800/310-3220 or 626/449-3220, ⓦ www.distantlands.com.

Elliott Bay Book Company 101 S Main St, Seattle, WA 98104 ⓣ 1-800/962-5311, ⓦ www .elliottbaybook.com.

Globe Corner Bookstore 28 Church St, Cambridge, MA 02138 ⓣ 1-800/358-6013 or 617/730-3901, ⓦ www.globercorner.com.

Map Link 30 S La Patera Lane, Unit 5, Santa Barbara, CA 93117 ⓣ 805/692-6777 or 1-800/962-1394, ⓦ www.maplink.com.

Rand McNally ⓣ 1-800/333-0136, ⓦ www .randmcnally.com. Around thirty stores across the US; dial ext 2111 or check the website for the nearest location.

The Travel Bug Bookstore 2667 W Broadway, Vancouver V6K 2G2 ⓣ 604/737-1122, ⓦ www .travelbugbooks.ca.

World of Maps 1235 Wellington St, Ottawa, ON K1Y 3A3 ⓣ 1-800/214-8524 or 613/724-6776, ⓦ www.worldofmaps.com.

In the UK and Ireland

Blackwell's 48–51 Broad St, Oxford OX1 3BQ ⓣ 01865/792 792 or 20 Trinity St, Cambridge CB2 1TY ⓣ 01223/568 568 ⓦ www.blackwells.com.

Easons Bookshop 40 O'Connell St, Dublin 1 ⓣ 01/873 3811, ⓦ www.eason.ie.

The Map Shop 30a Belvoir St, Leicester LE1 6QH ⓣ 0116/247 1400, ⓦ www.mapshopleicester.co.uk.

National Map Centre 22–24 Caxton St, London SW1H 0QU ☎020/7222 2466, ⊛www.mapsnmc.co.uk.

Newcastle Map Centre 55 Grey St, Newcastle-upon-Tyne, NE1 6EF ☎0191/261 5622, ⊛www.newtraveller.com.

Ordnance Survey Ireland Phoenix Park, Dublin 8 ☎01/8025 349, ⊛www.osi.ie.

Ordnance Survey of Northern Ireland Colby House, Stranmillis Court, Belfast BT9 5BJ ☎028/9025 5755, ⊛www.osni.gov.uk.

Stanfords 12–14 Long Acre, WC2E 9LP ☎020/7836 1321, ⊛www.stanfords.co.uk, ⓔsales@stanfords.co.uk. Maps available by mail, phone order, or email.

The Travel Bookshop 13–15 Blenheim Crescent, W11 2EE ☎020/7229 5260, ⊛www.thetravelbookshop.co.uk.

In Australia and New Zealand

The Map Shop 6–10 Peel St, Adelaide, SA 5000 ☎08/8231 2033, ⊛www.mapshop.net.au.

Mapland 372 Little Bourke St, Melbourne, Victoria 3000, ☎03/9670 4383, ⊛www.mapland.com.au.

MapWorld 173 Gloucester St, Christchurch, New Zealand ☎0800/627 967 or 03/374 5399, ⊛www.mapworld.co.nz.

Specialty Maps 46 Albert St, Auckland 1001 ☎09/307 2217, ⊛www.wise5maps.co.nz/.

Costs, money, and banks

Though the cost of buying an apartment in Miami may be skyrocketing, for the visitor it's still a city that you can afford to see on a budget. South Beach, which contains most points of interest, is compact and walkable; there's better-than-average public transport; and you can still (just about) find some cheap hotel deals. The abundance of Cuban lunch counters provides a low-cost meal, though it's worth saving up and splurging at least once on one of the city's increasingly noteworthy upscale eateries. The biggest expenses you're likely to incur are if you decide to hit Miami's nightlife: bottle service at $250 per bottle in clubs isn't uncommon, while the price of cocktails at swanky lounges will never dip below $12 per drink.

Average costs

Accommodation will be your biggest single expense: the cheapest reasonable double hotel rooms go for $100–125 per night, although hostels will of course be cheaper. That said, within this range, you should be able to haggle during the offseason, especially during the hit-and-miss weather months of July and August – see p.129, "Accommodation" for further suggestions. After you've paid for your room, count on spending a minimum of $35 a day for breakfast, lunch on the run, a budget dinner and a beer, but not much else. Eating fancier meals, taking taxis and drinking will mean allowing for more like $60–70 per day. If you want to go regularly to the theater or major concerts, rent a car, take a tour, or seriously shop, double that figure.

Youth and student discounts

Once obtained, various official and quasi-official **youth/student ID cards** soon pay for themselves in savings. Full-time students are eligible for the International Student ID Card (ISIC; ⊛www.isiccard.com or www.isicus.com), which entitles the bearer to special air, rail, and bus fares and discounts at museums, theaters, and other attractions. The card costs $22 for Americans; Can$16 for Canadians; Aus$16.50 for Australians; NZ$21 for New Zealanders; and £7 in the UK.

You only have to be 26 or younger to qualify for the **International Youth Travel Card**, which costs US$22/£7 and carries the same benefits. Teachers qualify for the **International Teacher Card**, offering similar discounts and costing US$22, Can$16, Aus$16.50, and NZ$21. All these cards are available in the US from Council Travel, STA, Travel CUTS, and, in Canada, Hostelling International; in Australia and New Zealand from STA or Campus Travel; and in the UK from Usit Campus and STA.

Several other travel organizations and accommodation groups also sell their own cards, good for various discounts. A university photo ID might open some doors, but is not easily recognizable, as are the ISIC cards. However, the latter are often not accepted as valid proof of age, for example in bars or liquor stores.

Currency

US currency comes in **bills** of $1, $5, $10, $20, $50, and $100, plus various larger (and rarer) denominations. All are the same size and same green color (except for twenties, which now have almost aesthetically pleasing splashes of pink, blue, and yellow in the middle), making it necessary to check each bill carefully. The dollar is made up of 100 cents (¢) in coins of 1 cent (usually called a penny), 5 cents (a nickel), 10 cents (a dime), 25 cents (a quarter), 50 cents (a half-dollar), and one dollar. The $2 bill and the half-dollar and dollar coins are seldom seen. Change – especially quarters – is needed for buses, vending machines, and telephones, so always carry plenty. For current exchange rates check ⓦwww.x-rates.com.

Banks and ATMs

With an **ATM card** (and PIN number) you'll have access to cash from machines all over Miami, though as anywhere, you may be charged a fee for using a different bank's ATM network. Foreign cash-dispensing cards linked to international networks such as Cirrus and Plus are also very widely accepted – ask your home bank which branches you can use, as otherwise the machine may simply gobble up the card. To find the location of the nearest ATM in South Florida, call: **Amex** ☎1-800/CASH-NOW, **Plus** ☎1-800/843-7587, or **Cirrus** ☎1-800/424-7787.

Most **banks in Miami** are open Mon–Fri 9am–3pm and a few open on Saturday 9am–noon. If you need to change money, facilities are available at the airport, at American Express offices, and the following locations: Bank of America, 100 SE 2nd St (☎1-800/432-1000), and SunTrust Bank, 777 Brickell Ave (☎305/591-6000), both Downtown, as well as the Union Planters Bank, 2800 Ponce de Leon Blvd (☎1-800/776-1205), in Coral Gables. For banking services – particularly currency exchange – outside normal business hours and on weekends, try major hotels: the rate won't be as good, but it's the best option in a tight financial corner.

Travelers' checks, credit and debit cards

Travelers' checks should be brought in US dollars only – they are universally accepted as cash in stores or restaurants, as long as you have a photo ID. It's best to bring them in smaller denominations, as some stores will balk at cashing a $100 check. The usual fee for travelers'-check sales is one or two percent, though this fee may be waived if you buy the checks through a bank where you have an account. You can also buy checks by phone or online with Thomas Cook and American Express. Make sure to keep the purchase agreement and a record of check serial numbers separate from the checks themselves. In the event that checks are lost

---

Tipping

When working out your daily budget, allow for **tipping**, which is universally expected. You really shouldn't depart a bar or restaurant without leaving a tip of at least fifteen per cent (unless the service is utterly disgusting); twenty percent is more like it in upmarket places. About the same amount should be added to taxi fares – and round them up to the nearest 50¢ or dollar. A hotel porter should get $1 a bag, $3–5 for lots of baggage; chambermaids $1–2 a day; valet parking attendants $1.

or stolen, the issuing company will expect you to report the loss immediately; most companies claim to replace lost or stolen checks within 24 hours.

For many services in the US, it's simply taken for granted that you'll be paying with plastic. When renting a car or checking into a hotel, you will be asked to show a **credit card** – even if you intend to settle the bill in cash. Most major credit cards issued by foreign banks are honored in the US: locally, Visa, MasterCard, American Express, and Discover are the most widely used. If you use your credit card at an ATM, remember that all **cash advances** are treated as loans with interest accruing daily from the date of withdrawal; there may be a transaction fee on top of this.

Wiring money

Having money wired from home using one of the companies listed opposite is never convenient or cheap, and should be considered only as a last resort. It's also possible to have money wired directly from a bank in your home country to a bank in New York. If you go this route, your home bank will need the address of the branch bank where you want to pick up the money and the address and telex number of the Miami main office, which will act as the clearing house. Money wired this way normally takes two working days to arrive, and costs around £25/$40/Can$54/Aus$52/NZ$59 per transaction.

Financial services

American Express Moneygram UK ☎0870/600 1060, ⊛www.americanexpress.co.uk; US and Canada ☎1-888/269-6669, ⊛www .americanexpress.com.
Thomas Cook US ☎1-800/287-7362, Canada ☎1-888/823-4732, UK ☎01733/318 922, Belfast ☎028/9055 0030, Dublin ☎01/677 1721, ⊛www .thomascook.com.
Travelers Express Moneygram Canada ☎1-800/933-3278, UK ☎0800/6663 9472, US ☎1-800/926-9400, ⊛www.moneygram.com.
Western Union US and Canada ☎1-800/325-6000, Australia ☎1800/649 565, New Zealand ☎09/270 0050, UK ☎0800/833 833, Republic of Ireland ☎1800/395 395, ⊛www.westernunion .com.

City transportation

Getting around Miami is a cinch, mostly because the compact layout of the tourist hub of South Beach means that the easiest option is to walk. If you plan to linger exclusively in this area, there's no need for a car: there's always the Electrowave Shuttle or taxis if your feet need a rest, or you could even rent some rollerblades (for rental info, see p.183 – be aware, though, that many stores won't let customers inside wearing skates). Elsewhere in the city, Coconut Grove is also compact enough to handle on foot while many people staying in Key Biscayne rely on biking; otherwise, in Coral Gables, along the Biscayne Corridor or in Little Havana, a car will make sightseeing much quicker and more convenient.

However, if you do stick to **public transport**, you'll be surprised at how easy it is to use, despite locals' constant grumbling. The buses and trains are all cheap, clean, and run on regular schedules; the one caveat is that bus and train networks are not well coordinated, so connecting between them can involve 5- or 10-minute hikes on foot.

Buses

Both buses and local trains are run by **Metro-Dade Transit** (information line open

Useful bus routes

Unfortunately, there's little logic to the lettering and numbering of **bus routes**: as a guide, most, but not all, lettered buses include some part of the beaches in their track.

Useful routes from Downtown's Government Center hub are as follows:

South Beach – #C, #K (along Washington Ave), #S (along Alton Road)

Miami Beach – #K, #S

Coral Gables – #24

Miami International Airport – #7

Key Biscayne – #B

Little Havana – #8

Coconut Grove – #48

Biscayne Corridor – #3 (along Biscayne Blvd)

Mon–Fri 6am–10pm, Sat & Sun 9am–5pm, ☎305/770-3131, ⓦ www.miamidade .gov/transit/). Maps for all Metro-Dade services can be picked up at Government Center Station, 101 NW 1st St, which is the main bus terminal; alternatively, there are route maps inside each bus. Travel by bus is not a speedy option, so allow plenty of time; it's a good choice if you're staying Downtown or at the beaches, but connecting from Coconut Grove or Key Biscayne to anywhere else by bus is a painfully long process – you'll normally need to take one route to Government Center and then change onto a second bus to reach your destination.

Even so, **buses** in Miami are surprisingly pleasant; they're clean and chillingly air-conditioned, and the network crisscrosses the city 24 hours a day. **Fares** require $1.25 in exact change, including dollar bills; there's a 25¢ surcharge for a **transfer slip** that can be used to connect with another bus or service in the Metro-Dade network, like Metrorail (see opposite). These transfer slips are time-stamped to prevent you from lingering too long between connections – they're valid for two hours from the moment you board the first bus.

If you're planning on staying in town for a while, consider buying a monthly **Metropass**.

Available from any store displaying the Metro-Dade Transit sign, it costs $60 and is on sale from the 20th of each month. It provides unlimited rides on both Metrobus and Metrorail services (see below).

A jaunty alternative in **South Beach** is the **Electrowave Shuttle** (info line ☎305/535-9160). It runs on two routes, one that cruises up and down Washington Avenue and Lincoln Road, the other that circles Collins Avenue at the northern end of South Beach. These multicolored minibuses come in all shapes and sizes and cost 25¢ per ride. They're a good option on steamy days in July for a 5-minute cool-down, or for getting around quickly at night without a car (Mon–Sat 8am–1am, Sun and holidays 10am–1am). **Coral Gables** has just launched its own **free shuttle service**, which has made the city drastically more convenient for anyone without a car (route maps and info at ⓦ www.coralgables.com/CGWeb /trolley.aspx). This old-fashioned trolley follows two routes: the first, a north–south course along Ponce de Leon from the Metrorail station, runs every 10–15 minutes (Mon–Thurs 6.30am–8pm, Fri 6.30am–11pm); the second, known as the Miracle Mile Twilight Route, zigzags through the main commercial drag and hits sights like the Venetian Pool and the *Biltmore Hotel* (Mon–Thurs 3–7pm, Fri 3–10pm).

Local trains

Metrorail trains, also run by Metro-Dade Transit (see above), amble along a single line connecting the northern and southern suburbs, hugging Hwy-1 through Coconut Grove and Coral Gables (daily 5am–midnight, with reduced service after 6pm). Useful stops are Government Center (for Downtown and the main bus depot), Vizcaya (2-minute walk to the mansion, see p.120), and Coconut Grove. Douglas Road and University are the designated Coral Gables stops; best to use the former during daylight hours, as you can connect with the trolley service. Frankly, though, the most direct way to Coral Gables way is to hop on a bus from Government Center that deposits you at the heart of the Miracle Mile. Single-journey **fares** on the Metrorail are $1.25 (exact change only) – buy a token from one of the machines and drop it into the turnstile at the foot of the stairs.

Tips on parking

Parking is no problem in most areas – Coral Gables has plenty of spaces, as does Downtown. The two shopping centers (see p.115) in Coconut Grove have ample facilities, and everywhere there's streetside parking (25¢ for 15 minutes) for the nimble and patient: just keep plenty of quarters in the car.

The beaches are a somewhat different story, though don't be put off by doomsayers who liken finding parking on South Beach to winning the lottery. Avoid the jams on Ocean Drive whatever the time; if you're looking for roadside metered parking, your best shot is away from the beach around Alton Road, or along the lower edges of Washington Avenue. There are three municipal lots in South Beach which normally have ample space, costing $1/hour: their overnight parking rates vary – 7th Street and Collins Avenue is $14/night, 13th Street and Collins Avenue is $8/night, and 17th Street and Washington Avenue will set you back $8/night. Few of the old Art Deco hotels have their own lots, so they offer pricey valet parking – though this often entails paying someone else to drive your car to one of the municipal lots; you'll save plenty by doing it yourself.

The **Metromover** system is a **free** auto-mated monorail that ribbons around the Downtown central business district. The inner loop cinches the main sights including Government Center and Bayfront Park; the outer loop extends service to the Omni Mall north and the Brickell business district south of the river (inner loop runs daily 24 hrs, outer loop runs daily 5.30am–midnight, later during events at the American Airlines arena; ☎305/770-3131). The Metromover is reli-able, fast, and clean, if a little limited – take it for a good view of the city and to get your bearings when you arrive.

The **Tri-Rail** system is a local commuter train service that was introduced in 1989 in an attempt to cut congestion along the coastal corridor between Miami and West Palm Beach. It's primarily aimed at com-muters, with service heaviest during rush hours and only 7 trains (each way) daily at weekends (weekdays 6am–8pm, Sat 7.15am–9.30pm, Sun 7.15am–7.30pm). If you want to use it for day-trips out of town – there are 18 stops, including Hollywood, Fort Lauderdale, and Fort Lauderdale airport – take the Metrorail to the station at 1149 E 21st St and hop onto the Tri-Rail there; **fares** vary according to distance: round-trip $3.50–9.25, weekend all-day pass $4.

Taxis and cars

Taxis are abundant on the streets, and drivers will stop when they see you waving. Alternatively, you can call to book a taxi – try Central Cab (☎305/532-5555) or Metro Taxi (☎305/888-8888). Aside from the flat-rate services from the airport, fares aren't

The streets of Miami

Driving in Miami Beach is relatively easy, since the grid system of streets is logical and consistent; but back on the mainland, the city's **street-ordering system** can at first seem rather confusing. To make it more manageable follow this simple system:

The city's grid is centered on the junction of Flagler Street and Miami Avenue: from that point, the four quarters tagged NE, NW, SW, and SE fan out. To find a street once you know its quarter, use the **PARC mnemonic**: Places, Avenues, Roads, and Courts run north–south, while everything else runs east–west.

In a maddeningly typical display of autonomy, **Coral Gables** ignored this system. Instead, the area was artistically streetscaped as per the City Beautiful tradition, its spaghetti-loop suburban roads and dead ends perhaps its most European feature. To find your way around here, keep the map at the back of this book ready at hand.

especially cheap – $1.70 for the first eleventh of a mile, and 20¢ for each additional eleventh of a mile. In case of complaints, call ☎305/375-2460.

Driving in Miami is practical and reasonably easy: the city's crisscrossed by a network of **expressways** that will shuttle you quickly from district to district – we've listed the key roads (and their various names) in the box on p.28. As in any city, expect these freeways to be heavily congested during rush hour so allow extra time, for example, if you're trying to make a flight in Fort Lauderdale.

Most of the **bridges and causeways** that connect the islands to the mainland are free – two exceptions are the Rickenbacker Causeway from Key Biscayne ($1) and the Venetian Causeway (toll booth closed for construction at time of writing; 10¢).

Tours

Given that Miami is one of the prime tourist destinations in America, there are surprisingly few **walking or bus tours** on offer. We've listed the scant few options below – reservations are always recommended, and you can find more information by visiting each tour operator's website or contacting the CVB. Astonishingly, there are no regular tours of historic Coral Gables, though occasionally the city does run walking tours – call the City Hall at ☎305/446-8800 for information.

David Brown is one of the few solo tour operators in the city (☎305/663-4455, ⓦwww.miamiculturaltours.com). He specializes in Miami's ethnic neighborhoods, including Little Haiti and Liberty City, with a focus as much on culture (sampling food, meeting locals) as on history. Tours cost $49 per person including a meal. The nonprofit **Dade Heritage Trust** ($35; ☎305/358-9572, ⓦwww.dadeheritagetrust.org) runs bus tours of the city, with varied themes, including Women's Miami and Miami's Ghosts. Meet at its office, 190 SE 12th Terrace.

If you're interested in the history of the CBD, the **Downtown Miami Partnership** runs tours of the area, which take in the historic buildings along Flagler Street and around (weekdays 10.30am; ☎305/379-7070, ⓦwww.downtownmiami.net). You can also pick up a handy self-guided walking tour of Historic Downtown from the CVB or the Downtown Miami Partnership's own info office.

Historical Museum of South Florida's walking tours are led by a local academic (no tours July & Aug; $17 and up; ☎305/375-1621, ⓦwww.historical-museum.org). Passionate about the city's history, he leads trips that include cycle tours around Little Havana and excursions to Key Biscayne by boat – there are 25 different, rotating itineraries so call or check the website for what's on offer. Each tour lasts 2–3 hours.

Unmissable as an introduction to the architecture of South Beach, **The Miami Design Preservation League** (Wed, Fri, Sat & Sun 10.30am, Thurs 6.30pm; $20; ☎305/672-2014, ⓦwww.mdpl.org) offers volunteer-run jaunts around South Beach's greatest hits, which are always lively and informative. Meet at the MDPL offices at 1001 Ocean Drive. If you're not able to make any of these pre-scheduled appointments, there's always a self-guided audio tour of the district that you can rent from the League ($15; daily 10am–4pm).

The North Beach Development has finally organized the first MiMo tours (Fri 10.30am; $10; ☎305/865-4147, ⓦwww.gonorthbeach.com), which meet at the North Shore Band Shell, Collins Avenue and 73rd Street, and include the major residential and commercial Miami Modernism sights in the area.

Phones, mail, and email

You should have little problem staying in touch while in Miami. Every hotel comes equipped with a **phone** (though these can be expensive to use), public pay phones are widespread, and there are enough places offering **Internet access** to keep you up to date with your email. You can buy stamps at **post offices** throughout Miami and Miami Beach, and mailboxes are easy to find.

Telephones

Miami has two **area codes**, the original ☎305 having been joined by ☎786. If dialing from one code to another, you'll need to dial 1 plus the full number, even for local calls. Note, too, that although the Keys share the same code, calling Key West from Miami is charged as a long-distance call. Toll-free calls (usually prefixed ☎888 or ☎800) also require a 1, no matter where you're calling from. Detailed information about calls, codes, and rates in Miami can be found at the front of the telephone directory in the *White Pages*.

In general, telephoning from your hotel room is considerably more expensive than using a pay phone, costing up to $1 for a local call; that said, some budget hotels offer free local calls. International calls can be dialed direct from public phones; the lowest rates for calls to Europe are usually between 11pm and 8am (plus all day Sat and all day Sun except 5–11pm). Don't even think of calling abroad from a hotel phone – you'll be charged a small fortune.

Calling home from Miami

One of the most convenient ways of phoning home is via a **telephone charge card** from your phone company back home. Using a PIN number, you can make calls from most hotel, public, and private phones that will be charged to your account. Since most major charge cards are free to obtain, it's certainly worth getting one at least for emergencies; enquire first though whether your destination is covered, and bear in mind that rates aren't necessarily cheaper than calling from a public phone.

In **the UK and Ireland**, British Telecom (☎0800/345 144, 🌐www.chargecard.bt.com)

Useful telephone codes

To make international calls **from the US**, dial **011** followed by the country code (note that if you're calling **Canada**, you simply need to dial a 1, then the area code and number, as though you were making a domestic call):

Australia 011 + 61 + number
Canada 011 + 1 + number
New Zealand 011 + 64 + city code
UK and Northern Ireland 011 + 44 + city code
Republic of Ireland 011 + 353 + city code

will issue free to all BT customers the BT Charge Card. The US access codes are ☎1-800/44 55 688 for AT&T, ☎1-800/854-4826 for MCI and ☎1-800/825-4904 for Sprint. Another option is AT&T (dial ☎0800/890 011, then 888/641-6123 when you hear the AT&T prompt to be transferred to the Florida Call Center, free 24 hours), which offers the Global Calling Card.

To call **Australia and New Zealand** from South Florida, telephone charge cards such as Telstra Telecard or Optus Calling Card in Australia, and Telecom NZ's Calling Card can be used to make calls abroad, which are charged back to a domestic account or credit card. Apply to Telstra (☎1800/038 000), Optus (☎1300/300 937), or Telecom NZ (☎04/801 9000).

Mobile phones

Non-Americans wishing to use their **mobile phones** in South Florida need to check with their phone provider if it will work abroad, and what the call charges are. Unless you have a tri-band phone, it is unlikely that a mobile bought for use outside the US will work inside the States and vice versa, with many only working within the region designated by the area code in the phone number, ie 212, 415 etc. If you're lucky enough to have a phone that works Stateside, you'll have to inform your phone provider before going abroad to get international access switched on. You may get charged extra for this and you're also likely to be charged extra for incoming calls when abroad, as the people calling you will be paying the usual rate. If you want to retrieve messages while you're away, you'll have to ask your provider for a new access code, as your home one is unlikely to work abroad. Tri-band phones will automatically switch to the US frequency, but these can be pricey, so you may want to rent a phone if you're traveling to the US. For further information about using your phone abroad, check out Ⓦ www.telecomsadvice .org.uk/features/using_your_mobile_abroad.

Mail

All mail between the US and Europe generally takes about a week. Letters that don't carry the **zip code** are liable to get lost or at least delayed; phone books carry a list for their service area and post offices – even abroad – have directories. There's also a handy zip-code finder at Ⓦ www.usps.com.

Letters sent to you c/o **General Delivery** (known elsewhere as **Poste Restante**) must include the post office zip code and will only be held for thirty days before being returned to sender, so make sure there's a return address on the envelope. You can also usually ask to have mail held at a hotel or, if you're a card holder, at an American Express office – see p.194, "Directory," for local branches.

Email

One of the best ways to keep in touch while traveling is to sign up for a free **Internet email address** that can be accessed from anywhere, for example YahooMail or Hotmail – available through Ⓦ www.yahoo.com and Ⓦ www.hotmail.com. Once you've set up an account, you can use these sites to pick up and send mail from any Internet café, or hotel with Internet access.

Miami doesn't have a huge number of **Internet cafés**, but there are plenty in heavily touristed locations like South Beach: we've listed the handiest locations on p.195, "Directory." Expect to pay around $7/hr. If money's tight, head to the public library where there's free 45-minute access for all – you'll have to sign up in advance, and expect a wait.

The media

Miami's **media** has a laser-like focus on issues. Put simply, the news media here is obsessed with tourism and real estate and anything to do with Cuba. For international and national news, you're best picking up a copy of the locally printed *New York Times* or tuning into a cable network. Where Miami does shine, though, is in its magazines – as befits as glossy a city as this, the homegrown lifestyle mag, *Ocean Drive*, is a superb, if frothy, read.

Newspapers and magazines

There's only one local **newspaper** in Miami, the *Miami Herald* (35¢ weekdays, $1 Sunday), which also publishes a daily Spanish-language edition, *El Nuevo Herald*. The best day to buy is Friday, when the *Herald*'s comprehensive weeklong entertainment supplement is bundled free with the main paper. It's a rather toothless publication, though recent Pulitzer Prize–winning columnist Leonard Pitts Jr is a high point. An alternative is the Fort Lauderdale–based *South Florida Sun-Sentinel*, which is gaining ground on the complacent *Herald*, mostly thanks to its extensive network of local bureaux. For exhaustive detail on the area in which you're staying, pick up one of the weekly local rags – there's the *Islander News* on Key Biscayne and the *Coral Gables Gazette* for starters.

For a snarkier take on what's happening in the city, the anti-establishment freesheet *New Times* (ⓦwww.newtimesmiami.com) is a must-read – it's also terrific for listings. Published weekly, the *New Times* is available from drop boxes across the city. There are several other handy **freesheets**: top picks are the *Biscayne Boulevard Times* (ⓦwww.biscayneboulevard.com), an invaluable source for that neighborhood's new developments and *Miami Today* (ⓦwww.miamitodaynews.com), which focuses on business deals and dealings in the city.

Miami has plenty of local magazines – after you need something to browse on the beach. The elder statesman is South Beach-centric *Ocean Drive*, jammed with ads for the latest clubs and photographs of local celebrities; you can buy it on newsstands, but it's usually available free at most hotels. Two competitors have recently appeared, *Lincoln Road* magazine and *The Loft*, though frankly neither beats *Ocean Drive*'s original cocktail of breathless profiles and trend-chasing. *Key Biscayne* also has its own namesake glossy, though its editorial content is rather thin and it's mostly a vehicle for real-estate ads. If you do see a copy of the monthly *GADA* (Go Anywhere, Do Anything), pick it up – not widely distributed, but it has the most reliable listings and insider info of all. Finally, there's always *TWN*, a weekly gay and lesbian freesheet (see p.166, "Gay Miami").

Spanish speakers are in for a treat – aside from *El Nuevo Herald*, most newsstands in the city carry Spanish-language editions of big-name magazines like *Glamour* and *Harper's Bazaar*.

Television

In Miami, you'll have access to all the usual stations, from major **networks** like ABC, CBS, and NBC to smaller netlets like the WB and UPN. Expect talk shows in the morning, soaps in the afternoon, and marquee-name comedies and dramas during primetime. If that's all too maddeningly commercial-heavy, there's always PBS, the rather earnest, ad-free station, which fills its schedule with news, documentaries, and imported period dramas. The precise channel numbers vary from area to area. One must-see local show – if only to groan at the low production values – is the evening entertainment news program, *Deco Drive*, which runs on Fox affiliate, WSVN Channel 7.

There's a wider choice on **cable**, including CNN for news and music on MTV; well-regarded premium channels like HBO and Showtime are often available on hotel TV systems, showing original series and blockbuster movies.

Radio

Unsurprisingly, you'll find many of South Florida's **local radio stations** either specialize in Latin music or keep Latin megastars like Shakira or Marc Anthony in heavy rotation. As in the rest of America, hip-hop has become a staple on every station. On FM, try mainstream pop-loving Y-100 (100.7 FM), the nonstop club mix of Party (93.1 FM), or the easy-listening Lite FM (100.5 FM). On any station, expect commercials interrupted by an occasional tune during drivetime (6–9am and 4–7pm); also note that many stations have astonishingly limited playlists, and songs in heavy rotation will often be played half a dozen times a day.

A safe harbor if you're struggling to find satisfying local news is to tune to **National Public Radio (NPR)**, the listener-funded talk station with a refreshingly honest take on news and chat (in Miami, 91.3FM, though frequencies vary in the Keys and Fort Lauderdale). To check for local frequencies for the World Service log on to the **BBC** (ⓦ www.bbc.co.uk/worldservice/index), **Radio Canada** (ⓦwww.rcinet.ca), or the **Voice of America** (ⓦwww.voa.gov). It's best to skip most specialty stations on the AM frequency – although AM chat shows, with their often angry, confrontational callers and hosts can be hilarious and illuminating, if not in the intended sense.

Opening hours and public holidays

The **opening hours** of specific attractions are given throughout the Guide, with websites and/or phone numbers provided for those sights that are open irregularly, closed until further notice, or require a reservation.

On the national **public holidays** listed in the box below, stores, banks, and public and federal offices are liable to be closed all day. The traditional winter tourism season, when many attractions have extended opening hours, runs from December through March.

Opening hours

As a general rule, Miami isn't a morning city – all that late-night partying can take its toll. Most offices will be fully staffed by 9.30am, but often stores won't open until late morning around 11am or so, especially in Miami

Beach. The counterpoint to this is that most amenities will be open later than in many other cities: expect stores in places like Lincoln Road to stay open until 10pm most nights, bars until 4 or 5am, and restaurants to continue serving until 1am. The one major exception is in Coral Gables, where local licensing laws mean bars must shutter by 2am.

Tourist attractions are more forgiving: most museums will be open 10am–6pm and a few art galleries stay open until 9pm or so once a month. Smaller, private museums close for one day a week, usually Monday or Tuesday.

Public holidays

The following are public holidays on which banks, post offices, and many (although by no means all) shops and attractions will be closed:

Jan 1 **New Year's Day**

Third Mon in Jan **Martin Luther King Jr's Birthday**

Third Mon in Feb **Presidents' Day**

Last Mon in May **Memorial Day**

July 4 **Independence Day**

First Mon in Sept **Labor Day**

Second Mon in Oct **Columbus Day**

Nov 11 **Veterans' Day**

Fourth Thurs in Nov **Thanksgiving**

Dec 25 **Christmas Day**

Crime and personal safety

In the 1980s, Miami had the worst reputation for crime of any major metropolitan area in the US, but these days, tourist carjackings and random shootings are long gone. In fact, the city's now largely a safe and easy place for visitors to wander round, whatever the time of day or night – the streets of South Beach, for example, are still packed with people at 1am so you shouldn't feel isolated walking home alone from a bar. Downtown may be deserted outside business hours, but largely crime-free. The only areas where it's still important to be vigilant are Overtown and Liberty City, which can be nasty come nightfall; the Biscayne Corridor's rapidly gentrifying, but the Boulevard's a better place to drive than stroll down.

Security at many public buildings and museums has been significantly increased since the terrorist attacks on America in September 2001. There are more visual, physical, and covert checks on anyone entering museums, galleries, and public buildings. You can expect to wait in line and have your bags searched before entering, while metal detectors and other security devices are in place at sites throughout the city. Sadly, some places, like the World Economics Gallery in Downtown have been closed to the public in response to security concerns.

As far as your personal responsibility goes, you should **carry ID at all times**. Two pieces should suffice, one of which should have a photo: a passport or driver's license and credit card(s) are best. (Incidentally, not having your license with you while driving is an arrestable offence.) A university photo ID might be sufficient, but is not always easily recognizable. An International Student Identity Card (ISIC) is often not accepted as valid proof of age, for example, in bars or liquor stores. Overseas visitors (often surprised to learn that **the legal drinking age is 21**) might want to carry their passport, unless they have a photo-style driving license.

Mugging and theft

Most people will have few problems, and if things do go wrong, foreign visitors tend to report that the police are helpful and obliging, although they'll obviously be less sympathetic if they think you brought the trouble on yourself through carelessness.

The fact that Miami attracts so many tourists means that it has more than its share of petty crime, simply because there are plenty of unsuspecting holidaymakers to prey on. Keep your wits about you in crowds; know where you wallet or purse is; and, of course, avoid parks, parking lots, and dark streets at night. Be careful when using ATMs in untouristed areas; try to use machines near Downtown hotels, shops, or offices, and during daylight. And if you have to ask directions, choose carefully whom you ask (go into a store, if possible).

Should the worst happen, hand over your money and afterwards find a phone and dial ☏911, or hail a cab and ask the driver to take you to the nearest police station. There, **report the theft** and get a reference number on the report to claim insurance and travelers'-check refunds.

Always **store valuables** in the hotel safe when you go out. When inside, keep your door locked and don't open it to anyone you are suspicious of. If they claim to be hotel staff and you don't believe them, call reception to check. In hostels and budget hotels, you may want to keep your valuables on your person, unless you know the security measures to be reliable.

Needless to say, **make photocopies** of everything important before you go (including the business page of your passport) and keep them separate from the originals. If the worst happens, go to the nearest consulate and get them to issue you a temporary passport, basically a sheet of paper saying you've reported the loss, which will get you back home.

Emergency numbers

For lost cards and checks, the following numbers are useful:

American Express Cards
☎1-800/992-3404

American Express Checks
☎1-800/221-7282

Citicorp ☎1-800/645-6556

Diners Club ☎1-800/234-6377

MasterCard ☎1-800/826-2181

Thomas Cook/MasterCard
☎1-800/223-9920

Visa Cards ☎1-800/847-2911

Visa Checks ☎1-800/227-6811

Keep a record of the numbers of your travelers' checks separately from the actual checks; if you lose them, call the issuing company on the toll-free number above. They'll ask you for the check numbers, the place you bought them, when and how you lost them, and whether it's been reported to the police. All being well, you should get the missing checks reissued within a couple of days – and perhaps an emergency advance to tide you over.

Finally, it goes without saying that you should **never hitchhike** anywhere in or around South Florida, or indeed the entire US.

Car crime

Crimes committed against tourists driving rental cars have garnered headlines around the world in recent years – Miami was renowned for a spate of violent **carjackings** in the early 1990s, including one that resulted in the murder of a German tourist – but there are certain simple precautions you can take to keep yourself safe. Any car you do rent should have nothing on it – such as a particular license plate – that makes it easy to identify as a rental car. When driving, under no circumstances stop in any unlit or seemingly deserted urban area – and especially not if someone is waving you down and suggesting that there is something wrong with your car.

Similarly, if you are "accidentally" rammed by the driver behind, do not stop but drive on to the nearest well-lit, busy area and phone the police at ☎911. Keep your doors locked and windows never more than slightly open. Do not open your door or window if someone approaches your car on the pretext of asking directions. Hide any valuable out of sight, preferably locked in the trunk or in the glove compartment (any valuable you don't need for your journey should be left in your hotel safe).

Travelers with disabilities

Florida law requires that all public buildings must be **wheelchair accessible** and have appropriate bathrooms, and Miami's city buses have handgrips for wheelchair users and are all able to 'kneel' to make access easier; the Tri-Rail and Metromover systems are also adapted for full disabled access. The one frustration for disabled travelers to Miami is likely to come in South Beach: the rooms and elevators in the old hotels there are tiny and so can often feel cramped for wheelchair users. In fact, disabled travelers might be better staying at a newer resort elsewhere in the city and commuting to sightsee and sunbathe on South Beach – there's a disabled access point to the beach at 10th Street close to the MDPL headquarters.

Planning your trip

It's always a good idea for people with special needs to alert their travel agents when booking: things are far simpler when the various travel operators or carriers are expecting you. A medical certificate of your fitness to travel, provided by your doctor, is also useful; some airlines or insurance companies may insist on it.

Most airlines do whatever they can to ease your journey and will usually let attendants of more seriously disabled people accompany them at no extra charge. Almost every Amtrak train includes one or more coaches with accommodation for passengers with disabilities; guide dogs travel free and may accompany blind, deaf, or disabled passengers in the carriage. Greyhound buses are not equipped with lifts for wheelchairs, though staff will assist with boarding, and the "Helping Hand" scheme offers two for the price of one tickets to passengers unable to travel alone (make sure to carry a doctor's certificate).

The American Automobile Association produces the *Handicapped Drivers Mobility Guide* for disabled drivers (available at bookstores or online). The larger car rental companies provide cars with hand controls at no extra charge, though only on their full-sized (in other words, more expensive) models; reserve well in advance.

Contacts for travelers with disabilities

In the US and Canada

Access-Able ☻www.access-able.com. Online resource for travelers with disabilities.

Directions Unlimited 123 Green Lane, Bedford Hills, NY 10507 ☎1-800/533-5343 or 914/241-1700. Tour operator specializing in custom tours for people with disabilities.

Mobility International USA 451 Broadway, Eugene, OR 97401, voice and TDD ☎541/343-1284, ☻www.miusa.org. Information and referral services, access guides, tours, and exchange programs. Annual membership $35 (includes quarterly newsletter).

Society for Accessible Travel & Hospitality 347 5th Ave, New York, NY 10016 ☎212/447-7284, ☻www.sath.org. Nonprofit educational organization that has actively represented travelers with disabilities since 1976.

Twin Peaks Press Box 129, Vancouver, WA 98661 ☎360/694-2462, ☻home.pacifier.com/~twinpeak/. Publisher of the *Directory of Travel Agencies for the Disabled* ($19.95), listing more than 370 agencies worldwide; *Travel for the Disabled* ($19.95); the *Directory of Accessible Van Rentals* ($12.95); and *Wheelchair Vagabond* ($19.95), loaded with personal tips.

Wheels Up! ☎1-888/389-4335, ☻www.wheelsup.com. Provides discounted airfare, tour, and cruise prices for disabled travelers; also publishes a free monthly newsletter and has a comprehensive website.

In the UK and Ireland

Holiday Care 2nd floor, Imperial Building, Victoria Rd, Horley, Surrey RH6 7PZ ☎0845/124 9973, Minicom ☎0845/124 9976, ☻www.holidaycare.org.uk. Provides free lists of accessible accommodation abroad. Information on financial help for holidays available.

Irish Wheelchair Association Blackheath Drive, Clontarf, Dublin 3 ☎01/818 6455, ☻www.iwa.ie.

Useful information provided about traveling abroad with a wheelchair.

Royal Association for Disability and Rehabilitation 12 City Forum, 250 City Rd, London EC1V 8AF ☎ 020/7250 3222, Minicom ☎ 020/7250 4119, ⊛ www.radar.org.uk. A good source of advice on holidays and travel.

Tripscope Alexandra House, Albany Rd, Brentford, Middlesex TW8 0NE ☎ 0845/7585 641, ⊛ www .tripscope.org.uk. This registered charity provides a national telephone information service offering free advice on UK and international transportation for those with mobility problems.

In Australia and New Zealand

Australian Council for Rehabilitation of the Disabled PO Box 60, Curtin ACT 2605 ☎ 02/6282 4333, ⊛ www.acrod.org.au. Provides lists of travel agencies and tour operators for people with disabilities.

Disabled Persons Assembly 4/173–175 Victoria St, Wellington, New Zealand ☎ 04/801 9100, ⊛ www.dpa.org.nz. Resource center with lists of travel agencies and tour operators for people with disabilities.

Senior travelers

South Florida's popularity with so-called "**snowbirds**" from the Northeast means that there are often senior-specific discounts and packages offered by hotels here. Amtrak, Greyhound, and many US airlines offer percentage discounts to anyone who can produce ID that proves they're over 62: don't expect hefty price breaks, but it's always worth checking. Museums and art galleries are better, and most will charge a reduced student/seniors rate, often to those 55 or older.

Any US citizen or permanent resident aged 62 or over is entitled to free admission for life to all national parks, monuments, and historic sites, using a **Golden Age Passport**, for which a once-only $10 fee is charged; it can be issued at any such site. This free entry also applies to any accompanying car passengers, or for those hiking or cycling, and the passport-holder's immediate family. It also gives a 50 percent reduction on fees for camping, parking, and boat launching.

Contacts for senior travelers

In the US and Canada

American Association of Retired Persons ☎ 1-800/304-4222, ⊛ www.aarp.org. Can provide discounts on accommodation and vehicle rental.

Membership open to US and Canadian residents aged 50 or over for an annual fee of US $12.50 ($29.50 for 3 years).

Elderhostel ☎ 1/877-426-8056, ⊛ www .elderhostel.org. Runs extensive educational and activity programs, including art appreciation, glassblowing, and historic sightseeing. Programs generally last 3–5 nights and costs are in line with those of commercial tours.

Vantage Deluxe World Travel ☎ 1-800/322-6677, ⊛ www.vantagetravel.com. Specializes in worldwide group travel for seniors.

In the UK

Saga Holidays ☎ 0800/096 0078 or 44 1303/771 190, ⊛ www.saga.co.uk. The country's biggest and most established specialist in tours and holidays aimed at older people.

The City

The City

Downtown Miami

With its profusion of gleaming office buildings towering over smaller Cuban-owned businesses, **Downtown Miami**, also known as the Central Business District (or CBD), simultaneously shows the city at its most Anglo and its most Latin. From a distance, the sparkling high-rises make Miami look much like any other modern American metropolis; it's only when you're standing below those skyscrapers, surrounded by jostling crowds and noisy traffic, that the feel of a Latin American capital takes over. If the place all feels a bit overwhelming, don't be discouraged – Downtown is actually one of Miami's most compact districts, and holds two of the area's best museums, while offering the clearest sense of the everyday influence Cuba has on the city, from office workers lighting at tiny streetside cafés for a midmorning *cafecito*, or Cuban coffee, to the bilingual signage in almost every store. The vibrant Cuban music spilling from almost every store onto the sidewalk is likely these days to be accompanied by the banging and crashing of construction; Downtown's the target for much of the new high-rise condo development mushrooming around the city. Though at the time of writing there are under a thousand residents in the CBD, more than 30,000 new homes are set to hit the market in the next five years and look likely to transform not just the skyline but also the atmosphere here.

Geographically, the Miami River divides Downtown: on the south bank, big business and big buildings line **Brickell Avenue**, known as "Millionaires Row" in the early twentieth century. The surrounding area, bounded by I-95 to the west, Coconut Grove to the south, and Biscayne Bay to the east, is known as **Brickell**; boasting one of the densest concentrations of new high-rise homes, it is becoming the district of choice for Miami's young professionals.

North of the river, things are less modern but more interesting. **Flagler Street** functions as the city's central artery, joining **Bayfront Park** with the **Metro-Dade Cultural Center** to the west. It's a commercial bazaar that hums with jewelers, fabric stores, and cheap electronics outlets. There are few name-brand shops here: this is a place of diners and discounters, stores in low-slung buildings playing loud music and spilling their wares out onto the sidewalk. At the same time, Flagler Street also offers up a successful showcase of the architecture on which modern Miami was built, beginning with the **Alfred I. DuPont Building**.

Further north, past the iconic, if derivative, **Freedom Tower**, lie **Overtown** and **Liberty City**, two of Miami's historically black neighborhoods. Both are areas that the strenuous tourist gloss applied by the city in the late 1990s has yet to reach, and can still be somewhat dicey. Though they've yet to benefit from the economic upsurge elsewhere in the city, they exude a fierce sense of history, and it's worth visiting one or both during the day or on an organized tour.

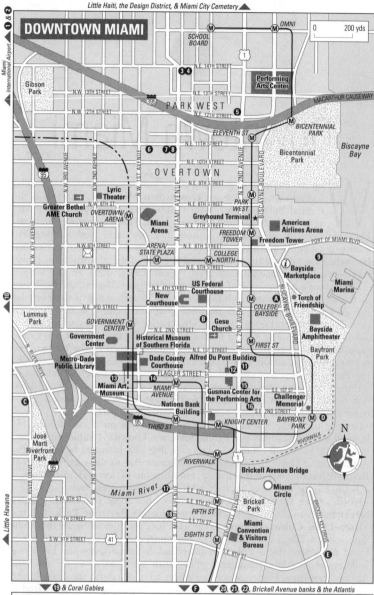

DOWNTOWN MIAMI

Little Haiti, the Design District, & Miami City Cemetery ▲

Miami International Airport ◄

❶ & ❷

DOWNTOWN MIAMI

Miami Beach & the Art Deco District ►

0   200 yds

SCHOOL BOARD

OMNI Ⓜ

❸ ❹

N.E. 14TH STREET

N.E. 13TH STREET

Gibson Park

N.W. 13TH STREET

Performing Arts Center

N.W. 12TH STREET

PARK WEST

N.E. 12TH STREET

MACARTHUR CAUSEWAY

❺

ELEVENTH ST

Ⓜ

BICENTENNIAL PARK

Biscayne Bay

❻

N.E. 11TH STREET

Bicentennial Park

❼ ❽

N.E. 10TH STREET

OVERTOWN

N.E. 9TH STREET

Lyric Theater

N.W. 8TH ST

N.E. 8TH STREET

PARK WEST

Greater Bethel AME Church

OVERTOWN/ARENA Ⓜ

N.W. 7TH ST

Miami Arena

N.E. 7TH STREET

Greyhound Terminal ★

Freedom Tower Ⓜ

American Airlines Arena

PORT OF MIAMI BLVD

Miami Beach & the Art Deco District

Port of Miami ►

N.W. 6TH STREET

ARENA/STATE PLAZA

N.E. 6TH STREET

Freedom Tower

✉

N.W. 5TH STREET

COLLEGE NORTH Ⓜ

N.E. 5TH STREET

❾

Ⓘ Bayside Marketplace

Lummus Park

N.E. 4TH STREET

US Federal Courthouse

Ⓜ COLLEGE BAYSIDE

Ⓐ

● Torch of Friendship

Miami Marina

New Courthouse

N.E. 3RD STREET

Ⓑ

Gesu Church

Ⓜ

Bayside Amphitheater

GOVERNMENT CENTER

N.E. 2ND STREET

Government Center

Ⓜ

Historical Museum of Southern Florida

Ⓜ FIRST ST

Bayfront Park

Metro-Dade Public Library

Dade County Courthouse

Alfred Du Pont Building

Ⓒ

⑫ ⑪

FLAGLER STREET

⑬

Miami Art Museum

⑭

MIAMI AVENUE

Nations Bank Building

⑮

Gusman Center for the Performing Arts

Challenger Memorial

S.E. 1ST STREET

José Martí Riverfront Park

⑯

S.E. 2ND STREET

Bayfront Park

Ⓓ

KNIGHT CENTER

Ⓜ

THIRD ST

Little Havana ◄

RIVERWALK

Ⓜ

RIVERWALK

Miami River

⑰

RIVERWALK

Brickell Avenue Bridge

Ⓜ

Ⓞ Miami Circle

S.E. 5TH STREET

Brickell Park

⑱

S.W. 6TH STREET

S.E. 6TH ST

FIFTH ST

S.W. 7TH STREET

S.E. 7TH ST

Miami Convention & Visitors Bureau

41

EIGHTH ST

Ⓜ

S.W. 8TH STREET

S.E. 8TH ST

N ✦

⑲ & Coral Gables ▼

Ⓕ ▼

⑳, ㉑, ㉒, Brickell Avenue banks & the Atlantis ▼

48

ACCOMMODATION		EATING				DRINKING & NIGHTLIFE	
Four Seasons Miami	F	Big Fish Mayami	15	Morton's		Club NV	6
Holiday Inn		Garcia's Seafood Grille	10	Steakhouse	20	Club Space	8
Marina Park –		Gili's Sandwich Bar	3	Mosaico	21	i/o lounge	4
Port of Miami	A	La Loggia	14	Raja's	11	M-Bar	E
Intercontinental	D	La Paris	16	Rosinella	22	Nocturnal	7
Mandarin Oriental	E	Las Palmas	15	Royal Man I	1	Pawn Shop Lounge	5
Miami River Inn	C	Lo Spaghetto	12	Tobacco Road	16	Tobacco Road	18
Miami Sun Hotel	B	Los Ranchos	9	Top Hat Deli	13		
				Tutto Pasta	19		
				Zion Bakery	2		

DOWNTOWN MIAMI (vertical, left margin)

❶ (circled, left margin)

The CBD is definitely a place to visit during the day – at weekends and in the evening, restaurants usually shut down since few of the would-be tenants have yet moved into their new Downtown homes. However, public transportation is thorough and an elevated monorail, the free **Metromover** (see p.35), circles Downtown's main loop, making it a handy way to orient yourself.

Flagler Street and around

The heart of Downtown Miami is **Flagler Street**, choked with cheap fabric stores, electronics shops, and, for some reason, dozens of discount shoe outlets. The other notable industry here is gemstones: the **Seybold Building**, which sprawls for a block between Miami and NE 1st avenues, is a hotbed hub of diamond trading – expect fair prices, but also be informed and prepared to haggle (it's not for amateurs). Although at lunchtime the area's throbbing with life, by 6pm it's deserted: unlike many other American city centers, Miami is in the early stages of its residential revitalization, and there are few apartment complexes or converted lofts Downtown open yet, though with the ferocious construction currently under way, scores of residents (by some estimates, up to 40,000 people) will move in over the next two years or so and likely enliven the area come nighttime.

Along the street are a few architectural highlights, as well as the mother lode of Miami's cultural elite (at least for now): the **Metro–Dade Cultural Center**. This ochre-colored, low-slung building stands out amid the gleaming metal and glass that dominates the rest of Downtown; it's full of grand intentions as a public space, but frankly falls a little flat. Architectural legend and pioneer Philip Johnson designed the complex to ape an old fort, echoing the Mediterranean Revival style found elsewhere in the city: the result is a series of anodyne ranch buildings around a communal piazza that remains eternally empty thanks to the punishing Miami sun. Still, at the moment, the Center boasts two of Downtown's top attractions, the **Historical Museum of South Florida** and the **Miami Art Museum**.

The Alfred I. DuPont Building and the Gusman Center for the Performing Arts

Two notable buildings stand along the eastern portion of Flagler Street. Near SE 2nd Avenue, the **Alfred I. DuPont Building**, at no. 169, is one of the best examples of Depression Moderne design in the city, with its simple but imposing black facade. Now home to the Florida National Bank, the first floor is open to the public, so feel free to wander through during office hours and catch its spectacular and ornate interior. Note especially the fanciful wrought-iron screens, frescoes of Florida scenes, and bronze bas-relief elevator doors with egrets and herons.

Opposite the DuPont Building, at no. 174, **the Olympia Theater at the Gusman Center for Performing Arts** (☎305/374-2444, ⓦwww .gusmancenter.org) was built in 1926 as a vaudeville house. Much like the Mathesons and their mustard-gas millions (see p.123), the Gusmans profited through government contracts in World War I; theirs was to provide condoms for departing American soldiers. The building's hodgepodge of architectural styles best approximates a Spanish-Moorish theme, with turrets, towers, and intricately detailed columns, and recent renovations have brought out the stunning moldings in its lobby ceiling; it's also noteworthy as the first air-conditioned building in Miami. However, the only way you'll be able to see inside the whole building (and not just the lobby) is by catching a performance (see p.163 for ticket information) – if you do, note the kitschy ceiling in the auditorium, twinkling with fake stars and the illusion of slowly moving clouds.

Burdine's and the Coppertone sign

Further west along Flagler, on the corner with Miami Avenue, stands the first in the **Burdine's** department store chain at no. 22 (now owned by, and recently rebranded as, Macy's). The structure's notable for its Streamline Moderne design, all hard edges rounded off and corners curved to convey gentle movement; the extension across Miami Avenue was put up immediately after World War II. This first outpost of "Florida's department store" was founded as a dry goods shop in 1898, a mere two years after the city was incorporated, by William Burdine, who traded refined sugar, cloth, and nails for Native American pelts.

Crossing over Miami Avenue onto West Flagler Street, look for the giant relief of the famous **Coppertone sign** – a young girl whose pet dog is tugging down her bikini bottom – that was based on a seaside snapshot (it's not, as urban legend sometimes has it, Jodie Foster). Originally located along Biscayne Boulevard, the iconic sign was moved here when the building to which it was attached was demolished; it's showcased simply because the office block was owned by a preservation-minded member of the Dade Heritage Trust, which spearheaded the campaign to save the sign.

The Miami-Dade County Courthouse

Continue west along the street and you'll hit the four forbidding Doric columns which mark the entrance to the **Dade County Courthouse**, at no. 73 W Flagler St (☎305/275-1155). Built in 1926 around a still-extant courthouse – where public hangings used to take place – this was Miami's tallest building for fifty years until it was superseded by the 55-story First Union Financial Center on South Biscayne Boulevard. Its night lights use to show off a distinctive stepped pyramid peak intended to serve as a constant reminder to would-be wrongdoers of where they'd end up. It was no idle boast: originally, this peak was the location of the courthouse's onsite jail, prisoners were known to throw dampened toilet paper down onto passersby, so the holding cells were moved in 1961.

The Historical Museum of Southern Florida

Looming above the piazza's western flank, the **Historical Museum of Southern Florida** (Mon–Wed, Fri & Sat 10am–5pm, Thurs 10am–9pm, Sun noon–5pm; $5, $6 combined ticket with Miami Art Museum; ☎305/375-1492, ⓦwww.historical-museum.org) is home to detailed, interactive displays covering Florida from the prehistoric up until the present. Some of the exhibits are a little worn around the edges, but there's plenty to entertain kids including dress-up boxes with period clothes and pioneer toys, while for adults, there's a small but instructive map collection that shows the gradual European charting of the area.

Where perhaps the museum is strongest, though, is its post-1950s display: a pair of tiny boats used by Cuban and Haitian refugees to reach Miami in the late 1970s sits next to TVs running archive news footage showing local hostility to the Mariel Boatlift in 1980. Also well chronicled are the fluctuating fortunes of Miami Beach, from its early days as a celebrity vacation spot – with amusing photos of Twenties Hollywood greats – through to the renovation of the Art Deco district. In its first-floor **research facility**, the Historical Museum houses the archives of the now-defunct *Miami News*, the city's first daily newspaper, and walk-in visitors are welcome to scan the decades of news photography on site.

The Miami Art Museum

Directly across the Metro-Dade Cultural Center piazza from the Historical Museum, the **Miami Art Museum**, at 101 W Flagler St (Tues–Fri 10am–5pm, third Thurs of each month 10am–9pm, Sat & Sun noon–5pm; $5, $6 combined ticket with Historical Museum, free admission second Sat of each month and every Sun; ☏305/375-3000, ⊕www.miamiartmuseum.org), holds a remarkable collection of postwar art, setting acknowledged modern masterpieces alongside quirky, newer works. The first floor of the building offers a rotating selection, refreshed four times yearly, from the museum's own collection. It's accessible and intelligently curated: among notable works, look for sketches by Robert Rauschenberg and art stuntman Christo (see p.72, "South Beach"), not to mention surrealist pioneer Marcel Duchamp's *Boîte en Valise*, which consists of witty *maquettes* of his previous masterworks, all in a handy carrying case. Yet it's the museum's conceptual art collection that is most stunning, especially the bevy of works by the late Cuban-American artist Felix Gonzalez-Torres. His organic pieces, designed to change through viewing – such as a stark ream of embossed paper that visitors are intended to sample sheet by sheet, or a help-yourself pile of candy stacked in a stark white corner that dwindles with every hungry passerby – are truly remarkable. The museum often manages to hook prime traveling exhibits, too, which are mounted in its gallery space on the upper floor. It's set to decamp to a state-of-the-art site on the waterfront, as part of the Museum Park Miami project (see p.56), though no firm date's been set yet.

Opposite the museum looms the **Main Public Library** (Mon–Sat 9am–6pm, Thurs 9am–9pm, Sun 1–5pm; closed Sun in summer), which, besides the usual lending sections, has temporary painting and photography exhibits showcasing local literary and artistic talents – the narrow focus of which typically makes them worth checking out – as well as a massive collection of Florida-related magazines and books.

The Gesú Church

Just north of the Alfred I. DuPont Building stands the **Gesú Church** (☏305/379-1424), at 118 NE 2nd St (Mass held Mon–Sat 8.15am (bilingual), 11am (Spanish), 12.10pm (English), additional vigil mass Sat 4pm, Sun 8.30am & 11.30am (English), 10am & 1pm (Spanish), home to Miami's oldest Catholic parish. The original wooden building, called the Church of the Holy Name, was completed in 1898 on land that Henry Flagler had donated to the city for use as a church and school. This large Mediterranean Revival replacement was built in 1925 and sticks out amid the cramped storefronts of Downtown, painted as it is in colors of peach sherbet and lemon meringue. However, the church's foamy, baroque appliqué exterior is more noteworthy than its stout inner sanctum – designed without posts or pillars so that the Jesuits would have unobstructed sightlines for their fiery sermons; the interior's framed by modern stained glass from Munich.

The US Federal Courthouse

Two blocks northwest from the Gesú Church, the unremarkable 1931 Neoclassical structure at 300 NE 1st St was originally the city's post office, but was commandeered a year later to serve as the **US Federal Courthouse** (Mon–Fri

8.30am–5pm; ☎305/523-5100). Most voluntary visitors stop by for a glimpse of Denman Fink's 25-foot mural, *Law Guides Florida's Progress* – depicting Florida's evolution from swampy backwoods to modern state – in the small courtroom on the second floor (for more of his work, head over to Coral Gables – see p.109). The WPA work is more impressive for its size rather than skill, but look for Fink's portrait of his young nephew, George Merrick, the founder of Coral Gables, delivering produce. The mural's usually accessible to visitors, provided there's no closed-door court case in session – call in advance to check and make sure to **bring photo ID**. Merrick's isn't the only notable public artwork in the building – in 1985, fresco artist David Novros was commissioned to decorate the building's medieval-style inner **courtyard**, to which his bold, colorful daubs make a lively addition.

The **New Courthouse** next door replaced this older structure as the city's main legal facility in the late 1960s, when Miami's soaring crime rate outstripped its capabilities (main entrance on N Miami Ave; Mon–Fri 8.30am–5pm). It's a gruesome creation of concrete and glass, and was poorly designed – it's difficult, for instance, for lawyers to present evidence clearly to the audience in the courtroom. The major advantage of the new courthouse – other than size – is that jurors can pass in and out unobserved – "Getting them out without getting them dead," as one judge commented. Now, even this courthouse is to be superseded by a soaring new $120m structure a few blocks away at 400 N Miami Ave, that's set to open in summer 2005; it's to be named after the late black judge Wilkie D. Ferguson and designed by Arquitectonica. Its odd location, diagonally in the middle of a block, was a security measure influenced by the Oklahoma City bombing – don't miss the gardens masterminded by Maya Lin, who shot to fame as the designer of the Vietnam War Memorial in Washington, DC.

Bayfront Park

At the east end of East Flagler Street lies **Bayfront Park**, at 301 N Biscayne Blvd (☎305/358-7550, ⊛www.bayfrontparkmiami.com). It's a pleasant enough urban greenspace, dotted with sculpture and large, leafy trees, though the lack of significant shade around its wide benches makes them a less than comfortable spot to dawdle for most of the year. There's no specific local connection to Isamu Noguchi's white geometric *Challenger Memorial* at the park's southwest corner – it's simply here because the park's current design was completed in 1986, around the same time as the space shuttle exploded mid-flight, and the designer included the monument as a late addition. Before that, Bayfront Park – laid out on reclaimed land dredged from the bottom of the bay in the 1920s – was best known as the site of the attempted assassination of President-elect Franklin D. Roosevelt by a disaffected Italian bricklayer, Giuseppe Zangarra (Roosevelt survived, but then-mayor of Chicago Anton Cermak, who was standing close by, died of his wounds; Zangarra went to the electric chair just over a month later).

At the opposite end of the park stands the highly charged **Torch of Friendship**, which commemorates a burning local issue and another, more controversial president. Built in 1960, then rededicated in JFK's memory four years later, it centers on a lighted torch, surrounded by crests of every Latin American country save one. Cuba's emblem is purposefully omitted, leaving a pointed blank space between Costa Rica and the Dominican Republic, intending to add her symbol only when Cuba was free of communism. That said, the site's now rather forlorn and the city takes little interest in it; it's also missing many of the original crests, which means that Cuba's omission no longer stands out.

△ The Brickell skyline

At its northern tip, the park leads into the **Bayside Marketplace** (usual hours Mon–Thurs 10am–10pm, Fri–Sat 10am–11pm, Sun 11am–9pm; ☎305/577-3344, ⑭www.baysidemarketplace.com), which features the usual upscale chain stores and restaurants in an open-air complex by the water, and is usually packed with tourists. There's also a small, unofficial tourist information booth at its entrance that's good for maps.

South of Miami River

To reach the southern portion of Downtown, head through the square surrounded by high-rise towers known as **DuPont Plaza**, and walk across the bridge – crowned by a moody, modern statue of a crossbow-toting Tequesta warrior and his wife – and you'll pass from the soul of the city to its wallet.

This area, known as **Brickell** (rhymes with "pickle"), is the city's financial center. Money was the original foundation of this area, and early developers Mary and William Brickell, who ran a trading post nearby, planned a wide tree-lined avenue that could be built up with mansions for their friends. In doing so, they created the city's most desirable neighborhood – it was *the* address in 1910s Miami – and Brickell Avenue soon earned the nickname **Millionaires Row**.

From the late Seventies, Miami emerged as a corporate banking center, cashing in on political instability in South and Central America by offering a secure home for Latin American money, some of which needed laundering. Since then, Miami has maneuvred to become second only to New York in serving as the headquarters of international **banks**; and the forest of mirrored buildings that cluster along Brickell Avenue sprouts new offshoots every year. Recent years have seen the Brickell area returning to that gleaming heyday, as the intensive construction of luxury residential condos and high-end condo-hotels like the *Four Seasons* have drawn wealthy young professionals to live close to their offices Downtown.

The Miami Circle

Local developer Michael Baumann purchased the triangle of land east of Brickell Avenue wedged against the Miami River – once the site of a 1950s apartment complex – for $8 million in the mid-1990s and planned to throw up a premium-priced high-rise. Archeologists were hired to clear the area for construction as per local ordinances and, unfortunately for Baumann, they found something – a coral rock circle, 38 feet in diameter and carved four feet deep into the bedrock, carbon-dated to be at least 10,000 years old and now known as the **Miami Circle**.

Its age is the only indisputable thing: experts argue over the circle's original purpose, whether it was a religious, community, or commercial center, or even who might have built it. While they debate, others are considering how best to display this find for the local community; no final decision's been made, and thus you can't visit yet. It will likely take at least five years before people can visit the Miami Circle close up – check with the Dade Heritage Trust (☎305/358-9572, ⊛www.dadeheritagetrust.org) for updates. If you're determined to see it close up, stay in the nearby *Sheraton* (☎305/373-6000, ⊛www.sheraton.com), and ask for a room that overlooks the site - at least until the hotel's razed by its new owners to make way for yet more high-rise waterfront condos. Don't weep for Baumann, though – he was able to strongarm the city into paying $26.7 million to purchase the land back from him, turning a tidy profit of more than $18 million without laying a single brick.

The Atlantis

At 2025 Brickell Ave, **the Atlantis** apartment complex is the project that turned the Arquitectonica design team, husband and wife architects Laurinda Spear and Bernardo Fort-Brescia, from wannabes to A-listers; it was built on the site of one of the grandest mansions on Millionaires Row, the Mitchell-Bingham residence, home to Mary Tiffany Bingham, sister of glass guru Louis. Like a cored apple, the Atlantis complex has a square hole through the middle, filled with a single palm tree, a Jacuzzi, and a fire-engine-red spiral staircase. Built some twenty years ago, its playful design is even more eye-catching now amid the earnest bombast of nearby skyscrapers; it clearly owes much to the stylish mischief of mid-century pioneers like Morris Lapidus. You won't be allowed inside unless you know someone who lives there, which might be just as well: even its designers admit the interior doesn't live up to the exuberance of the exterior, and claim the building to be "architecture for 55mph" – in other words, seen to best effect from a passing car.

North of Downtown

North of the Downtown loop, sights thin out considerably and neighborhoods grow rougher: patches like **Bicentennial Park** are closer to the crime-hobbled Miami of the 1980s than the glossy city of today. The **Port of Miami** is still one of the busiest cruise-ship docks in the world, though, and on any given day you can drive down MacArthur Causeway to the beach to see half a dozen mammoth ships queuing patiently at the dock.

△ The Atlantis building

One of the most arresting additions to the local skyline is the **American Airlines Arena** on the old Port of Miami site. A high-profile project for local design celebrities Arquitectonica, the AA Arena is an origami building floating by the bay, its stark, rounded walls like stowed wings. It's the site of many big-name concerts as well as home to the Miami Heat basketball team (see p.181), currently resurging thanks to the recent signing of superstar (and commercial icon) Shaquille O'Neal. Directly opposite the Arena is the **Freedom Tower**, new headquarters of the Cuban-American National Foundation.

Freedom Tower

Often called "Miami's Ellis Island," the ornate **Freedom Tower** (☎305/416-4456, @www.terradevelopers.com), at 600 N Biscayne Blvd, served not only as an immigration processing post but also as a community center for the more than 360,000 Cuban refugees who arrived between 1961 and 1974. It was one of three replicas of Seville's Giralda belltower built in Miami by the same architects, Schutze and Weaver, who designed New York's Grand Central Station: the others were the *Roney Plaza* hotel in Miami Beach (since demolished), and Coral Gables' *Biltmore* hotel (see p.110).

Since its 1925 construction as the headquarters of the *Miami Times* newspaper, this Mediterranean Revival structure has lain more often empty than occupied thanks in part to its impractical and eccentric shape, with a high, narrow turret, and little versatile office space. Its most recent owners were the **Cuban-American National Foundation**, whose late head, telecom billionaire Jorge Mas Canosa, bought the place in 1997 amid much fanfare with plans to open a massive museum. After his death, the plans foundered amid in-fighting and arguments over what was appropriate to feature – exhibits were scheduled to showcase refugee raft simulations, Cuban art exhibits, as well as a public research center. The building's been sold again, this time to local real estate conglomerate Terra Developers. The company's not yet confirmed its intentions, only saying that it will open some form of cultural space in the Freedom Tower, perhaps administered by a partner university, while using the land around it to construct high-rise condos.

Bicentennial Park

Troubled from the day it opened in 1977 (the men running the food stands on opening night were mugged for the day's takings), **Bicentennial Park**, at 1075 N Biscayne Blvd, is a problematic eyesore for the city to which little attention has been paid. For over 25 years, its 35 acres – originally an oily storage lot for shipping containers from the nearby Port of Miami – have served as a refuge for the area's homeless and is not a place to dawdle, especially at dusk. That's set to change in the next five years, as a monumental new construction project gets underway. Known as Museum Park Miami, this cultural hub will combine the Museum of Science, currently in Coconut Grove (see p.122), and the Miami Art Museum (see p.51) on a single site, alongside a satellite location for the Historical Museum of Southern Florida; the park will also boast a four-acre sculpture garden and a large zoo.

To date, progress has been slow and the project highly controversial, mostly owing to the debate of building here rather than creating an unbroken, open greenspace. However, in late 2004, voters approved funds to begin the construction and relocation, though no schedule's been confirmed at time of writing: check ⓦwww.miamiartmuseum.org for updates or call ☎305/375-1700.

Overtown

Northwest of Downtown lies **Overtown**, originally known as Coloredtown, one of the oldest neighborhoods in Miami. Local zoning laws forbade the sale of land to blacks except in this area after Miami was founded in 1896, and it was soon securely cordoned off from the rest of Downtown by the railroad. Even so, a settlement developed that was larger even than the existing black neighborhood in Coconut Grove. By the 1930s, Coloredtown was a vibrant entertainment district: NW 2nd Avenue between 6th and 10th streets was variously known as "Little Broadway," "The Strip," and even "The Great Black Way."

One of the driving forces behind Little Broadway was the black promoter **Clyde Killens**, who started out as a drum accompanist for silent movies. From there, the outlandish Killens achieved pre-eminence managing hotels and nightclubs, not to mention being one of the first black Miamians to register to vote. He succeeded in part thanks to the segregationist policy that ensured that while black entertainers like Dorothy Dandridge were wowing white crowds at sell-out shows on Miami Beach, they would have to stay at hotels in the Overtown ghetto.

Although the postwar years proved tough for the local economy, Overtown's decline accelerated rapidly in the 1960s, as the **construction of the I-95 Expressway** devastated the area. It was nothing more than an act of urban social vandalism with 20,000 people forcibly displaced and disconnected from all social amenities. The neighborhood never recovered, and it became a poster child for Miami's crime problem in the late 1980s. Now, although it's slowly clawing its way back to economic health, the district's still a dangerous place for visitors even in the daytime, and the best way to see it is on an organized tour (see p.36).

The Overtown Historic District

If Coloredtown was Miami's Harlem, then its counterpart to the Apollo Theater is the **Lyric Theater**, at 819 NW 2nd Ave. It's at the center of a rather desolate two-block area now known as the **Overtown Historic District**, and is owned and promoted by the Black Archives (see p.58). The theater was built in 1913 by black entrepreneur Geder Walker, who dreamed of rivaling Europe's grand opera houses, though by the late 1940s it had been converted into a church. Recently restored to its original opulence, it is the only standing reminder of the district's funky heyday, when the likes of Nat King Cole and Lena Horne were regular visitors. It's still in sporadic use thanks to the efforts of the Black Archives; the new glass atrium currently being added to its northern edge is intended to make it appealing for corporate events but sadly detracts from the simplicity of the building's original design.

Nearby stands the Black Archives' other attraction here, the 1915 **D.A. Dorsey House** at 250 NW 9th St; the interior's not open to the public, as it houses some of the charity's administrative offices. It's famous as the home of the city's first black millionaire – fittingly, given today's building boom, he made his money in real estate. Dana Albert Dorsey started out as a carpenter and shrewdly racked up his money by buying land, building houses, and renting them to blacks. Astonishingly, his real-estate portfolio included the land that's today hyper-exclusive Fisher Island (see p.72); he'd intended to build an upscale black resort there in 1918 before changing his mind and selling his holdings a few years later. Built as a wedding gift to his new wife, the house had high-tech touches like electricity in every room; sadly, the structure that currently stands is actually a replica, albeit an authentic one. The other major sight of interest is the **Greater Bethel A.M.E. Church**, at 245 NW 8th St, notable mainly as the oldest black congregation in Miami (dating back to the year of the city's incorporation, 1896) and for its large Mediterranean Revival structure.

The Miami City Cemetery

Just north of Overtown, at 1800 NE 2nd Ave lies Miami's original cemetery (☎305/579-6938, ⓦwww.ci.miami.fl.us/Parks/pages/park_listings/cemetery .asp), founded in 1897. With its separate black section to the west plus white and walled Jewish sections to the east, the **Miami City Cemetery** is the final resting place for early pioneers, including Julia Tuttle (see p.254). The cemetery's now in a rundown part of town and so can be rather dangerous – many of the graves are littered with used syringes, anything valuable has been stolen and the family vaults of early Miami bigwigs have had their doors torn off by the homeless seeking shelter – so it's best seen on an organized tour (☎305/375-1621, ⓦwww.historical-museum.org), though, frankly, the Woodlawn Cemetery (see p.101) has richer pickings for grave hunters.

Liberty City

Much further northwest, **Liberty City** has wider streets and more parkland than Overtown, but can be just as dangerous and again is best visited during the day by car or with a tour.

The district centers on **Liberty Square**, at NW 12th Avenue between 62nd and 67th streets. This sprawling low-rise development, nicknamed "Pork'n'Beans" by locals on account of its pinkish-orange color, was the first public housing project in the state, opening in February 1937; thanks to its modern amenities, like indoor plumbing, it quickly began drawing blacks from Coloredtown. Today, the identical row houses, separated by threadbare lawns and barely affording residents any privacy, are much less appealing – note the remnants between 63rd and 64th streets of the six-foot-high segregation wall erected to keep the black and white communities separate. Look, too, for tributes to the late civil rights leader Martin Luther King: there's a particularly moving

The Liberty City riots

May 1980 was a grueling month for race relations in Miami. First, thousands of Cuban refugees poured into the city as part of the **Mariel Boatlift** (see p.259), causing widespread resentment. Then, the tinder of tensions waiting for a spark in Miami's black community finally ignited. There had been sporadic protests before: notably, what officials called a **"civil disturbance,"** which claimed the lives of four people in Liberty City in 1968, at the same time Richard Nixon was accepting the Republican presidential nomination at the Convention Center on the beach. The disturbance grew out of a protest against perceived bias in the criminal justice system as well as high local levels of unemployment, and it's ironic to note that one reason the Republicans picked Miami was the county's promise that urban unrest so common in other cities at the time, notably Chicago, could never happen here.

But the O.J. Simpson trial of its day was the **Arthur McDuffie murder case**, which set Miami's black neighborhoods ablaze. McDuffie was a black former Marine turned insurance salesman with no criminal record, who was stopped by four white police officers in December 1979 and beaten to death. They later claimed that he had provoked them by making an obscene gesture as he rode past on a borrowed motorbike. Tried in Tampa to avoid inflaming local passions, the four police officers were found not guilty (by an all-white jury) on **May 17, 1980**, six months to the day after McDuffie's death; the news came at 2.42pm and by 6.02pm, the riots had started. The citywide curfew that followed lasted nearly a week: by then, disturbances had reached as far south as Homestead. Whereas previous riots had been primarily aimed at property, in protest at slum conditions, this was racial violence: shocking stories, notably that of a young white motorist dragged from his car and mutilated by the mob, made headlines across America. When it was over, eighteen people had died, both white and black, with more than 400 injured – not to mention that the property destroyed was valued at more than $200 million.

mural at NW 62nd Street and 7th Avenue, the hub of the local economy and home to a few interesting stores and restaurants.

On the southwestern fringes of Liberty City, the **Black Archives History and Research Foundation of South Florida**, at 5400 NW 22nd Ave (Mon–Fri 9am–5pm; ☎305/636-2390), houses historical documents gathered from the local community. It's not, however, designed for drop-in visitors; call ahead if you want to use the facilities or go on a **tour** of Overtown and Liberty City (groups of ten or more necessary). The only other local attraction is the **African Heritage Cultural Arts Center**, at 6161 NW 62nd St (☎305/638-6771, ⊛www.miamidade.gov/parks/parks/african_heritage.asp), which offers Afrocentric classes in performing and fine arts along with a small gallery and theater.

South Beach

To most visitors to Miami, the charms of the rest of the city are eclipsed by seductive, chic **South Beach**, a colloquial designation for the area that stretches from the southernmost tip of Miami Beach north to 23rd Street (for the rest of Miami Beach, see "Central Miami Beach and north," Chapter 3). This is the place most people visualize when Miami is mentioned, and the partying and palm trees here perpetuate the image. Here, row upon row of Art Deco gems – especially along the much-photographed **Ocean Drive** – look exactly as they do on film: sleek, classic, and ultra cool.

Stretching from just south of 5th Street to just past Lincoln Road, bounded by the ocean to the east and Meridian Avenue to the west, the **Art Deco Historic District** holds almost every building that has made modern Miami famous. Walk around the area along the two main commercial drags, **Washington and Collins avenues**, or through the artsy **Española Way**, and you'll see dozens of architectural masterpieces, although don't forget to look up – some of the best signage and ornamentation is on the upper stories or the roofs of these buildings. While the tip of the island, **South Pointe**, is still gentrifying and a little edgy, there are parts of the District, notably along Ocean Drive between 5th and 10th streets, which have been worryingly Disneyfied despite the stringent preservation orders. This is where you'll find sidewalk cafés showcasing congealed samples of menu items and ferocious carnival-barker staff hailing passersby to take a table. Further north, though, it's as fun and stylish as ever: there are funky restaurants and hotels in the area around the junction of Collins Avenue and Lincoln Road, and **Lincoln Road Mall** is a great place to stroll even if you don't plan to spend. Floating just off the coast of the South Beach sandbar, a smattering of mostly man-made **islands** is notable largely for their celebrity residents.

Some history

Although the pioneer **John Collins** had lamely tried to launch fruit farming in the early 1900s further up the beach near what's now 41st Street, it wasn't until he joined forces with the money and determination of entrepreneur **Carl Fisher** that South Beach germinated. When Fisher drew up his original plan, he wanted to create a winter playland, to be called "Fairyland" – a story that many gay locals recount with ironic relish. His dream of a resort came true, if not his plans for its name: by the 1920s and 1930s, it was the heart of wealthy America's winter season. But after World War II, when soldiers (including Clark Gable) billeted here for training left, the smart set moved north to newer hotels in Central Miami Beach, and the district began to crumble.

By the 1980s, South Beach had become a no-go area, shared by geriatric retirees and criminals, many of them undesirables left over from the Mariel

SOUTH BEACH

Central Miami Beach

Sunset Island No. 4

Bass Museum of Art

Collins Park

Bayshore Municipal Golf Course

Holocaust Memorial

Miami Beach Convention Center

Miami Beach Chamber of Commerce

Jackie Gleason Theater of Performing Arts

Delano Hotel

Belle Isle

LINCOLN ROAD MALL

Lincoln Theater

Colony Theater

Art Center of South Florida

Flamingo Park

Miami Beach Post Office

Parking Garage

Parking Garage

Miami Beach Police

Versace Mansion

Beach Patrol Station

The Wolfsonian-FIU

Art Deco Welcome Center

South Shore Hospital

Parking Garage

Park Central Hotel

Electrowave Park N Ride

SOUTH POINTE

Sanford L. Ziff Jewish Museum of Florida

ATLANTIC OCEAN

Causeway Island

Miami Beach Marina

Terminal Island

Biscayne Bay

First Street Beach

South Pointe Tower

South Beach Pier

Government Cut

South Pointe Park

South Beach Pier

N

Electrowave Shuttle route

Art Deco Historic District

SOUTH BEACH

0   100 yds

Fisher Island

ACCOMMODATION				EATING					DRINKING	
Albion	G	The Ritz-Carlton		Cafeteria	16	Toni's Sushi	34	Mynt		
Aqua	K	South Beach	J	Casa Tua	7	Touch	13	Ultra Lounge	2	
Hotel Astor	X	Royal Hotel	gg	David's Café	38	Van Dyke Café	14	Nikki Beach	58	
Best Western		Sagamore	I	Eleventh St Diner	37	Verandah Café	5	Onda Lounge	32	
South Beach	T	Shelborne	C	Front Porch Café	28	Wish	ff	Opium Garden	53	
Brigham Gardens		Hotel Shelley	bb	Gino's	43	Yuca	10	Pearl	58	
Guesthouse	P	The Shore Club	B	Jerry's Famous Deli	22			Privé	53	
Clay Hotel		Standard Miami	H	Joe's Stone Crab	59			Purdy Lounge	1	
and Hostel	M	Townhouse	A	Joia	52	**DRINKING**		Raleigh Bar	D	
Clinton Hotel	aa	The Tropics		La Sandwicherie	30	**& NIGHTLIFE**		Rok Bar	4	
Delano	F	Hotel & Hostel	L	Le Provence	19	The Abbey		The Room	56	
Doubletree		Hotel Victor	S	Macaluso	6	Brewing Company	20	The Rose Bar	F	
Surfcomber	E	Villa Paradiso	N	Metro Kitchen & Bar	X	Amika Loft Lounge		Rumi	17	
Essex House	W	The Wave	jj	Miss Yip Chinese Café	8	& Discotheque	21	Sky Bar	A	
Fairwind Hotel	V	Whitelaw Hotel	ee	News Café	42	Automatic Slim's	33	The Spire Bar	ff	
The Hotel		Winterhaven	Q	Nobu	B	B.E.D.	39	State	18	
International	ff			Pacific Time	9	Blue	24	Studio Nightclub	C	
Travelers Hostel	Z	**EATING**		Pizza Rustica	41	Club Deep	47	Sushi Samba		
Island House	O	A La Folie Café	25	Prime 112	55	Club Deuce	31	Dromo	15	
Jefferson House	U	Ago	B	Puerto Sagua	45	Crobar	23	Ted's Hideaway		
Lily-Leon	cc	B.E.D.	39	The Smoothie Shop	35	DiLido Beach Club	J	South	51	
The Loft Hotel	Y	Balans		Sushi Samba Dromo	15	Honey	46	The Tides Bar	36	
Hotel Ocean	R	Lincoln Road	12	Tambo	3	Jazid	29	Touch	13	
The Park Central	ii	Bari	11	Tantra	27	Lost Weekend	23	W6 Lounge	49	
Pelican Hotel	dd	Big Pink	54	Tap Tap	50	Mansion	35	Wet Willie's	44	
The Raleigh	D	Bond St	A	Taverna Opa	57	Mango's	40			
				Taystee Bakery	26					

Boatlift (see p.259, Contexts: History). Its hip rebirth came at the end of the decade, when German catalog photographers discovered South Beach's unique combination of spectacular early-morning light, rock-bottom prices, and lack of expensive shooting permits. They started spending extended periods in South Beach, and soon developers noticed its advantages, too – not to mention the beautiful people who had begun to enjoy them. One of the first groups to decamp to the area in the late 1980s was Miami's **gay community**, which was soon rehabbing the area piecemeal much as the developers were on a larger scale, re-creating the resort and its funky, fabulous scene. Even if many in the local gay community have now moved on (especially further up the coast, either to Normandy Isle, p.81, or Fort Lauderdale, p.207), South Beach retains its glossy, glamorous reputation.

△ Miami Beach

②

The Jews of South Beach

The British and the Spanish were all too happy in the eighteenth century to encourage settlement of their new colony by anyone who was willing – even **Jews**, who can be found in the earliest records of the Sunshine State.

Jews were among Miami Beach's first settlers in the early twentieth century, too – founding **Joe's Stone Crab** restaurant in 1913, for one thing (see p.144 for review) – though they were ghettoised by an edict (supported by the staunchly anti-Semitic **Carl Fisher**) that prevented them buying land north of 5th Street. It wasn't until such laws were loosened after World War II that the local Jewish population exploded – though no local historian can offer a definitive explanation as to why. The most commonly accepted thesis cites the large portion of **soldiers** billeted here in converted hotels for training during the war; many, it's noted, were from New York or elsewhere in the Northeast and a large chunk of them were Jewish. After the war was over, suffering from the condition nicknamed "sand in their shoes," they returned to live in the sunny resort of which they had such fond memories. They were joined by another group made rootless by the same war: **Holocaust survivors**, whose community here was, at one point, the second largest in America.

By the 1970s, the Jewish community reached its peak: it's estimated that 90 percent of South Beach's population was Jewish, largely retirees from the Northeast who'd long spent winters here. Since then, the number has tailed off under pressure from gay gentrification and the increasingly mass appeal of the area, though experts still say that 15 percent of South Florida's current population is Jewish, making it one of the highest concentrations of Jews in the country.

Along Ocean Drive

You may not see many photo shoots taking place **along Ocean Drive** at 7am any more, but the early-morning light is still spectacular; it's easy to understand why South Beach became the fashion location of choice in the early 1990s and is well worth getting up early one morning to enjoy. One of the first hotels to cater to the fashionistas was the **Park Central** at no. 640, with its signature octagonal porthole windows. It's famous, too, as the place where the Vampire Lestat lodges when he visits Miami in Anne Rice's *Tale of the Body Thief* (1992); after repeated visits, the author was such a fan of the hotel that she lodged Lestat there, too. Today, the hotels here are being joined by increasing numbers of condo conversions, as the final few Art Deco shells like the *Adrian Hotel* complex are spiffed up and sold as luxury lofts.

The place to strut a well-toned, well-tanned body is **Lummus Park**, bordering Ocean Drive between 5th and 15th streets. It was named after pioneer brothers, J.E. and J.N. Lummus, who ran competing banks in Miami's early days (J.N. was also elected the first mayor of Miami Beach); the Lummus family were also real estate speculators, and sold the waterfront land to the city with the proviso that it always be a public beach – in the process, securing the value of the hotels they owned overlooking it. Although the gleaming beach seems quintessentially Miami, the fine white sand was actually imported from the Bahamas to replace the too-coarse local variety. You can rent deckchairs and umbrellas from one of many concessions on the waterfront, and there are bathrooms and showers on the grassy boardwalk that separates the beach from Ocean Drive. Open-air concerts are often staged here and it's also the site of the throbbing Winter Party each March (see p.166, "Gay Miami"). Notice too the quirky, ornamental lifeguard towers painted in neon colors and designed by local artists including Kenny Scharf – they're a fun addition to the seafront, if rather bedraggled now.

Casa Casuarina

Undeniably one of the most popular tourist sights on the beach, **Casa Casuarina** (T305/672-6604, Wwww.casacasuarina.com), the former home of murdered designer Gianni Versace, at 1114 Ocean Drive, is not open to the public. The original structure was built in 1930 as a spare-no-expense private home by Alden Freeman, who inherited $80m from family interests in Rockefeller's Standard Oil company (freespending Freeman vowed to die poor, and almost managed it, despite his staggering wealth). Freeman's pad was intended as a replica of the Alcázar de Colón in Santo Domingo, the home built by Christopher Columbus's son in 1510, which is claimed to be the oldest house in the Western Hemisphere. A friend of Freeman's called it Casa Casuarina, or House of the Pine, after a lone Casuarina or Australian pine tree that survived 1926's devastating hurricane. Upon Alden's death seven years later, it was sold to one of his friends who chopped it up into apartments; the complex became known as the Amsterdam Palace and limped along until 1992, by which time it was little more than a hovel. Versace, however, saw potential in the place, and snapped up the whole complex; he then spent $30m transforming it into his dream home, shipping in mosaic artists from Italy and frescoing ceilings with abandon, like a modern counterpart to Hearst Castle in California. Naturally, locals nicknamed it the **Versace Mansion**.

What Versace is most remembered for by history-minded locals, though, was one brazen act of architectural vandalism. Just before a preservation order could be enacted, he also purchased the adjoining *Revere Hotel*, a masterpiece of Miami Modernism, and promptly knocked it down to build a swimming pool and guesthouse (see p.262, Contexts: Architecture). That aside, Versace was a popular, easygoing member of the South Beach community, often spotted in local bars and clubs, and his murder on the steps here by serial killer **Andrew Cunanan** in 1997 shattered the safe illusion of South Beach's hedonistic abandon. After his death, it was snapped up by developer Peter Loftin, who's said to have paid around $19m for the place but declined to buy its furnishings, too, which were ultimately sold off piecemeal at auction. In 2004, after four years of dithering as to whether he'd open a hotel, a fashion museum, or a club, Loftin finally committed to transforming the place into a jet-set members-only pad: initiation fees run to $20,000 and annual dues alone are $3500.

The Art Deco Welcome Center

Headquarters of the Miami Design Preservation League, the Art Deco Welcome Center (Mon–Fri 10am–5pm; T305/672-2014, Wwww.mdpl.orgsits), at 1001 Ocean Drive on Lummus Park, are located in a jaunty Nautical Deco building, complete with faux smokestack and portholes on its lower decks; it is also still the headquarters for the local Beach Patrol.

The ambling, informative tours run by the League are unmissable (see p.36), plus there's a small free museum that makes a smart starting point for a comprehensive Art Deco tutorial. The League also arranges the Art Deco Weekend each January in the Historic District (see p.189, "Festivals and events").

Washington and Collins avenues

Named in honor of one of Miami Beach's pioneers, **Collins Avenue** (also known as Hwy-A1A) is the main traffic artery running the length of the island and, eventually, leads north to Fort Lauderdale's beachfront. At its southernmost end, one block west of Ocean Drive, it's crammed with hotels in all price ranges, as well as South Beach's swankiest shopping strip between 5th

Miami became a haven for Art Deco in large part owing to the wrecking power of South Florida's **hurricanes**. In 1926, the city was leveled by a devastating storm, and architects taken with Art Deco rebuilt whole blocks in the newly modish style. Cheap and sleek, it was ideal for developers anxious to throw up fresh hotels as quickly as possible, although shoddy construction methods doomed some treasured buildings to demolition less than fifty years later.

By that time, in the mid-1970s, many buildings, sound or unsound, were seen as old-fashioned and scheduled to be razed for condo construction – at least they were until one woman, **Barbara Baer Capitman**, began a relentless campaign for their preservation. Thankfully, she succeeded, and in 1979 the 1200-building **Art Deco Historic District** was formally declared in South Beach.

While Art Deco style is by no means uniform – one of its core features was its ready absorption of local influences – the pastel colors usually associated so strongly with it were a marketing gimmick Capitman & Co. devised in the 1980s. Originally most buildings were whitewashed, their features picked out in dark brown or navy blue.

Deco styles

Tropical or **Miami Deco** (most popular in the 1920s–1930s) is the base style from which all the other Deco types spring. Look for ornamental **"eyebrows"** above the windows, the signature mark of Miami Deco, which proved more than decorative, casting shade that kept rooms cool in the days before air conditioning (as a rule, the wider the eyebrow, the later the building). Observe, too, **repetitions of three** – windows or columns, for example – as well as **decorative reliefs and murals**, whose frequent palm tree, fountain, and flamingo subject matter localized the style. Even when first constructed, rooms in Deco hotels tended to be sparse and stark, and expense was focused on common areas. Some of the most typical examples of these reliefs can be found on the Lincoln Theater on Lincoln Road (see p.67), while most of the earlier hotels along Ocean Drive and Collins Avenue display the obsession with three so characteristic of Tropical Deco.

Depression Moderne (1930s) appeared with the onset of the Great Depression, and was **less ostentatious and ornamental** than its predecessor. Money was spent subtly on interior spaces, like murals and ironwork. The US Post Office (see p.66) is the best example of this style in South Beach; Downtown's Alfred I. Du Pont Building is another outstanding local example (see p.49).

Streamline Deco (1930s–1940s) bridges the simplicity of early Deco and the goofy playfulness of Miami Modern, or MiMo, the space age architectural style of the 1950s so obsessed with speed (for more on MiMo, see box, p.82). As in many MiMo designs, all elements of Streamline buildings are designed to give a **feeling of movement**, and the hard edges are **rounded off** – see the adjoining *Cardozo* and *Carlyle* hotels on Ocean Drive (see p.62). A more extreme version of fluid movement is **Nautical Deco**, which uses fake smokestacks, porthole windows, and railings to mimic grand oceangoing liners – see the *Albion Hotel* (see p.130) or the Miami Design Preservation League headquarters at 1001 Ocean Drive.

Not all local buildings are part of the Deco family, though. **Mediterranean Revival** (1920s–1930s) was a contemporary alternative for those, like Carl Fisher, who disliked the sleek modernity of Art Deco: about a third of the district's buildings are classified as Mediterranean Revival. Many at the time sniffed that this was how gangsters and movie stars – those with more money than taste – liked to commission houses. Structures in this style are **asymmetrical** to give the impression of organic extension over time, and often have **ornate ironwork** and **tile roofs.** Two strong examples of this style are Casa Casuarina on Ocean Drive (see p.63) and the whole of Española Way (see p.66).

For more on Miami's architecture and the full story of Capitman's crusade, see Contexts: Architecture (p.262) at the end of this book.

△ The Albion Hotel

and 8th streets (see p.172, "Shopping"). Look, too, for the squat, flat-roofed bungalow cobbled together from irregular blocks of the porous local stone on the corner of 9th and Collins: known as the **Coral Rock House**, it is one of the oldest single-family homes on Miami Beach. It was built in 1918 by Avery Smith, who operated the first ferry service from the mainland to the beach; at the time of writing, having lain derelict for more than three years after its last tenant, a restaurant, closed down, the house was under threat of demolition for structural reasons.

If the preservationists don't manage to save the coral bungalow on Collins Avenue, there is at least one other example of Miami Beach pioneer architecture nearby that's in no danger of demolition: the **Coral House**, at 1030 Washington Ave, a further block west from the beach, that's now part of the *Best Western South Beach* complex. It was built in 1922 by French immigrant Henri Levy, who went on to found Normandy Isle (see p.81); the hotel plans to reopen it as a restaurant but as yet there's no firm date set. Otherwise, Washington Avenue is South Beach's commercial heart, where supermarkets and schools stand alongside nightclubs and cheap cafés. Although the low-rise buildings seem architecturally unappealing, most have simply had their Art Deco features hidden behind false frontage, and are gradually being restored as the strip gentrifies. Even so, Washington Avenue is still as gritty as the Deco district gets, and having a stroll here is a welcome antidote to the vacation atmosphere of the other main drags. It also holds two star attractions: the **Wolfsonian-FIU** and the rotunda-topped local **Post Office**.

Wolfsonian-FIU

Built around one private collection, **The Wolfsonian**, at 1001 Washington Ave (Sat–Tues noon–6pm, Thurs & Fri noon–9pm; $5; free every Fri 6–9pm; ⊕305/531-1001, ⊕www.wolfsonian.fiu.edu), showcases the vast acquisitions of Mickey Wolfson, heir to a local TV and movie fortune and scion of the Wolfson family (see p.71). He was one of the pioneers of South Beach's renaissance, and his museum is dedicated to decorative and propaganda arts from 1885 to 1945 – fitting for a resort, like South Beach, that was built half on publicity and half on pretty buildings. Wolfson's trinkets are housed in a solid Mediterranean Revival building, with ornamental flourishes around the doors and windows, which originally served as the headquarters of Washington Storage. This was one of the companies that catered to the wealthier residents of South Beach in the 1920s, stashing the contents of their holiday homes for safekeeping during hurricane season – there are several contemporary photographs in the museum's lobby.

The best sections focus on the dozen or so World's Fairs held in the early twentieth century: the anachronistic propaganda that companies used in such showy pavilions is superbly jarring to modern visitors. Take, for example, Heinz and its tribal Deco statuary, representing happy natives from the different countries that joyfully contributed ingredients to Heinz's 57 varieties. Another standout is the Wolfsonian's large collection of political propaganda, including bombastic, highly stylized posters promoting the Fascist cause between the wars. Yet despite some outstanding individual pieces (look for work by British Arts and Crafts pioneers like William Morris as well as Art Nouveau icon Charles Rennie Mackintosh), the museum's confusingly laid out, since different areas muddle together as you walk around; and, overall, it is frustrating in its lack of focus. The temporary exhibitions it hosts, though, are often high profile and more satisfying; check the website for up-to-date schedules.

Note the 1939 **Bridge Tender's House**, a funky steel hut on the sidewalk in front of the building that was shipped in from the 27th Street Bridge to save it from demolition in the 1980s. It's been used for some time as a home for temporary modern art exhibitions overseen by the museum, but at time of writing it was closed for renovation.

United States Post Office

The main branch of Miami Beach's **Post Office** (Mon–Fri 8am–5pm, Sat 8.30am–2pm; ⊕305/672-2447, ⊕www.usps.com), 1300 Washington Ave, is a 1937 architectural gem built in 1937 during the Great Depression and funded by the WPA. Its sweeping curved Depression Moderne exterior stands out like a smooth, squat turret against the rows of boxy Deco buildings nearby; note the classically inspired touches like the loggia and cupola. During business hours, it's worth stepping inside to see the ornately bombastic metalwork that fills the rotunda, the decoration of the roof with the dome of heaven as well as the geometric murals by realist Charles Hardman, which were added in 1940. The three panels depict the conquest of Florida's Indians, and were only cooked up after Hardman's original plan to showcase the pleasures of the state – boating and beaches, mostly – was dismissed as not dignified enough. Look, too, at the post office boxes in the smaller room behind the loggia: they're original and still feature the fascias of the original alphabetical combination locks.

Española Way

Continue north along Washington Avenue past 14th Place, and you'll reach the six-block Mediterranean Revival development known as **Española Way**, or the "Spanish Village Historic District." The popular story's that the street was masterminded by entrepreneur Carl Fisher as an antidote to growing enthusiasm for Art Deco, a concrete statement in favor of the Mediterranean Revival style which he preferred. In fact, the pedestrianized strip, a mustard and ochre explosion of narrow alleys and deliberately uneven buildings, was conceived in 1925 as an artists' colony by hotelier Newton Roney, who devised it as Miami's answer to Greenwich Village in New York or Paris's Montmartre. Thanks to the collapse in real estate the next year, Española Way limped along until the arrival of Cuban bandleader Desi Arnaz (later to find fame as the real- and TV-life husband of *I Love Lucy*'s Lucille Ball). Arnaz is the hero of the frequently repeated and self-promoting (if dubious) story that the rumba dance craze of the 1930s kicked off here on Española Way before taking the US by storm. Arnaz is said to have written *The Miami Beach Rhumba* while playing at his home venue here, the *Village Tavern*, located inside the then swanky hotel that is now the *Clay Hostel* (see "Accommodation," p. 135).

The strip's at its most aggressively faux-dilapidated between Washington and Drexel avenues, where you'll also want to avoid the cluster of mediocre sidewalk cafés. There's a patchy artisans' market here Friday through Sunday (Fri 7pm–midnight, Sat 10am–midnight, Sun 11am–9pm) with rather too many home-made candles for sale, as well as small craft stores and a few artists' studios.

Lincoln Road Mall

Along the northern edge of the Art Deco Historic District stands **Lincoln Road Mall**. Originally laid out in 1912 by pioneer Carl Fisher, it was always intended as Miami Beach's commercial hub. By the 1940s, Lincoln Road was home to upscale department stores like Bonwit Teller and Saks, as well as swanky car showrooms for Fleetwood and LaSalle. But the boom further north on the beach, powered by mega-hotels like the *Fontainebleau* (see p.78), drew upscale shops away; it was only natural for the local council to tap store-designer-turned-architect Morris Lapidus, the man behind the *Fontainebleau*'s opulent design, to revive and rethink the strip here in 1959. Lapidus claimed that he "designed Lincoln Road for people – a car never bought anything," and to do this, pedestrianized six blocks and installed whimsical space-age structures to provide intermittent shade for strolling shoppers. The pricey stores and restaurants trickled back, and for a while, it was again "The Fifth Avenue of the South." But, as South Beach as a whole declined in the 1970s, those chi-chi shops dribbled away yet again (they're now mostly in Bal Harbour to the north). Lincoln Road's current renaissance – its second, so far – began in the mid-1990s. Now crammed with trendy restaurants, sidewalk cafés, and boutiques, Lincoln Road is where South Beach struts its stuff every Sunday afternoon – rollerblading, dogwalking, or window-shopping; the place has arguably replaced Ocean Drive as the local heart of the area.

The mall itself is bookended by two Art Deco theaters: the sleek, low-rise **Colony Theater**, at no. 1040, and the pristine **Lincoln Theater** at no. 541, home to the always reliable New World Symphony (see p.163, "Performing arts and film"). The Lincoln, especially, has some remarkable Tropical Deco reliefs, featuring trippy, triffid-like palm trees painted in deep shades of green; the interior, sadly, retains few of its original features.

One of the quirkier attractions on Lincoln Road, the **Art Center of South Florida** at nos. 800, 810, and 924 (studios daily 11am–11pm, gallery space summer Mon–Wed 4.30–10pm, Thurs–Sun 11am–11pm, winter Mon–Wed

1–10pm, Thurs–Sun 11am–11pm; ☎305/674-8278, ⓦwww.artcentersf.org), was founded in 1984 when real estate prices had hit rock bottom. This collective spreads across three buildings and provides 52 studios for artists and sculptors: alongside traditional painters, you'll find plenty of edgier works in mixed media, photography, and even textiles. Each artist works and exhibits on site, so feel free to wander around the studios or stop by the official gallery space at no. 800 – the work's better than its location (now highly commercial) might suggest.

North of Lincoln Road

Stepping **north of Lincoln Road** and beyond the Art Deco Historic District, you'll find that the sights thin out as the buildings become larger, more eclectic and ramshackle. The Deco-esque hotels along upper Collins Avenue, like the swirly *Shelborne* at no. 1801 and Ian Schrager's *Delano* at no. 1685, with its Aztec headdress-like turret, were constructed later – and are therefore larger and more space age – than their counterparts further south. Some of their playful architectural flourishes are precursors of the style known as Miami Modernism (MiMo), that would explode after World War II. These days, this upper end of Collins Avenue in South Beach is home to many of the best bars in town, and has usurped Ocean Drive's position as the place to party (for reviews, see "Drinking," p.152).

A block inland, at 1700 Washington Ave, just above 17th Street, stands the **Jackie Gleason Theater of Performing Arts** (☎305/673-7300, ⓦwww .gleasontheater.com). Originally the Miami Beach Auditorium, it was renamed in honor of the star of the classic TV show *The Honeymooners* after his death in 1987. Comedian Gleason was lured down to Miami by Hank Meyer, who was in charge of Miami's publicity in the 1960s. Meyer knew Gleason was tired of New York's long winters and had a passion for golfing, so he worked with the CBS network to bring Gleason and his entourage down to the city in a blaze of publicity. It worked and from 1964, *The Jackie Gleason Show* was filmed here, acting as little more than a weekly primetime advert for the joys of life in South Florida. Gleason's show was cancelled after five seasons, so in the 1970s, Morris Lapidus was tasked with transforming his auditorium into a performing arts theater; it now hosts regular Broadway tryouts and commercial smashes (see "Performing arts and film," p.162). The sexy, abstract sculpture in front of the main entrance with its blonde ponytail is pop art pioneer Roy Lichtenstein's *Mermaid*.

Nearby, at 1901 Convention Center Drive, are the massive white walls of the **Miami Beach Convention Center** (☎305/673-7311). This was once a premier venue for prestige exhibitions, although it's now long been bypassed by newer, warehouse-like convention centers elsewhere. It was here that Richard Nixon received the Republican Presidential nomination in August 1968, just as Miami's racial tensions finally flared into violence with the Liberty City riots (see p.58).

Further north, the cramped offices of the **Miami Beach Chamber of Commerce** (Mon–Fri 9am–6pm, Sat & Sun 10am–4pm; ☎305/672-1270 or 1-800/666-4519, ⓦwww.miamibeachchamber.com), 1920 Meridian Ave, offers maps and details on tours of the area, although it's often easier and more pleasant to stop by the Miami Design Preservation League's Art Deco Welcome Center on Ocean Drive (see p.63).

The Holocaust Memorial

A visit to the **Holocaust Memorial** just blocks from the sidewalk cafés and jostling crowds of Lincoln Road, at 1933–1945 Meridian Ave (daily 9am–9pm;

$2 donation; ☎305/538-1663, ⊛www.holocaustmmb.org), is a contemplative, sobering experience. Its presence here is a reflection of the large number of Holocaust survivors who chose to make Miami Beach their home.

Graphic and unflinching, the memorial centers on a sculpture by Tony Lopez; it's a massive, cast bronze hand stretched in desperate supplication to the sky, reaching up through a cluster of dozens of agonized human figures that tumble from, and cling to, the arm like spindly insects. The attention to detail here is astonishing, from the memorial's address noting the years of European persecution of the Jews last century to the Auschwitz ID number tattooed to the sculpture – Lopez was careful to choose a fictitious one.

To reach his central sculpture, visitors pass through curved black granite colonnades, etched with archive photographs that pull no punches in their depiction of concentration camp horrors, then down a darkened tunnel that echoes with the voices of modern Israeli children singing songs from the Holocaust era. The dark walls around the hand are filled with the names of those who died in the death camps. The memorial is bracketed by two eloquent sculptures: it begins with a depiction of a mother protecting her two fearful children, punctuated by a quote from *The Diary of Anne Frank*: "… that in spite of everything I still believe that people are really good at heart." As you exit, there lie the original mother and children, now dead, accompanied again by Anne's words: "… ideals, dreams and cherished hopes rise within us only to meet the horrible truths and be shattered."

The Bass Museum of Art

The only fine art museum on Miami Beach, the **Bass Museum** (Tues–Sat 10am–5pm, Sun 11am–5pm; $6; ☎305/673-7350, ⊛www.bassmuseum.org), 2121 Park Ave, began as the local public library when a bunch of local socialites donated a few hundred books to the city. It later became a museum to house the private collection of European art accumulated by local bigwigs John and Johanna Bass, who donated the place to the city in 1963. The Bass was long housed in a stark, temple-like 1930 Art Deco building designed by Russell Pancoast, the architect grandson of beach pioneer John Collins. Whenever further exhibition space was needed for the Basses' 3000-strong holdings, Pancoast himself was recruited for the extension, ensuring a harmonious design; he built the south and north wings, for example, in 1937 and 1950. Japanese architect Arata Isozaki was brought in for a renovation/expansion project intended to triple the display space while uniting the museum with the Miami City Ballet (see p.163, "Performing arts and film") and the local library to form the **Miami Beach Cultural Park**. Isozaki's swooping white box with its wide central ramp was grafted unobtrusively onto the Park Avenue side of the plot, and is an ideal exhibition venue.

It's a shame the holdings themselves are so hit and miss. At first glance, the collection seems studded with star names like Jordaens and Van Dyck; but most are represented by minor or studio works – even Rubens' much admired *Holy Family* is disappointing, clearly as much the work of his assistants as the master himself. Standouts include the sixteenth-century Flemish tapestry *The Tournament*; a notable drawing collection with gems by Daumier and Toulouse-Lautrec; and a sunny altarpiece jointly painted by Ghirlandaio and Botticelli. The temporary exhibitions are far more impressive, ranging from a recent review of the key architects, like L. Murray Dixon, who shaped Miami Beach's skyline, to paintings, sculpture, and furniture from the Art Deco period in Paris.

△ The Bass Museum extension

South Pointe

Towards the tip of the island, **South Pointe** is pimpled with high rises you won't see elsewhere in South Beach, owing to sluggish preservation orders that, until recently, allowed developers to bulldoze buildings at will: the first of these high-rises, South Pointe Towers, has been joined by several more, approved before new zoning laws came into effect.

South of Fifth (or "SoFi" as local realtors have taken to calling it) was origi- nally the city's Jewish ghetto since Fifth Street marked the northernmost point where Jews could buy housing. By the late 1980s, though, it had been taken over by crack houses and criminals, spurred by the arrival of undesirables in the wake of the Mariel Boatlift. For this reason, gentrification has proceeded more slowly here than elsewhere in South Beach, and it's a still a little more raw than the manicured streets further north. There are many unpleasant examples of late 1980s Neo-Deco garishness – angular concrete buildings in turquoise, ochre, and raspberry, conjuring an image of Art Deco with shoulder pads. Even so, it's worth checking out one notable old building, the former **Brown's Hotel** at 112 Ocean Drive, now home to hip steakhouse *Prime 112* (see p.145, "Restaurants"). This small, boxy 1915 structure was the first hotel built on Miami Beach. When it was restored in 2001, the new owners moved it a few feet west of the original site and, in the process, helped dispel a long-held local legend that *Brown's* was built on top of a shipwreck; no relics of any kind were found.

At the end of Washington Avenue, there's a pleasant waterfront greenspace, **South Pointe Park** (daily 8am–sunset), with wide lawns and good facilities that's a sleepy place to pass the afternoon; it's worth stopping by on Friday evenings when its open-air stage is the venue for enjoyable free **music events** (details are posted up around South Beach). **Surfers** should note that the waves here are widely regarded as the best in the area.

The park looks out over **Government Cut**, a waterway first dredged by Henry Flagler in the nineteenth century to create easy access to the growing Port of Miami. In so doing, he amputated the southernmost tip of South Beach to create exclusive **Fisher Island** (see p.73). The waterway has been substantially deepened since then, and is now the main route by which Miami's endless parade of cruise ships on the Caribbean circuit reaches the main harbor. Even these days, you might also witness an impounded drug-running vessel being towed along by the authorities. Don't be surprised, either, to hear the neighing of horses: Miami Beach's police horses are stabled on the eastern side of the park.

The Sanford L. Ziff Jewish Museum of Florida

Housed in a deconsecrated Art Deco synagogue at 301 Washington Ave, the **Sanford L. Ziff Jewish Museum of Florida** (Tues–Sun 10am–5pm; $6; ☎305/672-5044, ⊛www.jewishmuseum.com) commemorates the history of Jews in Florida from the late 1600s until today. Finished in 1936, the building is one of architect Henry Hohauser's earliest local projects, and has been lovingly restored at a cost of more than $2m, including the eye-catching Moorish-style copper dome.

In addition to temporary shows, the building houses a permanent exhibition that's compact, but so crammed with information that it's almost overwhelming in its thoroughness; make sure to ask one of the many docents bobbing around the building to take you on an informal tour – they're extremely knowledgeable and friendly. Though the early documents and photographs are interesting enough, the museum's at its strongest when exposing how recently anti-Semitism continued unchecked in South Beach, with hotel signs from the 1950s that guaranteed guests "Always a view, never a Jew" (prejudice that is even more astonishing given that Mitchell Wolfson, father of Wolfsonian museum-founder Mickey, had been elected mayor of the city in 1941). One of the most awkwardly poignant documents is a brief letter written in 1929 by the mayor of St Louis to Carl Fisher: in it, he asks Fisher if he would get "his best friend of Earth, Mr. William Lewin," courtesy in his golf club. The mayor goes on to write that he would be "everlastingly grateful," as he knows that, "on account of [Lewin's] nationality," it could be a problem. For more on the history of the Jews in South Beach, see box, p.62.

The Islands

Miami Beach is surrounded by dozens of small islands, most of them man-made and residential like **Fisher Island** and unlikely to detain a casual visitor; the exception is recently redeveloped **Watson Island**, site of both the Miami Children's Museum and the new Parrot Jungle. And though there are no specific sights on islands like **Star** and **Palm**, it is there that wealthy South Beachers live undisturbed, and a drive through these or the chain of **Venetian Islands** shows what everyday life is like, far from the boutiques and hotels of Ocean Drive.

This isolation may change soon with the transformation of the decrepit *Lido Spa* resort on **Belle Isle** into a sceney spa-hotel, *The Standard Miami*, which looks likely to draw more, high-profile, visitors (for a review, see p.132). The last time the islands made headlines was over twenty years ago, when art stuntmaster **Christo** wrapped eleven of them in 200-foot-wide bright pink plastic skirts for two weeks in 1983 – a project he called *Surrounded Islands*.

It's tough to reach any but Watson Island by **public transport** (see opposite) and there are no official tours; instead, you'll need a car to cruise along the Venetian or MacArthur causeways and to explore the hushed, mansion-lined streets.

The Venetian Islands and the Flagler Memorial Monument

This necklace of six islands is threaded together by the Venetian Causeway toll road; what's now the Causeway was originally the site of the Collins Bridge, the first permanent connection between the beach and the mainland, built in 1913. The Causeway now runs between five neat artificial islands – **Rivo Alto**, **DiLido**, **San Marino**, **San Marco**, and **Biscayne** – as well as the raggedy but natural **Belle Isle** (picturesquely renamed from the original Bull Isle). There's little to see on any of them other than the exteriors of upscale private residences, but a casual drive along the Causeway is a pleasant detour (plus it's a great place for jogging) – while their names serve as yet another example of Miami's glaring obsession with Venice.

Just south of the Venetian cluster, the **Flagler Memorial Monument** sits on its own specially constructed island, a byproduct of the extensive dredging nearby during the late 1910s. In 1920, this sculpture was built there, commissioned by Carl Fisher in memory of the father of Miami, railroad magnate Henry Flagler; with this gesture, Fisher hoped to align himself with Flagler's hallowed memory. The monument itself consists of four giant statues representing Industry, Prosperity, Education, and Pioneering, who stand looking out over the water, their backs to an enormous obelisk. The statues are falling apart, missing chunks of their faces or hands, and riven with deep cracks thanks to pollution, neglect, and vandalism; its profile hasn't been helped by the fact that it's impossible to visit without a private boat. Thankfully, in late 2004, $250,000 was allocated by the city for its restoration; no word yet on when or how visiting the site might be made more convenient.

Palm, Hibiscus, Star, and Fisher islands

While **Palm** and **Hibiscus** islands were dredged expressly for luxury housing in the early twentieth century, **Star Island** was initially designed to house the Miami Beach Yacht Club and was only converted to residential use in the 1920s. Certainly prime real estate now, they are crammed with swanky private homes.

Residents of the aptly named Star Island include talk-show queen turned lesbian poster-girl Rosie O'Donnell; renaissance man P. Diddy; and expat Cuba's answer to Prince Charles and Lady Di, Emilio and Gloria Estefan. Upon his arrival, Miami Heat basketball player Shaquille O'Neal snapped up a mansion here – one of the largest on the island, it was built by a former Heat player, so has handy eight-foot doorways to accommodate his 7'1" frame.

As for Palm Island, its most infamous ex-resident is Al Capone, who snagged a lavish house there by using a local lawyer as his frontman for the purchase; Capone finally succumbed to syphilis here in 1947. All three islands are public and accessible from MacArthur Causeway – just tell the gatekeeper that you're sightseeing and he should let you through, although the high fences and thick hedges around most of the homes means there's little to see.

Fisher Island, just across Government Cut, has always been the poshest of all the islands. In the 1920s, Carl Fisher sold it to William Vanderbilt and his wife Rosamund, who built a spectacular winter estate here. It's passed through several hands since then, and is now an exclusive resort, virtually inaccessible to anyone other than hotel guests or full-time residents of the new condo developments and then only by boat (☎305/535-6000, ◍www.fisherisland.com).

Watson Island

Eighty-six-acre **Watson Island** has been transformed with the arrival of two-high profile attractions, Parrot Jungle and the Miami Children's Museum. Before then, it was an embarrassing eyesore for the city, known mostly as a landing area for seaplanes and haven for local vagrants. Current city plans to scrap the seaplane terminal and replace it with a luxury development known as Island Gardens, complete with hotel and mooring space for mega-yachts are facing fierce opposition from locals, who claim what's left should remain open parkland. Note that there's plentiful, if pricey parking, on the island if you're coming by car. Otherwise, you can catch **bus** #S, #K, or #C from either Downtown or South Beach.

For decades, **Parrot Jungle** (daily 10am–6pm; $24.95, parking $6 per vehicle; ☎305/258-6453, ◍www.parrotjungle.com), on 1111 Parrot Jungle Trail, was a charming oddity on the southern reaches of Miami. Thanks to millions of dollars and a nifty deal that allowed a private institution like this to be built on city land as a catalyst for other development, the aviary has reopened on a brand new, specially constructed site on Watson Island (its charming old location, filled with lush vegetation, is now a park). It was opened in 1936 by Franz Scherr, a parrot-loving Austrian immigrant, who – inspired by Monkey Jungle (see p.203) – rented some land and bought two dozen squawky macaws to display them to the curious public. Now, the vast aviary-cum-gardens are home to more than 3000 parrots as well as 500 or so other creatures, including monkeys and reptiles. Their new site here was purpose built, and though its smooth walkways and antiseptic foliage lack some of the original site's haphazard charm, it's still a must-see, thanks largely to the moody, gaudy birds – whether flying free in the Manu exhibit, intended to replicate a Peruvian mountain top, or in cages dotted around the park. The birds are very loud yet very tame – bring plenty of quarters if you want to feed them, as there are seed vending machines throughout. There's also a parrot nursery for hatchlings, as well as the Monkey Bars, where primates play, and an Everglades habitat to showcase local fauna (including an albino alligator that looks like it was molded from white chocolate). But the most mesmerizing sight of all is the flock of tame, candy-colored flamingos that stand motionless and eerily identical to their plastic, ornamental counterparts.

Parrot Jungle also oversees the newly rebuilt **Ichimura Miami-Japan Garden**, best known for its fat laughing statue of the god Hotei. Built in 1961, it had fallen into disrepair by the 1980s, when vagrants used it as a flophouse; that original site was leveled to make way for Parrot Jungle's move. But as part of the deal, Parrot Jungle's owners were compelled to rebuild and administer it

△ Flamingos at Parrot Jungle

on a new site nearby. While the garden itself – all stone lanterns and boulders – is wrapped in a cocoon of concrete for tranquility's sake, the Buddha sits outside the wall smiling at the passing cars. Note that the flora here, aside from a few bonsai and some black bamboo, isn't indigenous to Japan; rather it's a next-best re-creation amid Miami's tropical climate.

Housed in a specially constructed building designed by Arquitectonica, the brand new **Miami Children's Museum** (daily 10am–6pm; $10; $3 parking per car; ☎305/373-5437, ⊛www.miamichildrensmuseum.org), at 980 MacArthur Causeway, sits like a row of jagged white teeth, studded with cavity-like portholes, on the southern edge of Watson Island. It's an ideal place to distract younger children for an afternoon, with exhibits aimed firmly at the pre-school crowd, who can learn through play. The displays themselves are impressive: a bank where you can chance to design your own currency or lend precious objects to be temporarily displayed for other visitors in "safe deposit boxes"; or a farm-cum-supermarket, where you harvest produce and then follow its path to the store.

It's a shame, however, that everything within sight blares with corporate sponsorship – even the Emergency Room is branded by a local hospital. Upstairs, the blatant branding continues; even so, the cruise ship complete with wooden food buffet and dress-up box for would-be showgirls and -boys is a delight, as is the world music studio, which encourages kids to discover musicians and instruments from other countries. Aside from all that, to burn off any excess energy, head for the central atrium's Castle of Dreams, a mosaic-encrusted house bursting with slides and tunnels.

Central Miami Beach and north

A rt Deco and all-night parties give way to Modernism and massive tower
blocks as South Beach settles out into **Miami Beach** proper. Although
most visitors rarely stray up Collins Avenue past 23rd Street, there's
plenty to see here – notably some fine mid-century architecture – even
if the sights are more scattered than in South Beach. One surefire reason to
brave the trek, though, is for the beaches: the strips of sand here are uniformly
wider, cleaner, and better maintained than the scraps packed with people at
the southern tip.

This chapter covers a necklace of confusingly named neighborhoods, strung
one after the other along the artery of **Collins Avenue**, which runs the entire
length of the Miami Beach sandbar. The forty blocks from 23rd to 63rd streets
form what's known as **Central Miami Beach** (also sometimes known as
Middle Beach): this area is home to a mix of mid-century hotels and monolithic condo complexes. Between 63rd Street and 87th Terrace, **North Beach**
is increasingly recognized for its mine of fine Miami Modernist buildings,
including the cluster on the old world–obsessed **Normandy Isle**. **Surfside**,
an unfussy but unremarkable ten-block middle-class settlement of shops and
bungalows, collides with the toniest local spot **Bal Harbour**, home to the
namesake luxury mall, housed in a decidedly un-chic concrete center. Beyond
the shops lie the nude beaches at **Haulover Park**, plus the most sumptuous
sands on the island, unfortunately located in the package-holiday destination of
Sunny Isles Beach. Continuing on, Collins Avenue passes through **Golden
Beach**, the northernmost community on the sandbar, before eventually reaching Fort Lauderdale (see p.207).

Central Miami Beach

Though it wouldn't develop to its extent until after South Beach, **Central
Miami Beach** was in fact settled first. In the 1920s and 1930s, the oceanfront here, especially north of what's now 44th Street, boasted multimillion-
dollar mansions owned by rich families like the Firestone Tire clan. But these
sprawling estates were demolished in the 1950s to make way for condos and
grand hotels. Those hotels presented Rat Pack celebrities like Frank Sinatra
or Sammy Davis Jr an A-list hang-out in what was then a true seafront Vegas,
whether they were performing or vacationing. When the smart set moved on,

CENTRAL MIAMI BEACH & NORTH

EATING		ACCOMMODATION	
Arnie & Richie's Deli	11	Best Western	
Bistro at 39	F	Thunderbird Resort	A
Buenos Aires Bakery	6	Bizcaya Hotel	E
Café Prima Pasta	8	Circa 39	F
Christine Lees	2	Eden Roc	C
The Forge	12	Fontainebleau	D
Lure Cafe	9	The Golden Sands	B
Madame's	1		
Miami Juice	3	**DRINKING & NIGHTLIFE**	
Rascal House	4	Chamber Lounge	13
Santa Fe News & Coffee	5	Club Tropigala	D
Tamarind Thai	7	Lemon Twist	10

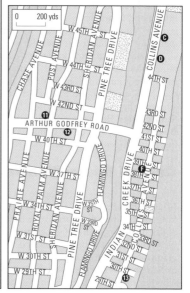

housing here split between two groups: Latin expats looking for *pied-à-terres* and seniors wanting to spend their last years soaking up the sun. Inevitably, this diminished the area's vibrancy, and it's only now that Central Miami Beach is starting to warm up again as a holiday destination.

This underappreciated area is where the **Miami Modern**, or MiMo (MY-moe), style first flourished; it's at its fiercely whimsical best in places like the *Fontainebleau Hilton* and *Eden Roc* hotels (for more on MiMo, see box, p.82). The value of these and other buildings has been recognized with the creation of the **John S. Collins Oceanfront Historic District** between 22nd and 44th streets, bestowing the same protection (if not prestige) on landmarks here as in South Beach's Art Deco Historic District (see p.63). North from here, above 44th Street, Collins Avenue continues on through what's known as **Condo Canyon**, an endless row of residential skyscrapers, brightly colored but architecturally bland, eventually crossing 63rd Street, the northern boundary of Central Miami Beach.

△ Ocean Terrace

Pine Tree Drive and North Bay Road

West of Collins Avenue across the intracoastal waterway of Indian Creek (see below), the mansions of Miami Beach's old-money families can be found on and around **Pine Tree Drive**. This was one of the first areas to be tamed when Europeans settled on the beach and is named for the windbreak of Australian pines that one of those settlers, John S. Collins, planted here upon his arrival.

Though Pine Tree is the main drag through this residential area, visitors will be far more interested in **North Bay Road**, a block or so west. This is where many of the boldface names who call Miami home – at least part-time – have bought mansions, and though there are no publicly organized tours here, there's also nothing to stop a casual visitor cruising up and down the streets here to check out the manses. North Bay Road between 40th and 60th streets is known as **Millionaires Music Row**, as there's barely a house that isn't owned by a major pop star – at least on the west side. It's a must-live option for two reasons: the spectacular sunset-facing views and the fact that the eastern mansions are overlooked by that crowd of towers in Condo Canyon, where apartments can easily be rented by pesky paparazzi.

The 5700–5900 block is a BLT sandwich – that's Bee Gees–Latin Temptress. Jennifer Lopez lives in an epic $9m pad here; either side of her is one of the surviving falsetto songsters. Just as it's easy to tell when the Queen of England's at home in Buckingham Palace (a flag flies), the sign that JLo's in Miami is a clump of guards outside the main gate. Michael Jackson has spent much of the time since leaving his California ranch at no. 5930, known as "Whitehall"; while Ricky Martin recently sold his place on the 4400 block, a surprisingly modest ochre-and-brown house, for $5.75m to Calvin Klein. Close by, the four artificial Sunset Islands are also popular with celebrities like Lenny Kravitz and Anna Kournikova.

Forty-first Street

It was on the site of what's now **41st Street** that Collins established his first plantation, growing potatoes, avocados, and bananas, though there's no evidence of his early farm today. Instead, the strip is the heart of Miami Beach's Jewish community – tagged, ironically enough, Arthur Godfrey Road in honor of the 1940s radio personality, a notorious anti-Semite (a hotel he co-owned in Bal Harbour, the now-demolished *Kenilworth*, had a sign informing guests: "No dogs or Jews allowed"). Today, 41st Street is dotted with kosher restaurants and neighborhood stores, busiest on a Saturday when the local orthodox community gathers for temple. Stop by **Arnie & Richie's Deli** for a true taste of the local flavor (see review, p.139): open for more than fifty years in the same spot, it's one of the few survivors of the many New York–style kosher cafés that once littered Miami Beach and catered to its huge Jewish population.

The Fontainebleau Hilton and the Eden Roc Hotel

One of the masterpieces of Miami Modernism, **the Fontainebleau** (☎305/538-2000, ◎www.fontainebleauhilton.com), at 4441 Collins Ave, resembles a giant white space station perched on the beach. Designed by store-dresser-turned-architect **Morris Lapidus** (who called his style "the architecture of joy") and opened in 1954 on the site of the former Harvey Firestone mansion, the central chateau building was loathed by critics at the time for its swooping, curved wings and outlandish decoration.

Despite the architectural drubbing, the hotel quickly became ground zero for glamour: it snagged big-name stars as guests – including Judy Garland and

Elvis Presley – as well as making cameos in the hottest movies (the James Bond classic *Goldfinger*, for one). Frank Sinatra, the most regular visitor, had a suite permanently set aside for his use. Besides reliably brattish movie-star behavior – starting a scrambled-egg fight in the coffeeshop and hurling deckchairs off his balcony, among other things – he also shot many scenes here as the private-eye hero of sixties classic *Tony Rome*. (Indeed, the *Fontainebleau's* still popular with filmmakers – Will Smith shot scenes for the boxing biopic *Ali* here recently).

Though its gleaming white facade is still much as Lapidus intended, the building's interior has suffered greatly over the years from aggressive and unsympathetic modernization. Recent plans look set to restore much of its tarnished glamour: the brutal 1970s escalators that once dominated the entranceway have been torn out, and its focal point will once again be the terrazzo floor, patterned with Lapidus's trademark bow ties, as well as the immense, *Poseidon Adventure*–like Belgian glass chandeliers. Two brand-new condo towers are expected to be completed in 2005; just before his death in 2001, Lapidus approvingly called them the exclamation point to his original design.

Little wonder. Lapidus's aesthetic was driven not just by excess but also by a sense of theater. A trademark touch was the way he incorporated unnecessary staircases into his buildings to enable "grand entrances" – look for one example leading from the left of the lobby to the mezzanine balcony that was often used by ballgown-clad debutantes in the hotel's heyday (their escorts simply took the elevator directly to the main floor).

The nearby **Eden Roc** hotel, 4525 Collins Ave (☎305/531-0000 or 1-800/327-8337, ⊛www.edenrocresort.com), is another curvy Lapidus confection,

Towering ego

Morris Lapidus's half-moon-shaped main hotel was actually built on the instructions of original **Fontainebleau** owner **Ben Novack**, but Lapidus – never a shrinking violet – was all too happy to take credit for its innovation. The two new condo towers that are being added to that structure aren't, in fact, the first additions – that distinction goes to the 17-story northern wing tacked on in the 1960s. And the reasons behind its construction – as much emotional as financial – offer a clear glimpse of the larger-than-life characters of Lapidus and Novack.

Ben Novack was, by all accounts, a tricky boss, and few lasted long in his employ. ; An exception was his right-hand man, **Harry Mufson**, who secretly bought the patch of land immediately to the north of the hotel and tapped then-rising star Lapidus to design a hot new rival to the *Fontainebleau*, an ocean-liner-inspired design intended to trump his past masterpiece. Mufson's mischievous plan worked perfectly: after opening in 1956, his **Eden Roc** was the venue for Elizabeth Taylor's birthday bash, and Jayne Mansfield honeymooned in one of its suites.

Incensed, the ornery Novack had an ingenious and equally vengeful response. He put up the monstrous **tower** on the *Fontainebleau's* northern edge, instructing his new architect – Lapidus refused to be involved – that every guestroom should face south. That way, he reasoned, there would be nothing but a massive concrete wall abutting the *Eden Roc*; and even better, Novack's tower would block the sun from reaching the newer hotel's lavish new pool. Mufson sued and lost; there was (and, in fact, still is) no law protecting access to sunlight. Instead, the city allowed him special permission to build a second pool closer to the beach out of shadow's reach.

Ironically, standing near to the *Eden Roc's* so-called sundeck pool is the best way to see the nastiest touch in Novack's so-called "Spite Wall": five tiny windows cut into the beachfront corner of the top two floors. They mark the site of his own apartment and allowed him alone to look down on the cheeky upstart hotel.

crowned with a giant green sign intended to ape the smokestack of an ocean liner. Unfortunately, its rooms retain none of their signature MiMo features, but the sleek modernist lobby has been snappily restored to its original design, and its sunken sofas are a slinky throwback to the times of Sammy Davis Jr. (For reviews of these hotels, see p.133, "Accommodation.")

Indian Creek

In Central Miami Beach, Collins Avenue skirts along the edge of the wide, peaceful intracoastal waterway known as **Indian Creek**. The boats grow larger as you travel further north, like ocean-bound answers to the luxury condos that overlook them.

It was on one of these moored houseboats that **Andrew Cunanan**, the serial killer who murdered Gianni Versace in 1997 (see p.63), was found dead from a self-inflicted gunshot wound. To avoid ghoulish profiteering, the boat itself was seized by the city for demolition – although not before the owner's onsite manager was able to offer impromptu crime-scene souvenirs for sale to passersby.

Despite this bloody incident, the canal is a soothingly calm place; the shady benches dotted regularly along the grassy path make for a glorious, lazy stroll by the water. It's also the site of one of Miami's most exciting and unusual residential developments: **Aqua** (ⓦwww.aqua.net), on lozenge-shaped Allison Island on the creek's northern tip. Taste-making real estate magnate Craig Robins – who first promoted South Beach and then revived the Design District (see p.89) – is now building his own $225m urban utopia, handily gated to keep out the riff-raff (though visitors shouldn't have a problem sneaking a look around). To design this brand new village, Robins has tapped boldfaced architectural names like Hariri & Hariri, Walter Chatham, and Alison Spear; there are low-rise condo clusters as well as individually designed single-family homes all set for completion in late 2005, plus the public art for which he's become known (the showstopper is Richard Tuttle's massive mural *Splash* along the side of Chatham's building, a Jackson Pollock–style paint splatter on a massive scale).

North Beach and Normandy Isle

By the end of the 1980s, the area between 63rd Street and 87th Terrace, or **North Beach**, began absorbing those who'd been economically or socially expelled from the newly cool South Beach. They brought with them social problems of their own as crime rates rose and the infrastructure of this working class community frayed. Now North Beach is at last picking up, thanks to aggressive investment in businesses and buildings. There are also some good restaurants (see p.146) around the area's heart at 71st Street, as well as a huge oceanfront park; plans are under way for a boardwalk, to be completed in 2006, which will run the length of the beach.

Another reason for renewed interest is that the area offers the densest concentration of **MiMo architecture** anywhere in the city, from hotels to apartment complexes and even single-family homes. Preservationists recently scored a triumph when eight blocks of the eastern side of Collins Avenue from 63rd to 71st streets were designated the North Beach Resort Historic District. This area includes masterpieces like the **Sherry Frontenac** hotel at 65th and Collins, with its jazzy neon signs, and the stone-grill-fronted **Golden Sands** at 69th and Collins. Sadly, such conservation efforts came too late to protect the **Carillon**, a MiMo gem at 69th and Collins – it has been hollowed out and turned into upscale condos; the sign, at least, was preserved, as were the weird holes in the overhang of its rooftop. In fact, the architect's original plan for the place called for bells to hang in those holes, but the developer's money ran out and the bells were never cast. Just outside the district stands **Ocean Terrace**, a two-block slice of low-rise MiMo buildings between 73rd and 75th streets.

Head west across the 71st Street Bridge to find the buzziest spot around here, **Normandy Isle**. It's home to a swelling number of gentrification-minded gays, many refugees from increasingly mainstream South Beach drawn here by its fine **MiMo buildings** like the salmon-colored Bayside Apartments, 910 Bay Drive, or the complex at 125–135 North Shore Drive, its angular entrance like two snaggle-toothed incisors. Normandy Isle was, unsurprisingly, developed by a Frenchman, Henri Levy, who immigrated in 1900 and quickly made his fortune running moviehouses in Cincinnati; after moving to Miami, Levy snapped up two large but uninhabited mangrove islands on the bay side of Miami Beach (his own home, the Coral Rock House on Washington Avenue in South Beach, still stands; see p.65). Levy then parceled off the land and sold it ready for construction; to evoke the exoticism of his homeland he named the roads after French towns and provinces – hence Normandy and Biarritz drives.

△ The Normandy Isle Fountain

CENTRAL MIAMI BEACH AND NORTH | North Beach and Normandy Isle

81

Woggles. Cheeseholes. Delta fins. Pylons. Not the names of the latest NFL teams, these are the most prominent design touches that distinguish **Miami Modernism**, or MiMo. This umbrella term for local mid-century buildings was only coined in 1999 by preservationists hoping to call attention to the clusters of long-overlooked buildings they were then fighting to save, much as Barbara Baer Capitman had crusaded on behalf of Art Deco three decades earlier (see p.64).

These particular 1950s and early 1960s structures have the same clean lines and graphic shapes of their contemporaries across the country. But what sets Miami Modernism apart are the heat- and beach-specific touches: **bright, poppy colors** (contrast this with Art Deco's original all-white schemes) and **maritime imagery**. Landmarks in a city where vacations were a way of life, these buildings were intended to divert and amuse, hence the proliferation of playful, non-functioning touches like **woggles** (a term Morris Lapidus coined for floating amoeba-like shapes) and **cheeseholes** (where holes are bored through concrete like bubbles in Swiss cheese). In fact, Lapidus had **eight guiding principles** whose impact can be seen on almost every building he oversaw: get rid of corners; use sweeping lines; manipulate light to create unusual effects; introduce drama whenever possible; keep changing the floor levels; keep people moving; use plenty of color; and take advantage of what he called the Moth Complex – the fact that people are attracted to light.

MiMo styles

While Deco's prevailing style shifted over time, MiMo manifested itself in different ways simultaneously – the explosion of construction in the 1950s, buoyed by America's postwar optimism and the birth of mass consumer culture, allowed architects plenty of wiggle room with their woggles. There are three main styles:

Resort MiMo is the best known. Used mostly in Miami Beach's hotels, it twinned clean-lined towers with jazzy entranceways, usually a car-friendly *porte cochère*. It was the interiors, though, which really stood out – always movie-set glamorous, they were intended to turn holidays into Hollywood: staircases for grand entrances (a signature Lapidus touch), lashings of marble, and gold-plated aluminum. Sadly, few examples of such impressive interiors remain – the restorations of the *Fontainebleau* and *Eden Roc* are the best approximation – but two other hotels on Collins, the *Sherry Frontenac* at no. 6565 and the *Dezerland Hotel* at no. 8701, have exemplary exteriors.

Think of **Iconic Modernism,** the second style, as appliqué architecture. Most of these buildings are very simple, often square boxes, but are spiffed up with goofy, eye-catching details: boomerang and delta shapes, pylons, or parabolic arches. Two strong examples are the shopping center entranceway at 6616 Collins Ave and the stunning, bright yellow synagogue, Temple Menorah, designed jointly by Gilbert Fein and Morris Lapidus at 620 75th St.

Vernacular MiMo marks the most restrained and practical of the styles. It still has plenty of MiMo's playfulness – vertical fins and stucco reliefs as decoration or snazzy balcony rails – but the buildings themselves are much more in keeping with the austere International Style prevalent in that era. This was the cheapest way to erect a MiMo building, and was often used on apartment blocks rather than public spaces like hotels. An exception is the *Golden Sands* at 6901 Collins Ave, with its radiator-grille facade; as for apartments, a fine example is the bubblegum-pink complex at 6890–6896 Abbot Ave.

For more on MiMo's place in Miami's architectural timeline, see Contexts: Architecture (p.262) at the end of this book or check ⓦ www.mimo.us.

Local preservationists give weekly **tours**, on Fridays at 10.30am, leaving from the bandshell at 73rd Street and Collins Avenue – for more information, see Basics, p.36.

Surfside and Bal Harbour

Moving north along Collins Avenue, the next major settlement, **Surfside** is a self-contained, unremarkable beachside community that spans from 88th to 96th streets. The blocks here are full of one- and two-story single-family homes, as well as neighborhood amenities along Harding Avenue including a post office, drugstore, and banks.

Unless you need to make a pit-stop there, skip Surfside in favor of the tony **Bal Harbour**, which begins at 96th Street. Bal Harbour's most telling feature is its name, anglicized to underscore pretensions to culture, history, and wealth; it's somewhat ironic, then, that Miami Beach's most self-consciously ritzy area should have such humble beginnings. It was originally nothing more than a soldiers' training camp in World War II; and the town only incorporated in 1946 when many of those soldiers – who fondly remembered Miami – came back from the war and settled here permanently.

Most visitors today, though, come to Bal Harbour for one thing: the **Bal Harbour Shops**, at 9700 Collins Ave (☎305/886-0311, ⓦwww .balharbourshops.com). This bi-level, open-air mall positively drips with designer names: Fendi, Prada, and Gucci all have their Miami outposts here, although the exclusivity is becoming diluted with the arrival of everyday stores like Banana Republic and the construction of a competing luxury mall in Coral Gables, the Village at Merrick Park (see p.109). It may be a fun place to window-shop, but don't expect any bargains – even the cafés are premium-priced. Clearly, though, someone's spending: Bal Harbour usually ties with the Caesars Mall in Las Vegas as the most lucrative mall per square foot in the whole country.

Haulover Park and north

Moving on north from Bal Harbour brings you to the nude beaches at **Haulover Park** – in fact far more salubrious than their racy reputation might suggest. The golden coastline here stretches for several sand-packed miles before delivering you to the mouth of package-holiday hell – though, admittedly, it's a golden-sand-capped hellmouth – in **Sunny Isles Beach**.

Haulover Park

Famous for being Miami's one nude beach, Haulover Park (daily sunrise–sunset; free, parking $4 per car; ☎305/944-3040, ⓦwww.miamidade.gov/parks /haulover_park.asp), at 10800 Collins Ave, is far more than that: the glorious, wide sands make a visit here worth the trip, wherever you're staying, not to mention the excellent facilities – showers, picnic tables, and bathrooms – along the boardwalk that runs parallel to the oceanfront.

The "clothing optional" section to the north is clearly marked by warning signs on the footpath, although you don't have to strip off to sunbathe even there: either way, there's a volleyball court for sporty nudists, and an unofficial gay section at the northernmost end between sections 27 and 29. Sniffier local residents have been mounting a sneaky campaign to nix the nudists, petitioning the city for a new school to be built nearby; standard zoning laws would apply and so forbid nude bathing. The fact that Bal Harbour's population is largely retirees with grown children means that they're unlikely to succeed, though at time of writing, no final decision's been taken; however, call the number listed to check if you're determined to bathe in the buff.

The barefoot mailmen

Visitors to the Haulover Beach boardwalk will notice a plaque commemorating a forgotten piece of Florida history – the barefoot mailmen.

Florida was the last state east of the Mississippi to join the US, gaining full statehood in 1845, and its civic amenities were often primitive until a widespread railway network was established in the 1920s. The postal service was especially underdeveloped: mail traveled between settlements in South Florida on a circuitous route that sometimes took a letter to New York and back again before delivering it.

This frustrating and impractical service ended in 1885 when **the Barefoot Mailman service** was established. For seven years, mail traveled between scattered coastal settlements the only way it could – on foot. Eleven mailmen used the beach as their road for the trek **from Palm Beach to Miami**. The 136-mile journey was a six-day round-trip, and included 56 miles in a small boat and 80 by land. Overnights were spent at houses of refuge run for shipwrecked sailors in Orange Grove and Fort Lauderdale, and individual travelers wanting to walk with the postmen for their own safety could pay $5 to join the trip. The barefoot mail route ended when a new country road was built connecting Palm Beach with Lemon City, then the largest settlement in the Miami area, and a stagecoach service began.

Sunny Isles Beach

Poor **Sunny Isles**. This blatant Las Vegas rip-off was founded in 1952 expressly as a holiday resort and dozens of natty motels quickly sprung up here along the ample beach; two were even named *Sahara* and *Suez* in Vegas's honor. However, the resort soon lost its luster and spent much of the rest of the century languishing as an undesirable package-holiday destination clogged with bargain-minded sunseekers, mostly from Europe.

The sumptuous **beaches** here do provide some saving grace, however. While elsewhere in southern Florida, resorts have been bedeviled by coastal erosion, Sunny Isles' heavy investment in renourishment – basically, Rogaine for beaches, where dredged sand is dumped onto thinning shoreline – has paid off. Unfortunately, there is a downside to this oceanfloor harvesting: shifting the massive sands has altered tideflow here and created dangerous new riptides that can catch swimmers off guard.

Aside from its glorious sands, though, there's little reason to visit: ritzier, soulless skyscraper hotels from the likes of Donald Trump are swallowing up the cramped but charming motels. Many of the kitschier buildings thrown up in the 1950s are being torn down, but there are a few fun examples of Sunny Isles' showmanship left along Collins Avenue. Concrete sheikhs and camels guard the entrance to the now-closed **Sahara**, at no. 18335; white and gold mini-sphinxes like marzipan statues look out on the driveway of the **Suez** at no. 18215; while there's even a grand Native American homage – which looks disturbingly like a tablecloth pattern from the 1950s – on the facade of the **Thunderbird** at no. 18401. Go see them now while you can; there are no preservation laws protecting this strip of coastline, and with development proceeding so aggressively, it's likely not long until little evidence at all is left from Sunny Isles' heyday.

Golden Beach

Golden Beach holds little of interest for the visitor. As A1A threads through this subdivision, drivers are thrown back into the Miami of the early 1980s when there were so many seniors in Miami Beach that it earned the nickname "God's Waiting Room." The aligning houses and condos are still stocked with old ladies enjoying the warm weather and tanning through retirement, yet the number of blue hairs has certainly dwindled in the last twenty years.

If you stay on A1A, it will eventually, via the nondescript resort town of Hollywood, bring you to Fort Lauderdale (see p.207), although it's a roundabout route and you're better off using faster, interior roads like I-95.

4

North along the Biscayne Corridor

O n Miami's rundown north side lie chunks of the city that have only recently appeared on visitor itineraries. It wasn't always that way: the main drag here, **Biscayne Boulevard**, was once the central artery flowing between Miami and Fort Lauderdale, bringing traffic, motels, and diners to the area in equal measure. But when that connection was severed by the construction of the I-95 freeway in the 1960s (see p.259, Contexts), everything changed. In the heady days of the cocaine cowboys, Biscayne Boulevard became the OK Corral. The playful, poppy MiMo motels that once catered to commuters soon started renting rooms by the hour; while the classic mid-century mansions nearby became crack dens. But when the economic high from cocaine deals dwindled, the more law-abiding locals slowly started reclaiming the stunning buildings and in the past five years, that renaissance has rapidly accelerated.

The most noteworthy example of its rebirth is in the southernmost area, **north of the OMNI Mall**. This chunk of land is being transformed by music, both classical, played in the newly built mega-venue, the Miami Performing Arts Center, and contemporary, throbbing in the warehouse clubs of Park West. Heading north, the **Design District** exudes a funky, if somewhat artificial, vibe: the stores here sell swanky, stylish furniture and fixtures, while developers have made an effort to erect buildings of modern architectural interest. **Wynwood** next door is the city's new arts district, combining painters in residence with a glut of new galleries, as well as two of Miami's best museums.

Little Haiti further north is rather different. A robust neighborhood, it has grown up in the last twenty years thanks to the arrival of thousands of Haitian refugees, and though it has few sights it is refreshingly authentic and a great place to try cheap, tasty Caribbean food. Biscayne Boulevard snakes up into the lower-middle-class suburbs, starting with **North Miami**, incongruously home to the snazzy Museum of Contemporary Art-North Miami, and then hitting the confusingly named mainland settlement, **North Miami Beach**, home to a reconstructed medieval monastery from Spain.

The OMNI Mall and north

Built twenty years ago to revitalize the area, the **OMNI Mall** at 14th Street and Biscayne Boulevard failed miserably. Now, however, the OMNI area looks set to

Museum of Contemporary Art ▲

BISCAYNE CORRIDOR

Vagabond Motel

DuPuis Building

Caribbean Marketplace

LITTLE HAITI

Legion Park

Legion Park Picnic Islands

Belle Meade Island

Morningside Park Picnic Islands

MORNINGSIDE

Morningside Park

N

DESIGN DISTRICT

Living Room Building

Design & Architecture Senior High School

Melin Building

Moore Park

BUENA VISTA YARD

Rubell Collection

Margulies Collection

FASHION DISTRICT

Bacardi Building

Margaret Pace Park

Biscayne Island

ARTS & ENTERTAINMENT DISTRICT

OMNI

VENETIAN CAUSEWAY

Performing Arts Center

BICENTENNIAL PARK

Watson Island

MCARTHUR CAUSEWAY

JULIA TUTTLE CAUSEWAY

AIRPORT EXPRESSWAY

0   500 yds

South Beach

ACCOMMODATION
Normandy South   A

DRINKING & NIGHTLIFE
Churchill's Hideaway   8
The District   11
Grass Lounge   13
Magnum Lounge   3
The Pawn Shop Lounge   18

EATING
Café Café   7
Cane a Sucre   15
Caribbean Café Shop   17
Citronelle   5
COMA's   14
The District   11
Dogma   6
Enriqueta's   16
Lacaye Restaurant   4
Lakay Bakery   9
Laurenzo's   1
Mike Gordon's
  Seafood Restaurant   2
OLA   10
The Secret Sandwich   12
Soyka   7

thrive thanks to the construction of Cesar Pelli's showstopping Performing Arts Center next to the mall. North of here, the street's lined with motels, which mushroomed when Biscayne Boulevard was the throughway to Fort Lauderdale: most are crack dens, but their names – the *Gold Dust, Shalimar, Sinbad* – and jaunty signs hearken back to the Swinging Sixties. The most notable, **The Vagabond Motel** at 7301 Biscayne Blvd, has just been sold to new owners who plan to upgrade it; built by Robert Swartzburg, the same architect behind the Aztec-inspired *Delano* (see p.130), it's a MiMo masterpiece, complete with jagged streetside neon sign.

Close to the Performing Arts Center lies **Park West**, a warehouse district the city has cannily designated a nightlife zone, granting 24-hour liquor licenses to a cluster of clubs along 11th Street with the idea that it will draw traffic and congestion away from South Beach's choked nightlife. It's working, albeit slowly – the crowd here may be smaller, but it's much hipper than at most of the venues across the Causeway. For information on Park West's clubs, see p.157, "Nightlife."

The Miami Performing Arts Center

Masterminded by architect Cesar Pelli, the enormous **Miami Performing Arts Center** (☎305/372-7611, ☒www.pacfmiami.org), on Biscayne Boulevard between 13th and 14th streets, comprises three linked but separate performance spaces. The **Carnival Symphony Hall** is a 2200-seat shoebox-design space intended to maximize acoustics; the slightly larger **Ziff Ballet House** is devoted to opera, dance, and Broadway-style shows; and the tiny **Studio Theater**, with a flexible 200-seat auditorium, is available to local arts groups. The one old landmark on the site, the octagonal Art Deco Tower, was part of the now-demolished 1929 Sears flagship building and will now house a café; with its vaguely crenellated top, it was one of the first Art Deco–style buildings in the area.

Scheduled to debut in late 2004, the center has been dogged by problems that have put its opening back by two years and swelled its budget. It's only when the doors open for the first time that anyone will know for sure whether this investment has paid off, although the city's rabid commitment to the space means it's likely to receive hefty financial and promotional support for some time to come.

The Performing Arts Center will be home to four companies: the **Florida Grand Opera**, the **Miami City Ballet**, the **New World Symphony**, and the **Concert Association of Florida** – for ticket information, see p.163, "Performing arts and film."

The Bacardi Building

Looming above the street like a gleaming robot, the **Bacardi Building** (☎305/573-8511, ☒www.bacardi.com), at 2100 Biscayne Blvd, is a masterpiece of Modernist architecture, best known for the white and blue floral murals that sprawl across its northern and southern facades. Designed and installed by Brazilian artist Francisco Brennand in 1963, they're made from individually fired ceramic tiles. There's a small museum of uninteresting Bacardi memorabilia on the main floor here – a satellite of the original in Cuba – but it's only sporadically open to the public: call to check about access. Nearby, the squat, square building was an addition to the complex ten years later; its interior walls are made almost entirely of stained glass.

The Design District

Bounded by 36th Street and 41st Street between Miami Avenue and Biscayne Boulevard, **the Design District** was originally a pineapple plantation owned by Theodore Moore, known as the "Pineapple King of Florida." On a whim, Moore opened a furniture showroom in 1921 on NE 40th Street and created what became known as Decorators' Row. During Miami's Art Deco boom of the 1920s and 1930s, this was the center of the city's design scene, filled with wholesale interiors stores selling furniture and flooring. By the early 1990s, though, the district was derelict, crime-ridden, and filled with factories, with only a handful of interiors shops still holding out – most had been lured to move north to Fort Lauderdale's new Design Center of the Americas building. That's when developer **Craig Robins**, one of the masterminds behind the gentrification of South Beach as well as the new Aqua community (see p.80, "Central Miami Beach and north"), moved in and began buying buildings, spearheading the regeneration process with aggressive plans, including an emphasis on public art and sculpture.

He's succeeding – and little wonder, given that the city is in the middle of a building boom rivaling that of the 1920s; after all, those thousands of new apartments need fixtures and furniture. Almost overnight, the Design District's main drag along **40th Street** has been reborn as a temple to the *Wallpaper** lifestyle of conspicuous but elegant consumption, and the district is now dotted with funky, high-priced houseware boutiques alongside marquee names like Knoll and Holly Hunt. The showrooms are all open to the public, so feel free to browse – although prices are steep enough that browsing's likely all you'll be able to do. The two blocks between 2nd and Miami avenues along 40th are also the site of the **Decorators' Walk of Fame** – a tenuous claim at best – where stars embedded into the sidewalk honor long-forgotten interiors pashas from the area's first heyday, like Aaron T. Euster.

This whole neighborhood is set to transform even further during phase two of Robins' plans: fifteen new buildings, mostly high-rise condo towers, will soon sprout among the low-slung streets while a new square, Oak Plaza, will be constructed between 39th and 40th streets around an existing cluster of trees. The aim is to remedy the Design District's lack of energy: the showrooms are gleaming, but the sidewalks often seem deserted, so Robins plans to lure residents to join his business tenants.

For now, the district is liveliest during business hours Monday through Saturday, or on **Gallery Walk** night – dates vary, so check ⓦwww.designmiami .com for schedules. The website also has information on the area's twice-yearly sample sales (usually February and August) that offer a chance to pick up relative bargains from all the showrooms.

The Living Room Building

A neighborhood mascot of sorts for the district, **The Living Room Building** can be found at 4000 Miami Ave, at the junction with 40th Street. A whimsical landmark, with a sense of the district's campy fun rare elsewhere in Miami, the low-rise office building's signature feature was designed by local husband-and-wife architects Rosario Marquart and Roberto Behar. It's an entranceway that has been turned inside out and decorated with 40-foot walls, a giant concrete couch, and oversized lamps, all painted in fruity pinks and oranges. Topping it off, there's even a "painting" on the wall – or, rather, a gloriously simple hole through which the sky and shifting clouds can be seen. Sadly, at the time of writing, the building had not yet found a tenant, and so is unopen to the public;

after years of vacancy, the sculpture's now a little forlorn, but at least from a distance is still an unmissable photo opportunity.

The Melin Building

Two blocks east, the headquarters of Robins' real estate firm is located inside the enormous **Melin Building**, at 3930 NE 2nd Ave, where the thing to see is the sculptural oddity in the atrium. It's a giant hybrid shoe-gondola, designed to fit the Statue of Liberty's foot, and created by Antoni Miralda for the Venice Biennale in the early 1990s. Truly bizarre, the high-heeled sculpture has a black lacquer body flecked with foamy silver appliqué shapes, and a slatted, reinforced interior like that of a boat.

Design and Architecture Senior High

Design and Architecture Senior High (☎305/573-7135, ⊛www.jump2net .com/dash/), or DASH, is what's known as a magnet school – publicly funded, but selective in its students. Fittingly given the neighborhood, this high school at 4001 NE 2nd Ave specializes in the arts, and is housed in a former mall for design showrooms that was converted by Arquitectonica in the late 1980s. Only 500 teenagers study here, each of whom tests in via a portfolio and onsite art exam in the eighth grade. A year later, each must choose a major among architecture, film technology, graphic design, and fashion to complement the regular school curriculum. It's an unusual school in other ways, too: there's no mandatory phys ed, for instance, and no football team, either – instead, students can play golf, soccer, bowling, and basketball or take rhythmic dance classes. Of course, there's no public access to the school's interior but look for the twin column sculptures in the playground, again by Marquart and Behar, and yet another example of Robins' commitment to public art. *Kids!* is a pair of polychrome life-sized statues of a boy and girl; their animated gestures are based on the two central figures in Raphael's *School of Athens* fresco in Rome.

Wynwood

Immediately south of the Design District, **Wynwood** is hemmed in by major roads on each side – I-95, I-195, I-395, and Biscayne Boulevard. Long a predominantly working-class, Puerto Rican neighborhood, its low rents were discovered by artists two or three years ago, and they subsequently began to commandeer its spaces as workshops-cum-homes. At one point, New York's Whitney Museum was eyeing the area for a new satellite site, but those plans are now on hold; even so, there are plenty of vibrant new **galleries** speckled throughout, especially along N Miami Avenue. Pick up a map of these exhibition spaces anywhere in the neighborhood, or download it from ⊛www .wynwoodartdistrict.com – note that the sites are rather spread out, so it's best to tour by car rather than on foot. The liveliest time to stop by is the second Saturday of each month; that evening, from 7 to 10pm, all the galleries are open, with drinks available and artists on site – there's even valet parking.

The big change to the area is set to come in late 2006, with the opening of a sprawling 56-acre development on the eastern side of N Miami Avenue called **Midtown Miami**. The old buidlings of the Buena Vista Railyards, where freight trains were garaged, have been razed to make way for new townhomes and condos, as well as a massive mall. For more on the progress of this, check ⊛www.midtownmiami.com. In the meantime, there are two irresistible reasons to spend time in Wynwood: stunning private collections open to the public that

△ Arquitectonica sculpture at the DASH

vie to be Miami's answer to London's Saatchi Collection, the **Rubell Collection** and the **Margulies Collection at the Warehouse**. Indeed, these two galleries are set to be joined by a third sometime in 2006: collectors Dennis and Deborah Scoll have just bought an old boxing gym on 23rd Street to showcase their own holdings.

The Rubell Collection

Housed in a cavernous warehouse once used by the DEA to store evidence, the **Rubell Collection**, at 95 NW 29th St (Wed–Sat 10am–6pm, 2nd Sat of each month 10am–10pm; $5; ☎305/573-6090). In 2004, the exhibition space here was more than doubled to allow the Rubell family to showcase more than a fraction of its astonishing holdings, and the warehouse superbly displays a range of works that afford a comprehensive survey of the last thirty years in contemporary art. The family has snapped up oddities and masterpieces by American and international artists in equal measure. There's work by Cindy Sherman, including one of her earliest photographs, plus punk modernist Jeff Koons, Jean-Michel Basquiat, and graffiti master Keith Haring, whom the Rubells championed early on in his career. The showstopping piece is undeniably Charles Ray's eight-figure fiberglass orgy group: each of the sexually contorted figures is astonishingly a self-portrait copulating with its mirror image. Alongside such big names sit many lesser-known but equally interesting pieces by tomorrow's superstars – don't miss the filigree paper collages by British artist David Thorpe.

The Margulies Collection at the Warehouse

A stark showcase for the collection of a local developer with a passion for modern art, the **Margulies Collection** (Sept–May Fri & Sat 11am–4pm,

Sun noon–4pm; free; ☎305/576-1051, ⊛www.margulieswarehouse.com), at 591 NW 27th St was, like the Rubells', enlarged in 2004. Frankly, of the two, this is the more user-friendly space, with nooks and crannies where individual works can be effectively spotlit. Margulies is known for his **photography**, whether classics by Walker Evans and Eudora Welty or modern installations by the likes of Vanessa Beecroft. But the rest of his holdings are equally intriguing: take Ernesto Neto's dripping, sensual sculptures made from nylon stockings or Do-Ho Suh's bizarre re-creation of his New York apartment corridor in pink netting, light switches and door handles included. Two other unmissable stand-outs are Julian Opie's hypnotic, sexy computer animation *Monique Walking* and the half-dozen wax figures by Gilles Barbier, which show arthritic superheroes in an old-age home.

Little Haiti

Bounded on the east and west by Biscayne Boulevard and I-95, and running from 54th to 85th streets, **Little Haiti** is a residential neighborhood seldom visited by tourists. Unlike Little Havana (see p.96), this is an economically struggling district, and, unlike Miami's Cubans, the city's Haitian community has yet to make significant inroads in politics or business (though the city of North Miami Beach did recently elect the first Haitian–American mayor in the country).

Originally known as **Lemon City**, it was, along with Coconut Grove, one of the area's earliest European settlements. Haitians first started arriving here en masse in the late 1970s, fleeing the corrupt Duvalier regime, and Miami became the second most popular destination after New York City; almost 60,000 Haitians had arrived here by 1981. Today, Little Haiti is an undiluted immigrant neighborhood, with residents who live, shop, and work within its confines. Street signage is in both English and Kreyol, and you'll also hear French spoken in some stores.

To get some of the local flavor it's best to wander along the central drag of NE 2nd Avenue, and simply enjoy the Caribbean colors, music, and smells. Do be mindful, though: the area is relatively safe, but it's still a good idea to stick to both the main streets and the daytime.

NE 2nd Avenue

With buildings painted in ripe colors of raspberry and lime, and daubed with hand-written signs, not to mention music blaring out of the odd record store, **NE 2nd Avenue** has a distinctly Caribbean feel to it. Adding to the effect is the brightly colored ironwork of the **Caribbean Marketplace** at no. 5927, modeled after a similar bazaar in Haiti's capital, Port-au-Prince, and designed as an urban renewal project to showcase Haitian crafts while drawing tourist dollars to the area. Unfortunately, the bank foreclosed on the venture owing to bad management, and the Marketplace has been in commercial limbo for several years.

Don't be surprised to see chickens wandering round among the pigeons at the unnamed park three blocks north at 62nd Street and NE 2nd Avenue, which marks one of the hubs of the neighborhood. Next to the park stands the simple, Modernist **Notre Dame** church, which acted as a processing center for the stream of Haitian immigrants who arrived in Miami in the late 1970s. The church is still the heart of the neighborhood, attached to the Pierre Toussaint Center, which provides everything from medical care to job listings for local residents.

△ The DuPuis Building

On the corner of 62nd Street and NE 2nd Avenue, one of the oldest houses in Miami, the **DuPuis Building**, sits in what was once the heart of Lemon City. This white porticoed structure, built in 1902, first housed Lemon City's doctor, John DuPuis, and his pharmacy; at the time, it was the only concrete building north of Downtown. Later it was turned into the local post office before finally being abandoned several decades ago. Now derelict, it's still a rare remaining sign of how early European settlement took place here. Plans are afoot to transform the building into a tourist office, though they are still in the early stages.

Fifty-fourth Street

The heart of Miami's *voudou* and *santéria* culture (see box, p.94) is **54th Street**, especially along the blocks immediately west of NE 2nd Avenue, where it's lined with several *botanicas*. Here, believers can purchase ritual potions, candles, and statuettes. Almost all will permit a casual visitor to browse their merchandise, although the (mostly female) owners are notoriously tight-lipped with strangers. It goes without saying that photographing the racks of gaudy statuary and glass jars packed with herbs is both rude and foolish.

North Miami

Continuing along Biscayne Boulevard, the ten square miles or so from 103rd to 163rd streets comprise the suburban sprawl of **North Miami**, one of the many nondescript but pleasant enough subdivisions stretching north of the city proper. It's noteworthy solely for the avant-garde artspace, **Museum of Contemporary Art-North Miami** located here.

Museum of Contemporary Art-North Miami

At 770 NE 125th St (Tues–Sat 11am–5pm, Sun noon–5pm, last Fri of each month open 7–10pm; $5, Tues donation suggested; ☎305/893-6211, ⑳www.mocanomi.org), the large modern **Museum of Contemporary Art-North Miami** is set back from the shopping strip on an open plaza. Home mostly to traveling shows it presents at least eight different displays each year,

Santéria

A secretive Caribbean religion with an oral tradition, **santéria** was one of the many spiritual hybrids created by colonial rule. Despite their forcible baptizing, the conversion of slaves brought from their homes in Africa to the New World proved to be largely cosmetic. To preserve their own religions, the gods, or **orishas**, in the African pantheon were "translated" into Christian saints, so that they could be worshipped without fear of reprisal. (Thus, the popular male *orisha* Shangó, who's quick-witted and –tempered, ruling drums and dance, bizarrely became St Barbara.) Even the name *santéria* began as slang, when colonial Spaniards noticed how greatly their African slaves venerated the saints rather than Christ.

Much like the gods of Ancient Greece, *orishas* have flaws and favorites: each is identified with a given color, food, and number, and all require **animal sacrifices** and human praise for nourishment. Altars in *santéria* temples will often be covered with offerings of cigarettes or designer perfume – the *orishas* are apparently all too human in their vulnerability to flattery and expensive gifts. Religious services, conducted in secret by a priest or priestess, involve channeling the gods through dances and hypnotic trance.

While in Africa, each priest was associated with a single god and channeled that one alone, but as the religion came under threat in slave times, many priests began communing with the entire pantheon to preserve the worship of all the gods. This had two effects: firstly, that some *orishas* holy in the Caribbean are no longer venerated in Africa, since the city-states that held them dear were wiped out by the slave trade. Secondly, that the gods in American *santéria* became more closely linked in myth and practice than was traditionally the case.

Santéria's certainly a flexible religion, and there are many different incarnations – the Mexican version, for instance, is known for extensively incorporating local icons like the Virgin of Guadeloupe. The Cuban strain, though, is very African, and is strongest in the poor, sugarcane-farming Oriente province; it's closely related to, although distinct from, Haiti's **voudou** tradition.

Estimated numbers of those practicing *santéria* worldwide vary wildly, from 60,000 up to 5,000,000; regardless, it has a hidden but powerful role in local Miami society, as many people are at least part-time believers. Wandering round the city, you'll see signs of *santéria* activity if you look hard enough – **streetside offerings**, usually nailed to holy kapok trees, are common in Little Havana and Little Haiti. There's also much sensationalist reporting when *santéria* offerings are discovered near local courthouses, supposed attempts by family members to invoke the *orishas'* help during trials.

focusing on contemporary art – whether solo retrospectives on Keith Haring or surveys of the latest video installation techniques. A small permanent collection, including painting by Julian Schnabel and sculpture by Mariko Mori, is on rotating display alongside the pop art installation on the wall of the museum's interior courtyard by Jack Pierson that spells out the word "PARADISE" using mismatched, multicolored neon letters. The onsite giftshop is impressive for its unusual selection of art books and funky kids' toys, like arty finger puppets and bizarre sequined purses.

North Miami Beach

Cross 163rd Street and you'll arrive in the confusingly named and somewhat deprived suburb called **North Miami Beach** – not the safest neighborhood, so keep your wits about you if you plan to wander. Like so many subdivisions in the city, its founders wanted to leverage an association with the glamour of Miami Beach when first selling land plots, and decided that the small matter of being on the mainland rather than the sandbar proper was no reason not to call the place North Miami Beach. Here you'll find one of the city's oddest sights, William Randolph Hearst's **Ancient Spanish Monastery**.

The Ancient Spanish Monastery

Oddly anachronistic among the gas stations and strip malls, the **Ancient Spanish Monastery**, at 16711 West Dixie Hwy (Mon–Sat 10am–5pm, Sun 1.30–5pm; free; ☎305/945-1461, ⓦwww.spanishmonastery.com), is an unremarkable medieval building, the 1133 Monastery of St Bernard de Clairvaux from Segovia, Spain. But its complicated history is far more interesting than the surprisingly diminutive structure itself.

Early in the twentieth century, media magnate **William Randolph Hearst** scoured Europe for beautiful architectural souvenirs, snapping up whatever took his fancy; he then dismantled everything and shipped it to America, where most items were stitched together as part of Hearst Castle in California. The monastery, though, didn't make it – these ruins were quarantined by customs on arrival in New York, thanks to an outbreak of foot-and-mouth disease in Spain. The boxes never reached the West Coast – problems with Hearst's finances obliged him to auction them off, and the rubble gathered dust in a Brooklyn warehouse for almost thirty years. It wasn't until the early 1950s that the forlorn chunks were purchased – and reassembled - as a tourist attraction by Allen Carswell, who rebuilt the Cloisters Museum in northern Manhattan.

Unfortunately, though, the 11,000 crates were opened during the quarantine so that hay within could be burned; at the time, no one had noted which block belonged in which box – with the result that there were dozens of spare stones left after the eventual reconstruction. (Those stones were recycled, and now form part of another church building, the Parish Hall, on the same site.) The Monastery is a working Episcopal church with a tiny chapel that was formerly the monks' refectory; the cloisters themselves are small and rather frayed around the edges.

The site's difficult to reach without a car – **bus** #3 from Downtown and #H, #E, and #V from the beaches drop you off at the corner of 163rd and West Dixie Highway; if you're determined to make the trip, call ahead to check whether it's open, especially at weekends, as hours can be erratic.

5

Little Havana

A quiet district of sherbet-colored, low-rise buildings and dilapidated houses, **Little Havana,** southwest across the river from Downtown, is where the vibrant Cuban streak that colors Miami is most vividly seen. Wandering the streets, it's not unusual to see statues of Cuba's patron saint, the Virgin Mary, in residential gardens, and rare to find a newspaper box on the street that sells the English-language *Miami Herald* rather than *El Nuevo Herald*. Along **Calle Ocho** (aka SW 8th Street), the neighborhood's main drag, tiny stores and restaurants with hand-painted signs stand elbow to elbow; the other main thoroughfare, the **Cuban Memorial Boulevard,** is a quiet residential street rimmed with modest bungalows with a collection of monuments to the motherland clustered along its median. If the weather's co-operating, it's easy to forget you're not in Latin America: salesmen will come into restaurants to peddle videos or CDs while you eat, and the neighborhood *McDonald's* even serves *café cubano* alongside its Big Macs and apple pies.

What is now Little Havana only became largely Latin after Fidel Castro took power in 1959, and Cuban refugees – drawn here by the proximity and low rents – soon set about creating a replica of their homeland in America. They were unofficially fettered by the Miami city council, which attempted to deny business licenses anywhere north of 8th Street to those who didn't speak English, thereby confining newcomers to southwest Miami. Soon, though, upwardly mobile refugees gained an economic foothold in their adopted city – so much so, in fact, that Little Havana is increasingly a misnomer, as the successful Cuban community, especially the YUCAs (Young, Upwardly-Mobile Cuban Americans), decamps to wealthier neighborhoods, especially Coral Gables.

That said, this is still a heavily Latin residential area, and proper sights are few and far between: most visitors come to eat authentic Cuban food like *vaca frita* (fried beef), buy a hand-rolled cigar made from tobacco grown from Cuban seeds, or just browse the shops. Take time, though, to walk around the back streets – at least in daylight hours – for this is where you'll see the real signs of a transplanted ethnic community: there may be a man selling fruit from his van on a quiet corner or crude posters haranguing passersby about the latest political injustice in local government. The city council is also trying to energize the area through a program called **Cultural Fridays**: on the last Friday of each month, Calle Ocho between 10th and 15th avenues is transformed into a venue for music and street stalls, in an attempt to turn the neighborhood into more of a destination.

Along the map:

LITTLE HAVANA

0 ___ 400 yds

N

836

Miami River

N.W. 9TH ROAD
N. RIVER DRIVE
N.W. 9TH AVENUE
N.W. 8TH ROAD
N.W. 9TH STREET
N.W. 8TH ST
N.W. 7TH ST
N.W. 6TH ST
N.W. 5TH ST
N.W. 4TH ST
N.W. 3RD ST
N.W. 2ND ST
N.W. 1ST ST

S.W. 7TH AVENUE

N.W. 8TH CT
13TH AVE
I-95

4TH ST
N. RIVER DRIVE
3RD ST

Orange Bowl Stadium

LATIN QUARTER

N.W. 6TH ST
N.W. 5TH ST
N.W. 4TH ST
N.W. 3RD ST
N.W. 2ND ST
1ST ST
FLAGLER TERRACE
N.W. 1ST ST

WEST FLAGLER STREET

S.W. FLAGLER TERRACE

WEST FLAGLER STREET

S.W. 1ST STREET

S.W. 2ND ST
S.W. 2ND ST

S.W. 2ND ST

Riverside Park

José Martí Riverfront Park

A

Downtown

S.W. 3RD ST
S.W. 4TH ST
S.W. 5TH ST
S.W. 6TH ST
S.W. 7TH ST

933

Máximo Gómez Park

41 90
S.W. 8TH ST (CALLE OCHO)

Bay of Pigs Museum

Tower Theater

Brigade 2506 Memorial

S.W. 9TH STREET
S.W. 10TH STREET
S.W. 11TH STREET
S.W. 11TH TER
S.W. 12TH STREET

Cuban Memorial Boulevard

S.W. 14TH STREET
15TH ST
16TH ST
16TH TER
17TH ST
17TH TER
18TH ST
19TH TER

S.W. 22ND STREET (CORAL WAY)

VIZCAYA M

Museum of Science and Space Transit Planetarium

Villa Vizcaya

SAMANA DRIVE
SHORE DRIVE
BAYSHORE DRIVE
HIGH OLE DR
TIGERTAIL AVE
WA KEE NA DR

Coconut Grove

Left margin markers: ① Unidos en Casa Elián ② ③ ④⑤⑥&⑦ Woodlawn Cemetery ⑧ ⑨ ⑩ ⑪ ⑩, ⑮ & Coral Gables

ACCOMMODATION

Miami River Inn B&B — A

EATING

Ayestaran	5
Casa Juancho	6
Casa Panza	12
El Cristo	9
El Fogon	16
El Palacio de los Jugos	2
Guayacan	8
Habana Vieja	14
Hy Vong	7
Karlo Bakery	17
Los Pinarenos	13
Nuevo Siglo	10
Sergio's Cafeteria	15
Versailles	4
Yambo	3

DRINKING & NIGHTLIFE

Club Tipico Dominicano	1
Hoy Como Ayer	11

Along the Cuban Memorial Boulevard

The Cuban Memorial Boulevard, SW 13th Avenue between Calle Ocho and SW 12th Street – close to the houses of many former political prisoners and Brigade 2506 members – is home to several monuments, often draped in Cuban flags. The hexagonal **Eternal Torch in Honor of Brigade 2506**,

Cubans in Miami

Proximity to the Caribbean island has long made Florida a place of refuge for Cuban dissidents and economic migrants. A raft ride from Cuba's northern shore, propelled by prevailing currents, can take four days to arrive in South Florida. From **José Martí** in the 1890s to Fidel Castro in the early Fifties, the country's radicals have come to campaign and raise funds, and numerous deposed Cuban politicians have whiled away their exile in Florida. However, until Fidel's time, New York, not Miami, was the center of Cuban émigré life in the US.

It was during the mid-Fifties, when opposition to the Batista dictatorship – and Cuba's subservient role to the US – began to assert itself, that a trickle of Cubans started arriving in the predominantly Jewish section of Miami called Riverside, moving into low-rent properties vacated as the extant community grew wealthier and moved out. In fact, when **Fidel Castro** took power in 1959, he was enthusiastically welcomed here as part of his eleven-day tour of the USA (it was only later, after he broke off diplomatic relations, that the world found out how bloody and widescale his oppression of political dissidents had been). Back home, though, the affluent Cuban middle classes who stood to lose the most under Castro's increasingly hardline communism were soon packing their bags en masse and moving to Miami. These doctors, lawyers, and entrepreneurs helped transform the small existing Cuban community into what's now known as **Little Havana**.

Many regarded themselves as the entrepreneurial sophisticates of the Caribbean. Stories abound of formerly high-flying Cuban capitalists who arrived penniless in Little Havana, took menial jobs, and, over the course of two decades (and aided by a formidable network of old expats) toiled, wheeled, and dealed their way to positions of power. Their influence stretched further than South Florida; leading Miami Cubans also exerted considerable influence over the US government's policy toward Cuba with their 800,000 votes and hefty campaign contributions.

The second great Cuban influx into Miami was of a quite different social nature and racial composition: the **Mariel Boatlift** in May 1980 brought 125,000 predominantly Black islanders from the Cuban port of Mariel to Miami. Unlike their more worldly predecessors, these arrivals were largely poor and uneducated, and a fifth of them were fresh from Cuban jails – incarcerated for criminal rather than political crimes. Bluntly put, Castro had dumped his criminals and misfits on Miami. Only a few of them wound up in Little Havana: most *marielitos* settled in South Beach, where they

at the corner of SW 13th Avenue and Calle Ocho, is topped with a metal lamp that memorializes one of the fiercest incidents in Cuban exile politics. Named after the ID number of one of the brigade's fallen members, it features the brigade's crest, commemorating the incident that put JFK below only Castro in many Cuban-Americans' esteem. In April 1961, a ragtag band of US-trained Cuban exiles landed at the Bay of Pigs in an abortive attempt to overthrow Castro's regime. They were all either captured or killed – 117 men died fighting or drowned when their ship sank, while 1180 were taken prisoner. Depending on personal political affiliations, locals will tell you that the reason the invasion failed was either the soldiers' lack of preparation or JFK's lack of interest in Cuba – he withheld air support that may have changed the battle's outcome. Each year on April 17, a dwindling number of veterans gather here in their fatigues to reaffirm pledges of patriotism in exile to their Cuban homeland.

A block or so south stands a cluster of other monuments: there's a simple stone column commemorating **José Martí** and a moody bronze bust of **Antonio Maceo**, both heroes of Cuba's War of Independence with Spain.

proceeded to terrorize the local community, becoming a source of embarrassment to Miami's longer-established and determinedly respectable (and white) Cubans.

Yet local division gives way to fervent agreement when the subject turns to Fidel Castro: he's still universally detested. Cubans even suspected of advocating dialogue with Castro have been killed; one man had his legs blown off in the Eighties for suggesting that violence on the streets was counterproductive, and the Cuban Museum of the Americas was firebombed for displaying the work of Castro-approved artists and closed down because of it.

The energy and money expended against Castro is phenomenal. The late telecoms billionaire **Jorge Mas Canosa**, who acted as unofficial king of Miami's Cuban community, earmarked much of his fortune for massive lobbying attempts in Washington to keep Castro economically isolated and politically vilified. He helped nurture **the Helms-Burton Bill**, passed in the early 1990s under sponsorship of the right-wing senator Jesse Helms. Broadly speaking, this act prevented any president from changing America's hardline approach to Cuba. Bill Clinton initially baulked at these political handcuffs and only signed the bill after a long delay in response to Cuba's downing a US military helicopter. Even so, Cuban lobbyists' reach in DC is dwindling, and until recently, when he tightened restrictions on family visits, George W. Bush has shown an indifference to Cuba that would have been unthinkable in the Reaganite Republican 1980s.

Of course, the biggest headline-grabber was the case of **Elián González**, the little boy returned to his father in Cuba after his mother died during an abortive raft trek as a refugee. Mention of the case still rouses loathing for Clinton in Miami's Cuban community – by supporting the legality of the boy's repatriation he made himself the least popular president since JFK among locals. This sad mess, which has seemed to blight everyone involved, did produce two winners: **Manny Diaz**, the lawyer who defended Elián's right to stay in America, is now mayor of Miami; while his media-genic cousin, **Maryslesis**, whose ability to cry on cue was tailormade for primetime soundbites, now runs Maryslesis Hair Design, her own salon, on the western end of Calle Ocho at 73rd Avenue.

But no doubt the biggest test for Miami's Cuban community lies ahead, after Castro's death, when the Cuban-exile leadership will eventually be able to return to the island, and the armchair politicians from Miami face the daunting task of governing a very different country from the one they left behind.

Notice the doleful statue of the Virgin Mary – she cradles a decapitated baby Jesus, whose state of disrepair underscores the brooding isolation of the monuments – as well as the stark **Island of Cuba Memorial** featuring a large bronze map. Looming over the loose group of monuments on the Cuban Memorial Boulevard is a massive kapok tree, holy to the Afro-Cuban religion of *santéria* (see box, p.94): you'll frequently see offerings left at its base.

Calle Ocho and around

Southwest 8th Street runs through the whole of Miami, morphing into the Tamiami Trail as it skirts Coral Gables' northern boundary and shoots out into the Everglades. It's between SW 8th and 27th avenues, though, where it earns the moniker of **Calle Ocho**, as a staunchly Spanish-speaking commercial drag, lined with stores and restaurants plus local landmarks like **Máximo Gómez Park** and the **Tower Theater**.

△ A kapok tree on Cuban Memorial Boulevard

Máximo Gómez Park

West along Calle Ocho from the Brigade 2506 memorial, **Máximo Gómez Park**, at the corner of SW 14th Avenue (daily 8am–6pm), is officially named after a hero of the Cuban War of Independence (even if he was Dominican-born). This gated concrete hideaway is nicknamed "Domino Park" – despite the clichéd image, old Cuban men really do gather here to play dominoes and spend the day arguing about politics. In fact, access to the park's open-air tables is (quite illegally) restricted to men over 55. Bear in mind that these old-timers are camera-fierce rather than camera-shy, and don't take kindly to the attentions of enthusiastic visitors. The fence and key cards that guard its entrance aren't geared to prevent tourist intrusion, though – they were installed after a spate of shootings in the 1980s. You shouldn't have any problem stopping by during the day, though, as the gates will normally be open.

The Tower Theater

Two blocks of the street west of the domino players has just been gussied up into a pedestrianized park and renamed Domino Plaza, but it's an unappealing and artificial place to dawdle. Instead, stop and admire the astonishing exterior of the **Tower Theater** at 1508 SW 8th St, a 1930 Art Deco masterpiece, with its shiny, rounded steel signage, and sleek blue and white spire. Notable as the first theater in Miami to add Spanish subtitles in 1960, it's now owned by the

City of Miami and operated by Miami Dade College, which runs sporadic film programs – for details, see p.164, "Performing arts and film."

The Bay of Pigs Museum

The small **Bay of Pigs Museum**, at 1821 SW 9th St (Mon–Fri 10am–9pm, Sat 10am–2pm; free; ☎305/649-4719, ⊛www.brigada2506.com), is crammed with ephemera associated with the invasion, also commemorated on the Cuban Memorial Boulevard. There are maps, uniforms, guns, military plans, and of course, a full roll call of Brigade 2506 plus extensive photographs. The snapshot of Cuban history it offers is intriguing, but it's mostly of interest to specialists and partisans – it was set up, of course, as little more than a myth-sustaining exercise and yet another bastion of anti-Castro propaganda. There's also an onsite library, largely in Spanish, with documents on Cuban history and the Bay of Pigs invasion itself.

Woodlawn Cemetery

Even further west, at 3260 SW 8th St, lies the enormous, serene **Woodlawn Cemetery** (daily sunrise–dusk; ☎305/445-5425), crowded with mausolea and statuary and filled with the manicured graves of many prominent local figures. The father of Coral Gables, **George Merrick**, is buried here, but not in the Merrick plot: his wife Eunice Peacock – whose parents had been pioneers in Coconut Grove (see p.116) – had him moved into her own family's area two decades after he died. It's also the final home for several expat Cuban bigwigs, including two deposed presidents: **General Gerardo Machado**, unseated in 1933, and **Carlos Prío Socarras**, one of the prime movers behind Machado's downfall, who was himself driven from office (and the country) in 1952. Also interred in the mausoleum (and marked only by his initials) is **Anastasio Somoza**, dictator of Nicaragua until overthrown by the Sandinistas in 1979, and later killed in Paraguay; look, too, for the black marble wall, a tribute to the **Unknown Cuban Freedom Fighter**, one of the many killed during the abortive Bay of Pigs invasion.

Northern Little Havana: Unidos en Casa Elián and the Orange Bowl

Northwest of the heart of Little Havana at 2319 NW 2nd St stands **Unidos en Casa Elián** (Sun 10am–6pm; free), the house where Elián González stayed during his stormy time in Miami. Elián was a flashpoint in Miami politics: after his mother was killed trying to reach America with her son on a raft in November 1999, he was forcibly returned to his father who'd remained in Cuba by the federal government, despite enormous local protest. This house has been turned into an oddly discomforting museum in his honor by great-uncle Delfin González: display cases house Elián's playthings, alongside dozens of photocollages and mawkish poems written in tribute by local residents. Frankly, the only reason to come here is in an attempt to understand how raw and vivid a wound the Elián controversy carved into Miami's Cuban community – as this house shows, it's far deeper than an outsider might suspect.

Unless you're taking in a concert or a game (see p.184, "Sports, fitness and ocean activities"), there's nothing to draw you to the vast **Orange Bowl**, due north from Máximo Gómez Park at 1501 NW 3rd St. Home to the University of Miami's perennially successful college football team, the Hurricanes, the Orange Bowl is also known locally as the place where JFK accepted the

△ Food vendor at the Calle Ocho Festival

Brigade 2506 flag after the Bay of Pigs debacle and promised to return it in "free Havana." Older Cuban exiles grimly joke that he was referring to a well-known bar in Miami, rather than the city.

6

Coral Gables

A curate's egg of urban planning, **Coral Gables** is separated from Miami proper by more than just politics. It has a distinct local council and residential regulations, and seems to regard itself as an upper-class cousin to Miami, sandwiched as it is between gritty Little Havana and oddball Coconut Grove. Its twelve square miles of broad boulevards and leafy streets are lined by elaborate Spanish- and Italian-style architecture; you'll also find civic amenities like fountains and even a swimming pool dotted throughout the area. Intended by founder George Merrick to inspire civic pride in its residents, some say the plan for this European-style city has worked a little too well: this is the snootiest part of Miami, and its architectural beauty is somewhat blighted by a suburban smugness you won't find elsewhere.

That said, it's a fascinating place to visit, largely because almost all the landmarks that sprouted during its development still stand. The **Merrick House**, George Merrick's charming family home, remains, as do projects like the majestic **City Hall** and the **Miracle Mile** downtown. The grandiose **Biltmore Hotel** has reopened for business, while the delightful **Venetian Pool** is an unmissable Miami sight. The **International Villages** and **the Entrances** are spectacular follies, born jointly of Merrick's grand vision and sales savvy, adding further variety to the city's European-style architecture. Indeed, even the street layout is European, with winding roads that amble through a haphazard grid of residential streets and tiny, ground-level white rocks that act as street signs – remember to bring a map to navigate, especially if you're driving.

Some history

Whereas Miami's other early property developers built cheap and fast in search of a quick buck, the creator of Coral Gables, **George Merrick**, fired by the **City Beautiful Movement** (see Contexts: Architecture, p.263), was equal parts entrepreneur and aesthete. He was inspired by the Shaker Heights suburb in Ohio, a City Beautiful project planned by a pair of wealthy brothers that boasted wide greenspaces and fancy buildings. Merrick's pedigree was impeccable – his preacher grandfather had made millions with a questionable cure-all called "Fink's Magic Oil" – and he himself would become a fleeting millionaire through a combination of idealism, ego, and sheer salesmanship. Merrick appointed his uncle, artist **Denman Fink**, as Coral Gables' creative director; recruited **Phineas Paist**, one of the architectural masterminds behind Villa Vizcaya (see p.120), to plan the plazas, fountains, and artfully aged stucco-fronted buildings; and employed **Frank Button**, a landscape gardener who'd worked on Chicago's Lincoln Park enlargement, to oversee all the greenspaces.

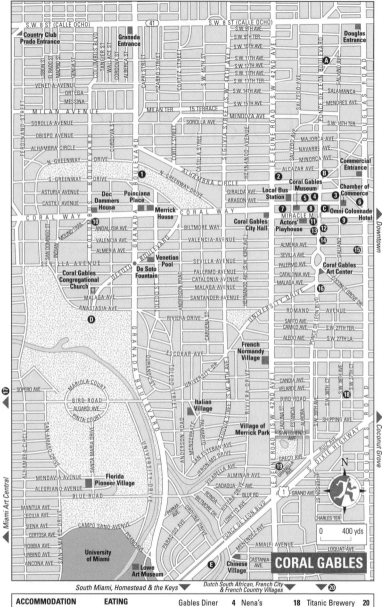

Miami International Airport & Little Havana

South Miami, Homestead & the Keys   Dutch South African, French City & French Country Villages

CORAL GABLES

ACCOMMODATION		EATING		Gables Diner	4	Nena's	18	Titanic Brewery	20
Best Western		Books & Books Café	5	The Globe	2	Norman's	15		
Chateau Bleau	A	Bugatti's	13	Havana Harry's	19	Ortanique		DRINKING	
Biltmore	D	Burger Bob's	1	House of India	6	on the Mile	11	& NIGHTLIFE	
Gables Inn	E	Caffe Abbracci	7	Les Halles	12	Picnics at Allen's		The Globe	2
Hotel Place St Michel	B	Canton	14	Miss Saigon		Drug Store	17	John Martin's	8
Omni Colonnade Hotel	C	Christy's	16	Bistro	3	Restaurant		Titanic Brewing	
		Estate Wines	9	Mykonos	10	St Michel	A	Company	20

Merrick envisioned a **Floridian Venice**, a city floating on, and by, the water. He further declared that no two houses could be the same, and that all designs had to be approved by the official city architect. The layout and buildings of Merrick's own suburb quickly took shape, according to his plans, often working around potential disasters. He transformed an abandoned quarry (used to supply the plentiful porous **coral rock** that gave his own homestead and later the whole city its name) into the Venetian Pool and disguised the construction ditches that ringed the infant Coral Gables into a network of canals (see p.113).

As the city took shape, Merrick focused on his own flair for selling, combining snappy sloganeering ("Where Your Castles in Spain are Made Real") with publicity stunts like a Spanish-themed land auction in 1921, or the ninety coral pink buses he bought to ferry in prospective residents from across Florida. This relentless hard sell worked – after all, Merrick spent a then mind-boggling $3m on marketing in less than four years; in that same time, the city had brought in more than $150 million.

Coral Gables' heyday was short-lived, though: soon after the **Biltmore Hotel** first opened, Miami was devastated by a major hurricane in 1926, and its tourism lifeblood was cut off. Ironically, the carefully built, ornamental city of Coral Gables was the district least damaged by the winds – even the towering *Biltmore* held firm. But the Great Depression set in before the local economy could recover, and Merrick's money soon disappeared. He retreated to Matecumbe Key in the Florida Keys to run a resort that his wife Eunice's parents had bequeathed her until it, too, was wrecked by a hurricane. Merrick finally returned to the area to serve as postmaster of the City of Miami until his death in 1942; he's buried next to Eunice in Woodlawn Cemetery (see p.101).

Merrick's dream lives on, however, as local residents have collectively embraced his grand design, enacting stringent ordinances on everything from appropriate color schemes to the size of "For Sale" signs in yards (5"x8") and even the times during which unsightly trucks may be parked outside a private house (in fact, the city even publishes a handy booklet, *Frequent Code Violations*, so that locals will know what they can and can't do). As affluent, second-generation **Cuban-Americans** have begun to move into the area, some say that Coral Gables, not Little Havana, is the new center of Miami's Cuban community. Still, there's little commercial evidence of Cuban presence here – this is one place in Miami where it's hard to find a quick *cafecito*.

The Entrances

Merrick was an entrepreneurial showman, and his plan to ring Coral Gables with eight impressive **entrance gates** was another theatrical flourish; he reasoned that these entranceways would evoke a sense of place before there were even houses here. He had originally planned on eight entrances to frame the main access roads, but only four were completed before funds ran out. Three of these, all along a two-and-a-half-mile stretch of SW 8th Street, are well worth seeking out.

At the junction with Douglas Road, the million-dollar **Douglas Entrance**, also known as the Puerta del Sol, was the most ambitious, consisting of a gateway and tower with two expansive wings of shops, offices, and artists' studios. During the Sixties, it was almost bulldozed to make room for a supermarket, but survived to become a well-scrubbed business area, still upholding Merrick's Mediterranean themes. Sadly, it's soon to be dwarfed by the inevitable high-end condo complex set to be built on its south side where there's currently a parking lot. Further west, at the junction with Granada Boulevard, the sixty-foot-high vine-covered **Granada Entrance** is based on the entrance to the city of Granada in Spain – a massive Renaissance gateway erected by Carlos V in the sixteenth century. The **Country Club Prado Entrance**, at the junction with Country Club Prado is an elaborate re-created Italian garden, bordered by free-standing stucco and brick pillars topped by ornamental urns and gaslamps. The fourth entrance, **Commercial** (also known as the Alhambra), is at the corner of the Alhambra Circle and Douglas Road but doesn't come close to matching the others in flair or style.

If you don't particularly wish to see the Entrances, the best way into Coral Gables from points east is along SW 24th Street, Coral Way, which turns into the Miracle Mile between Douglas Road (SW 37th Avenue) and LeJeune Road (SW 42nd Avenue).

The Miracle Mile and around

The so-called **Miracle Mile** wasn't the main commercial drag in Merrick's plan (that was Ponce de Leon Boulevard); rather, this strip of stores was cooked up in the 1940s by George and Rebyl Zain, married entrepreneurs who moved to Coral Gables from New York (there's a plaque commemorating them at the Mile's western end). Until recently, this strip was rather forlorn, filled with cobwebby ladies' boutiques and bridal emporia, yet it's now recharging its retail batteries with an aggressive redevelopment plan that's lured casual cafés and shops, like local designer Rene Ruiz, back to the main street. Another major incentive to pedestrians is the new free **trolley service** (☎305/460-5070) that shuttles along two routes Downtown that intersect at the heart of Miracle Mile: one north–south jaunt runs along Ponce de Leon Boulevard from the Metrorail stop to Calle Ocho (Mon–Thurs 7am–7pm, Fri 7am–10pm), the other east–west from the Alhambra Circle moves along the Miracle Mile to the *Biltmore Hotel* (Mon–Thurs 1.30–7pm, Fri 1.30–10pm). There are stops on almost every block.

As for nightlife, the local government has also loosened liquor laws, allowing bars to remain open until 2am (rather than midnight) in the hope of re-energizing this segment of Downtown. In large part, it's working; the area's at its liveliest and least hollow on weekday evenings when staff from many of the

△ The Miracle Mile

big-name businesses that have offices locally stop by for drinks or dinner after work. Architecturally, this strip is filled with Mediterranean Revival buildings of only passing interest, save for the occasional standout.

The Omni Colonnade Hotel

Halfway west along the Miracle Mile, the **Omni Colonnade Hotel** (☎305/441-2600) can be found at 180 Aragon Ave (just north of the Mile), at the corner of Ponce de Leon Boulevard. The Colonnade building initially was to house Merrick's local real-estate sales office – but was completed only months before the 1926 hurricane that wiped him out, and he never moved his offices from across the road. It served as a sometime movie soundstage in the 1930s and 1940s until Los Angeles decisively eclipsed Miami as the home of America's infant film industry; during the war, it became an army training facility and parachute factory. Today, it's an upscale yet unremarkable hotel and one of the more architecturally impressive buildings on the Miracle Mile – be sure to take note of its ornate center fountain, as well as the stylistic spiral and peak flourishes on the structure itself.

The Actors' Playhouse at the Miracle Theater

Originally built in the 1940s as Coral Gables' main cinema, the **Actors' Playhouse**, at 280 Miracle Mile (☎305/444-9293, ☻www.actorsplayhouse .org), was converted to a theater in the mid-1990s to provide a home for an acting company displaced by Hurricane Andrew. The classic theater has been sensitively restored, and stylish accents like the intricately etched glass in the lobby and a gleaming, metallic ticket booth embellish the otherwise rather plain Art Deco building, a standout among Coral Gables' usual ye olde building style. In addition to hosting traveling productions, the Playhouse's two small auditoria feature readings by local writers and performances by the resident children's theater company. For ticket information, see p.162, "Performing arts and film."

The Coral Gables Museum

Set to open in late 2006 or early 2007, the **Coral Gables Museum** (☻www .coralgables.com), at 285 Aragon Ave, will finally showcase decades of memorabilia that has been stashed in boxes in the Coral Gables Merrick House (see p.109). The collection, ranging from line drawings and plans for the *Biltmore* to old letters, will be housed in the former police and fire station, designed by Phineas Paist. A Depression-era WPA project, it was built later than many of his other designs – look for the muscular busts of firemen sculpted as reliefs above the garage doors.

Coral Gables City Hall

At the western end of the Miracle Mile, **Coral Gables City Hall**, at 405 Biltmore Way (Mon–Fri 8am–5pm; ☎305/460-5217, ☻www.coralgables .com), was planned as the heart of the city. This coral rock building, designed by the prolific Paist, is set at the busiest intersection in downtown Coral Gables – a pity, since the noise and traffic diminish its impressive facade: fronted with twelve stately columns as well as a replica of the city's seal, it's topped off by a multi-tiered, Spanish-inspired clock tower and plenty of ornamental moldings. Paist drew direct inspiration from the City Hall of Philadelphia, but tweaked the design by incorporating local elements like marine animals frolicking on the column's capitals. Inside, you'll see sales posters from Coral Gables' heyday, as well as newspaper clippings that illustrate how frenzied the Florida land boom of the 1920s truly was. There's also a blandly decorative **mural** of the *Four Seasons*, painted by the ubiquitous Denman Fink, in the belltower; it was recently spiffed up after years of neglect – note that while three of the seasons are represented by young women, winter's the old man.

Coral Gables Art Center

Merrick was careful to keep his sales and artistic staff separate: he built what's now the Colonnade for the former, while Denman Fink, Phineas Paist, and their staffs were housed at the **Coral Gables Art Center** at 2901 Ponce de Leon Blvd. Each person had an office that overlooked the magnificent spiral staircase in the main turret; the blue and white cloud painting on the ceiling was Merrick's nod to the building's artistic purpose. Today, the Art Center is simply a multi-tenant office building, but there's free public access to the turret's lobby during business hours.

Coral Way and DeSoto Boulevard

The forced rebirth of downtown Coral Gables is most glaring as the Miracle Mile turns back into **Coral Way** immediately west of LeJeune Road (or SW 42nd Street). Here, Mediterranean Revival high-rises proliferate, nurtured by a canny scheme that rewards those who construct in a locally appropriate style: called a Mediterreanean Bonus, which allows any such new structure to be 20 percent larger than a modernist counterpart, say sixteen stories rather than thirteen. Even so, Coral Way is an oddly soulless strip, and there's little to detain the casual visitor. The most pleasant detour is a wander round the residential streets south of Coral Way, canopied with enormous banyan trees. Stop by Fink's **DeSoto Fountain** near the Venetian Pool: it's an imposing centerpiece at the junction of Granada and DeSoto boulevards and another example of Merrick's determination to provide aesthetic as well as civic amenities, in accordance with City Beautiful precepts. Most streets here are named for Spanish provinces and towns, usually pilfered by Eunice Merrick from Washington Irving's book, *The Alhambra*. The few that aren't (Bird Road and Douglas Road, for example) were chosen not by officials of Dade County and honor notable early locals.

Move west along Coral Way and you'll come across three interesting houses after crossing Toledo Street. **Merrick House**, the first, was George's family home and is now a museum (see opposite). Further west stands **Poinciana Place** at no. 937, one of the earliest structures in the city, built close to Merrick's home when he married Eunice Peacock in 1916: its Mediterranean Revival style would serve as a template for later constructions. **Doc Dammers House**, at no. 1141, is unfortunately hard to see, stashed behind lush greenery on a large corner plot at Columbus Boulevard. This elaborate two-story home (now a private residence) belonged to New Yorker Dammers, a smooth-talking auctioneer who'd come to the area on the bidding of Carl Fisher to sell land in Downtown Miami. He was then employed by Merrick to bring his magic to Coral Gables: his tricks included gifts like boxes of grapefruit and trinkets given to the audience in between each lot, which guaranteed him a healthy crowd. Once a plot had been sold, the building plans and coral rock needed to construct a house were provided free of charge. When the city was incorporated, his fame among locals was high enough to secure him the post of first mayor of Coral Gables.

The Coral Gables Merrick House

Designed by George's eccentric and artistic mother Althea, the **Coral Gables Merrick House**, at 907 Coral Way (Wed 1–4pm, Sun 1–4pm or by appointment; $5; ☎305/460-5361), has been ably restored into a compact showpiece of Floridian shotgun design, its central ventilating hallway and wraparound veranda ideal for muggy South Florida summers. The simple wooden structure at the rear of the building was home to the Merricks when they arrived here in 1889 from New England to run a 160-acre fruit and vegetable farm. The venture was such a success that the shack was later augmented by a grander house of coral rock and termite-resistant local pine: it was christened Coral Gables, passing its name on to the city that later grew up around the family farm. The dual blows of the property crash and a citrus blight led to the gradual deterioration of the house, until restoration began in the Seventies. The house now showcases artwork by Denman Fink, as well as various Merrick memorabilia, along with an informative video that gives an overview of Coral Gables history. Upstairs, look for the chest Merrick received from King Alonso XIII of Spain, who decorated him in 1927 for creating a Spanish-inspired city in North America. There's a pleasant rustic grotto decorating the entrance to the small servant's house at the rear: the grotto was once much larger, until Merrick's practical mother sold some land to pay for her grandsons' dental work.

By the entrance to the car park, don't miss one oddball remnant of Coral Gables' past that demonstrates how aesthetic considerations always overruled practical ones in Merrick's vision. His traffic STOP signs were originally at ankle level to avoid interrupting vistas – until, of course, they proved rather unsafe; there's an example of one in the undergrowth here.

Venetian Pool

South of the Coral Gables Merrick House, along DeSoto Boulevard, you'll find the magical **Venetian Pool**, at no. 2701 (Nov–March Tues–Sun 10am–4.30pm; April–May & Sept–Oct Tues–Fri 11am–5.30pm, Sat & Sun 10am–4.30pm; June–July Mon–Fri 11am–7.30pm, Sat & Sun 10am–4.30pm; Sept–Oct, April–Oct 13 & up $9.50, children under 13 $5.25; Nov–March $6.25, children $3.25; ☎305/460-5356, ⊛www.venetianpool.com), originally known as the Venetian Casino. As local coral rock was plundered to build the original homes in Coral Gables, an unsightly quarry developed in the heart of the area, which Merrick, along with uncle and artist Denman Fink, ingeniously transformed into one of Miami's most appealing attractions. Merrick knew from the outset it was one of Coral Gables' most appealing features – this was his makeshift sales center in the earliest days of the city. Officially intended as another civic project for the benefit of local residents, it's a delightful place to spend an afternoon.

Despite its ornamentation, the pool was never designed with the social elite in mind; admission was cheap and open to all, and even today, local residents get a special discount. Surrounded by shaded porticos, wrought-iron railings, palm-studded paths, and Venetian-style bridges, the deep-blue water winds its way through coral rock caves and spills over two waterfalls – there's even a landlocked beach for sunbathers. Locker rooms are spotless, as are the tiled colonnades that display photographs of the pool in its heyday, when watersport celebrities like Johnny Weismuller (later famous as the first onscreen Tarzan) and Esther Williams performed here, or Olympic champion Pete Desjardins gave daily diving exhibitions. Until recent changes in labor laws, one of the perks of employment as the head lifeguard at the pool was to live onsite, in the ornate turret above the ticket hall.

Coral Gables Congregational Church

Just southwest from the Venetian Pool, the **Coral Gables Congrega-tional Church**, 3010 DeSoto Blvd (☎305/448-7421, ⓦwww.coralgables congregational.org), is another of Merrick's lofty civic projects, designed as a replica of a church in Mexico – he donated the land and dedicated the building to his late father, a Congregational minister. The church itself is a bright, ornate Spanish Revival flurry whose belfry echoes the imposing tower of the *Biltmore* across the street. The interior is dark – more Spanish Inquisition than Spanish Revival – with much elaborately-wrought ironwork and fine acoustics, especially notable during the regular jazz and classical concerts held here (see p.163, "Performing arts and film"). Sunday services are held at 9.15am and 11am.

The Biltmore Hotel

Merrick's crowning achievement – aesthetically if not financially – was no doubt the **Biltmore Hotel**, at 1200 Anastasia Ave (☎305/445-1926 or 1-800/727-1926, ⓦwww.biltmorehotel.com), which wraps its broad wings around the southern end of DeSoto Boulevard. The third in a trio of Miami towers inspired

△ The Biltmore Hotel

Before the *Biltmore* was constructed as his showpiece, Merrick had put up six smaller **hotels** where he could host prospective residents when they came down for site inspections of their real estate deals. One, the Hotel Seville, became today's *Place St Michel* hotel (see p.134); the best preserved, though, is the Cla Reina – now the *La Palma* restaurant (116 Alhambra Circle). The exterior, with its enclosed courtyard and decorative ironwork, looks much as it did during Merrick's heyday.

by the Giralda belltower in Seville, Spain (the others were the now-demolished *Roney Plaza* hotel in South Beach and Downtown's Freedom Tower, see p.55), the *Biltmore* looms majestically over Coral Gables. Its architecture is Mediterranean Revival with a strong Moorish influence shown in its ornate surface decorations: in fact, the hotel looks like a movie set, with 25-foot-high frescoed walls, vaulted ceilings, and immense fireplaces. When it was built, it was the last word in elegance, especially notable for an enormous chevron-shaped pool, and it attracted celebrity guests like Judy Garland and Bing Crosby (not to mention Al Capone, who hosted splashy parties on the 13th floor in what's still unofficially known as the "Capone Suite").

Surprisingly, given its grand scale, the hotel took less than a year to construct: from March 1925, workers lived in a tent city nearby and worked 24 hours a day to meet the opening date of January 15, 1926. One thousand VIPs were brought down from New York on a luxury train and genuine Venetian gondoliers punted guests through the Coral Gables waterways to the nearby beach. Since then, the *Biltmore* has weathered rough seas: the hotel was sold to new owners during the Depression, became a military hospital for burn victims after World War II – the pool was fenced in, a small store opened in the lower courtyard to sell candy and the giant ochre building was whitewashed. Then, following the hospital's closure, it was an illicit hang-out for local teenagers. Eventually, it was renovated at a cost of $55 million, a project that included partially filling in the pool, as it was too deep for modern safety regulations. The *Biltmore* reopened as a hotel in 1993 but the new owners promptly went bust and it closed again for two years before current management took over.

If you can't afford to stay here (for a review, see p.134), at least step in to marvel at the space. It's easy enough to wander round without a guide: otherwise, there are **free tours** every Sunday at 1.30, 2.30, and 3.30pm – though these are mostly disappointing. For a sprightlier take on its history, stop by each Thursday evening when a local historian recounts the grisly stories of ghosts and murders at the *Biltmore* – including the death of Al Capone's bodyguard, Fats Walsh, killed while his boss was supping at the Prohibition-era speakeasy stashed on the 13th floor of the tower. Meet at the main lobby by the fireplace at 7pm.

The neighboring **Biltmore Country Club**, also open to the public, is as stately as it sounds. You can poke your head inside for a closer look at its painstakingly renovated Beaux Arts features, but most people turn up to knock a ball along the lush fairways of the **Biltmore Golf Course**, which, in the glory days of the hotel, hosted the highest-paying golf tournament in the world.

South Coral Gables

The southern reaches of Coral Gables are primarily residential, aside from the campus of the **University of Miami**, built in the 1920s on land donated by

Merrick (with the theory that a world-class city would need a world-class university). The school almost went bankrupt in its early years, but is now a thriving institution, known especially for the successful Hurricanes football team (see p.184, "Sports, fitness, and ocean activities").

The International Villages

Even before the great hurricane of 1926, the market for housing in Merrick's new city had begun to soften. To revive interest, he worked with Myers Y. Cooper, a banker and former governor of Ohio, to cook up a gimmick that's now one of the area's signature features: the **International Villages**. Fourteen were planned, each representing a different style and each overseen by different architects. Unfortunately, constraints of time and money dictated only seven were built: the hoped-for remainder had showy themes like Japanese, African Bazaar, Persian Canal, and Tangier, as well as the more restrained Italian Country, Neapolitan Baroque, and Mexican Hacienda. Today, the seven standing are among the priciest real estate in the city. They include:

The eight buildings of the **Chinese Village** (bounded by Sansavino Ave, Castania Ave, Menendez Ave, Maggiore St, and Riviera Drive) were designed by Henry Killam-Murphy, who'd lived in the Far East and just completed buildings for Yale University in China. They're arguably the most dazzling, notable for their brightly colored roofs and ornately carved balconies; ironically, though, they're the least saleable and fetch the lowest real-estate prices of all. Another photogenic cluster, the **French Normandy Village** (the 400 block of Viscaya Ave at LeJeune Rd), looks thoroughly Elizabethan, thanks to its thick, chocolate-brown-beam-studded stucco facade and red-tile roofs. It has weathered surprisingly well, too, given that it was once owned by the University of Miami and housed five fraternities, then was turned over to soldiers' barracks in World War II.

Close by, the **Dutch South African Village** is less eye-catching (the 6600–6700 block of LeJeune Rd). Look for the gabled and dormered roofs inspired by the houses that were built by wealthy Boer settlers in South Africa, as well as connecting windows that make the two-storied houses look like bungalows. In contrast, see the grand colonial-style mansions of the **Florida Pioneer Village** (the 4300–4600 block of Santa Maria St); in the Greek Revival style, they feature pillars and verandas as well as incongruous white-picket fences.

Eighteenth-century-style townhouses make up the **French City Village** (the 1000 block of Hardee Rd); you'll know them by the four-foot-high walls that surround the buildings, enclosing courtyards and kitchen gardens. Its rural companion, the **French Country Village** (the 500 block of Hardee Rd and around) includes buildings designed to echo French farmhouses, with steeply pitched, crossed-gabled roofs, wrought-iron balconies, and, best of all, huge back yards.

Finally, the **Italian Village** (bounded by San Antonio Ave, San Esteban Ave, Monserrate St, and Segovia St) is a larger, looser collection of homes in Italian country and Venetian styles, and as a result stand out less from their Mediterranean Revival neighbors; to identify them, look for exterior stairways and walled gardens.

For some time, six of the seven quirky clusters were designated as National Historic Landmarks – with all the prestige and red tape that brings to the owners. Until recently, though, residents of the French City Village held out against this bothersome honor. All it took for them to reconsider was one owner's garish exterior paintjob – a deep mustard that had been approved by the city but offended his neighbors – for them to petition to join the other six settlements on the register. Even the Villages have become part of the development mania that's sweeping through Miami: real-estate speculators, following Merrick's lead, are planning a new round of villages, starting with a Bermuda-style cluster close to the South Dixie Highway.

Merrick's late additions to the city plan, architectural stunts known as the **International Villages**, are mostly in this area (see box, opposite), and it's here you'll find the **canals** which sparked Coral Gables' claim to be the Venice of America. In fact, much like the Venetian Pool, they're simply dolled-up byproducts of construction: having hewn chunks of coral rock from the ground to build houses, Merrick simply filled the holes with water and called them canals, employing real gondoliers every night to authenticate his claim.

The Lowe Art Museum

From its beginnings in 1950 as Miami's first professional exhibition space in a few rooms on the University of Miami campus, the **Lowe Art Museum**, at 1301 Stanford Drive (Tues, Wed, Fri & Sat 10am–5pm, Thurs noon–7pm, Sun noon–5pm; $5; ☎305/284-3535, ⓦwww.lowemuseum.org), has grown through acquisitions and renovations to be one of the largest museums in Florida. Its collection is large and diverse, featuring nineteenth-century, contemporary, Native American, and Renaissance art, even a sizeable amount of Cuban ephemera, thanks to a donation from the controversial Cuban Museum of the Americas in Little Havana, which closed its doors in 1999. Unfortunately, though, that diversity is its downfall: the Renaissance collection is sprawling and nondescript, while the Impressionist works are primarily small, early canvases by Sisley and Monet. Works that do stand out include the eerily lifelike *Football Player* by local sculptor Duane Hanson, and some paintings by pop innovator Roy Lichtenstein. Overall, it's pleasant enough, but not a patch on better collections at the Miami Art Museum Downtown (see p.51) or at the Margulies and Rubell collections in Wynwood (see p.91).

Miami Art Central

On the border with South Miami, **Miami Art Central** (Tues–Sun noon–7pm; $5; ☎305/455-3333, ⓦwww.miamiartcentral.com), at 5960 SW 57th Ave, is the newest art venue in Miami's mushrooming modern scene. A 30,000-square-foot space, it only displays temporary shows housed in a simple 1940s telephone building. The place was organized and funded by Venezuelan philanthropist and art lover Ella Cisernos, who taps avant-garde artists to come in and curate exhibitions. Past shows have included artistic reaction to the question "How do we want to be governed?" and "10 Floridians," which, despite its title, invited international curators to give their own perspectives on Miami.

7

Coconut Grove

The latent pioneer spirit of South Florida surfaces in **Coconut Grove**, an area known for being both tolerant and, at times, ornery. It's always seemed uneasy about being a part of Miami, which annexed it in the late nineteenth century. Eccentrics and artists have made their homes here for more than a century (the local Hare Krishna temple is just off Virginia Street), and older locals will usually treat outsiders with politeness plus a little suspicion. In recent years, the area has gentrified somewhat, blighted by bland shopping centers and towering bayview apartments, but it has somehow managed to remain a refreshingly off-kilter, resoundingly real place.

From its beginning, the Coconut Grove community has been diverse: having sprung up after the Civil War around the tropical plantation of a Confederate doctor, the area was originally home to migrant Bahamian laborers and liberal-minded Anglo settlers, as well as characters like wacky philosoper-environmentalist Ralph Middleton Munroe (who built the house at the Barnacle State Historical Site – see p.116). Facilities in the town were highly developed by 1896, with a library, churches, a yacht club, and the first school in Dade County. Up until then, a chunk of dense hardwood hammock had kept the new city of Miami at bay, but city growth and Henry Flagler's railroad merged the two, and Coconut Grove was soon annexed. The populace – galvanized by their early independence, as well as the many liberal-minded artists and leftists who migrated here thanks to tolerant attitudes – has tried to secede several times since then; there are still activists pushing the cause today.

Separatist attitude aside, Coconut Grove is still part of Miami proper – in fact, the **Miami City Hall** moved here to the Dinner Key Marina on Biscayne Bay in the 1950s. Geographically, the southwestern portion of the area is leafy and residential, with chunks of thick hammock and enormous canopies of greenery on most streets, while pedestrian-friendly **central Coconut Grove** holds two well-known shopping centers. East from here, there's the once countercultural, now well-tended **Peacock Park**, as well as the sublime **Barnacle** building and the superb **Kampong** botanical garden. Moving north up Bayshore Drive past City Hall, Biscayne Bay is lined with greenspace before arriving at **Villa Vizcaya**, the spectacularly overwrought mansion built by millionaire James Deering.

Central Coconut Grove and around

The **Grove's central district** is compact and walkable, with shops and restaurants fanning out northwest from the intersection of Main Highway and Grand Avenue. **CocoWalk**, a hacienda-inspired outdoor mall, was a revitalizing force for the neighborhood when it was built in the early 1990s, though the more

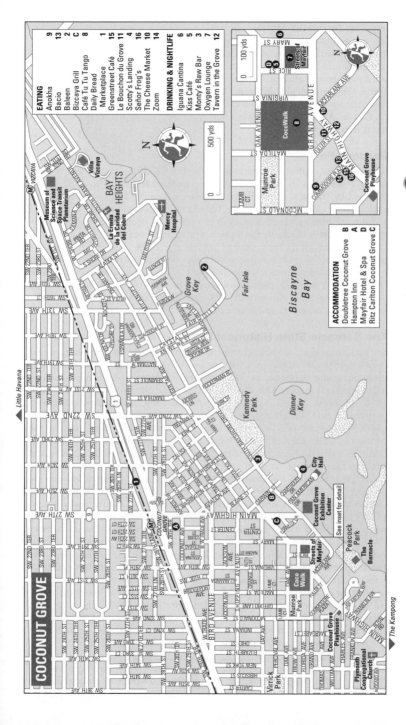

COCONUT GROVE

EATING
Anokha	9
Bacio	13
Baleen	C
Bizcaya Grill	2
Café Tu Tu Tango	8
Daily Bread	1
Marketplace	
Greenstreet Café	15
Le Bouchon du Grove	11
Scotty's Landing	4
Señor Frog's	16
The Cheese Market	10
Zoom	14

DRINKING & NIGHTLIFE
Iguana Cantina	6
Kiss Café	5
Monty's Raw Bar	3
Oxygen Lounge	7
Tavern in the Grove	12

ACCOMMODATION
Doubletree Coconut Grove	B
Hampton Inn	A
Mayfair Hotel & Spa	D
Ritz Carlton Coconut Grove	C

CocoWalk

Munroe Park

Coconut Grove Playhouse

Streets of Mayfair

Biscayne Bay

Little Havana

Bay Heights

Museum of Science and Space Transit Planetarium

Villa Vizcaya

La Ermita de la Caridad del Cobre

Mercy Hospital

Grove Key

Fair Isle

Dinner Key

Kennedy Park

City Hall

Coconut Grove Exhibition Center

See inset for detail

Peacock Park

The Barnacle

The Kampong

Virrick Park

Coconut Grove Playhouse

Plymouth Congregational Church

Coco Walk

Munroe Park

7

COCONUT GROVE | Central Coconut Grove and around

imposing **Streets of Mayfair** shopping center just across Virginia Street was less successful: while it has a good range of stores (including one of the few large bookstores within reach of Downtown; see p.172) it's oddly monolithic and unappealing, with its zigzagging walkways and copper sculptures. Better to head south, and grab a coffee at one of the many sidewalk cafés lining Main Highway. While there, you might also want to take a look around the south Grove – or, as it's known colloquially (if unfortunately) – "Black Coconut Grove." Centered on Charles Avenue, this somewhat depressed area throws the wealth surrounding it into sharp relief.

Peacock Park

South of these centers and overlooking the bay stands **Peacock Park**, the site of the *Peacock Inn*, the first hotel to open in the Miami area in 1882. It was designed by Barnacle owner Ralph Middleton Munroe and owned by British settler Charles Peacock and his wife, Isabella. After the building was demolished and the site became a park, it was the epicenter of Coconut Grove counterculture in the 1960s thanks to the hippies who camped out here.

Today, thankfully, it's been spruced up and is the best of several local greenspaces, with a few public tennis courts and some peculiar abstract sculptures sprinkled throughout; this is where most of Coconut Grove's festivals take place (see p.189). It's especially pleasant for the superb views of the bay it affords – and if rollerblading along the catwalk of Ocean Drive in South Beach is a little intimidating, come here and practice first.

The Barnacle State Historical Site

Set back from the road behind tropical hardwood hammock (the foliage that once covered the whole of what's now Coconut Grove), one of the city's most intriguing sights lies at 3485 Main Hwy: Ralph Middleton Munroe's pagoda-pioneer house, **The Barnacle** (Fri–Mon 9am–4pm; tours depart at 10 & 11.30am, 1 & 2.30pm; $1; ☎305/442-6866, ⊛www.floridastateparks.org/thebarnacle/default.asp).

Munroe was one of Miami's first snowbirds, drawn from New York by the weather in a vain attempt to cure his dying wife's TB in the 1870s. Despite her death, he stayed, and became wealthy through the salvage business, rescuing and reselling the cargo of wrecked commercial ships. Munroe built the Barnacle in 1891 to showcase his own eco-friendly engineering theories. He quickly became an eccentric curiosity to locals, mostly thanks to his devotion to Transcendentalism (which advocated self-reliance, a love of nature, and a simple lifestyle) and his close friendship with Bahamians and Seminoles. By the 1920s, when tourists first started scoping out his home, he was a confirmed oddity.

Munroe used local materials plus tricks he learned from nautical design to make the house as durable as possible. For one, he built the house completely above ground to prevent flooding and improve airflow – helping to alleviate some of the discomfort of living year round in Miami's humidity – and, after remarrying in 1908, raised the building further, adding a floor under the original one when his growing family needed extra room. There's also a recessed veranda that enables windows to be open during rainstorms and skylights that allow air to be drawn through the structure. The wide overhangs on each story, designed to give shade from the sun, exudes a vaguely oriental vibe.

The only way to see inside the house is on a guided tour; inside, you'll see many original furnishings alongside some of Munroe's intriguing photos of pre-settlement Coconut Grove. The grounds are also a pleasant place to dawdle:

once a month major fundraisers are held here, featuring live classical music played from the veranda while the audience lolls on the waterfront lawn – call for details of the next concert.

117

△ The Barnacle State Historical Site

Coconut Grove Playhouse

Opposite the Barnacle on the main road, the blue-and-white Mediterranean Revival building at 3500 Main Hwy started as a movie theater in 1926; its first production was *Sorrows of Satan* starring Adolphe Menjou. The place became the **Coconut Grove Playhouse** (☎305/442-2662, ⓦwww.cgplayhouse.com) in the mid-1950s when an entrepreneur bought the abandoned building hoping to bring Broadway to Coconut Grove. He certainly invested heavily in its refurbishment – there were lavish onsite apartments for the stars with gold plumbing fixtures in some bathrooms – and, at least initially, he succeeded, luring performers like Tallulah Bankhead and Chico Marx. The theater's greatest claim to fame, though, is that Samuel Beckett's *Waiting for Godot* (starring Bert Lahr, of *Wizard of Oz* fame) had its US premiere here in 1956. Now, the interior's less compelling than the ornate exterior, and there's little reason to go inside other than to take in a performance. For ticket information, see p.162.

Charles Avenue

In the nineteenth century, there was a small Bahamian village called Kebo on the site that Coconut Grove now occupies, and many black immigrants settled here during Miami's construction boom, notably along what's become **Charles Avenue**. It's remained a largely black, working-class neighborhood and is noticeably less chichi than surrounding areas.

There aren't many specific sights, other than a few so-called "shotgun" houses on the 3200 block of Grand Avenue, built in the 1920s and 1930s around long, narrow hallways: cheaply made at the time from local hardwoods, they're now cherished for the same reason. Notice how the cemetery, at no. 3650, is tiled with gravestones: owing to the combination of hard coral rock and a close-to-the-surface water table, coffins here could not be sunk deep into the ground, and so the dead were buried in unusually shallow graves.

Plymouth Congregational Church

On the southern edge of the district, close to Black Coconut Grove, stands the small neighborhood church of **Plymouth Congregational**, 3400 Devon Rd at Main Highway (Mon–Fri 8.30am–4.30pm; ☎305/444-6521, ⓦwww .plymouthmiami.com). It has a striking, vine-covered coral-rock facade – and remarkably, this finely crafted exterior was the work of just one man. The 375-year-old main door, hand-carved in walnut, looks none the worse for its journey from an early seventeenth-century monastery in the Basque region of Spain. The dark interior of the church sadly doesn't live up to its spectacular exterior – but if you're determined to poke around inside, call ahead to the church office and make an **appointment**.

The Kampong

The 11-acre **Kampong** garden ($10; ☎305/442-7169, ⓦwww.ntbg.org /kampong) at 4013 Douglas Rd is a hard-to-find gem – look for the semi-circular entrance and tiny street-number sign along a stretch of residential mansions. The nearby Fruit and Spice Park (see p.202) may be better known but the Kampong (a Malaysian word meaning "cluster of houses" or "extended family") is far more impressive, home to an extraordinary range of more than 5000 tropical flowering and fruit trees or plants.

The collection was cultivated by the late lumber heiress Kay Sweeney, who bought both house and plot from botanist David Fairchild. Like him, Sweeney was not just a plant fiend but confirmed globetrotter, and picked up interesting specimens on her travels then sent them back to be planted at her Florida home alongside Fairchild's existing species. The result was an eclectic, far-reaching display with an emphasis on Asia: highlights include wide-leafed philodendra, used as impromptu umbrellas, and *ylang ylang* plants, whose pungent fragrance is the basis for Chanel No. 5. There are also more than fifty species of mango, as well as offbeat fruits like the round, dark-skinned *bael* from India, a hard-shelled citrus that Fairchild himself used to eat daily as a natural laxative.

The Asian-inspired (and less intriguing) house is crammed with native artifacts and most significant locally as the site of the meeting where Fairchild and activist Marjorie Stoneman Douglass conceived the Everglades charter designed to protect that drying-up wilderness from development (see p.218).

Bayshore Drive and around

From Peacock Park, **Bayshore Drive** heads northeast, skirting Biscayne Bay and running by most of the sights in the area. Southwest off of Bayshore Drive, along Pan American Drive, you'll find the **Miami City Hall**, as well as the Marina, a mooring for lines of ultra-pricey yachts.

Continuing north you'll come across **Silver Bluff** between the 1600–2100 blocks. This limestone ridge is where the earliest Coconut Grove settlers made their homes, on one of the highest and safest points in the flat and flood-prone city. These settlers were later joined by the well-heeled notables of 1910s Miami, and today the area remains a preserve of the tasteful and wealthy, with the early mansions replaced by equally expensive modern counterparts.

Finally, further up the drive you'll come to the last sights of Cococut Grove, just below Little Havana: magical **Villa Vizcaya**, kids' mecca the **Museum of Science** and the **Space Transit Planetarium**, and the Modernist church **La Ermita de la Caridad del Cobre** – a shrine to Our Lady of Charity.

Miami City Hall and around

The cheerful **Miami City Hall**, at 3400 Pan American Drive (☎305/250-5300), provides a rare dash of Deco in Coconut Grove. A flared white building flecked with blue reliefs, the structure was built on the bay in 1934 as a terminal for Pan American Airlines' seaplane service to Latin America – the reliefs of winged globes and rising suns are Pan Am's insignia. The company began flying from here in 1930, and its first passenger terminal was a houseboat dragged here from Cuba and anchored to pilings. That temporary structure was replaced by this swooping building, which was then commandeered to serve as naval base during World War II; Pan Am's last flight here was in 1945.

The building subsequently became an unlikely site for Miami's City Hall, mostly thanks to the age-old animosity between the city proper and its annexed, formerly independent subdivision; it didn't help matters when it was announced that Miami paid a then-astonishing $1 million in the 1950s to take it over, with much local grumbling about wasting public money. The grand globe that once graced its lobby is now in the Museum of Science, albeit in a sorry state (see p.122), and there's no public access to the building's interior – a pity, given the murals near the ceiling which record the history of flight, running from da Vinci to Pan Am, naturally. However, you can get close to a small plaque in front that reminds visitors this is where the veterans of the Bay of Pigs stepped ashore after their release from Cuba in 1962.

Just south of here, near the end of Bayshore Drive, **Dinner Key** can be found, named after a popular early twentieth-century picnic spot; it was a small island in Biscayne Bay until joined to the mainland for defensive reasons during the

△ Miami City Hall

World War I. Nearby, the former Dinner Key Auditorium, where Jim Morrison was charged with indecent exposure after allegedly dropping his leather trousers onstage in 1969 (see box opposite) – it's now called the Coconut Grove Exhibition Center.

Villa Vizcaya

In 1914, farm-machinery mogul **James Deering** followed his brother Charles (of Charles Deering Estate fame; see p.201) to Florida and blew $22 million re-creating a sixteenth-century Italian villa within the belt of vegetation between Miami proper and Coconut Grove. It took two years – and one thousand workers – 10 percent of Miami's then population – to build his monumental folly, **Villa Vizcaya** (daily 9.30am–4.30pm, grounds open until 5.30pm; $10,

The Lizard King takes off in Miami

Coconut Grove's famed eccentricity and tolerance of countercultures made it a natural refuge for hippies in the 1960s – although their mass arrival stirred up the area's other signature emotion, ornery crankiness, in equal measure. While the hippies slept in Peacock Park or lounged in the churchyards, locals grumbled about the dozens of stoned teenagers wandering the streets asking for money.

The crackdown on counter culture here came in March 1969, during the infamous Doors concert at the **Dinner Key Auditorium** at which **Jim Morrison** was said to have dropped his leather trousers and exposed himself to the crowd. It's impossible now to know the truth of what happened. Certainly, the concert's greedy promoter had oversold the venue by more than 8000 tickets, packing 13,000 people into a small building without air conditioning on a hot spring night. Unquestionably, Morrison was blind drunk when he took the stage, having missed his flight to Miami and filled the time until the next plane knocking back booze. When he appeared, very late and incoherent, the overcapacity crowd charged the stage. Although some who attended the concert still insist that he merely taunted the crowd and exposed nothing, a warrant (signed by a junior in the local attorney's office who'd attended the concert) was issued five days later. It claimed that Morrison had asked "Do you wanna see my cock?" before baring his crotch, an act that constituted, in the attorney's words, an "attempt to precipitate a riot."

Eighteen months later at his **trial**, he pleaded not guilty and was cleared of the felony charge of lewd and lascivious behavior. However, Morrison received hard-labor sentences totaling 240 days for exposure and profanity, which were still under appeal when he died in Paris in July 1971. Either way, reaction to this incident across the country was surprisingly vocal: many radio stations dropped Doors tracks from their airplay schedules, *Rolling Stone* printed a scathing article on the band, and many venues in the Doors' upcoming tour canceled their bookings. More than thirty years later, incensed and devoted fans are still campaigning for the Lizard King's pardon.

free tours every 40min; ☎305/250-9133, ⓦwww.vizcayamuseum.com) at 3251 S Miami Ave. A temporary spur was even constructed from the nearby railroad simply to bring materials into the courtyard during the building phase, and like an early twentieth-century Elton John, every day Deering filled each room of his villa with fresh flowers, and never let good taste get in the way of acquisition; in a grandiose PR stunt, he arrived by yacht on Christmas Day 1916 to move in. He and his decorator-in-chief Paul Chalfin spent several summers in Europe cherry-picking dozens of classical, Renaissance, and Rococo antiques, all geared to convincing Vizcaya's visitors that the structure was at least 400 years old. Taken individually, the rooms are appealing, but in a single house this orgy of styles is an architectural sugar rush.

Still, Vizcaya is an unmissable sight. Inside the villa, don't miss the spectacular ceiling in the East Hall, the earliest of all in the house, and the master clock in the Butler's Pantry, to which all other clocks at Vizcaya were linked to keep in sync. The villa was high-tech as well as old world, outfitted with elevators, fire sprinklers, and a telephone switchboard; every bedroom had an en-suite bathroom, and there were thirty servants living on site to minister to Deering and his guests' every need. Of course Deering was only in residence for four months of the year, through the winter – the rest of the time he spent back home in Chicago.

Notwithstanding its Spanish name, the house is another example of Miami's obsession with the watery old-world glamour of Venice, notably the waterfront *terrazzo* and stone barge; the sculptures of mermaids and mermen on the barge are by Sterling Calder, father of mobile designer Alexander. The rest of the **grounds** are undeniably beautiful – don't miss the orange jasmine maze garden or the mythological statues lining the walkways – though much reduced from their 180-acre, seven-island heyday; look for the map inside the house that shows a rendering of their initial opulence before the land was sold to developers building what's now Mercy Hospital. Making the place even more surreal, the walkways are often clogged with teenage girls, enveloped in gloriously over-the-top meringue dresses; they're being officially photographed for their *quince*, the Cuban version of a Sweet Sixteen.

The Museum of Science and Space Transit Planetarium

Dedicated to making science simple, the **Museum of Science** (daily 10am–6pm; $10; ☎305/646-4200, ◉www.miamisci.org), at 3280 S Miami Ave, virtually across the street from Vizcaya, is great for kids – but less so for adults – with interactive, engaging exhibits, and a rolling program of exhibits and live demonstrations from in-house educators. In its main hall sits the Pan Am Globe, which was once the centerpiece of the airline's terminal in Coconut Grove: the museum acquired it in 1960, and, in a fit of political correctness ten years later, repainted it to show geographical features rather than political boundaries.

Off the left of the main lobby in the same building, the **Space Transit Planetarium** features the standard domed auditorium, but its presentations are better than average, with shows on the hour. There's a wildlife refuge attached, which houses the usual injured birds and snakes, although the Miami Seaquarium's a better choice if you want to learn about animal rescue (see p.124).

The museum's been in stasis for some time while lawmakers argue over its proposed move to Museum Park Miami, a specially constructed complex Downtown it would share with the Miami Art Museum. At time of writing, there's still no firm date for the move or even start of construction.

The Church of La Ermita de la Caridad del Cobre

Looking rather like an angular meringue half-dipped in dark chocolate, the modernist church **La Ermita de la Caridad del Cobre** perches on the waterfront near Mercy Hospital at 3609 S Miami Ave (daily 8am–9pm; ☎305/854-2404), close to the southeastern border of Little Havana. Named for Cuba's patron saint, the Virgin of Charity, and known affectionately as "La Ermita," the church is the spiritual center of Cuba-in-exile. Built on 10¢ donations from newly arrived immigrants, it was consecrated in 1973 and significantly renovated (this time through $1 donations) twenty-five years later. Iconic and symbolic, every element of the building resonates with the island country: the six concrete columns forming the mantel represent the six traditional provinces that existed before Castro, while beneath the altar, there's Cuban soil, sand, and rock, salvaged from a wrecked refugee boat. Finally, an emotive, if patchy, sepia mural behind the altar traces the history of Cuban immigration, and the conical-shaped church is angled to allow worshippers to look out across the bay in the direction of Cuba.

8

Key Biscayne and Virginia Key

The island of **Key Biscayne**, with its luxury apartments and enormous mansions, has long been one of the most desirable addresses in Miami. It's not unusual to see old-fashioned, white-uniformed nannies wheeling their baby-buggy-bound charges between condo complexes, and the overall impression is of a secluded and wealthy community that's hardly ruffled by its proximity to the city. Most people, though, are drawn here by the **beaches** and **parks**, which are some of the lushest around the city.

So named because the island was thought to be part of the Florida Keys (it isn't), Key Biscayne is what South Beach would have become without the Deco and the decadence. It was settled at the same time during the 1910s, though as a farming community rather than as a resort. However, when wide-scale agricultural development quickly proved impractical – rabbits nibbled on the tasty coconut-palm shoots – the island fell largely into the hands of the Matheson family, who had made millions from the chemical industry, providing blue jean dye to Levi's and mustard gas to the US government during World War I. Once this first wealthy family made the island their secluded home, Key Biscayne became known as a privacy-cherishing place where the wealthy could live undisturbed; even President Nixon spent his winters here. Recently, its reputation for seclusion and safety has also attracted rich expats from Latin America, and it's estimated that two-thirds of the island's population is now Hispanic.

Unless you have access to a boat, **getting to Key Biscayne** will require taking the soaring Rickenbacker Causeway from Downtown ($1 toll for vehicles), which stops off at **Virginia Key** along the way. Since Key Biscayne was never intended as a resort, services for visitors are still patchy: public transport is almost nonexistent – you can take bus #B from Downtown (service ends at 7pm), or better still, rent a bike (see p.183, "Sports, fitness, and ocean activities").

Virginia Key

Nonresidential **Virginia Key** is an unavoidable, if scenic, obstacle on the way to Key Biscayne. The quiet island houses several marine research facilities, as well as the **Miami Seaquarium**. Besides this attraction, there's not much more to do here other than stretch out on fine **Virginia Key Beach** (daily 8am–sunset; cars $2; ☏305/571-8230, ⓦwww.virginiakeybeach), reached by a two-mile lane that winds through a cluster of woodland. Opened in 1945,

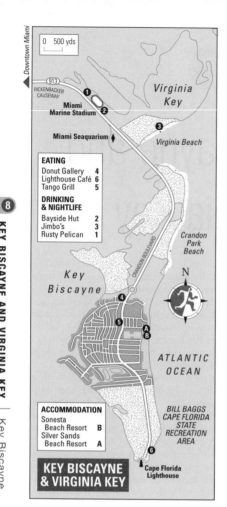

EATING
Donut Gallery   4
Lighthouse Café   6
Tango Grill   5

DRINKING
& NIGHTLIFE
Bayside Hut   2
Jimbo's   3
Rusty Pelican   1

ACCOMMODATION
Sonesta
  Beach Resort   B
Silver Sands
  Beach Resort   A

KEY BISCAYNE
& VIRGINIA KEY

during the years of segregation, this was set aside for Miami's black community (chosen, cynics might say, for its proximity to a large sewage works); it's still largely and unofficially a facility for the local African-American community. Otherwise, the beach is best known as the location of local institution *Jimbo's* (see review p.154), a place that's part-bar, part-junkyard – if you want to dodge the nominal entrance fee to the beach, tell the guard you're going to *Jimbo's* and it will be waived.

The Miami Seaquarium

The theme-park-style **Miami Seaquarium**, 4400 Rickenbacker Causeway (daily 9.30am–6pm, box office closes 4.30pm; $24.95, children 3–9 $19.95; ☏305/361-5705), is one of the city's major family attractions. It offers the usual performing spectacles, such as those starring Lolita the 8000-pound acrobatic killer whale, who leaps and jumps through one show daily at noon; and a trio of dolphins performs tricks to a thumping track of cheesy dance music. Feeding sessions throughout the day are ring-mastered by one of the park's rangers, who'll provide detailed background on the animal species in question. The crocodile sessions are especially fun; to see the reptiles at their hungriest and most ferocious, be sure to visit on a hot day, as the sun stimulates their appetites.

The Seaquarium's also one of the foremost marine-life rehab centers in the area: especially interesting are the turtles, often rescued from Biscayne Bay after eating plastic bags they've mistaken for jellyfish, and the some half-dozen manatees, a docile yet fiercely intelligent species now under constant threat of injury (and eventual extinction) by modern speedboats.

Key Biscayne

Key Biscayne is split roughly into three sections, on the axis of Crandon Boulevard, the island's main drag: the small **Village of Key Biscayne** is bookended by sprawling **Crandon Park** to the north and glorious **Bill**

△ Jimbo's bar

Baggs Cape Florida State Park at the south. Sadly, one of the more notorious sights in the Village was torn down in summer 2004: Nixon's Winter White House at 500 Bay Lane. A nondescript ranch-style home, it was where plans for the Watergate burglary were discussed and where Nixon picked up a copy of the *Miami Herald* one morning in 1972 to read of the break-in; the seemingly insignificant event (only featured by the paper because two Miami Cubans were involved) was to lead to Nixon's resignation two years later. The other notable residence here is also gone. Located at what's now the entrance to Hurricane Harbor, Mashta House (an Egyptian name meaning "home by the sea") was originally owned by chemical magnates the Mathesons; it was allowed to fall into disrepair and then the sea in 1950. At that time, the Mackle Company's cheap, prefab houses were mushrooming on the island; there is a movement to preserve them against the McMansion onslaught – look for the scattered, single-story homes in between the new buildings, squeezed awkwardly into smaller plots.

To find out more about these and other mostly vanished historical sites around the island, stop by the **Chamber of Commerce** at 87 W McIntyre, Suite 100 (Mon–Fri 9am–5pm; ☎305/361-5207, ⓦwww.keybiscaynechamber .org), which can provide an informative map. Other than that, there's little to do in the center of town and most visitors head straight for one of the nearby beaches.

Crandon Park Beach

As part of living in one of the best natural settings in Miami, the people of Key Biscayne have access to one of the finest landscaped beaches in the city – **Crandon Park Beach** (daily 8am–sunset; $5 per car; ☎305/361-5421, ⓦwww .miamidade.gov/parks/parks/crandon_beach.asp) a mile along the main drag, Crandon Boulevard. The three-mile stretch is popular with families, and it's easy to understand why: the golden beach is wide and glorious, and the ocean sandbar reduces waves and eliminates riptide, making swimming safe and easy.

However, be advised that on weekends the park is filled by the sounds of boisterous kids and hisses of sizzling barbecues – if it's peace and quiet you're after, you'd do better to head down to the less popular southern coast of the island.

Bill Baggs Cape Florida State Park

The luscious **Bill Baggs Cape Florida State Park** (daily 8am–sunset; $5 per car, $3 per car for solo drivers, $1 for pedestrians and bike riders; @www.dep.state.fl.us/parks/), named after the late Florida newspaper editor who campaigned for its creation, was leveled by Hurricane Andrew in 1992 – the many exotic plants that were here, such as the shallow-rooted Australian pine, could not withstand the 220mph winds. Over a decade later, it's slowly returning to normal through a rigid replanting program, which aims to reintroduce tougher, indigenous species, using as its guide a historical list of vegetation that could be found here in the nineteenth century.

Stretching the park's length, a wide **boardwalk** divides the picnic shelters from the soft, sandy beach. Along the boardwalk, the concession next to the *Lighthouse Café* has rentals for bikes, rollerblades, ocean kayaks, and windsurf boards, as well as deck chairs and umbrellas; you can also bring your tackle and try your luck on one of the eight fishing platforms. The **beach** itself is dotted by natural "umbrellas" of young palm trees – planted after Hurricane Andrew ripped out their predecessors.

At the southernmost tip lies the restored **Cape Florida Lighthouse**, an 1845 replica of one built twenty years previously which was destroyed in the first Seminole War. The lighthouse only remained in use until 1878, and now serves as a navigation beacon. It's only with the ranger-led **tour** (daily 10am & 1pm; free; limited to the first ten people to arrive) that you can climb the 118 steps up the 95-foot-high structure; there you'll see the lighthouse keeper's original quarters, as well as stunning **views** of Key Biscayne and South Beach to the north, and the last few huts of **Stiltsville** (see box, below) to the south.

Stiltsville

A few hundred yards off the southern tip of Key Biscayne, **Stiltsville** is an undeniable oddity. At the settlement's height, it comprised 27 houses standing on stilts above the ocean mudflats: now, only seven remain, their number winnowed down by successive hurricanes. The buildings themselves are nondescript, except one that resembles a jagged wooden ribcage like a row of arrows pointing to the sky.

Stiltsville's origins are murky: some claim that shacks first appeared in the bay as early as the 1920s for Prohibition-era parties, while others maintain that the settlement was erected by local fishermen as a tax dodge in the 1940s. Eventually, it became a regular party venue – one notable institution was the short-lived *Bikini Club*, a bar that opened in the early 1960s where any girl in a bikini got a free drink. Either way, it's now technically part of Biscayne National Park, and was for a while caught up in byzantine federal government regulations: owners couldn't carry out repairs, but the houses were also denied official historic status as none of the original buildings remain, and those that still stand are less than fifty years old. Local preservationists responded with a fierce campaign, Save Our Stiltsville (@www.stiltsville.org), which managed to persuade government politicos to establish a board that would not only oversee what public use the remaining buildings would serve, but also raise funds for their repair and restoration; to date, sadly, they're still not yet open for public visits or tours. And whether the rickety structures can survive many more of Florida's hurricane seasons, remains to be seen.

Listings

Listings

9

Accommodation

M iami has plenty of accommodation to suit travelers of all budgets and tastes, from chic boutiques to homely hotels, as well as a smattering of hostels. Starting prices for hotels hover around $100, but rocket in **high season** (January–March) or when major conventions are in town. A smart alternative is to come in May or December – rates will be much lower and, although the weather can be variable, it should be beachworthy most days. Also, if you're hoping to see Miami without renting a car, it makes most sense to stay Downtown or on South Beach, as connections by bus are most regular to these areas.

Unsurprisingly, a huge percentage of the hotels and guesthouses are clustered together on **South Beach**, most of them lining two streets, Ocean Drive and Collins Avenue – in fact, there are almost 14,000 rooms available on the beach. Increasingly, though, former budget hotels are being converted into swanky new luxury hot spots, so it's getting harder and harder to score a bargain in high season – budget accordingly. In some ways, it's money well spent, given the thrill of staying in one of the many photo-ready Deco masterpieces – but do remember that Deco hotels were built in a different era, and rooms can be tiny.

Heading north, the enormous 1950s hotels in **Central Miami Beach**, like the *Fontainebleau* and the *Eden Roc*, make fun, kitschy places to stay for any would-be Rat Packer. There's a smaller selection of pleasant places to stay in **Coconut Grove** and **Coral Gables**, though no incredibly compelling reason to stay in either neighborhood for most travelers. Otherwise, **Downtown** is crowded with sub-par or overpriced chain hotels, while Little Havana is not yet geared to providing visitor accommodation; steer clear of all the modernist motels along Biscayne Corridor for now – sadly, no one's snapped any up yet to transform them from crack dens or hourly rentals into haute hotels. If you're planning on spending a few days in Miami before heading down to the Keys, it's worth considering one of the guesthouses around **Homestead** or **Florida City** – although be aware that the trip to South Beach is quite a hike. Note that **prices are for lowest double room in high season** (which, in Miami, is January through March).

Hotels and guesthouses

Downtown

The Four Seasons Miami 1435 Brickell Ave ☎305/358-3535 or 1-800/819-5053, ⓦwww.fourseasons.com/miami. One of the new-comers on Brickell's main drag, this sleek 70-story condo-hotel is known for the impressive modern art scattered through the common areas, as well as the visiting sports teams, who often stay here because of its enormous onsite Sports Club LA facility and the three-pool complex on the roof of the sixth floor. The bathrooms with standalone tubs and showers are especially roomy. Rates start at $349.

Holiday Inn Marina Park – Port of Miami 340 Biscayne Blvd ☎ 305/371-4400 or 1-800/526-5655, ⓦ www.holiday-inn.com. Conveniently located near all the major attractions and public transport, this is an above-average option – especially given the rather ratty other chain outposts Downtown – with clean, large rooms close to the waterfront. Rooms from $100.

Intercontinental 100 Chopin Plaza ☎ 305/577-1000 or 1-800/327-3005, ⓦ www.interconti .com. The pick of Downtown's chain hotels, this *Intercontinental* high-rise boasts spectacular views of Biscayne Bay and the Port of Miami. The rooms themselves are stylishly furnished, with good amenities for business travelers, like power outlets built into the desktops. From $229.

Mandarin Oriental 500 Brickell Key Drive, ☎ 305/913-8288 or 1-800/622-0404, ⓦ www.mandarin-oriental.com. Vying with the *Four Seasons* (see overleaf) for the title of Downtown's top luxury hotel: the *Mandarin* certainly has a spectacular setting – on its own island just off the main business district. The infinity-edged pool is a lush place to lounge, and the rooms are large, with a vaguely Asian theme (as befits the hotel's name), but the snooty staff is a major letdown. $395 and up.

Miami Sun Hotel 226 NE 1st Ave ☎ 305/375-0786. The rooms at this budget motel are far more attractive than the lobby, with its fake leather sofas and forlorn disco ball, might suggest. They're very basic but clean, with bright floral bedspreads, and have fridges: the four-person suites are a steal for $55. Standard rooms from $35.

South Beach

Albion 1650 James Ave ☎ 305/913-1000, ⓦ www.rubellhotels.com. A sensitive conversion of a classic Nautical Deco building houses one of the best hotels in the city that's only two blocks from the beach. It's a top choice, thanks to its affable, unflappable staff, gorgeously simple rooms, and a whimsical, elevated pool that has portholes cut into its sides. From $190.

Aqua 1530 Collins Ave ☎ 305/538-4361, ⓦ www.aquamiami.com. This motel conversion has preserved little other than the original Sea Deck sign out front. The superb, spartan-chic rooms have raw concrete floors with tart tangerine and bright blue accents – IKEA-inspired and funky. All rooms look over a tranquil courtyard, and there's a private sundeck, too. From $199.

Hotel Astor 956 Washington Ave ☎ 305/531-8081 or 1-800/270-4981, ⓦ www.hotelastor .com. Distinguished from other boutique hotels by its easygoing and helpful staff, the *Astor* is renowned on the strip. As for the rooms, they're standardly stylish, though larger than many of the others on the beach, with swivel TVs mounted on poles, and rainhead showers. $165 and up.

Best Western South Beach 1020 Washington Ave ☎ 305/532-1930 or 1-888/343-1930, ⓦ www.bestwestern.com/prop_10320. A cluster of four hotels (the *Kenmore*, *Taft*, *Bel Aire*, and *Park Washington*) owned and operated by *Best Western*, this is one of the remaining cheaper options on the beach. The rooms have been renovated to remove all character, but amenities have been added; ask for a junior suite in the *Taft* building, as those rooms have kitchenettes at no additional cost. $129 and up.

Brigham Gardens Guesthouse 1411 Collins Ave ☎ 305/531-1331, ⓦ www.brighamgardens .com. The *Guesthouse* is actually a hamlet of buildings, with 23 rooms in the hotel, crowding round a shady courtyard, and is one of the best low-cost options in the area, with friendly management and an onsite laundry. The quirky, individual rooms have an eccentric, Caribbean feel thanks to delightfully mismatched furniture; fully equipped kitchenettes in the studio rooms are worth the extra expense. Standard rooms from $100, studios $25 extra per night.

Clinton Hotel 825 Washington Ave ☎ 305/938-4040, ⓦ www.clintonsouthbeach.com. This Art Deco gem lay empty for years but has finally been revived as a boutique hotel with a vaguely S&M twist – there are laced corset motifs on the mirrors, banquettes, and backs of chairs, while the massive bathrooms have luxurious two-person showers. Rooms from $169.

Delano 1685 Collins Ave ☎ 305/672-2000 or 1-800/555-5001, ⓦ www.morganshotelgroup.com.

Ian Schrager–owned and Philippe Starck–designed, the *Delano* was one of the first high-profile celebrity hang-outs on the beach. The all-white rooms have Starck's signature witty touches –such as the single green apple left for you on its own sconce "to keep the doctor away" – but the staff can be snotty and the service touch-and-go. For a while, the *Delano* was suffering in the shadow of its sister hotel, *The Shore Club* (see overleaf), but the buzz is picking up again here, especially at the *Rose Bar* (see p.155 for review). $490 and up.

▽ The Delano

Doubletree Surfcomber 1717 Collins Ave ☏ 305/532-7715 or 1-800/853-0264, ⓦ www.surfcomber.com. A fashion and media favorite, this unassuming hotel has direct beach access, a full-sized pool, and spacious, airy rooms. Camera crews often use its terrace to film TV shows, and – always a good vote of confidence – it's one of the places that locals will lodge their relatives when they visit. Rooms from $245.
Essex House 1001 Collins Ave ☏ 305/534-2700 or 1-800/553-7739, ⓦ www.essexhotel.com. The *Essex House* has bland, corporate-style rooms that are luxurious but could be anywhere. The building, though, is a gem, with a superbly restored Egyptian Deco lobby full of ziggurats – plus, the management is friendly. From $159.

Fairwind Hotel 1000 Collins Ave ☏ 305/531-0050 or 1 -888/944-6835, ⓦ www.fairwindhotel .com. A good mid-range option, the *Fairwind* offers basic, brightly colored rooms that are clean and convenient – but watch out for the noisy bar/restaurant in the hotel's courtyard; ask for a quiet room when you book. There are a few suites in a separate onsite building with kitchenettes (fridge, microwave). Rooms start at $100.
The Hotel 801 Collins Ave ☏ 305/531-2222, ⓦ www.thehotelofsouthbeach.com. Designer Todd Oldham oversaw every element in this hotel's renovation, using zesty colors on everything from the lobby to the bathrobes. The luxurious rooms are like a millionaire's tropical hideaway, their stylish look only part of a thoughtful aesthetic of smart improvements – for example, the shower control is not under the shower head, so you won't have to scald yourself every time you turn on the water. Expensive, but a treat. For a review of *The Hotel*'s rooftop bar, *The Spire*, see p.155. $275 and up.
Lily-Leon 835 Collins Ave ☏ 305/535-9900 or 1-888/742-6600, ⓦ www.lilyleonhotel.com. Owned by the same people as the *Shelley* and the *Whitelaw*, the *Lily* has bigger rooms but more basic furniture, and can be noisy, as several of the suites are on the roadside ground floor. The rooms all have fridges and CD players, though, and it's still well-situated for a night out. Though it recently bought the *Leon* next door and combined the two hotels, there's little difference in room size or decor. Rooms start at $175.
The Loft Hotel 952 Collins Ave ☏ 305/534-2244, ⓦ www.thelofthotel.com. A sleek low-rise building converted from apartments, the *Loft* has a chic, rather LA feel with modern, wrought-iron furniture and an airy garden filled with lush trees. Its rooms all have down comforters, kitchenettes, and VCRs. From $139.
The Park Central 640 Ocean Drive ☏ 305/538-1611 or 1-800/727-5236, ⓦ www.theparkcentral .com. One of the first hotels to be reborn during the South Beach renaissance of the early 1990s, the *Park Central* is showing its age a little. The rooms, with crisp white linens and pale green walls, have a colonial safari feel, an effect augmented by the black-and-white photographs throughout the hotel; a full renovation is planned soon, so check for updates when booking. There's

also a sky-high roof deck for sunbathing and sightseeing. Rooms start at $185.

Pelican Hotel 826 Ocean Drive ☎305/673-3373, ⓦwww.pelicanhotel.com. Owned by the Italian jeanswear company Diesel, the *Pelican* injects a welcome touch of campy humor into the earnest coolness of South Beach. Each room is themed, with either refurbished flea-market finds or specially constructed furniture: try the "Deco(cktail)" room for a touch of Twenties glamour, or the "Best Little Whorehouse" room, with deep red wallpaper and plenty of lush black lace. You'll also be given two chairs and an umbrella to use on the beach opposite the hotel. $155 and up.

The Raleigh 1775 Collins Ave ☎305/534-6300 or 1-800/848-1775, ⓦwww.raleighhotel.com. Once languishing in dusty if elegant dotage, the *Raleigh* has been transformed after a sensitive recent refurbishing that retained signature touches like the huge garden, curvy pool – where many 1920s synchronized swimming movies were shot – and the dark, wood-paneled bar; with its cream sofas and colonial feel, it's very Gable and Lombard. The rooms, though, are where the difference really shows, with orthopedic beds and sumptuous linens. $225 and up.

The Ritz-Carlton South Beach 1 Lincoln Rd ☎786/276-4000 or 1-800/241-3333, ⓦwww.ritzcarlton.com. The former *DiLido* hotel was another Morris Lapidus confection – see the *Fontainebleau* p.134 – and its new owners have sensitively spruced the place up. The design of the lobby is exactly as it was in its 1950s heyday, though using more durable materials – such as cherry wood instead of stucco on the walls. The rooms themselves are large but bland; try to snag one overlooking the pool where there's a tanning butler available to slather free lotion on you at weekends. Rooms from $309. For a review of the *DiLido Beach Club* bar, see p.155, "Drinking."

Royal Hotel 758 Washington Ave ☎305/673-9009 or 1-888/394-6835, ⓦwww.royalsouthbeach.com. Fantastic new bargain hotel, with a candy-colored lobby covered in Art Deco posters. The room decor is all white and Jetson-inspired – marble floors with injection-molded plastic bed-frames and a swirly love seat with TV stand built in. There are microwaves, coffee makers, and even free toothpaste in the bathrooms. Note that the entrance is behind the hotel on Pennsylvania Avenue. $99 and up.

Sagamore 1671 Collins Ave ☎305/535-8088 or 1-877/242-6673, ⓦwww.sagamorehotel.com. A low-key luxury hotel, with enormous rooms decorated in muted shades of chocolate and taupe. There's a beachfront pool, where you can swim a few laps then climb out straight onto the sands. Even if you aren't staying here, stop in to the lobby to gawp at the stunning modern artwork dotted around the public areas, including works by Cindy Sherman and Cathy de Monchaux; it's the private collection of one of the owners. Rooms from $450.

The Shelborne 1801 Collins Ave ☎305/531-1271 or 1-800/327-8757, ⓦwww.shelborne.com. Site of the early Miss Universe pageants, the *Shelborne* offers all the usual amenities (free onsite fitness center, pool) and is well located at the northern end of the beach, right on the ocean. The rooms are unremarkable in decor, but have small kitchenettes, DVD players, and high-speed broadband Internet access. With 200 rooms, this is one of the larger hotels on the beach, so often has space in peak season when other smaller properties are booked up. $235 and up.

Hotel Shelley 844 Collins Ave ☎305/531-3341 or 1-800/414-0612, ⓦwww.southbeachgroup.com. A budget boutique hotel, the *Shelley* is stylishly spartan, with the usual all-white rooms. There are some great comp add-ons, like a free open bar every night from 6 to 10pm and discounted gym passes, but there's no elevator, so don't stay here unless you are traveling light. High-season rates are often reduced on negotiation and can even be slashed in half during the summer. $150 and up.

The Shore Club 1901 Collins Ave ☎305/895-3100 or 1-800/640-9500, ⓦwww.shoreclub.com. Ian Schrager swooped in to save this high-end hotel when it floundered only months after opening, and it's now *the* place to stay on the beach. Rooms are small and minimalist in style, decorated in bright colors rather than all-white, but you probably won't spend long inside when you can be lounging with the beautiful people in the poolside *Sky Bar* (see review, p.155). Rooms start at $345.

Standard Miami 40 Island Ave ☎305/673-1717, ⓦwww.standardhotel.com. Andre Balazs, owner of the *Raleigh*, has just opened this Miami outpost of his budget-minded *Standard Hotels* in LA; he has transformed a forlorn hotel on Belle Isle, on the bayside of South Beach, into a spa hotel – so don't expect a scene here. It's designed as a sanctuary from the craziness elsewhere on the beach, with onsite Turkish baths, Roman waterfall hot tubs, nude mud baths, and an onsite yoga center. From $95.

Townhouse 150 20th St ☏ 305/534-3800 or 1-877/534-3800, ⊛ www.townhousehotel.com. Many boutique hotels promise much but deliver little – *Townhouse* is an exception. Stark, white (of course) rooms are well-thought-out and comfortable; the staff is attentive but laid-back, and there's an indulgent roof deck filled with crimson waterbeds for sybaritic sunbathing. It sits on the beachfront behind the *Shore Club* – only a 2min walk to the water. $135 and up.

Hotel Victor 1144 Ocean Drive ☏ 305/428-1234, ⊛ www.hotelvictorsouthbeach.com. The latest lavish hotel to open in a hush-hush *Hyatt* project. The decor's apparently inspired by jellyfish – there's a tank-full in the lobby – and it's intended as a clubby, Ibiza-style hotel, complete with in-residence DJs spinning daily throughout the hotel until midnight. The rooms all have deep soak tubs, LCD TVs, and even a hot button on the phone to Neiman Marcus in Bal Harbour for last-minute shopping urges. Rooms from $475.

Villa Paradiso 1415 Collins Ave ☏ 305/532-0616, ⊛ www.villaparadisohotel.com. More basic and retro than its sibling the *Loft* (see p.131), *Villa Paradiso* features *Miami Vice* decor and leather futons. However, the place is clean, the rooms are large, and all have their own kitchenettes; there's also an onsite coin laundry. Good discounts for longer stays. Rates from $89.

The Wave 350 Ocean Drive ☏ 305/673-0401 or 1-800/501-0401, ⊛ www.wavehotel.com. Nestled in the increasingly buzzy SoFi area below 5th Street and close to *Prime 112* (see p.145, "Restaurants"), this hotel has small but fully equipped rooms, each with a mood machine so you can drift off to sleep to the sound of crashing waves as well as the usual jungle or soothing nighttime sounds. The huge free breakfasts are a major plus. $159 and up.

Whitelaw Hotel 808 Collins Ave ☏ 305/398-7000 or 1-888/554-3123, ⊛ www.whitelawhotel.com. The *Whitelaw* has stylish, if overdesigned, all-white rooms complete with CD players and some good add-ons are offered, too,

such as free airport pick-up and an open bar in the hotel every night. From $175.

The Winterhaven 1400 Ocean Drive ☏ 305/531-5571 or 1-800/395-2322, ⊛ www.winterhavenhotelsobe.com. One of the best values on the beachfront, the *Winterhaven* offers rooms that are standard and comfortable enough. The real draw, though, is the lobby, restored to an identical replica of its original design – notice especially the antique etched mirrors and *terrazzo* floor – though the chairs were tweaked to accommodate more generous modern proportions. $115 and up.

Central Miami Beach and north

Best Western Thunderbird Resort 18401 Collins Ave ☏ 305/931-1700 or 1-800/327-2044, ⊛ www.bestwestern.com. No frills, but handy for both Miami and Fort Lauderdale; it's popular with families and has handy amenities like an onsite laundry. As in most other hotels in Sunny Isles Beach, you can step straight out of your room into the pool or onto the beach. The biggest bonus of staying here is the chance to admire its fabulously retro facade close-up. Rooms from $120.

Bizcaya Hotel 4000 Alton Rd ☏ 305/532-4411 or 1-800/532-4411. Off the beaten track, this large motel at the western end of 41st Street in Middle Beach is a terrific alternative if one of the other, more central hotels are full. Rooms are clean, bright, and furnished with the standard amenities like coffee-makers and irons. From $99.

Circa 39 3900 Collins Ave ☏ 305/538-4900 or 1-877/8-CIRCA39, ⊛ www.circa39.com. The old *Copley Plaza* is the latest to undergo a boutique hotel overhaul: the rooms here are, predictably, all white with pale blue accents, and feature CD players and flat-screen TVs. The common areas are more playful, with mismatched Modernist furniture scattered through the lobby, and a pleasant wading pool. Rooms start at $169.

Eden Roc 4525 Collins Ave ☏ 305/531-0000 or 1-800/327-8337, ⊛ www.edenrocresort.com. Now owned and operated by hotel giant *Marriott*, the *Eden Roc* has fully renovated rooms with standard, rather garish decor: clearly French-inspired, there are fleur-de-lys printed coverlets and faux Rococo furniture. Its greatest draw is its lobby, which alone of all the Miami Modern hotels has retained a

⑨

ACCOMMODATION | Hotels and guesthouses

133

feel of sleek Fifties glamour, with huge sofas and curvy stonework – though it's a pity about the snooty staff. $299 and up.

The Fontainebleau 4441 Collins Ave T 305/538-2000, W www.fontainebleauhilton .com. Once the ground zero of cool in the 1950s (see p.79), this hotel hosted Lucille Ball, Frank Sinatra, and Elvis, among others. Now, it's been haphazardly renovated – the multiple lobbies still show scattered Miami Modern touches, but the large rooms in the main building have been completely overhauled: they're comfortable, if corporate, and lacking quirky touches. Even better are the gleaming suites in the brand-new tower – pricier, but with business amenities like in-room high-speed Internet access. This is a favorite place for families, since it stands in enormous grounds, and there's a children's play area and pool designed around a large fiberglass octopus, known as "Cookie." Rooms from $269.

The Golden Sands 6901 Collins Ave T 305/866-8734, W www.goldensands.com. Nothing flashy and mostly filled by Europeans on package tours, the *Golden Sands* in North Beach is nevertheless likely to turn up some of the cheapest accommodation with a pool in this pricey area. $79 and up.

Little Havana

Miami River Inn Bed & Breakfast 118 SW South River Drive T 305/325-0045 or 1-800/468-3589, W www.miamiriverinn.com. The charming, offbeat *Miami River Inn*, a cluster of old buildings set around a secluded courtyard and small pool, is more like a B&B than a hotel – rooms are furnished in a floral country style, with antique beds and dressers, and there's a self-service home-made breakfast every morning. As it's somewhat off the beaten path, though, you really need a car to stay here. From $109.

Coral Gables

Best Western Chateau Bleau 1111 Ponce de Leon Blvd T 305/448-2634, W www .hotelchateaubleau.com. Don't let its oddly spelled, old-world name mislead you – this place is a 1960s-style concrete-box motel. However, it's great value if you're not worried about prettifying extras; there's an onsite, kidney-shaped pool, every room has a balcony and some have kitchenettes.

Ask for a room at the back, if you're a light sleeper. $69 and up.

The Biltmore 1200 Anastasia Ave T 305/445-1926 or 1-800/727-1926, W www.biltmorehotel .com. Miami's first grand hotel has been thoroughly restored – rooms are luxurious but unremarkable, though the giant chevron-shaped pool and onsite golf course are major pluses. The rooms themselves are somewhat reminiscent of a Spanish island villa – lots of gauzy drapes in peach and cream tones. For a more in-depth account of the *Biltmore* and its history, see p.110, "Coral Gables." Rooms from $359.

The Gables Inn 730 South Dixie Hwy T 305/661-7999, W www.thegablesinn.net. Coral Gables' version of a budget hotel, the *Gables Inn* is Mediterranean Revival in style, with arched walkways painted a deep ochre, and *Biltmore*-lite rooms: plenty of bottle green and dark wood, but this time with a linoleum floor. One of the few cheaper options in the area, it's located directly on Hwy-1 (or the South Dixie Hwy), so it can be noisy. From $78.

Hotel Place St Michel 162 Alcazar Ave T 305/444-1666 or 1-800/848-4683, W www .hotelplacestmichel.com. Country-style rooms in a small, charming hotel minutes from the center of Coral Gables. There are gold fixtures, mixed antiques, and overstuffed sofas in each room – even the elevator is vintage, complete with a sliding grill and hand operation. Ask for a suite if you can; the added expense is more than worth it for the extra room. Rooms start at $185.

Omni Colonnade Hotel 180 Aragon Ave T 305/441-2600, W www.omnihotels.com. The mahogany-decorated rooms are here all minisuites: a bedroom plus a sitting area filled with overstuffed, rather over-floral sofas. It's a historic spot – George Merrick's original rotunda-capped sales office on the Miracle Mile – and today the hotel is equally commerce-minded, geared as it is to the business traveler who needs to be close to Coral Gables business district. One upside: rates often plummet at weekends. Rates from $129.

Coconut Grove

Doubletree Coconut Grove 2649 S Bayshore Drive T 305/858-2500 or 1-800/222-TREE, W www.doubletree.com. Formerly the

Coconut Grove Hotel, this place has undergone a grandiose renovation, all dark wood and deep carpets. The rooms are large and nondescript – many look out over the bay, while some have balconies and small kitchenettes. Rooms from $145.

Hampton Inn 2800 SW 28th Terrace ☎ 305/448-2800, ⓦ www.hamptoninncoconutgrove.com. Basic but bright accommodation geared to the budget business traveler. Free local calls, onsite coin laundry, and complimentary continental breakfast make this a good base for exploring away from the beach. Rates start at $169.

Mayfair Hotel and Spa 3000 Florida Ave ☎ 305/441-0000 or 1-800/433-4555, ⓦ www.mayfairhotelandspa.com. Groovy new hotel in the heart of the Grove, intended as a spa or retreat. There are quirky touches everywhere – from the free *mojito* and scented towel on check-in to the iPods on loan by the rooftop pool. The best feature, though, is undoubtedly the two-person tubs on the balconies of every room. Rooms from $179.

Ritz-Carlton Coconut Grove 3300 SW 27th Ave ☎ 305/644-4680, ⓦ www.ritzcarlton.com. Much like the MiMo-inspired *Ritz-Carlton South Beach* (see p.132), this tiny hotel – just over 100 rooms – is a boutique operation: the decor of the common areas is Vizcaya lite, with lashings of marble and moldings, though the atrium's a surprisingly pleasant place to linger, especially in the evenings when there's live jazz. The rooms are large, with separate marble tubs and showers. There's even a waterfall in the grounds. From $289.

Key Biscayne

Silver Sands Beach Resort 301 Ocean Drive ☎ 305/361-5441, ⓦ www.key-biscayne.com/accom/silversands. There's little to recommend this bland motel, other than the fact that it's on the inexpensive side as far as Key Biscayne goes. It also huddles right on the beach – the pricier oceanfront rooms

allow you to step right out of your door onto the sand. $129 and up.

Sonesta Beach Resort 350 Ocean Drive ☎ 305/361-2021, ⓦ www.sonesta.com/keybiscayne. The Miami outpost of this family luxury chain has its own private beach and convenient facilities, but it's a little careworn at the edges – make sure to ask for a renovated room, which will be brighter and have more modern furniture. From $169.

South of the city

Best Western Gateway to the Keys 411 S Krome Ave, Florida City ☎ 305/246-5100 or 1-800/981-5100, ⓦ www.bestwestern.com. One of the most comfortable places to stay round here, recently renovated if bland – there are coffee makers, microwaves, and fridges in all rooms. The location's the handiest thing: Florida City's a good stop-off en route to the Keys. Note that all rooms are nonsmoking. Rooms from $120.

Greenstone Motel 304 N Krome Ave ☎ 305/247-8334, ⓦ greenstone.gzinc.com. Smack in the middle of Homestead, this motel is a quirky oddity. Linking with the local ArtSouth complex next door that aims to bring the arts to the masses, it has recruited local creative types to customize the bedrooms. If their styles put you off, there are also plain rooms available with full motel amenities. $45 and up.

Grove Inn Country Guesthouse 22540 SW Krome Ave, Homestead ☎ 305/247-6572 or 1-877/247-6572, ⓦ www.groveinn.com. On an old fruit farm, the *Grove Inn* makes for a comfortable South Miami base, with friendly, knowledgeable owners and an informal atmosphere. $75 and up.

Redland Hotel 5 S Flagler Ave ☎ 305/246-1904 or 1-800/595-1904, ⓦ www.redlandhotel.com. A historic inn, where every unit is named after a pioneer family, in the center of old Homestead. The decor's comfy, country florals with all modern conveniences, and there's a welcoming bar in the hotel. $89 and above.

Hostels

Clay Hotel and Hostel 1438 Washington Ave, South Beach ☎ 305/534-2988 or 1-800/379-2529, ⓦ www.clayhotel.com. Located in a landmark building on the corner of Española Way, the *Clay* has both private and dorm rooms at budget rates. It's a great place

to meet other travelers, and has a fully equipped kitchen, but unfortunately, some rooms are cleaner than others: ask to see one before you commit. Dorms from $17 YHA members or $19 nonmembers; rooms from $43.

International Travelers Hostel 236 9th St, South Beach ☎305/534-0268, ⊛www.sobehostel .com. The great location just blocks from the beach is the biggest selling point of this hostel: the dorm rooms are rundown and rather lovelorn, but reasonably clean. Dorms from $14, private rooms from $36.

The Tropics Hotel & Hostel 1550 Collins Ave, South Beach ☎305/531-0361, ⊛www.trop-icshotel.com. The private rooms are cheap but unappealing though that's no matter, as the real reason to stay here is the hostel accommodation: it's sparse yet clean, and each room sleeps four with a private bath. Dorms from $16, rooms from $50.

⑩

Cafés and light meals

From a quick Cuban coffee to a filling Jewish knish, Miami has plenty on offer in the way of **cafés**, snacks, and **light meals**. Two unmissable local specialties are the Cuban sandwich, made with pickles, cheese, smoked ham, and roast pork – all crammed into a fluffy roll that's toasted in a press – and the toxically sweet *cafecito*, a thimble-sized jolt of caffeine and sugar that's addictively energizing.

In addition, the city features New York–style pizza joints, vintage diners, home-style bakeries, and a range of cheap, filling breakfast spots – plus plenty of sidewalk cafés good for nursing a coffee while watching the crowds go by. Below we've listed some of the best options; all are fairly inexpensive. For listings of places more appropriate for a sit-down dinner, see "Restaurants," beginning on p.142.

Downtown

Garcia's Seafood Grille 398 NW North River Drive ☎305/375-0765. Join the customs guys at this lunch-only riverside fish café – it's bustling and efficient, serving tasty fresh fish at reasonable prices, with a small counter in the front and racks of waterfront picnic tables out back. The dolphin sandwich (actually mahi mahi) is delicious – as is the house special, lemon-grilled grouper.

Karlo Bakery 1242 SW Coral Way ☎305/858-1080. The European-style food at this bakery is delicious, especially the buttery soft croissants and frothy *café au lait*. The rich desserts are delicious, too, and just right for an indulgent picnic – smuggle them into Vizcaya's waterfront grounds a couple of blocks away.

La Paris 251 SE 2nd St ☎305/371-5181. Packed with office workers at lunchtime, *La Paris* is one of the better Cuban diners, serving basic dishes at rock-bottom prices (sandwiches $4, entrees $5). The place is absolutely without frills and there's limited counter seating, but the food is hearty and appetizing.

Las Palmas 209 SE 1st St ☎305/373-1333. Although there are plenty of similar Cuban lunch-counter cafés around Downtown

serving sandwiches and deep-fried treats at breakfast and lunchtime, *Las Palmas* is clean and the staff friendly.

Lo Spaghetto 169 E Flagler St ☎305/379-2000. Take a break from admiring the DuPont Building's interior at this Italian café inside serving delicious pasta, panini, and coffee from 7.30am to 3.30pm.

Raja's 33 NE 2nd Ave ☎305/539-9551. This no-nonsense restaurant serves South Indian staples like a *masala dosa* (potato pancake) accompanied by tangy *sambhar* (hot-and-sour soup). Prices hover around $6 per dish, and the portions are generous. Lunch only.

Top Hat Deli 150 W Flagler St ☎305/381-6337. Well-priced for the neighborhood, this café offers filling sandwiches for around $7 and has plentiful outdoor seating overlooking the Metro-Dade Cultural Center. Service can be rather slow, but it's a convenient stop-off when sightseeing.

Zion Bakery 659 NW 62nd St ☎305/758-6267. Vegan bakery in Liberty City, covered in brightly colored rasta-themed murals, that sells egg and dairy-free choc chip or peanut butter cookies, banana cream cake, and even baked fish or tofu patties. All the food is baked on the premises and prices are rock-bottom – around $1 an item. Closed Sat.

516 Española Way
484. Run by French expats, this dilapidated café serves authentic, crêpes and salads from $6 and is well stocked with European magazines. It's a refreshing respite from the tourist traps and conga music elsewhere on Española Way, and you're likely to sit beside locals rather than other visitors.

Balans Lincoln Road 1022 Lincoln Rd
☎305/534-9191. An outpost of a small British chain of gay restaurants, *Balans* serves its stylish brunches to visitors and locals alike – don't expect warm service, but it's a great place to see and be seen on Lincoln Road. Good weekday breakfast specials, and don't miss the chunky, crunchy *Balans* potatoes.

Bari 441 Lincoln Rd ☎305/534-1838. The best of the clutch of new *gelaterie* that have popped up across the city in the past few years, this Italian import displays swirled mounds of at least two dozen flavors of organic, all-natural ice cream. Try the white chocolate with walnuts, cheesecake, or *tramontana* (that's *dolce de leche* studded with Kit Kat balls) ice cream. Cups cost $2.75–4.95.

David's Café 1058 Collins Ave ☎305/534-8736. At this original outpost of the Cuban restaurant, suited expat businessmen sit alongside brassy teenagers. Try the great, filling Cuban sandwiches for around $6, along with a delicious coffee (60¢), or head to the Meridian Ave branch – *David's Café II*, at no. 1654 (☎305/672-8707) – for swanky dining-room seating and pricier food like *ropa vieja* for around $15.

Front Porch Café 1418 Ocean Drive ☎305/531-8300. Despite its over-touristed location, this really is where the locals go for breakfast. Portions are supersized: gigantic omelets, wholemeal pancakes as big as Frisbees, and doorstop sandwiches are all well-priced ($6–8 for most entrees). Come here early with a newspaper and check out the morning crowd.

Gino's 731 Washington Ave ☎305/673-2837. Open 24 hours a day, *Gino's* serves true New York–style pizza to shift workers and clubbers alike: each slice comes with a free, buttery garlic knot.

Jerry's Famous Deli 1450 Collins Ave ☎305/532-8030. This 24-hour deli, housed in a converted cafeteria, offers a menu so vast that you'll find almost anything you're craving (try the salad served in a pizza crust – it's better than it sounds). Sure, it's overpriced, but as a late night pit-stop, it's almost unbeatable.

La Sandwicherie 229 W 14th St ☎305/532-8934. Don't be put off by the pretentious name – open until 5am, this place serves serious sandwiches starting at around $6 from its open-air lunch counter; each giant French loaf could make two meals – if you can fit it in your mouth, that is – crammed with fresh, crunchy greens, and cold cuts.

Le Provence 1627 Collins Ave ☎305/538-2406. This French bakery close to the beach is a terrific place to stock up on baguettes and brioches before a day on the sands. The croissants are outstanding, as are the jewel-like fruit pastries. Daily 7am–8pm.

News Café 800 Ocean Drive ☎305/538-6397. The food may be nondescript, but its location at the corner of 8th and Ocean Drive has made the *News* ground zero for the South Beach scene since the early Nineties. Enjoy the fact that its brasserie approach lets you sit all afternoon over a single coffee without being shooed away.

Pizza Rustica 863 Washington Ave ☎305/673-8244. This is a cheap beach pit-stop serving huge slices of pizza for only $3.50. Un-Italian toppings like barbecue chicken combined with tangy tomato sauce make delicious snacks, and each slice is cut into six bite-sized pieces while still hot from the oven. Try the Rustica, piled high with artichoke, olives, ham, and sun-dried tomatoes. There are also branches at 667 Lincoln Rd ☎305/ 672-2334 and 1447 Washington Ave ☎305/538-6009 – but the pizza at the original branch is still the best.

Puerto Sagua 700 Collins Ave ☎305/673-1115. Larger and much cheaper than *David's*, this Cuban hang-out, with brown wood-effect Formica tables, has a decor that's unchanged since the late 1970s. Thankfully the traditional food is filling – try the hefty portions of rice and beans.

The Smoothie Shop 1229 Washington Ave ☎305/531-5633. The best place for lunch if you're planning on hitting the beach in the afternoon: nothing but healthy fruit shakes and protein bars here – small smoothies are $4, large $6. Try an appletini with apples, bananas, and cinnamon, or, if you're not worried about washboard abs, a sinfully rich It's Elvis, Baby, with peanut butter, banana, and milk.

Taystee Bakery 1450 Washington Ave ☎305/538-4793. Join the elderly clientele for breakfast from 6am in this super-cheap neighborhood bakery, serving old-fashioned kosher breads, pastries, and *empanadas* with various fillings at a couple of Formica tables tarted up with bright red tablecloths.

Van Dyke Café 1637 Jefferson Ave ☎305/534-3600. Newsstand-cum-café serving pastries and American-style coffees – cappuccinos, Americanos, lattes – with squish sofas, low tables, and plenty of reading material: the entire wall of magazines, both domestic and foreign language, is hands down the best selection on the beach. Daily 7.30am–11pm.

Verandah Café Richmond Hotel, 1757 Collins Ave ☎305/538-2331. Ditch the crowds on Collins Avenue and head into this secluded find, located poolside in this mid-range hotel. Sail past reception and through the central hallway to the back of the building; cheap sandwiches can be had for around $8. Breakfast and lunch only.

Central Miami Beach and north

Arnie & Richie's Deli 525 41st St ☎305/531-7691. In the bosom of Miami Beach's Jewish neighborhood, this deli serves standbys like pastrami sandwiches, knishes, and whitefish salad without fuss or fanfare – if you eat in, be prepared to share a table with the gaggles of local old ladies who stop in regularly or grab a meat-crammed sandwich for $7–8 to go. The fruit *rugelach* are also delicious.

Bistro at 39 *Circa 39* hotel, 3900 Collins Ave ☎305/538-4900. There aren't many appealing cafés on this stretch of Middle Beach, but if you duck into this hotel (see p.133 for review) to this small room off the lobby, you'll find comfy chairs – including one stool shaped like a giant pair of red lips – and salads or sandwiches for lunch and dinner running around $8.

Buenos Aires Bakery 7134 Collins Ave ☎305/861-7887. This gourmet Argentine bakery in North Beach serves mostly glistening handmade tarts and candies, as well as coffee and a small selection of ice cream by the cone.

Lure Café 6995 Collins Ave ☎786/355-5873. Wine bar/restaurant with dark wood fixtures

and walls lined with bottles that's one of the newest signs of North Beach's gentrification. It's open for lunch and dinner – huge sandwiches, like a veal *piccata* dripping in tomato sauce, cost around $7.50. There's also free onsite wireless DSL if you want to linger by the bar with a glass of wine and your laptop.

Miami Juice 16120 Collins Ave ☎305/945-0444. A welcome healthy alternative amid the diners and fast-food joints that cluster along this stretch of Collins Avenue in Sunny Isles. It's also good for Middle Eastern specialties like falafel and hummus.

Santa Fe News & Coffee Bal Harbour Shops complex, 9700 Collins Ave ☎305/861-0938. An unremarkable café that's notable simply as one of the few places to grab a quiet coffee in Bal Harbour, and the only eatery in the mall that isn't as premium-priced as the stores – coffee's just $1.85. There are magazines for sale, as well as gooey pastries and simple sandwiches ($6).

North along the Biscayne Corridor

Café Café 5580 NE 4th Court ☎305/754-6700. Eclectic, ramshackle Little Haiti café with mismatched furniture – overstuffed leather sofas, antique tables, bentwood café chairs – and a leafy grove-like patio shaded with umbrellas. It features the usual café staples as well as sandwiches and salads ($6–8) – try the salmon ceviche salad.

Cane à Sucre 3535 NE 2nd Ave ☎305/572-0111. Gourmet French bakery and café in Wynwood, serving pastries and sandwiches – it's a bargain for lunch: try Caesar salad & soup of the day for $4 or a brioche *croque monsieur* at the same price.

Caribbean Café Shop 2804 NE 2nd Ave ☎305/572-9282. With a tiny kitchen and the daily menu scribbled on a whiteboard, this Honduran hole-in-the-wall shares a Wynwood storefront with the local laundry. Sit down at the counter amid the washing machines and enjoy tasty soups like black bean or crispy fried savory treats for less than $5 a portion.

COMA's 3920 NE 2nd Ave ☎305/576-8109. Inside the Melin Buidling (see p.90), this small, trendy café from Spain tricked out with Philippe Starck furniture serves gleaming mini-croissants and -pastries at breakfast, while at lunch, there's a rotating menu, mostly sandwiches and salads for around

$10. The only place to get a good coffee in or around the Design District. Closed Sun and dinner.

Dogma 7030 Biscayne Blvd T 305/759-3433. Hipsters make pilgrimages to this stylish Little Haiti hot-dog stand on a sketchy part of Biscayne Boulevard. Sit at red and white tables and munch on cheap, filling dogs – try the best-selling chili dog (slathered with chili flown in specially from Los Angeles) or more exotic inventions like the Athens, topped with feta, oregano, and cucumber (both under $4).

Gili's Sandwich Bar 28 NE 14th St T 305/538-3600. Housed in a recycled one-story warehouse, this jazzy Park West café boasts animal print wallpaper and framed posters of Marilyn Monroe and James Dean. The food's a little less outlandish – standard salads and sandwiches for $7 or so.

Lakay Bakery 91 NE 54th St T 305/751-2912. This tiny bakery in Little Haiti produces outstanding home-made ice cream, using exotic and familiar fruits as flavoring – try the pineapple or the guava: two large scoops cost a paltry $1.50. There's also a small selection of flaky Haitian pastries.

▽ Lakay Bakery

Laurenzo's 16385 West Dixie Hwy T 305/945-6381. A local institution in North Miami Beach, the diner counter inside this Italian-American supermarket serves *zitti*, lasagna, and garlic-laced spaghetti for cheap and filling lunches. It's hardly the funkiest restaurant around, but the pasta portions are good value if you're in the neighborhood visiting the Old Spanish Monastery, and it's a glimpse of Old Miami.

The Secret Sandwich 3918 N Miami Ave T 305/571-9990. Spy-themed café in the Design District, with a massive world map spread across one wall, serving hearty sandwiches for around $7: try the flavorful Mata Hari (lime-marinated chicken with caramelized onions) and the deliciously creamy flan. It closes whenever the food's run out, usually around 4pm.

Little Havana

El Palacio de los Jugos 5721 W Flagler St T 305/264-1503. Locally renowned for its edgy seediness (it was busted as the headquarters for a major smuggling ring in 1998), this grocery store and café bustles with life. The take-out counter offers large portions of Cuban dishes, and there are cafeteria-style tables under a lean-to out back; unsurprisingly, the *batidos* (fresh juice shakes) here are excellent, too.

Los Pinarenos 1334 SW 8th St T 305/285-1135. Enormous *fruteria* sprawling along the southern side of Calle Ocho: for $2 you'll snag a flagon of juice squeezed to order. Even better, you'll rub elbows with the old-timers from the neighborhood who hang out here during the day. Breakfast and lunch only.

Nuevo Siglo 1305 SW 8th St T 305/854-1916. The pick of the many grocery-store cafés on Calle Ocho, this lunch counter along the back wall serves excellent *café cubano* as well as delicious pressed Cuban sandwiches with sweet pork, pickles, and ham.

Coral Gables

Books & Books Café 265 Aragon Ave T 305/448-9599. A low-key oasis off the Miracle Mile, this café serves crusty French-loaf sandwiches starting at $6, as well as rich, buttery pastries and sweets produced by a local bakery – try the fresh strawberry cheesecake. There's live music every Friday from 6–8pm.

Burger Bob's 2001 Granada Ave T 305/567-3100. Tucked away in the clubhouse of the public Granada Golf Course is one of Coral Gables' gems: this homely café, with its green Formica chairs, white plastic tables, and yellow mustard bottles, is where local politicos power breakfast alongside pensioners looking for a deal. The home-made chili's a steal at $2.50, but the reason to come here's as much for the vibe as the food. Breakfast and lunch only.

Estate Wines 92 Miracle Mile T 305/442-9915. This place started out a wine store but slowly evolved into the tastiest café in downtown Coral Gables. There are hot and cold sandwiches on offer – the gooey hot ham and cheese on a roll's delicious – as well as house-baked pastries like chocolate-doused macaroons or apple strudel, a nod to the owner's German roots. To stay, head to the rear of the store and pull up a stool at the large wooden communal table.

Nena's 3791 Bird Rd. No phone. *Nena's* is the lunchtime hub of Miami's power Cuban scene: within a derelict-looking building are two lunch counters and a couple of tables, with whiteboards on the wall describing the day's offerings – the *croqueta preparada* (Cuban sandwich) is juicy and delicious.

Titanic Brewery 5813 Ponce de Leon Blvd ☎305/667-2537. Unpretentious pub food served in a friendly bar just outside Coral Gables. The hamburgers are especially good and start around $6, and there are gourmet beers on tap. In addition, the *Titanic* hosts regular performances by local bands (see p.154, "Drinking").

Coconut Grove

Bacio 3462 Main Hwy ☎305/442-4233. Glorious sorbets and ice creams are sold at this modernist *gelateria*, staffed by Italians who give the place a laid-back, European feel. Ask for a sample before you order – the *frutti di bosco* (fruits of the forest) and *zuppa inglese* (trifle) are staff favorites. There's also a small counter for a quick *caffè*. There's another branch at 204 Miracle Mile in Coral Gables ☎305/442-6430.

The Cheese Market 3049 Main Hwy ☎305/446-8800. Trendy gourmet pickle and cheese shop with a lunchtime café attached: sample a chunk of one of its exotic cheeses at the counter and then order a baguette sandwich with whatever you prefer for $7.50: a Hollandia with gouda, or a Torero with manchego, for instance. There's also a short but reliable list of wines by the glass.

Daily Bread Marketplace 2400 SW 27th St ☎305/856-5893. Just over Hwy-1 from Coconut Grove proper, this Middle Eastern grocery store and cafeteria serves delicious lunches like falafel, *tabbouleh*, and ground-lamb pita kebab in a hurry.

Greenstreet Café 3468 Main Hwy ☎305/444-0244. The *Greenstreet's* terrific breakfasts of fragrant fruit pancakes and hefty omelets

make this café a real scene at weekends. Also, it has a large number of outdoor tables where you can dawdle undisturbed over a coffee.

Scotty's Landing 3381 Pan American Drive ☎305/854-2626. Though hard to find, tucked away on the water near City Hall, and service can be slow, there are few better places to taste local flavor than at *Scotty's* – sit out on the water at the Marina, order a fish sandwich (around $6), and join the locals for lunch.

Zoom 3117 Commodore Plaza ☎305/569-0009. Zesty juice bar serving huge smoothies in every flavor, as well as fresh salads: an excellent place for a healthy stop, and the fruit drinks are large enough to make a (liquid) meal on their own.

Key Biscayne

Donut Gallery 83 Harbour Drive ☎305/361-9985. Open at 5.30am, this old-time diner is an untouched classic on Key Biscayne, with its red vinyl stools, faded Formica tables, and sweet, greasy donuts. Breakfasts start around $4.

South to Homestead and Florida City

Main Street Café 128 N Krome Ave ☎305/245-7575. This laid-back Homestead café features home-made soups and plenty of vegetarian options, as well as gourmet coffee, beer, and wine. There's live entertainment, usually folk music, on Thursday, Friday, and Saturday nights.

Moreno's Tortilla Shop 439 West Palm Drive. No phone. Neighborhood café primarily catering to the large number of migrant Mexican workers in Florida City. Worth stopping by, though, for its excellent and authentic hand-made *tamales*.

Robert Is Here 19900 SW 344th St ☎305/246-1592. Started in the mid-1950s, when his farmer father put young Robert in charge of an impromptu roadside cucumber stall, this fruitstand is now a ramshackle institution. Part farmers' market, part café, Robert and his team sell fruity milkshakes, preserves, and tropical salad dressings. Close to the main entrance of Everglades National Park.

CAFÉS AND LIGHT MEALS | Coconut Grove • Key Biscayne

Restaurants

With cuisine from nearly every corner of the globe, including hearty dollops of Cuban, Haitian, Italian, and French, eating in Miami is an endless pleasure. This is the realm in which Miami's cosmopolitan, cobbled-together history produces plenty of flavor with none of the friction.

The dominant ethnic food is, of course, **Cuban** – though it's not for the weak-hearted: many of the juicy, tender meat dishes are fried, and glorious desserts like *tres leches* are artery-clogging. Cuban menus also often feature Spanish staples such as paella and black beans and white rice, known as Moros y Cristianos (literally, "Moors and Christians"). The ethnic style most in vogue in Miami, though, is **Haitian**: restaurants like *Tap Tap* in South Beach have opened outside the borders of Little Haiti, and the dishes – which place emphasis on ingredients like starchy tubers and goat, much like in Jamaican cooking – are hearty and satisfying.

The last few years have seen the evolution of a local cooking style, known variously as **Floribbean**, **Nuevo Cubano**, or **Tropical Fusion.** Miami's chefs have taken much from Cuban cooking (hearts of palm, avocadoes, and guava) and used those same ingredients in unusual combinations, often adding light but spicy tastes like ginger or bonnet peppers. This uniquely local style also uses plenty of fresh fruit and, since the key is to keep flavor high but fat low – a popular combination in body-conscious Miami – seafood is more common than meat. Miami's cultural fusion has also nurtured numerous **pan-Asian eateries**, as well as a growing number of sushi-ceviche restaurants that bring Latin American and Japanese flavors together.

As for where to go, **South Beach** unsurprisingly holds the largest grouping of trendy restaurants. Many of these establishments actually serve excellent food that lives up to the hype – though unfortunately, so do the prices; as with hotels, restaurants in South Beach are increasingly catering to an upscale, moneyed clientele rather than the poor and trendy types who first recolonized the place ten years ago. Note that the one strip here to avoid entirely is Ocean Drive, filled as it is with so-so eateries staffed by carnival-barking waitresses who lasso unsuspecting passersby into eating the food – skip anywhere other than the handful of places we've highlighted. Back on the mainland, **Coral Gables** is the other chichi place to dine – restaurants there are less sceney than their counterparts in South Beach, though often more formal. And the **Biscayne Corridor** renaissance is most evident in the profusion of trendy new restaurants that have sprung up over the past two years; it's one of the best options away from the beach.

Away from these two areas, though, the pickings thin out: **Coconut Grove** has only a small cluster of restaurants at its center, and **Downtown** is virtually bereft of good eateries, and those worth trying all tend to close early – plan to dine before 9pm. While in **Little Havana**, stick to Calle Ocho, as there are plenty of authentic choices on every block. Back on Miami Beach, Collins Avenue offers a few clusters of restaurants as it snakes northwards, notably around 41st Street and 71st Street. For the best Mexican food around, head south to **Homestead**, where several cheap canteens cater primarily to the migrant workers who staff the fruit farms each season.

The restaurant reviews below have been price-coded into five categories according to per-person meals: an inexpensive place will hover at less than $15, while a moderate restaurant should cost between $15 and $30. Expensive places will run between $30 and $45 per person, while the few very expensive establishments we've listed will cost $45 and up. Bear in mind that these quotes are based on a two-course meal, not including drinks, tip, or taxes.

Downtown

Big Fish Mayami 55 SW Miami Ave ☎305/373-1770. Known for its crab cakes, this riverside shack offers a taste of the Florida Keys without leaving Miami. The atmosphere's casual and the design ramshackle – for example, the bar is built around an enormous banyan tree. *Moderate.*

La Loggia 68 W Flagler St ☎305/373-4800, ⓦwww.laloggiarestaurant.com. La Loggia is a casual Italian pasta café with terracotta floors and plenty of Chianti bottles for decoration. There's bar and restaurant seating, plus a varied wine list. Entrees start around $10. *Moderate.*

Los Ranchos Bayside Marketplace, 401 Biscayne Blvd N-100 ☎305/375-0666. As this chainlet of Nicaraguan steakhouses has grown, its food has become more Americanized, but steak specials like *churrasco con chimichurri* (steak with spicy herb salsa) are tender and delicious, while the *cuatro leches* dessert outdoes the traditional Cuban *tres leches*. *Expensive.*

Morton's Steakhouse 1200 Brickell Ave ☎305/400-9990, ⓦwww.mortons.com. Clubby old-world steakhouse in the midst of skyscraping banks, serving juicy slabs of aged beef to an upscale clientele – try the Porterhouse or double filet mignon for around $30. One of the few places in Downtown to remain lively during the evening. *Expensive.*

Mosaico 1000 S Miami Ave ☎305/371-3473, ⓦwww.mosaicorestaurant.com. This brand-new Spanish-inflected eatery in Brickell is housed in a historic Mediterranean Revival building that was once a firehouse. Skip the interior space for a table on the huge wooden patio or a drink at the outdoor lounge; try the seared tuna with manchego

cheese ($13) followed by the soupy lobster risotto *arroz caldoso* ($27). *Expensive.*

Rosinella 1040 S Miami Ave ☎305/372-5756. At this outstanding family-run restaurant, you'll find classic Italian comfort food at reasonable prices. Even though all the bread and pasta are made on site, Mama Rosinella is best known for her soft, floury gnocchi. Another location is at 525 Lincoln Rd ☎305/672-8777. *Moderate.*

Royal Man I 6217 NW 7th Ave ☎305/758-8725. This homely Liberty City vegetarian rasta restaurant decorated in bright Caribbean colors serves spicy entrees made from tofu, *ackee*, and peppers. Lunch and dinner Mon–Thurs, lunch-only Fri & Sun. *Inexpensive.*

Tobacco Road 626 S Miami Ave ☎305/374-1198, ⓦwww.tobacco-road.com. This bar and live music venue (see p.160, "Nightlife") also serves surprisingly hearty and fresh American diner food. The burgers are juicy, and there are regular bargain specials like lobster for $10 – just don't come here if you're in the mood for a romantic dinner. *Inexpensive.*

Tutto Pasta 1751 SW 3rd Ave ☎305/857-0709. A small Italian restaurant, *Tutto* is one of the new cluster of eateries opening in southwestern Downtown. There's outdoor seating and the menu features standard Italian classics – not the place for a foodie's pilgrimage, but a strong option if you're in the area. *Moderate.*

South Beach

Ago Inside the Shore Club hotel, 1901 Collins Ave ☎305/695-3244, ⓦwww.shoreclub.com. The first of the *Shore Club*'s two celebrity eateries, this is an LA transfer, co-owned by Robert DeNiro, and is sceney if not especially celeb studded – for that, you'll have to head to *Nobu* next door (see opposite). Even so, the pricey Italian food is tasty enough, especially the home-made ravioli and crispy wood-fired pizzas. *Expensive.*

B.E.D. 929 Washington Ave ☎305/532-9070, ⓦwww.bedmiami.com. The name stands for Beverage-Entertainment-Dining, and the Frenchy food's shockingly good – try the duck breast with mascarpone polenta ($32) or hazelnut-crusted foie gras ($26) – given the restaurant's gimmicky premise: enormous white beds replace chairs, and diners recline around low tables while eating. There are two sittings every evening, at 8pm and 10.30pm – if you choose the earlier, don't expect to lounge for too long. *Very expensive.*

Big Pink 157 Collins Ave ☎305/532-4700, ⓦwww.bigpinkrestaurant.com. This cartoonish diner, decked out in pink lucite and aluminum, is famous for its TV dinners served on vintage trays. The huge menu offers good versions of traditional burgers and salads, as well as ample desserts; the cafeteria-style tables make the diverse crowd more intimate. Open till 5am weekends with a beer and food happy hour on Thursday evenings. *Inexpensive.*

Bond St Inside the Townhouse hotel, 150 20th St ☎305/398-1806, ⓦwww.townhousehotel.com. The Miami outpost of a chic New York scene eatery that is smaller but otherwise identical to its sibling: glamorous people, same sleek menu (the vegetarian sushi roll with sun-dried tomato and avocado for $6 is excellent) and same signature cocktail, the Saketini. Expect a wait at weekends, especially on Fridays when the hotel holds its rooftop sunset parties. *Moderate–expensive.*

Cafeteria 546 Lincoln Rd ☎305/672-FOOD. Huge, sprawling two-level New York transplant, this modern black-and-white café is a 24hr hang-out with ample outdoor tables plus comfy banquettes inside. The food consists mostly of sandwiches and staples like meatloaf ($9–18), though there's a nod to Miami in the Thursday special of *ropa vieja*. Look for the local scenesters photographed expressly to appear on the menu. *Moderate.*

Casa Tua 1700 James Ave ☎305/673-1010. Hands down, the priciest place to eat on the beach. Hidden behind a high hedge, this lounge-restaurant is a gourmet experience – portions of Italian food are tiny, so

don't come hungry, and most entrees will set you back close to $80 so save up. Of course, the sumptuous ingredients – truffles, asparagus, and artisanal cheeses – make it almost worth it. *Very expensive.*

Eleventh St. Diner 1065 Washington Ave ☎305/672-2000. Housed in a 1948 Art Deco–style diner car, specially shipped to South Beach from Pennsylvania, the feel here is local, diverse, and friendly. Open 24 hours, it has terrific down-home food – the spinach salad is good – chatty staff, and happy-hour specials from 5 to 7pm and again from 10pm to midnight on Monday to Friday. *Moderate.*

Joe's Stone Crab 11 Washington Ave ☎305/673-0365, ⓦwww.joesstonecrab.com. Synonymous with South Beach for decades, this packed, pricey restaurant serves fresh, steamed stone crabs to those prepared to wait up to three hours for the pleasure – though it's popular as much out of tradition than tastiness these days. Better to do as locals do and grab a portion to go from the take-out window next door. *Expensive.*

Joia 1500 Ocean Drive ☎305/674-8871, ⓦwww.joiamiami.com. In South Beach's early 1990s go-go days, Madonna hung out here all the time. Now, she may be gone but there's still ample reason to eat here – try to get a table in the outdoor loggia by the waterfall. The Italian food is simple and tasty; there's also a new sushi bar with terrific mango seafood ceviche. *Expensive.*

Macaluso 1747 Alton Rd ☎305/604-1811. Nestled in a strip mall by the canal at the northern end of South Beach, *Macaluso* serves unpretentious Italian food like fusilli with spinach and white beans or spaghetti *alle vongole* that's far better than many of the chic, overpriced Italian restaurants around Lincoln Road. *Moderate.*

Metro Kitchen & Bar Inside the Astor Hotel, 956 Washington Ave ☎305/672-7217, ⓦwww.metrokitchenandbar.com. One of the hottest eateries at the beach, thanks to its celebrity clientele, this sunken restaurant boasts a fine garden, simple but delicious Italian-inflected food, and killer cocktails – with the attendant celebrities and local hipsters. *Expensive.*

Miss Yip Chinese Café 1661 Meridian Ave ☎305/534-5488, ⓦwww.missyipchinesecafe.com. Owned by the same woman who helps run *Bond St*, this new Chinese spot looks likely to hold firm. The food is

Cantonese – *dim sum* at lunchtime ($4.95–6.95), staples like moo shu pork at night ($13.95) – while the decor's much trendier, with a vibe like a swanky café in Shanghai's decadent 1930s heyday. *Moderate–expensive*.

Nobu Inside the Shore Club hotel, 1901 Collins Ave ☎ 305/695-3232, ⓦ www.shoreclub.com. The top celeb-spotting place on the beach, sibling to the famous sushi restaurant in New York. Chef Nobu Matsuhisa serves up a similar menu here, offering his offbeat Japanese/Peruvian dishes alongside a selection of sushi, sashimi, and rolls. No one, however, really comes here for the food. *Very expensive*.

Pacific Time 915 Lincoln Rd ☎ 305/534-5979. The first upscale restaurant to open during Lincoln Road's renaissance, it's still a scene, but a welcoming one. Decor is shabby chic and food is a Floribbean fusion of Pacific Rim countries: unusual recipes like Mongolian lamb and steamed shrimp dumplings hit more often than they miss. *Very expensive*.

Prime 112 112 Ocean Drive ☎ 305/532-8112, ⓦ www.prime112.com. The toughest reservation on the beach, and arguably its hottest restaurant right now, *Prime 112* is housed in a converted 1915 hotel. The waiters are decked out in butcher aprons and the dining room's plastered with press cuttings – both from Miami Beach's early days and reviews of the restaurant from today. The steak-heavy menu is pricey but tasty – the $20 hot dog is more than worth it – but with patrons wedged so close together, it can be very noisy so don't come on a quiet date. *Very expensive*.

Sushi Samba Dromo 600 Lincoln Rd ☎ 305/673-5337, ⓦ www.sushisamba.com. At *Sushi Samba Dromo*, the cuisine and space fuse Tokyo with Rio: brightly colored tiles meet black lacquered wood while the sushi chef prepares sashimi and the samba chef whips up ceviche. It has a great vibe, thanks more to its central location, which attracts plenty of Lincoln Road evening strutters than the food: the sushi can be disappointing, but dishes like crispy whole red snapper work better. *Expensive*.

Tambo 1801 Purdy Ave ☎ 305/535-2414, ⓦ www.tambobeach.com. Tucked out of the way at South Beach's northern end, this fusion restaurant successfully combines South American and Japanese flavors: alongside fancy hand rolls, for example,

you'll be served nutty breads and Peruvian dipping sauce. The atmosphere's elegant and low-key, and it's good for a light snack and a glass of wine from the extensive list. *Expensive*.

Tantra 1445 Pennsylvania Ave ☎ 305/672-4765, ⓦ www.tantrarestaurant.com. Modern Indian cuisine with a Mediterranean slant served in a dense, sexy environment, where every element is designed to be sensual – there's grass on the floor, enormous embroidered cushions, plus hookahs and belly dancers. It may sound gimmicky, but it works – and even if the over-the-top design puts you off, risk it for the food, which is extremely good – if it's on the menu, try the Saffron Saigon Stew, with market seafood and lashings of coconut. *Expensive*.

Tap Tap 819 5th St ☎ 305/672-2898. One of the few restaurants outside Little Haiti that serves authentic Haitian food, *Tap Tap* often features intriguing specials – say, goat in a peppery tomato broth or a mango, avocado, and watercresss salad – and the drinks are cheap. Worth stopping by for the Caribbean art displayed on the walls or the live Haitian folk music every Thursday and Saturday. *Moderate*.

Taverna Opa 36–40 Ocean Drive ☎ 305/673-6730. This massive Greek restaurant – with its frantic table-dancing, loud music, and Mediterranean-themed decor – might at first seem like a tourist trap, but it's an absolute gem. Skip the forced bonhomie inside and grab a table on the patio out back; the food is delicious, and well priced – the tapas-style *meze* dishes run $3–5. *Moderate*.

Toni's Sushi 1208 Washington Ave ☎ 305/673-9368. *Toni's*, which claims to be the oldest sushi bar on the beach, is especially good for vegetarians, boasting a wide selection of vegetable and noodle dishes. There's classic sushi and sashimi as well as funky new options – try the Miami Heat roll, with tuna and peppery sesame oil. The staff is notoriously gruff, although the bartenders in the small bar can be friendlier. *Moderate*.

Touch 910 Lincoln Rd ☎ 305/532-8003, ⓦ www.touchrestaurant.com. The wackiness of this upscale eatery starts with its location – inside a converted synagogue, the Temple King Solomon. *Touch* boasts a whimsical and fun Goth Polynesian interior, featuring real palm trees; the portions are huge and the showy modern American food delicious – try the chicken stuffed with almonds and

Swiss cheese or lime-cured salmon fillet. *Expensive*.

Wish Inside The Hotel, 801 Collins Ave T 305/674-9474, W www.wishrestaurant.com. Daring Floribbean food, heavy on fruit, fish, and unexpected ingredients. Dinner here may not be cheap, but it's good value for a rare treat – though the cranked-up muzak can get rather overwhelming. Try the tuna ceviche, and finish your meal with one of the odd, interesting desserts like herbed pineapple sorbet. *Very expensive*.

Yuca 501 Lincoln Rd T 305/532-9822. Famed gourmet Cuban (or Nuevo Cubano) restaurant at the beach end of Lincoln Road – ask to sit outside. Perhaps past its trendy heyday the clientele is heavy on Anglo yuppies), its food is still remarkable – try anything with pork, or the gazpacho with cilantro oil. *Expensive–very expensive*.

Central Miami Beach and north

Café Prima Pasta 414 71st St T 305/867-0106. Everyone raves about this North Beach place, and for good reason: the pasta's home-made, the tiny main room charming, and the prices reasonable – it's no surprise, then, that the wait for a table can be on the long side, so come early with a newspaper or two. *Moderate*.

Christine Lees 17802 Collins Ave T 305/947-1717. *Christine Lees* is a Sunny Isles Beach standby that's been serving simple Chinese food for years: the cuisine is Szechuan-Cantonese, with an emphasis on fish and seafood – people swear by the steamed shrimp. The place rather lacks atmosphere, but the massive portions more than make up. *Moderate*.

The Forge 432 41st St T 305/538-8533, W www.theforge.com. Dining at this Middle Beach institution is an unmissable experience, not for the staggeringly huge wine cellar (available for tours if you ask nicely), the hearty and traditional steakhouse food, or the kitschy gilt decor, but rather for the vibrant scene, where you'll find hip locals eating the likes of goat-cheese-crusted rack of lamb or herbed filet mignon alongside sixtysomething Miami Beachers. *Expensive–very expensive*

Rascal House 17190 Collins Ave T 305/947-4581. Make a pilgrimage to this vintage standby, where portions of standard diner fare are huge, and breakfast is accompanied by dozens of baked treats, such as

bagels, *rugelach*, and muffins. Even better, what you don't finish you can take with you in the plastic "Waste Not" bag the waitress leaves along with your check. *Moderate*.

Tamarind Thai 946 Normandy Drive T 305/861-6222, W www.tamarindthai.us. One of the latest arrivals on up-and-coming Normandy Isle, this smallish restaurant's run by two Thai expats and cookery-book authors who whip up delicious, tangy dishes – many, naturally, accented with its namesake fruit – like crispy noodles with sweet tamarind or roast duck in tamarind sauce. *Moderate*.

North along the Biscayne Corridor

Citronelle 7300 Biscayne Blvd T 305/757-2555. Upscale Tropical Fusion eatery that was one of the pioneers on this strip: the decor's low-key, mahogany while Caribbean music quietly plays in the background. The food, though, is much showier, with fantastic risotto, skirt steak, or sour orange and lemon chicken for around $22 an entree. *Expensive*.

The District 35 NE 40th St T 305/576-7242, W www.thedistrictmiami.com. This trendy Design District spot features a palm-shaded court with a fountain out front, and a restaurant with a backlit Lucite bar in back with orchids enclosed in it. The gimmick here is that each dish is from a district, say Southeast or Northwest, but sadly, the food's so-so: best option is house salad with goat cheese and smoked red onions for $11. *Expensive*.

Enriqueta's 2830 NE 2nd Ave T 305/573-4681. This local diner bustles all day, serving no-frills Cuban sandwiches and massive steaks. Sit at the counter and watch the squad of old ladies who staff the kitchen nonchalantly preparing an assembly line of pressed sandwiches – try a Cuban sandwich, jammed with ham, pork, Swiss cheese, and pickles, for $4. *Inexpensive*.

Lacaye Restaurant 7499 NE 2nd Ave T 305/756-5054. In this low-slung coral pink building on Little Haiti's main drag, you can try Haitian specialties like fried pork or goat in a friendly environment at rock-bottom prices. *Inexpensive*.

Mike Gordon's Seafood Restaurant 1201 NE 79th St T 305/751-4429. A Little Haiti favorite, this mid-range seafood eatery on the bay is just as good as famed *Joe's Stone Crab* in South Beach (see p.144), but much cheaper, too. Skip the fancy dishes and stick with staples like stone-crab claws and lobster. *Moderate*.

OLA 5075 Biscayne Blvd ☎305/758-9195, Ⓦwww.olamiami.com. Local foodie superstar Chef Douglas Rodriguez has transformed this restaurant into a Tropical Fusion or pan-Latin eatery (hence the name: Of Latin America). It boasts an impressive ceviche bar with twelve different kinds of fish – try the scallop, marlin, or conch. His bartenders also make a killer *mojito*. *Expensive*.

Soyka 5580 NE 4th Court ☎305-759-3117. Soyka – the man behind the *News Café* on South Beach (see p.138) – is the mastermind of this large, cavernous space in Little Haiti, with its distressed concrete walls and simple wood furniture. The food is Mediterranean-American: huge salads and crispy thin pizzas, served alongside Italian touches like polenta and fried calamari. It's a cheaper option to stop by for lunch than dinner. *Expensive*.

Little Havana

Ayestaran 706 SW 27th Ave ☎305/649-4982. This unpretentious restaurant serves Spanish-Cuban food in a family-style setting – the sandwiches are good and daily lunchtime specials keep prices low: try the *arroz con mariscos* (rice with prawns). *Inexpensive–moderate*.

Casa Juancho 2436 SW 8th St ☎305/642-2452, Ⓦwww.casajuancho.com. Oddly reminiscent of either a Swiss chalet or Disney's idea of Old Cuba, this upscale Calle Ocho restaurant offers hearty, Spanish-inflected dishes, notably the fish. It's one of the few posh restaurants in the neighborhood, and makes for good people-watching. *Expensive*.

Casa Panza 1620 SW 8th St ☎305/643-5343. Less formal and more Iberian than many of the other Spanish restaurants hereabouts, with tapas, *raciones*, and main dishes prepared primarily in a Madrid style. Above-average prices ($16–20), but you get to watch free flamenco on Tues and Thurs–Sat from 8pm onwards. *Moderate–expensive*.

El Cristo 1543 SW 8th St ☎305/261-2947. Casual café, with mismatched brown Formica furniture indoors, a lunch counter, and a few white garden chairs propped up on the sidewalk. Come here for huge helpings of tangy ceviche for only $5 or *palomilla* steaks for just $8. There are around ten different daily specials, too – check the back of the menu for details. *Inexpensive*.

El Fogon 2091 Coral Way ☎305/856-3451. This out-of-the-way restaurant serves massive Mexican dinners at minimal prices: try the house special of *cochinita pibil* (shredded marinated pork) in one of its many preparations, or order real Mexican fajitas. *Moderate*.

Guayacan 1933 SW 8th St ☎305/649-2015. Tasty, fresh Nicaraguan food served either at the counter or in the small, unfussy dining

A brief Cuban food glossary

Aguacate Avocado

Ajo Garlic

Arepas Cornmeal pancake

Arroz con pollo Chicken and yellow rice

Buñuelos Cuban donuts

Cabra or chivo Goat

Camarones Prawns

Chorizo Spicy, greasy sausage

Churrasco Marinated and grilled beef tenderloin

Empanada Ground beef in a tortilla, either fried or baked

Escabeche Pickled fish

Langosta Florida lobster

Maduros Sweet, fried plantains

Mariscos Seafood

Moros y Cristianos Black beans and white rice

Paella Spanish dish, incorporating saffron rice with seafood or chicken

Papa Potato

Queso Cheese

Ropa vieja Literally "old clothes": shredded beef, fried with vegetables

Sesos Brains

Tostones Mashed, fried plantains

Tres leches Supersweet custard-like dessert, made from condensed, evaporated, and fresh milk, sometimes served with sweet caramel

Vaca frita Beef fried with onions

room to the back: it's known for its soups, with a different recipe served every day – and somehow, the unfriendly staff doesn't detract from the place's charm. *Inexpensive*.

Habana Vieja 3622 Coral Way ☎305/448-6660. In a sprawling cream building with a tiled red roof, this restaurant's known for its *vaca frita* and *fufu de plantano (*mashed plantains). High-spirited and friendly, the staff makes even non-Spanish speakers feel welcome. *Moderate*.

Hy Vong 3458 SW 8th St ☎305/446-3674. Glorious Vietnamese gem, tucked away on the western end of Little Havana. The decor's simple – bright lights, varnished pine tables without cloths – but the food is sumptuous: try *banh cuon* rolls made with home-made rice papers as an appetizer or beef and fresh rice noodle as an entree (prices hover around $15). The other major plus is an extensive beer list, taking in selections from Australia, the Bahamas, Jamaica, and, of course, Vietnam. *Moderate*.

Sergio's Cafeteria 3252 Coral Way ☎305/529-0047. Loud, noisy, and fun, *Sergio's* is a Cuban diner with plenty of attitude, welcoming late-night diners and offering a wide menu at fair prices. A great place to finish up a long Friday night and chow down on one of the best Cuban sandwiches in town. There's another branch at 13600 SW 152nd St, South Miami ☎786/242-9790. *Inexpensive*.

Versailles 3555 SW 8th St ☎305/445-7614. This local legend has retained its 1960s decor and mirrors despite several renovations, inspired by its namesake. Come here for the homestyle Cuban food, and watch a cross-section of Miami's Cuban community come together to enjoy it with you. Traditional, delicious dishes like *ropa vieja* and *vaca frita* should be followed with *tres leches*. Low-fat devotees will find little to eat here. *Moderate*.

Yambo 1643 SW 1st St ☎305/642-6616. This 24-hour Nicaraguan restaurant is one of Miami's treasures, with plentiful outdoor seating that's covered in mosaics and a bevy of bizarre items. Entrees like *puerca asada* (grilled pork) or fried whole snapper go for around $4 – grab them from the counter, then seat yourself – and expect to be offered videos or CDs by itinerant peddlers who thread through the crowd. There's little English spoken here. *Inexpensive*.

Coral Gables

Bugatti's 2504 Ponce de Leon Blvd ☎305/441-2545. An Italian restaurant run by a German in the heart of Cuban Coral Gables, *Bugatti's* food is surprisingly impressive – make sure to try the buffalo mozzarella, as well as the tender gnocchi. The only downside is the sometimes-sniffy service. *Moderate–expensive*.

Caffè Abbracci 318 Aragon Ave ☎305/441-0700. For a taste of local life in Coral Gables, visit this upscale Italian trattoria, which serves traditional pastas alongside more unusual combinations (try the pumpkin ravioli or the heart lentil soup There's a good wine list, too. *Expensive*.

Canton 2614 Ponce de Leon Blvd ☎305/448-3736. Chinese restaurant that offers a greatest-hits-style menu, with Cantonese, Mandarin, and Szechuan favourites – it's especially known for huge portions of honey garlic chicken. There's a good sushi bar as well. *Moderate.*

Christy's 3101 Ponce de Leon Blvd ☎305/446-1400, ⓦ www.christysrestaurant.com. Upscale restaurant with old-fashioned decor and a robust, steak-filled menu for carnivores only – if you dare splash out on the filet mignon, it won't disappoint; the Caesar salad, too, is tangy and delicious. Clubby, rather formal, and very Coral Gables. Very expensive.

Gables Diner 2320 Galiano St ☎305/567-0330, ⓦ www.gablesdiner.com. Fresh and unpretentious compared with many of the posh eateries around the Miracle Mile, this bistro serves good meatloaf, alongside standard sandwiches and salads, for around $10. *Moderate*.

The Globe 377 Alhambra Circle ☎305/445-5555. Yes, it's a rabid pick-up joint, but still good fun: the bar is lively at weekends, packed with a twentysomething Cuban crowd. The food is gimmicky but adventurous, drawn (as per the restaurant's name) from across the world: for an appetizer, try the Cajun egg rolls. *Expensive*.

Havana Harry's 4612 LeJeune Rd ☎305/661-2622, ⓦ www.havanaharrys.com. The homestyle food here comes in large, cheap portions and is authentically Cuban – try the *pollo a la plancha* (marinated grilled chicken) or the *vaca frita* (fried beef with onions). The space is tiny, though, so be prepared to wait at dinnertime. *Inexpensive*.

House of India 22 Merrick Way ⊕ **305/444-2348.** Quality catch-all Indian food including some excellently priced lunch buffets ($7 weekdays, $8 weekends). Not the chicest place, perhaps, but terrific value. *Inexpensive*.

Les Halles 2415 Ponce de Leon Blvd ⊕ **305/461-1099,** ⊛ **www.leshalles.net.** Almost too cozy, this packed French bistro serves excellent classics like steak *tartare* ($15.50) and *moules frites* ($17.50). The decor's a little overdone in its desperate attempts to reproduce every element of a true French restaurant, but the food makes up for it. *Moderate*.

Miss Saigon Bistro 146 Giralda Ave ⊕ **305/446-8006.** Sushi aside, it's challenging to find much good Asian food in Miami, but this family-owned Vietnamese restaurant hits the mark. The food's light and zesty – the noodles with lemongrass and chicken are particularly tasty, as are the spring rolls; what's more, the staff is welcoming and great fun. *Inexpensive–moderate*.

Mykonos 1201 Coral Way ⊕ **305/856-3140.** Greek food in an unassuming atmosphere. *Spanakopita* (cheese and spinach filo pastry pie), lemon chicken soup, gyros, *souvlaki*, and huge Greek salads are among the offerings, along with good vegetarian options. *Moderate*.

Normans 21 Almeria Ave ⊕ **305/446-6767,** ⊛ **www.normans.com.** Superchic, top-notch restaurant, owned by chef Norman Van Aiken, one of the pioneers of New World cuisine. This is another local restaurant where fish is especially good – the inventive paella's a standout – but expect nouvelle cuisine–size portions. *Very expensive*.

Ortanique on the Mile 278 Miracle Mile ⊕ **305/446-7710,** ⊛ **www.cindel-group.com /ortanique_miami.** Another chic eatery in downtown Coral Gables, *Ortanique* serves innovative, adventurous Tropical Fusion food in a lush tropical setting, almost like a terrace garden. Deliberate as the atmosphere may be, the food's sumptuous and creative, there are always reliable fish specials, while the chocolate mango tower is a heavenly dessert. *Expensive–very expensive*.

Picnics at Allen's Drug Store 4000 Red Rd ⊕ **305/665-6964.** Home-style cooking, featuring such staples as freshly made burgers, in an old-fashioned drugstore complete with a jukebox that blasts golden oldies. *Inexpensive*.

Restaurant St Michel Inside the Hotel St Michel, 162 Alcazar Ave ⊕ **305/446-6572.** Inside the B&B-like hotel, this rustic country restaurant is unapologetically old-fashioned, romantic, and French. The food is tastiest when least fussy – stick with simple dishes to be safe, such as the delicate crêpes. *Expensive*.

Coconut Grove

Anokha 3195 Commodore Plaza ⊕ **786/552-1030.** Just off the main drag in Coconut Grove, this tucked-away Indian restaurant is arguably the best of its kind in Miami, for the tangy *biryanis* and *tandooris* as well as a satisfying fiery chicken *vindaloo*. The evening menu's à la carte, while lunch is an $8.95 all-you-can-eat buffet. *Moderate*.

Baleen Inside the Grove Isle Hotel, 4 Grove Isle Drive ⊕ **305/857-5007.** The food at *Baleen* – like the house special, lobster "martini" served on truffled roast potatoes – is good but too expensive. The views, however, are priceless: situated on a private island just off Coconut Grove, the waterfront patio looks out over Biscayne Bay – undeniably one of the most romantic dining spots in town. *Very expensive*.

Bizcaya Grill Inside the Ritz-Carlton Coconut Grove, 3300 SW 27th Ave ⊕ **305/644-4670.** Sure, it's inside a hotel on the mainland but this buzzy restaurant deserves its excellent reputation. It's all down to the fantastic food; best described as simple but flavor-packed – try the stone-crab ravioli or parmesan-crusted beef tenderloin. There are cute touches to the venue, too – every woman's handed a "purse stool" specially designed for her handbag to rest on while she eats. *Expensive*.

Café Tu Tu Tango Inside CocoWalk, 3015 Grand Ave ⊕ **305/529-2222.** This gimmicky restaurant offers Brazilian and belly dancers, onsite tarot-card readers, and even in-residence artists daubing every day from 1.30pm. But forget all that and come just for the reliable, tasty food: the pizzas ($7.50–10) are terrific, especially the tomato with roasted garlic and shallot puree, as are the "sticks and bones" selections of skewers, chops, and ribs. *Moderate*.

Le Bouchon du Grove 3430 Main Hwy ⊕ **305/448-6060.** Ramshackle chic with its designer-dilapidated signage, *Le Bouchon* is a treasure at the heart of the Grove – funky but posh, it's a restaurant that the locals still love, serving French favorites like chicken *en papillote* and home-made patés in a brasserie atmosphere that lets you linger. *Moderate–expensive*.

Señor Frog's 3480 Main Hwy ☎305/448-0900, ⓦ**www.senorfrogsfla.com.** Don't be put off by the name – the food here is terrific, tasty, and affordable, with most entrees hovering around $10 for a plate piled high with Tex-Mex standbys like burritos and enchiladas. The cavernous ceilings stifle any atmosphere, unfortunately. There's another branch at 616 Collins Ave ☎305/673-5262. *Moderate*.

Key Biscayne

Lighthouse Café Bill Baggs Cape Florida State Park, 1200 S Crandon Blvd ☎305/361-8487. Tucked away in the Cape Florida State Park, this is a casual beachside café by the historic lighthouse. With plenty of outdoor seating, it's worth the trip for the tasty fresh fish, Cuban specials, and, of course, the views. *Inexpensive*.

Tango Grill 328 Crandon Blvd, suite 112 ☎305/361-1133. A small Argentine grill in one of the Key Biscayne Village strip malls, *Tango Grill* serves superb *bife de chorizo* (sirloin steak) and other South

American specialties to a heavily Latin crowd. *Expensive*.

South to Homestead and Florida City

Rosita's Restaurante 199 West Palm Drive ☎305/246-3114. Located off Hwy-1 at the junction for the Everglades and Biscayne National Park, *Rosita's* serves glorious Mexican food at budget prices, accompanied by spicy salsa, creamy refried beans, and tangy cheese toppings. There's canteen-style seating at basic Formica tables, all set to a backdrop of loud Hispanic talk radio. Well worth the detour south. *Inexpensive*.

Sango Jamaican and Chinese Restaurant 9485 SW 160th St ☎305/252-0279. Somewhat of an offbeat combination (and the Caribbean food is far better than the Chinese confections), this is still a worthwhile stop in South Miami, especially given its low prices. Try the curried goat and jerk chicken. Mainly a take-out joint, but there are a few tables if you want to linger. *Inexpensive*.

Shorty's Bar-B-Q 9200 South Dixie Hwy, South Miami ☎305/670-7732. A log-cabin institution, *Shorty's* is now more than fifty years old, with a perennial line outside waiting for the splendid, rich barbecue – even the crinkly fries taste smoky. *Inexpensive*.

Drinking

Oddly enough, Miami is not a hard-drinking town. There's little distinction between bars, clubs, and restaurants and in most places you'll be able to eat dinner – or at least snack heartily – with your cocktails. There's also a thriving **hotel bar scene**, some highlights of which we've included in the box at the end of this chapter.

As you might guess, **South Beach** is the place to head first for a night of drinking: there are plenty of options, and its compact, walkable center means you won't need to designate a driver for the evening. Weeknights here are just as good as weekends for going out, if not better: locals haughtily dismiss the so-called "Causeway Crowds" from across the bridges who flood the beach on Friday and Saturday nights, often clogging up smaller lounges. While there are still plenty of South Beach's signature lounges to choose from, the vogue at the moment here is for dive bars, whether ersatz upscale newcomers or rediscovered old gems; an added plus is that prices here tend to be much lower, too.

Beyond South Beach, the scene **along the Biscayne Corridor** is exploding, as hip new bars and night spots open every month, powered by the option of a 24-hour liquor license **Downtown**; while **Coral Gables** has a less trendy selection of places to drink, but is a great destination for a quality beer. There are a couple of detour-worthy spots on **Key Biscayne**, yet **Coconut Grove**, which once hoped to swipe South Beach's crown in funky nightlife, has admitted defeat – bars here are less sceney, to the point of being disappointingly quiet (except at weekends).

Licensing hours vary by neighborhood: South Beach spots are usually serving until 5am, although the incumbent mayor's campaigned – so far, unsuccessfully – to tighten licensing laws so reveling would end three hours earlier. Expect mainland spots to shutter by 2am at the latest, except in the club hub of Park West (see p.88), where there's an experiment in 24-hour licensing. Miami is also a hotbed of bottle service, where swankier boîtes will reserve seating only for those willing to shell out upwards of $150 for a single bottle of liquor, so be prepared to stand at these places if you're on a tighter budget.

All bars are open to those 21 and over only, so remember always to bring photo ID.

Downtown

Tobacco Road 626 S Miami Ave ☏ 305/374-1198, ⊛ www.tobacco-road.com. This late-night dive bar lives off its reputation: it purportedly received the city's first liquor license in 1912, and the place is gloriously gritty. The bar food is standard American – burgers and fries – but the drinks list is more adventurous. There are also two stages where nightly live acts (primarily blues and traditional R&B) perform – see p.160, "Nightlife."

The Abbey Brewing Company 1115 16th St
☎ 305/538-8110, ⓦ www.abbeybrewingco.com.
A hops-fueled antidote to the South Beach
scene, *The Abbey* is as close to a neighborhood pub as the area gets. The tiny space
is themed on a church – hence the wooden
pew seating – and the homebrewed range
of beers is superb: try the popular Oatmeal
Stout or one of twelve other varieties on tap.

Automatic Slim's 1216 Washington Ave
☎ 305/695-0795. Loud and lively, velvet-
rope-free locals' favorite: come here to
down cheap beers (only $2 from 4 to 8pm),
dance to classic rock or 80s hip-hop, and
ogle the foxy bartenders who gyrate on
the bar throughout the evening. Refreshingly unpretentious spot amid the swanky
lounges of South Beach.

Blue 222 Española Way ☎ 305/534-1009. Opin-
ions are divided over this tiny, lively bar: it's
cool but a little clichéd, and popular with
travelers from the nearby *Clay Hostel*. Either
way, expect house music with decor – you
guessed it – in different shades of blue.

Club Deuce 222 W 14th St ☎ 305/531-6200.
Grimy, noisy grunge bar, this remnant from
pre-fabulous South Beach is equally fabulous in its own way. This is one of Miami's
premier dive bars: drinks are cheap, plus it
features a dartboard and pool table and it's
open until 5am every night.

Honey 645 Washington Ave ☎ 305/604-8222.
Don't let the sexy, soft-toned decor at
this venue fool you (although the flattering
lighting will take ten years off anyone): the
crowd's insatiable and it's carving out a
reputation for itself as a VIP hot spot thanks
to sceney weekly events. There's plenty
of lounge-style seating plus a massive
mahogany bar, although drinks are pricey.
The best night of the week is Thursday's
1980s-obsessed Vintage Vinyl party.

Lario's on the Beach 820 Ocean Drive
☎ 305/532-9577. The sole reason to come to
Gloria Estefan's restaurant on the beach is
its mojitos, the signature Cuban concoction
of crushed mint and rum – most people
concede that *Lario's* serves the best mojitos
on the beach. Unfortunately, the food is so-
so, so stick with the cocktails.

Lost Weekend 218 Española Way ☎ 305/672-
1707. Divey sports bar that's popular with
backpackers from the nearby *Clay Hostel*.
There are more than 100 different beers on

offer from around the world, as well as every
bar game, from foosball and billiards to air
hockey.

Onda Lounge 1248 Washington Ave ☎ 305/674-
4464, ⓦ www.ondalounge.com. Swish, upscale
newcomer whose name means "wave"
in Italian; the interior's nautical, in foamy
greens and blues, with huge gauzy curtains
dividing the main dancefloor from the VIP
room at the rear. Best of all, there's ample
comfy seating, mostly overstuffed sofas, so
you should always be able to find somewhere to crash.

Pearl 1 Ocean Drive ☎ 305/538-1231, ⓦ www
.penrods.com. Swathed in orange lights, this
neo-space-age all-white eatery has a champagne bar in the center of the main room.
Drinks are ultra-expensive, so it's really a
place to go for one glass and plenty of
rubbernecking before heading off elsewhere
for the evening.

Privé 136 Collins Ave ☎ 305/674-8630, ⓦ www
.opiumiami.com. Attached to the *Opium
Garden* nightclub, this lounge is tucked
away in a back alley. The door policy is one
of the tightest around, especially on Friday
nights, so make sure to sashay like a VIP
if you want to sip with the A-list behind the
silk curtains.

Purdy Lounge 1811 Purdy Ave ☎ 305/531-4622,
ⓦ www.purdylounge.com. This groovy, out-
of-the-way lounge is big enough that you
should be able to grab a table without too
long a wait, no matter the night. The vibe's
overwhelmingly local and the decor vaguely
Arabian with minaret-shaped seat backs
in a sludgy gold and purple color scheme;
but it's the pool tables and late license that
really matter – *Purdy* stays open and busy
till 5am every night.

Rok Bar 1805 Collins Ave ☎ 305/535-7171.
Co-owned by rocker Tommy Lee and the
team behind *Mynt* next door (see p.157),
this is like an upscale dive bar, with its artily
decorated walls are covered in pictures of
hard rockers, dim but flattering rosy lighting,
and a VIP room accessible only by a ladder.
Frankly, it's not the hot spot most expected,
but Tommy and his celebrity pals do occasionally drop by.

The Room 100 Collins Ave ☎ 305/531-6061.
Lookalike Miami outpost of a minimalist
New York bar, with raw concrete floors,
industrial metal tables, and low lighting. One
wall's lined with high leather banquettes and
metal tables; the other's home to the large

bar. The low-key crowd's generally a mixed selection of locals and tourists.

Sushi Samba Dromo 600 Lincoln Rd ☎305/673-5337, ⓦwww.sushisamba.com. While primarily a restaurant (see review, p.145), *Sushi Samba Dromo*'s large lounge is one of the funkiest places in the city to snack and drink, and there's a nifty champagne and sushi bar to the left of the entrance. The waitstaff is sweet, but don't expect speedy service.

Ted's Hideaway South 124 2nd St ☎305/532-9869. Twice-daily happy hours (from noon–7pm and again from 1am–3am) make this local spot popular: the atmosphere's basic and homely, and the cheap beer really is the only draw.

Touch 910 Lincoln Rd ☎305/532-8003. Great fun, this *grande dame* of the South Beach bar scene is one of the best places in Miami to sample a Cuba Libre. A restaurant as well (see p.145), *Touch* is decorated with palm trees in Gothic Polynesian style, the round bar at the front is another great spot for people watching – plus it's easy to make eye contact with other barflies. The staff is friendlier than usual in a place this hip, and is happy to chat on quieter nights.

W6 Lounge 619 Washington Ave ☎305/532-4445. Understated, thanks to its lower South Beach location, this artsy lounge draws direct inspiration from New York's SoHo. Here, though, the drink prices and bartenders are pleasant, making for a stylish fallback if you don't pass the doorman's muster at the mega-clubs.

Wet Willie's 760 Ocean Drive ☎305/532-5650, ⓦwww.wetwillies.com. Frat boy central, this raucous Ocean Drive bar has its own upstairs terrace packed with youngish tourists from lunchtime on. The frozen drinks are served from washing-machine-sized mixers – be sure to try a rumrunner – and, at only $5, each giant helping is a bargain.

Central Miami Beach and north

Chamber Lounge 2940 Collins Ave ☎305/673-0338. Another of the dive bars staging a comeback in Miami, this basement gem in Middle Beach is found by looking for the large green awning. There's a jukebox rather than a DJ, and the drink list is more Scotch and beer than faddish cocktails. Even better, there's a happy hour on Fridays from 2–5am so it's a perfect refuge at the end of a night of bar-hopping.

Lemon Twist 908 71st St ☎305/868-2075. Though primarily a French-Mediterranean restaurant, this spot – one of the first to open in gentrifying Normandy Isle – is an even better place to grab a cocktail than a meal. There's cover-free live jazz most nights and shots of the namesake house liqueur, a version of limoncello, are usually given out gratis through the evening.

North along the Biscayne Corridor

Churchill's Hideaway 5501 NE 2nd Ave ☎305/757-1807, ⓦwww.churchillspub.com. Emblazoned all over with the Union Jack, this utterly out-of-place bar set deep in the heart of Little Haiti is home away from home for Miami's expat Brits. It serves good tap beer, and satellite soccer and rugby

---

Cocktails in Miami

Don't miss the chance to try one of Miami's signature **cocktails**. Potent and flavorful, they're often made with fresh ingredients and, of course, rum – yet another nod to Cuba's dominant influence in the city. Even if you're a confirmed cosmopolitan drinker, stray a little and sample something local, like the drinks listed below – it'll be worth it.

Cuba Libre A fancy name for rum, coke, and a splash of lime juice.

Mojito A sumptuous Cuban cocktail. Mint is pounded to release its full flavor, then stirred with sugar syrup, rum, lime juice, and soda water: many claim that *Lario's on the Beach* serves the best in town (see review, opposite).

Rumrunner Another rum-based cocktail, combined with a variety of fruit flavors, often banana or blackberry: whatever the combination, expect it to be heavily alcoholic. Though the classic place to sample a Rumrunner is Key West (see p.248), bars in Miami often mix a mean version, too.

matches are beamed into the main bar; check out the live band performances, too.

The District 35 NE 40th St ☎305/576-7242. The bar at this Design District restaurant is buzzy late at night: come to sit at the back-lit, pink Lucite counter or grab a chair in the open-air courtyard. Four-serving cocktail pitchers are a bargain option at $35 – try a Miamishine (Absolut, *crème de banane*, and orange juice). There's no velvet rope, so expect a mixed, hit-and-miss crowd.

Grass Lounge 28 NE 40th St ☎305/573-3355. This French-Polynesian restaurant in the Design District sports a large outdoor bar decked out as a designer tiki hut. It may be cooling as the hot spot *du jour*, but the crowd's still impressive and the door policy still brutal: dress up and look like you belong if you want to get past the bouncers, most of whom learned their door-barring trade at the similarly restrictive *Mynt*.

Magnum Lounge 709 NE 79th St Causeway ☎305/757-3368. This out-of-the-way Little Haiti restaurant-bar feels more like a bordello or a speakeasy, with its lush red banquettes and hidden entrance. The food's so-so, but the campy sing-alongs around the piano and stiff cocktails make it a fun detour for a drink or two.

The Pawn Shop Lounge 1222 NE 2nd Ave ☎305/373-3511, ⓦwww.thepawnshoplounge.com. Park West's *Pawn Shop Lounge* is a massive, converted pawn shop with an exterior unchanged since its seedier days and interior best described as Alice in Wonderland on acid. Inside, there's a whole school bus, its innards gutted and replaced with comfy banquettes; while boots and chandeliers dangle side by side from the ceiling, and a retro playlist heavy on 1980s classics throbs from the speakers.

Coral Gables

The Globe 377 Alhambra Circle ☎305/445-3555. On weekends, the bar at this popular restaurant is the place to be in Coral Gables, as it's invariably packed with a lively, twenty-something Cuban crowd; on Saturday, there's usually live jazz, too. Just don't go for a quiet drink or a date – it becomes a raucous pick-up joint by the end of the evening.

John Martin's 253 Miracle Mile ☎305/445-3777, ⓦwww.johnmartins.com. Run by two Irishmen, *John Martin's* is refreshingly authentic. In the restaurant section, the food includes potato soup and other hearty Irish staples; in the bar, it's all dark green drapes and wood paneling, where a wide mix of people down pints of Guinness in a relaxed atmosphere that seems a world away from tony Coral Gables.

Titanic Brewery 5813 Ponce de Leon Blvd ☎305/667-2537, ⓦwww.titanicbrewery.com. *The Titanic* brewpub offers its own terrific beers – try the Boiler Room brown ale or the amber known as Captain Smith's. They're served with deliciously greasy bar food, and often accompanied by live music. Since it's right next to the University of Miami, expect a youngish, mainstream vibe.

Coconut Grove

Kiss Café 2957 Florida Ave ☎305/461-4214. This funky retro lounge, decked out in modernist reds and whites, is a welcome addition to the rather mainstream nightlife in Coconut Grove. Drinks are moderately priced, and the crowd is a smooth mix of college kids and young professionals.

Monty's Raw Bar 2550 S Bayshore Drive ☎305/858-1431, ⓦwww.montystonecrab.com. Come to *Monty's* for the views: this outdoor tiki bar overlooks Biscayne Bay and offers stunning panoramas, especially at dusk. Drink prices are reasonable, and the vibe is more partying than posing – though when the house reggae band starts up it's often too loud to chat comfortably.
There's another branch is at 300 Alton Rd, South Beach ☎305/673-3444.

Oxygen Lounge 2911 Grand Ave ☎305/476-0202, ⓦwww.oxygenlounge.biz. Enormous lounge in the Streets of Mayfair shopping complex, where the futuristic decor helps makes up for its unprepossessing location – try to snag one of the comfy cubbyholes, where you can lounge on sofas as you sip.

Tavern in the Grove 3416 Main Hwy ☎305/447-3884. Down-to-earth locals' haunt with a bouncy jukebox and easygoing mood – TVs show the latest football game, and there's a popular dartboard. The real draw, however, is the rock-bottom drinks prices – beer is only $1.75/bottle every day until 8pm.

Key Biscayne and Virginia Key

Jimbo's Inside the park at Virginia Key Beach ☎305/361-7026. More like a junkyard with a place to drink attached than a real bar,

Hotel bars

You might normally associate **hotel bars** with middle-aged business travelers nursing a lonely Scotch, chatting wearily with the bartender. But in Miami, especially on South Beach, many of the funkiest spaces these days are inside hotels. We've listed a few suggestions below, but check *Street Miami* and the *New Times* for one-off events in other places like *Townhouse*, which often uses its glorious rooftop space for parties (see review, p.133).

DiLido Beach Club *Ritz-Carlton South Beach*, 1 Lincoln Rd, South Beach ☎786/276-4000. Dreamy beachfront club, with a large blue-tiled bar, day beds scattered through the gardens, and a small but tasty snack menu. Make sure to try the house special, a frozen mojito, but note that drinks are pricey even by South Beach standards ($14–15). Buzziest on a Sunday afternoon.

M-Bar *Mandarin Oriental Hotel*, 500 Brickell Key Drive ☎305/913-8288. This high-rise hotel bar boasts astonishing views across Biscayne Bay, as well as a martini list with more than 250 different options – try the Ruby Slipper, made from cranberry vodka & juice, gin, and sour mix. The snack menu is heavy on sushi and rolls.

The Rose Bar *Delano Hotel*, 1685 Collins Ave, South Beach ☎305/672-2000. Weave through the gauzy curtains draped around the Wonderland of a lobby, and head to the back of the main hall. On the right, you'll find the *Rose Bar*, spilling out into the walkway: snag one of the chunky bar stools if you can, and enjoy its seclusion – drinks are pricey, though.

Raleigh Bar *Raleigh Hotel*, 1775 Collins Ave, South Beach ☎305/534-6300. This beautifully restored wood-paneled bar is a chic, elegant place to grab a cocktail to a soundtrack of jazz and 1940s classics: try the bartender's namesake concoction Crispy's Pink Lady, made from Absolut citron, 7UP, cointreau, and cranberry juice. If you want a livelier time, come on Sundays, late in the afternoon, when legendary promoter Ingrid Casares hosts Soirée Sundays here.

The Spire Bar *The Hotel*, 801 Collins Ave, South Beach ☎305/531-2222. Brand-new rooftop bar, designed like *The Hotel* by fashion icon Todd Oldham. The overstuffed white couches are a muted touch, and there's zingy color everywhere else from bright red cushions to candy-striped floorboards. The small bar nestles in the shadow of the neon-lit sign: make sure to order the bartender's special, a champagne mojito ($13). Open Wed–Sun only.

Sky Bar *The Shore Club*, 1901 Collins Ave, South Beach ☎786/276-6771. Sprawling outdoor bar arranged around the hotel pool, with giant overstuffed square seats and a Moroccan theme thanks to desert-tent-like cabanas made from billowy gauze curtains. It's hottest on a Thursday night, but the velvet rope is restrictive, so dress to impress. Once inside, check out the smaller *Sand Bar* attached to it, with fine views of the beach and ocean.

The Tides Bar *Tides Hotel*, 1200 Ocean Drive, South Beach ☎305/604-5130. Inside the swanky restaurant at the *Tides Hotel*, you'll find a small bar with a few sleek stools. There's barely room for it to be busy, but it's a soothing stop-off after the elbow-rubbing crowds at most lounges, and the cocktails are tasty.

Jimbo's, on Virginia Key, is rundown, ramshackle, and renowned throughout Miami. Help yourself to a beer from a wheelbarrow full of ice and settle down on a broken plastic chair in the shade: a bit self-consciously stagey, but good fun nonetheless.

Rusty Pelican 3201 Rickenbacker Causeway ☎305/361-3818. The views from the terrace of Key Biscayne's *Rusty Pelican* are superb – an unbroken panorama of Downtown Miami's glittering skyscrapers. Buy a drink and settle back to watch one of Miami's sensational sunsets from the deck.

(12)

DRINKING | Key Biscayne and Virginia Key

Nightlife

F
or a city with a hard-partying image like Miami, it's surprising how few true nightclubs there are. Instead, most **nightlife venues** tend toward the hybrid bar-lounge-dancefloor, where you can choose whether to sip a cocktail, kick back, or dance – or, conveniently, all three. And although the whiplash from the velvet rope at some bars may be painful, most nightclub spaces are less snooty. That said, it's always worth looking sharp for an evening out in style-conscious Miami: doormen are very label-conscious and intolerant of anyone scruffy. As in any city, it's best to dress up, smile, and arrive in a well-mixed male-female group early in the evening.

Certainly, Miami's nightlife scene has sobered up slightly since its debauched and celebrity-studded heyday of the early Nineties, but there's still plenty of choice and – especially away from the beach – some intriguing options. Many of the major clubs (like *Space*) are located in **Park West**, a warehouse district just north of Downtown and the latest hot spot, though so far there's little to do here other than dance. Earlier in the evening, you're better off sticking to **South Beach** and one of the better bars for dancing, like *Rumi*. The playlist is now increasingly likely to lean heavily on hip-hop – house nights are growing less common, replaced with harder R&B and rap.

As for **live music**, the Miami scene is – unsurprisingly – strongest with regard to Latin clubs, and there are some good spots for salsa, merengue, and modern Latin fusion. The rock'n'roll scene is less exciting; there are a few rock-centric spots like *Churchill's Hideaway*, but otherwise, as a rule, don't expect world-class quality in the performers, and you'll have fun.

Clubs

Most clubs in Miami keep hours **from 10pm to 5am,** although thanks to less restrictive liquor licenses, many of the newer Downtown spaces are open even later than that – some even 24 hours a day. It's also worth going out during the week, as that's when the crowd will be most local, especially on South Beach. Generally, **cover charges** will be $15–20, although early in the evening they may be waived. Note also that many clubs in Miami are alcohol- and age-conscious, so you're likely to have problems if you're under 21: call individual venues to check. Finally, as parties and promoters change frequently, be sure to peruse the latest line-ups in the *New Times*, or call the phone numbers and check the websites in the reviews below.

Downtown and the Biscayne Corridor

Club NV 90 NE 11th St, Park West ☎305/373-2229. This determinedly after-hours spot boasts a 24-hour liquor license, so don't plan on getting here before 2am or so (the only reason to come early, frankly, is there's free admission if you do come early, though the admission's waived before 11pm). It's open Friday through Monday; sadly, *NV* hasn't managed to grab many nightlife headlines, and sits firmly in the shadow of *Club Space* – it's best known for the Saturday night gay party, Queen. Cover $15.

Club Space 34 NE 11th St ☎305/372-9378, ⓦwww.clubspace.com. Fri 10pm–Sat 10am, Sat 10pm–Sun 10am. This Downtown pioneer has moved to an even bigger warehouse space than its original spot a few blocks away, but thankfully it's retained the rough decor and illicit ambience with its acres of concrete and spartan bathrooms. Most people migrate here to its three levels of dancefloors when the other venues shut down; there's a lusher chill-out patio on the roof. $10.

Nocturnal 50 NE 11th St ☎305/576-6996, ⓦwww.nocturnalmiami.com. Park West's *Nocturnal* is as much about high tech as hard house: the rooftop terrace has a 360-degree IMAX-style screen where trippy images can be projected all night, while staff are equipped with wireless PDAs so they can not only summon a bottle to your table in around 5 minutes, but also send for your car via valet without a wait. As for the music space, it's the standard dark and cavernous dancefloor. $20.

South Beach

Amika Loft Lounge & Discotheque 1532 Washington Ave ☎305/534-1499, ⓦwww .amikamiami.com. Wed–Sun 9pm–5am. The owner here, a model-turned-promoter, created this space in a converted synagogue as a deliberate alternative to the nasty velvet ropes elsewhere on the beach – it's intended to cater to a dressy but mainstream crowd from the mainland. There's a small bar, clubby dancefloor, and a loft upstairs overlooking it all; the music, of course, is hip-hop and house. If you're feeling flush, splash out on a serving or two from the *Caviar Bar* ($25–75). $20.

B.E.D. 929 Washington Ave ☎305/532-9070, ⓦwww.bedmiami.com. Mon, Wed–Sat
11pm–5am. Primarily a restaurant (see p.142), this space – like many others in Miami – also doubles as a disco, especially on Wed and Thurs when there's a live DJ and a lively crowd. $20.

Club Deep 621 Washington Ave ☎305/532-1509, ⓦwww.clubdeep.com. Wed–Sun 10pm–5am. Satirized in the novel *Naked Came the Manatee* (see p.268, "Books"), *Club Deep* is a flashy space with exactly one selling point: its dancefloor stands on a 2000-gallon aquarium. Unfortunately, the hip-hop/R&B scene's as obvious as the tanks, so come for the spectacle more than anything. $15 and up.

Crobar 1445 Washington Ave ☎305/531-5027, ⓦwww.crobarmiami.com. Thurs–Mon 10pm–5am. There's no sign for this club, just a neon sign that reads "Cameo," the place's old name when it was an Art Deco movie theater. Although this *Crobar* isn't much compared to its venerated Chicago sibling, it's still the hardest-partying club on the beach. Expect young, frenetic dancers with a large gay and drag queen element, especially on Sundays for its new Glee Club – a rival to the long-term Anthem party that just defected to *Mansion* (see below). $15 and up.

Jimmy'z 432 41st St ☎305/604-9798. Tues–Sun 10pm–5am. *Jimmy'z* is best during the weekly parties on Wednesday nights, but even then it's not for ravers: the design here is sequinned 1980s, and the crowd is Eurotrash trustafarians. Good for kitsch glamour, but not the place to cut loose. No cover.

Mansion 1235 Washington Ave ☎305/532-1525, ⓦwww.mansionmiami.com. Tues, Thurs, Fri & Sat 11pm–5am. A sprawling nightclub complex, with six VIP areas, nine bars, and five different dancefloors, each usually showcasing a different style of music. What is new is the buzz around this place: it's now a fierce rival to *Crobar* for the title of hottest club on the beach especially for hip-hop on Tues night, and Sat, when an out-of-town B-list celeb is usually shipped in to "host" a party. It's also the new home to gay mega-party Anthem, which used to be staged at *Crobar*. $20 and up.

Mynt Ultra Lounge 1921 Collins Ave ☎786/276-6132, ⓦwww.myntlounge.com. Wed–Sat 11pm–5am. For the last few years, the lounge of the moment has been *Mynt*: remarkably in as fad-happy a city as Miami, it's held onto the title despite the opening of several young pretenders to its crown, like next door *Rok Bar* (see p.152). Deep green walls are washed in menthol green light, and delicate scent of mint supposedly wafts through the air vents; there's a 30-foot waterfall cascading through the main room and an enormous mosaic-tiled bar running the length of the room – a pity it's often so understaffed. *Mynt* is especially popular on Friday night when even the VIP room is packed; be prepared for a ferocious door policy. Up to $20.

Nikki Beach 1 Ocean Drive ☎305/538-1231, ⓦwww.nikkibeach.com. A restaurant in the Penrod's complex that was formerly frat central, *Nikki* isn't the hot spot it once was, but is still a laid-back place to drink and dance, its bar spilling onto the white-teepee-dotted private beach: take your drinks with you and watch the waves. The place is hottest on Sunday nights, the Indio Loco parties, when well-known local DJs are booked to spin. No cover.

Opium Garden 136 Collins Ave ☎305/531-5535, ⓦwww.opiummiami.com. Tues, Thurs–Sun 11pm–5am. A massive open-air complex with a vaguely Asian theme – Chinese lanterns and a smattering of golden Buddha statues – *Opium Garden* plays fierce, if populist, house. The central dancefloor is enormous and there are plenty of private booths scattered around when it's time to rest the toes. Not a classically clubby crowd, but everyone here knows how to dance. Up to $20.

Rumi 330 Lincoln Rd ☎305/672-4353, ⓦwww.rumimiami.com. Although it's no longer the number-one night spot in town, *Rumi* is still very chic. This restaurant-bar-dance-club features a geometric color scheme in ochre, rush, and eggshell, plus a small bar up front that spills over into the restaurant at the rear around 11pm, when tables are cleared for dancing. Saturday night's Latin house night is especially fun. No cover.

▽ Rumi nightclub

State 320 Lincoln Rd ☎786/621-5215, ⓦwww.statesouthbeach.com. Brand-new upscale club in the heart of Lincoln Road, *State* is huge, with dancefloors on three levels, but the vibe's lounge-like, thanks to the velvet couches, swinging chandeliers, and taffeta drapes. The best night to check out is Suite 320 on Saturdays, another celebrity-"hosted" party with a house/hip-hop soundtrack. $20.

Coconut Grove

Iguana Cantina 3390 Mary St ☎305/444-8081. Thurs & Sat 9pm–5am, Fri 5pm–5am. Both a bar and a club, the *Iguana* hosts a hard-partying, mainstream crowd. Don't come here for top-name DJs; instead, plan to drink plenty, sashay enthusiastically to Latin music, and grind with the flashy, up-for-anything people on the dancefloor. Not for wallflowers or club snobs. No cover.

Oxygen Lounge Basement of the Streets of Mayfair, 2911 Grand Ave ☎305/476-0202, ⓦwww.oxygenlounge.biz. Daily 6pm–5am. Enormous lounge-restaurant-club in an unprepossessing setting, with futuristic decor and funky staff uniforms, as well as an onsite waterfall. Although there's a live DJ every night, it's clubbiest on weekends with a house night on Friday and a Middle East-ern fusion DJ on Saturdays. The crowd's dressy and a little self-conscious. $10.

Live music

Unlike the club scene, which focuses on South Beach and the after-hours strip Downtown, **live music venues** are scattered throughout the city: *Club Mystique*, for example, one of the top salsa spots, is way out by the airport, while the indie rock club *Churchill's* is hidden away in Little Haiti.

Cover charges vary widely – up to $20 or more for bigger names, while local pub bands will run you around $5. Call the numbers or visit the websites we've listed below for up-to-date schedules, or check with the *New Times*.

Latin, Caribbean, and reggae

Bayside Hut 3501 Rickenbacker Causeway, Virginia Key ☎305/361-0808. Daily 11am–11pm. A rundown restaurant that's worth heading out to on weekends, when there's live music with a minimal cover: no big names, but groovy enough. The views of Biscayne Bay are great, too. $10–20 cover.

Café Mystique 7250 NW 11th St, Downtown Miami ☎305/262-9500. Thurs, Sat, Sun 9pm–4am, Fri 5pm–4am. Don't be put off by *Café Mystique's* out-of-the-way location – this is one of the premier salsa clubs in the city. And don't worry if you're a beginner: there are free dancing lessons offered on Thursday, given by in-house teachers. Friday and Saturday nights are reserved for big-name performers, but it's busy (and friendly) most every night. $10.

Casa Panza 1620 Calle Ocho, Little Havana ☎305/643-5343. Mon, Wed 11am–11pm, Tues, Thurs–Sun 11am–1.30am. A yuppiefied restaurant with a large dancefloor attached, *Casa Panza* is liveliest on Tuesdays and Thursdays when there are flamenco shows and a live guitarist. Otherwise, it's open to diners and drinkers every night for salsa and merengue; however, weekends are low-key. No cover.

Club Típico Dominicano 1344 NW 36th St, Little Havana ☎305/634-7819. Fri–Sun 11pm–5am. This restaurant transforms into a salsa and merengue club at the weekends; don't be put off by the low cover – the music's authentic and the crowd enthusiastic. $5.

Club Tropigala Inside the Fontainebleau Hilton, 4441 Collins Ave, Miami Beach ☎305/538-2000, ⊛www.clubtropigala.com. Shows Tues, Wed, Thurs & Sun 8.30pm, Fri & Sat 8pm. This superb supper club is Vegas by way of Latin America, featuring live acts and an orchestra in the grand setting of the MiMo masterpiece the *Fontainebleau Hotel*. Dress to the nines and salsa the night away with a friendly, diverse crowd, amid fabulously camp decor; Sunday brunch is also a lavish spectacle. $10–25.

Hoy Como Ayer 2212 Calle Ocho, Little Havana ☎305/541-2631. Wed–Sun 9pm–4am. This classic lounge, once home to old-fashioned live shows, now features Cuban fusion music, with old-time performers jamming alongside second-generation expats – it's one of the most adventurous and musically inventive venues in the city. Note that *Hoy*

Como Ayer's signature long-term party, Thursday night's ¡Fuácata!, has defected to *i/o lounge* (see below). $10–20.

Mango's 900 Ocean Drive, South Beach ☎305/673-4422, ⊛www.mangoscafe.com. Daily 11am–5am. Shamelessly tacky and gloriously over-the-top, *Mango's* offers nightly live pop music and dance shows by the waiters: the blaring music spills out onto the sidewalk – and so does the crowd. Cheesy, but fun, especially on weeknights when the crowd's a little more local. Free–$20.

One Ninety 190 NE 46th St, Design District ☎305/576-9779. Tues–Sat 6pm–midnight or later. This boho café serves fusion food and terrific brunches but is also known for its eclectic live music programming. Tues welcomes rock bands, Wed *bossa nova*, Thurs live tango; the best two nights, though, are Fri for jazz and the Sat *rumba cubana* party. Chef-owner Alan Hughes, himself a rock guitarist, sometimes takes to the stage. Free–$5.

Tap Tap 819 5th St, South Beach ☎305/672-2898. Sun–Thurs 5–11pm, Fri & Sat 5pm–1am. Best known for its excellent restaurant (see "Restaurants" p.145), gallery of brightly colored native art, and regular live Haitian music, usually without a cover – phone ahead for details.

Rock, R&B, and jazz

Churchill's Hideaway 5501 NE 2nd Ave, Little Haiti ☎305/757-1807, ⊛www.churchillspub.com. Daily 11am–5am. Unmissable, if inconveniently located, local rock venue that's nurtured emerging and local talent for twenty years: both Marilyn Manson and the Mavericks played here in their early days. While the bill is sometimes hit-or-miss, it's still an authentic glimpse at Miami's underground music scene; Monday open-mic night for jazz and rock bands is usually a highlight. $3–15.

i/o lounge 30 NE 14th St, Park West ☎305/358-8007, ⊛www.iolounge.com. Hot new club/live venue hybrid, known for playing more than just Miami's staple selection of R&B/hip-hop: expect indie rock, punk-pop, or drum'n'bass instead. There's a large bar with cheap drinks and an outdoor garden-chill room; the main space features live bands every night at 11pm – the best day to come is Thursday, for the ¡Fuácata! Party featuring DJ Le Spam and his AllStars, who jam along while spinning traditional Cuban music at 11.30pm and 1am. $3–20.

Jazid 1432 Washington Ave, South Beach ☎305/673-9372, ⓦwww.jazid.net. Daily 9pm–3am. The only R&B and jazz venue at the heart of club-obsessed South Beach. A welcome alternative, if only it had a little more edge. Granted, there's nightly music in both the jazzy downstairs space and upstairs in the sleek, modern section, but both decor and music are bland and tooth-less – in other words, *Jazid's* won't please jazz fanatics. $10.

John Martin's 253 Miracle Mile, Coral Gables ☎305/445-3777 ⓦwww.johnmartins.com. Mon–Sat 11.30am–1am, Sun 11.30am–11pm. This expat-run Irish pub (see review, p.154) hosts regular live music – often Irish folk – that's surprisingly enjoyable and high-quality for a pub space. No cover charge.

Luna Star Café 775 NE 125th St, North Miami ☎305/892-8522, ⓦmembers.aol.com/luna13star/. Closed Sun & Mon. There's an open-mic night on Saturday, poetry read-ings during the week, and occasional folk concerts at this largely vegetarian café. Phone before you go as it has erratic open-ing hours. No cover.

Scully's Tavern 9809 Sunset Drive, South Miami ☎305/271-7404, ⓦwww.scullystavern.net. Mon–Thurs 11am–1am, Fri & Sat 11am–3am, Sun 12pm–1am. *Scully's*, an unremarkable sports bar in South Miami, hosts local rock bands at 10pm every Friday and Saturday

night without a cover – decent, although *Churchill's Hideaway* (see p.153) is more worth the pilgrimage.

Studio Nightclub Inside the Shelborne Hotel, 1801 Collins Ave ☎305/695-1770, ⓦhometown.aol.com/louiestudio/Karaoke. Daily 10am–5am. Fantastically kitschy relief from the chic clubs elsewhere on the beach, this karaoke venue boasts more than 22,000 songs; on Sundays there's even a film crew on hand so you can make an impromptu music video. The best time to stop by is early in the morning, when the drunken singers are at their most boisterous. No cover.

Tobacco Road 626 S Miami Ave, Downtown ☎305/374-1198, ⓦwww.tobacco-road.com. Mon–Sat 11.30am–5am. This gritty, rather shabby Downtown bar features two stages, where nightly live acts perform. The tunes are mostly blues and R&B, and the place occasionally snags biggish names – so check listings for upcoming performances. On a regular night, the cover's around $7.

Van Dyke Café 846 Lincoln Rd, South Beach ☎305/534-3600, ⓦwww.thevandyke.com/jazz. Sun–Thurs 8am–12am, Fri & Sat 8am–2am. Aside from the main restaurant, there's an upstairs jazz lounge with a full bar and high-quality performances seven days a week – and don't come to chat, as enthusiasts will quieten you down if you disrupt the music. Owned by the same team as the *News Café* (see p.138), it serves a similar menu. $5–10.

Performing arts and film

M iami's **performing arts** scene is in transition. While one local theater company, the New Theatre, snags a Pulitzer Prize for a premiere, several of the city's other long-term lynchpins, from arthouse cinemas like the Mercury Theater to classical favorite the Florida Philharmonic (based in Fort Lauderdale), can disappear. The Philharmonic's an especially egregious loss, as it often performed less-well-known classical works alongside crowd-pleasing staples – perhaps one reason its finances were no longer viable.

The brightest hope comes in the form of the long-delayed **Performing Arts Center**, Cesar Pelli's sprawling temple to the arts, which will snatch several of the highest-profile local companies from their current venues and bring them together under one roof: the Florida Grand Opera, Miami City Ballet, New World Symphony, and Concert Association of Florida. It's currently set to open in late 2006; check with the various venues concerned for updates (for more on the Performing Arts Center, see p.88, "North along the Biscayne Corridor"). Locals expect this multi-million-dollar investment to turbocharge interest in the arts here and likely seed several new, smaller companies around town.

In the meantime, arguably the strongest scene is in **film**: there are plenty of alternative theaters dotted around, like the Miami Beach Cinemathèque, as well as a thriving Spanish-language circuit, plus megaplexes shilling the requisite Hollywood blockbusters. There are also annual events like the Miami Gay and Lesbian Film Festival (see p.191, "Festivals and events").

A close second is **dance**, thanks mostly to the nationally known Miami City Ballet; fringe Latin American troupes help add interest. **Classical music and opera** offerings, on the other hand, are average, although the New World Symphony in South Beach often delights with the quality of its performances.

As for **theater**, most productions are rather mainstream: the Broadway series at the Gleason Theater is usually showy and fun, while the New Theatre and Actors' Playhouse are both reliable. There isn't much call for, or interest in, avant-garde or experimental work: the best option there is Miami Light Project. Of them all, **comedy** and other **spoken word** performances are the city's weakest link: there are few venues, and the existing companies are hit-and-miss at best.

Getting tickets

For **tickets** to most performing arts shows, contact the ubiquitous Ticketmaster (☎305/358-5885, ⊕www.ticketmaster.com) or the venues directly – you're unlikely to have problems finding tickets for anything other than one of the pre-Broadway out-of-town tryouts that occasionally surface at the Actors' Playhouse (see below). Pick up the *Miami Herald*'s Friday edition for details of the following week's concerts or the essential freesheet *New Times*. Check these listings, too, for sporadic performances at other venues, like the Barnacle in Coconut Grove (see p.116), which hosts magical monthly moonlit concerts on its bayfront lawn.

Theater

Actors' Playhouse 280 Miracle Mile, Coral Gables ☎305/444-9293, ⊕www.actorsplayhouse.org. Built as a movie theater, this building has been extensively restored and now offers three performance spaces: a large auditorium with space for 600 downstairs, a smaller, 300-seat theater upstairs and a 100-person capacity black raw space on the third floor for experimental work. Many Broadway productions stop off here, and there's an in-house children's theater workshop that performs regularly.

African Heritage Cultural Arts Center 6161 NW 22nd Ave, Liberty City ☎305/638-6771. This community center offers classes in ethnic dance, drama, and art, and features sporadic performances – often community productions – in its Wendell A. Narasse Theater, a tiny black box venue with only 200 seats.

Coconut Grove Playhouse 3500 Main Hwy, Coconut Grove ☎305/442-4000, ⊕www .cgplayhouse.com. The Coconut Grove Playhouse made its name with the 1956 US premiere of Samuel Beckett's *Waiting for Godot*: unfortunately, since then its productions have grown safer, more commercial, and less exciting – little wonder, as there are more than 1000 seats to fill each night. This is the place to come for broad farce and gentle drama – nothing too taxing, and plenty of Neil Simon.

Colony Theater 1040 Lincoln Rd, South Beach ☎305/674-1040. Originally a moviehouse, this rehabbed Deco building was converted to a theater with a 500-seat auditorium. Programming is a mixed bag of famous comedians, dance concerts, and performances by local theater groups; it's also usually home to the Miami Gay & Lesbian Film Festival each spring (see p.191,

"Festivals," for info), though at time of writing, the Colony's under another renovation, set to end sometime in 2005, and the festival will take up temporary home across other venues in the city. The Colony's massive program promises not only to upgrade its technical facilities for performers, but also restore the original facade and lobby design.

GableStage Biltmore, 1200 Anastasia Ave, Coral Gables ☎305/445-1119, ⊕www.gablestage.org. Formerly known as the Florida Shakespeare Theater, this company has found a permanent home in the *Biltmore*, having shuttled around Coral Gables for almost fifteen years – though the hotel's said to be manoeuvering to wrest the space back, so call to check before stopping by. Artistic director Joe Adler is a local legend, who produces accessible, exciting shows. Performances take place Thursday–Sunday, and the season usually includes classic plays alongside Florida premieres of Off-Broadway hits.

Jackie Gleason Theater 1700 Washington Ave, South Beach ☎305/673-7300, ⊕www .gleasontheater.com. Its size and beachside location lead most people to presume the Jackie Gleason Theater will play host to aging Vegas lounge acts. On the contrary, at least until late 2006, it's home to the high-profile "Broadway in Miami Beach" program, where shows stop off during national tours on their way to New York City. At that time, the Broadway series will defect to the Performing Arts Center Downtown – no word yet on how the Gleason plans to replace its marquee attraction.

The Lyric Theater 819 NW 2nd Ave, Overtown ☎305/358-1146. Now owned and run by the Black Archives, this Overtown landmark is undergoing a massive renovation at time of writing (see p.56) with hopes to open it around the same time as the Performing Arts Center: call the number listed for

PERFORMING ARTS AND FILM | Theater

updates. Programming at the 400-seat auditorium here will focus on African-American acts – whether jazz, gospel, or theater – both national and from Miami.

Miami Light Project 3000 Biscayne Blvd, Biscayne Corridor ☎ 305/576-4350, ⓦ www.miamilightproject.com. Miami Light Project (MLP) is an umbrella organization that brings avant-garde theater, music, and dance to various city venues, including the Gusman Center Downtown (see p.49). Expect banner performers like Laurie Anderson and Kenny Muhammad, as well as less-well-known hip-hop groups or performance troupes. February's Here & Now festival, hosted onsite at MLP's own Light Box theater, is a showcase for new works from local performers.

The New Theatre 4120 Laguna St, Coral Gables ☎ 305/443-5909, ⓦ www.new-theatre.org. This 100-seat theater is an artsy gem that provides high-quality, adventurous theater: it's dedicated to putting on edgy productions, whether by well-known dramatists like Tony Kushner, of *Angels in America* fame, or by new, local playwrights – the Pulitzer Prize–winning *Anna in the Tropics* was commissioned here.

Classical music and opera

Coral Gables Congregational Church 3010 DeSoto Blvd, Coral Gables ☎ 305/448-7421, ⓦ www.coralgablescongregational.org. Built in the Mediterranean Revival style, this church has a dark interior with fine acoustics, perfect for classical music performances from local groups.

Florida Grand Opera 1200 Coral Way, Little Havana; info ☎ 305/854-1643, tickets ☎ 1-800/741-1010, ⓦ www.fgo.org. This company produces five operas each year; at time of writing, performances shuttle between the Broward Performing Arts Center in Fort Lauderdale and the Miami-Dade County Auditorium, 2901 W Flagler St, Little Havana. In late 2006, though, FGO will move into a specially constructed space at the new Performing Arts Center as its Miami base. English translations are projected above the stage during the performance.

Lincoln Theater 541 Lincoln Rd, South Beach ☎ 305/673-3330, ⓦ www.nws.org. One of the best venues in the city, Lincoln Theater is the current home base for the New World Symphony, composed of graduate students from across the country who endure rigorous auditions to secure a place on the Symphony's three-year fellowship program. It's a training ground for future orchestral superstars, and the quality of the performances is superb. Ticket prices vary, but can be as low as $12. Note that the New World will be moving to the Performing Arts Center Downtown in late 2006; no information's yet available on how the Lincoln Theater will replace it.

Miami Chamber Symphony Orchestra Gusman Concert Hall, University of Miami, Coral Gables ☎ 305/799-8856. A small, local organization that's reduced its season after the loss of many of the performers it once shared with the defunct Florida Philharmonic; it now only plays from June to September. The orchestra is best known for its unusual performance selections. Call for details of upcoming concerts; tickets cost $12–30.

Olympia Theater Gusman Center, 174 E Flagler St, Downtown ☎ 305/374-2444, ⓦ www.gusmancenter.org. This kitschy performance space (see p.49, "Downtown Miami") – arguably one of the best venues in the city – is home to a highbrow but eclectic program: there's classical music, dance, and offbeat touring productions, though it's suffering slightly after the loss of the Florida Philharmonic as its home company. The Olympia isn't all earnest worthiness, though – one of its biggest hits was a season of *Sing-A-Long Sound of Music*.

Dance

Maximum Dance Company 9220 SW 158 Lane, Downtown ☎ 305/259-9775, ⓦ www.maximumdancecompany.com. For first-class contemporary dance, there's no better local option than the Maximum with the Gusman Center as its home venue. Expect a varied program with mostly world premiere dances choreographed to the music of Stravinsky or the Brubeck Quartet. The quality's consistently high, and ticket prices start at only $25.

Miami City Ballet 2200 Liberty Ave, South Beach ☎ 305/929-7010, ⓦ www.miamicityballet.org. Currently, the Miami City Ballet performs at the Jackie Gleason Theater (see opposite) roughly once every two months: at other times, though, you can stop by to watch rehearsals at its studio here, specially designed so that passersby can watch dancers at practice. In late 2006, though, the ballet will pirouette across the water to the new Downtown Performing Arts Center, which will become its permanent home. Wherever its performances, Miami City Ballet is among the largest regional companies in the country and the quality of performances is consistently exceptional.

Miami Hispanic Ballet 900 SW 1st St, Downtown ☎305/549-7711, ⓦwww.miamihispanicballet .com. MHB is best known for producing the International Ballet Festival every September at venues across the city like the Gleason and Tower theaters; companies are brought in from across the world to perform here under artistic director Pedro Pablo Peña. He also produces classical and contemporary productions throughout the year – check the website for schedules.

Momentum Dance Company Mirador Apart-ments, 1200 West Ave, South Beach ☎305/858-7002, ⓦwww.momentumdance.com. This troupe performs around the city throughout the year at various festivals and events; its repertoire is all kinds of contemporary dance, with special emphasis on produc-tions for children. Momentum is also the driving force behind the Beach Dance Festi-val each April; most of the performances are at the Byron Carlyle Theater, 500 71st St, North Beach. This troupe's offices are in Coconut Grove, but its rehearsal space is on a quiet residential strip in South Beach – and aspiring Pavlovas of all ages can take a class there for only $12, ranging from ballet to modern dance or even pilates.

Film

AMC CocoWalk 16 3015 Grand Ave, Coconut Grove ☎305/448-7075 AMC Sunset Place 24 5701 Sunset Drive, South Miami ☎305/466-0450. Two of the many mall-based mega-plexes in the city, these are both reasonably close to central Miami. Both have the usual stadium seating and booming speakers to go along with all the latest releases.

Bill Cosford Cinema University of Miami Memo-rial Building, University of Miami campus, Coral Gables ☎305/284-4861. Named after the long-time film critic at the *Miami Herald*, this is an artsy, surprisingly plush cinema that specializes in foreign-language and indie films. The program is set by University of Miami professors, so expect an academic slant to its schedule.

Miami Beach Cinematheque 512 Española Way, South Beach ☎305/673-4567, ⓦwww .mbcinema.com. Tucked away on the west-ern end of Española Way, this fifty-seat rep house is home to the Miami Beach Film Society. The regular fare of movies is impressive, taking in arthouse classics or newbies as well as low-profile, high-quality documentaries.

Regal South Beach 18 1100 Lincoln Rd, South Beach ☎305/673-6766. Massive multiplex on South Beach showing the usual range of Hollywood blockbusters; it was hugely controversial when constructed as several old buildings were demolished to make way for this gleaming (and rather garish) new structure. It's well located for the nearby municipal parking at 17th Street.

Teatro Avante 744 SW 8th St, Little Havana ☎305/445-8877, ⓦwww.teatroavante.com. This Spanish-language theater company, turfed out of its long-term home by a greedy landlord, has landed new digs nearby which, at time of writing, it was intending to turn into a performance space for Spanish-language plays with English supertitles as before. Either way, it will still oversee and produce the International Hispanic Theater Festival each June (see p.192), with performances at various venues around town – check the website or call for schedules.

Tower Theater 1508 SW 8th St, Little Havana ☎305/643-6091, ⓦwww.mdc.edu/iac /towertheater/. A landmark Deco building, this cinema was purchased by the city of Miami to show Hollywood movies with Spanish subtitles as a cultural service to Little Havana. Now, run by Miami-Dade College, it is only sporadically open; when it is, expect Spanish-language films.

Comedy

The Improv Comedy Club Streets of Mayfair 3rd level, Coconut Grove ☎305/441-8200, ⓦwww.miamiimprov.com. Miami branch of a nationwide supper/comedy club: the food's mediocre, but the talent is not. One of the few places to see quality, big-name comics like David Allen Grier in the city.

Just The Funny Miami Museum of Science, 3280 South Miami Ave, Coconut Grove ☎305/693-8669, ⓦwww.justthefunny.com. This is one of the few comedy improv troupes in town and has shuttled from venue to venue over the years;

its current home is the Museum of Science where there are two shows every Fri & Sat ($10 for 9pm show; $5 for 11pm show).

Spoken word venues

Churchill's Hideaway 5501 NE 2nd Ave, Little Haiti ☎305/757-1807, ⓦwww.churchillspub .com. Daily 11am–5am. Renowned for supporting breakout local bands, *Churchill's* is now also a place to catch spoken word performances – the program's the most varied of all venues, mixing everything from story slam-style long-form rants to hip-hop-inspired rhymes.

Funk Jazz Lounge At Jade Lounge, 1766 Bay Rd, South Beach ☎305/695-0000, ⓦwww .jadesobe.com. This is the only regular

spoken event within walking distance of South Beach. Every Thursday, poets perform in the overstuffed couch-crammed art gallery/lounge space upstairs at this bar. Get there early – around 7.30pm or so – to try to snag a spot on the comfy four-poster bed.

Literary Café 12325 NE 6th Ave, North Miami ☎786/234-7638. Opened by a poetry-loving ex-con a few years ago, this offbeat spoken word venue is modelled directly after New York's legendary *Nuyorican Poets Café*: it's intended as a community gathering spot where local freestyle poets like the Lip, Tongue & Ear collective can perform throughout the week alongside aspiring newcomers on open-mic nights.

(14)

PERFORMING ARTS AND FILM | Spoken word venues

15

Gay Miami

For over two decades now, Miami has been viewed as one of the top **gay destinations** in the country, with the scene focused squarely on **South Beach**. It doesn't quite live up to the hype: while there's a definite gay-friendly vibe in the city, and the beach is still the epicenter of gay life in Miami, things have slowed since the frantic, musclebound party atmosphere of the early 1990s. Recently, a spate of closings – including the transformation of warehouse-like circuit-boy mecca *Salvation* into an Office Depot – has seriously reduced the hedonism of nightlife here, while gay community associations, like the South Beach Business Guild or the Dade Human Rights Foundation, have also closed because of dwindling funding.

Much as in Key West – whose anything-goes gay vibe is gradually vanishing (see p.249) – the shift owes itself to the increasing numbers of straight tourists filling hotel rooms here. Though Miami Beach has been popular with trendy straight travelers for more than fifteen years, the city's aggressive marketing campaign to attract beach-seeking families in the late 1990s helped change the tourist profile here and push many gay locals to the mainland, notably the **Morningside District near 79th street along Biscayne Corridor**, and Fort Lauderdale. In both places, they're again snapping up the cheap historic property that was once abundant here. It's still true that during the mammoth **White Party** each November, gay life wholly subsumes straight life in the city, but for the rest of the year – and certainly away from the beach – there's a limited number of clubs and bars for such a mythic gay hot spot.

Information and resources

There are plenty of free **newspapers and magazines** that illuminate what's going on in the gay and lesbian scene around Miami. For events around town, the standard resource is *TWN* (Ⓦ www.twnonline.org), a well-known, newsy freesheet. The glossy *Hot Spots* (Ⓦ www.hotspotsmagazine.com) and *Outlook* (Ⓦ www.outlook.com) cover the whole of Florida, with a heavy focus on the party scene; a local counterpart is the freesheet *The Wire*, which spotlights South Beach almost exclusively. *The Express* (Ⓦ www.expressgaynews.com) is geared to gay tourists and residents across the whole of South Florida, while the large-format glossy women-oriented *She* (Ⓦ www.shemag.com) spotlights the lesbian scene in the Sunshine State.

Lastly, the *Miami Herald* is unusual in having a reporter assigned to cover gay and lesbian issues – but if you really want to find smart coverage of gay news and politics in Miami, visit Ⓦ www.outinmiami.com online.

The Winter Party Early March

A huge week-long event, the Winter Party is the springtime counterpart to November's White Party, with special nights at most major South Beach venues. The festivities climax with an outdoor club on the beach at 14th St and Ocean Drive. ☎305/572-1924, ⓦwww.winterparty.com.

Pride South Florida March

Pitifully, Miami's Pride celebrations collapsed a couple of years ago, so you'll need to head up the coast (as many locals already have) to celebrate Pride South Florida in Fort Lauderdale, which is larger and livelier. ☎954/561-2020, ⓦwww.pridesouthflorida.org.

Miami Gay and Lesbian Film Festival Late April

The Colony Theater in South Beach features two weeks of gay-themed film programming, a mixture of amateur and professional movies, in both documentary and drama genres. ☎305/534-9924, ⓦwww.mglff.com.

Aqua Girl Mid-May

One of the few women-oriented events in the city, this four-day party of cocktails and clubbing – essentially, the first circuit party targeted at girls – raises money for the Women's Community Fund, an NFP that supports lesbian rights. ☎305/532-1997, ⓦwww.aquagirl.org.

The White Party Thanksgiving

The godfather of all circuit parties, this is a week when what few clothes people wear must be white, and takes in hotels and bars across South Beach. Don't miss the debauched, surreal White Party itself when the neo-Italian Villa Vizcaya (see p.120) is transformed into gay Miami's fabulous answer to the Venice Carnival, all to raise funds for local HIV-related charities. ⓦwhiteparty.net.

For any other questions, contact the **Miami–Dade Gay & Lesbian Chamber of Commerce** at ☎305/534-3336 or ⓦwww.gogaymiami.com.

Accommodation

There's plenty of **accommodation** in Miami specifically geared to gay and lesbian travelers, especially on South Beach. You'll also find that most mainstream hotels are gay-friendly: those listed below are especially so.

Gay accommodation

European Guesthouse 721 Michigan Ave, South Beach ☎305/673-6665, ⓦwww.europeanguesthouse.com. This secluded, 12-room clothing-optional B&B is rather out of the way on the western side of the beach. The rooms are eclectically furnished but comfortable. Amenities include an outdoor hot tub, leafy pool, buffet breakfast, and even a massive flat-screen TV. Note that it's very male-dominated and women may prefer to stay elsewhere. Shared bath from $89, private bath from $119.

The Island House 1428 Collins Ave, South Beach ☎305/534-0547 or 1-800/382-2422, ⓦwww.islandhousesouthbeach.com. Nothing special, the *Island House* is notable only as one of the larger gay guesthouses in the area. Rooms are standard, if a little shabby, but its rates are excellent and it's a good option, especially in high season. Shared bath from $59, private bath from $99.

Jefferson House 1018 Jefferson Ave, South Beach ☎305/534-5247 or 1-877/599-5247, ⓦwww.thejeffersonhouse.com. The nine rooms in this historic Art Deco house are tastefully decorated with a motley assortment of antiques, a raft of homoerotic art, and in-room facilities even stretch to VCRs. Every evening, there's a free cocktail hour. There's a two-night minimum in season, and a five-night minimum during White Party week; it's not clothing optional, but skinny-dipping's allowed in the pool at night. Shared bath from $139, private bath from $159.

Normandy South 575 NE 66th St, Biscayne Corridor ☎305/756 9894, ⊕www .normandysouth.com Three-building clothing-optional complex stashed away on Biscayne Corridor's historic and gay-friendly Upper East Side aimed at an older, less party-centric crowd. There's a pool and Jacuzzi, and the rooms range from budget shared-bath bunkbeds to apartments with kitchenettes. Shared bath from $75, private bath from $150.

Gay-friendly accommodation

Doubletree Surfcomber 1717 Collins Ave, South Beach ☎305/532-7715 or 1-800/222-TREE, ⊕www.surfcomber.com. The hotel is an active supporter of the White and Winter parties, so book well ahead if you want to stay here then; for more, see review on p.131. Rooms start at $245.

Grove Inn Country Guesthouse 22540 SW Krome Ave, Homestead ☎305/247-6572 or 1-877/247-6572, ⊕www.groveinn.com. Gay-owned and -operated, this is a charming guesthouse that makes a welcome – if inconveniently located – alternative to the South Beach scene. That said, it's a good base for many of the city's outer district attractions, though there's little nightlife nearby. Rates from $75.

Hotel Ocean 1230 Ocean Drive, South Beach ☎305/672-2579, ⊕www.hotelocean.com. Rooms in this French-owned hotel are offbeat, charming, and feature tiled floors, mismatched antique furniture, and light switches that only operate when you insert a room key; breakfast is included in the rates. Its location opposite the primarily gay 12th Street Beach section makes it a convenient choice, although it's a little overpriced for the amenities it offers. Rates start at $225.

The Shelborne 1801 Collins Ave, South Beach ☎305/531-1271 or 1-800/327-8757, ⊕www .shelbourne.com. Site of the early Miss Universe pageants, for some reason, this mainstream hotel's now popular with queens of a different type: there are a few nods to gay travelers (gay porn on the hotel pay-per-view channels, for instance) but the rooms themselves are unremarkable. $235 and up.

Bars and clubs

Inevitably, most of the gay bars and clubs can be found in **South Beach**, although, as the local gay population's migrated to gentrify the shabby but historic **Biscayne Corridor**, a new raft of night spots has opened up to cater to it nearby.

BLVD 7770 Biscayne Blvd, Biscayne Corridor ☎305/756-7770, ⊕www.boulevardnightclub .com. Brand new chest-shaven-and-shirtless circuit megaplex, with a massive dance-floor that's a mainland replacement for the now-shuttered *Salvation*. It's open all night Fridays and Saturdays – expect big-name DJs to stop by regularly. There's also a café (serving from 10am daily) and a small movie theater showing movies with gay appeal. $20.

Club Boi 726 NW 79th St, Little Haiti ☎305/836-8995, ⊕www.clubboi.com. A refreshing change from the circuit-boy scene on South Beach, this largely black club plays Hi-NRG hip-hop, house, and old-school R&B every Tuesday, Friday, and Saturday night. $5–12.

Club NV 90 NE 11th St, Park West ☎305/373-2229. An after-hours spot on the mainland with a 24-hour liquor license that's only open Friday through Monday; the crowd's mixed most nights, but is full of the local circuit boys who once partied at *Salvation* on Saturdays for the Queen party. $15.

Crobar 1445 Washington Ave, South Beach ☎305/531-5027, ⊕www.crobarmiami.com. This satellite branch of the legendary Chicago club is housed in the old Cameo Theater: the decor is industrial-theatrical, and the sound system is arguably the best in town. The crowd's varied, but youngish, with plenty of drag queens. The long-time Sunday party Anthem has been replaced by a new night known as Glee Club; Monday's also gay-friendly with its Backdoor Bambi night. $15 and up.

House 2041 Biscayne Blvd, Biscayne Corridor ☎305/438-0662, ⊛www.housemiami.us. The former *Cactus* has been spiffed up and reopened as the mixed gay/straight *House*: it boasts two dancefloors as well as a billiard room, pool, and outdoor garden. The most popular gay event at the club is the revived Church party – it starts every Sunday at 5am.

Jade Lounge 1766 Bay Rd, South Beach ☎305/695-0000, ⊛www.jadesobe.com. Vaguely Buddhist-themed mixed neighborhood bar/club with a smallish dancefloor and plenty of comfy couches for lounging. Fridays are a rotating gay party, while on Saturdays it's the site of one of the rare lesbian-targeted events in the city. $15.

Laundry Bar 721 Lincoln Lane, South Beach ☎305/672-7569. Stylish, glass-fronted laundromat-bar, where you can sip a beer while your bedlinens dry. The clientele here is young and pretty, and it's one of the few places that has a good mix of girls and boys.

Magnum Lounge 709 NE 79th St Causeway, Little Haiti ☎305/757-3368. Not strictly a gay bar, but this campy restaurant-lounge is popular with gay locals, mostly for its sing-alongs around the piano. The crowd's a little older than on the beach, but very friendly and low-key.

Mansion 1235 Washington Ave, South Beach ☎305/532-1525, ⊛www.mansionmiami.com. Formerly *Level*, this massive nightclub complex managed to steal away *Crobar*'s signature party, Sunday's gay mecca, Anthem, run by uberpromoter Michael Tronn ($20; ⊛www.anthemsundays.com).

Martini Tuesdays Gay promoter Edison Farrow runs this roaming party, which shuttles between different venues each Tuesday, 9pm–1am, and has a permanent home on Sundays at the *Delano* hotel from 6–10pm. The crowd's youngish and friendly, making most of the parties great fun. Call ☎305/535-6696 or check ⊛www .sobesocialclub.com for up-to-date listings. He also hosts similar events throughout the

week, including the Surreal Sundays party at the *Delano* – check the freesheets for venues.

O'Zone 6620 SW 57th Ave (Red Road), South Miami ☎305/667-2888. A huge suburban club with a sunken dancefloor and a predominantly Latin muscle-boy crowd, *O'Zone* is grooviest at the weekends when there's salsa and house music, as well as drag shows. Cover varies from $5 to $15.

The Palace 1200 Ocean Drive, South Beach. ☎305/531-7234. This restaurant and bar opposite the gay beach is more welcoming than most on the South Beach circuit, with a diverse clientele – old and young, buff and less so. The food's so-so but the circular bar that looks out onto the sidewalk's a pleasant place for a martini or two – look for the $4 drinks specials.

Score 727 Lincoln Rd, South Beach ☎305/535-1111, ⊛www.scorebar.net. Local video bar, with the usual amenities like a pool table and patio, plus a martini lounge. Open from 1pm, it's a good place to get an afternoon coffee and sit outside to watch the Lincoln Road runway. Wednesday night features an amateur strip contest. The owners have recently invested heavily in amenities, and now book big-name DJs every weekend to lure a livelier crowd. No cover.

Stallions 841 Washington Ave, South Beach ☎305/673-0GAY, ⊛www.stallionsmiami .com. This circuit club has taken over the after-hours space which once housed the Hi-NRG and go-go dancer-fueled *Pump*; expect much the same from *Stallions* as well as kitschy touches thanks to its weekly themes, like circus weekends featuring jugglers and clowns. Free–$10.

Twist 1057 Washington Ave, South Beach ☎305/538-9478, ⊛www.twistobe.com. A labyrinthine bar that just keeps expanding: there are two dancefloors, video screens in the main lounge downstairs, and a garden bar out back. The all-male crowd's friendly and more diverse than most South Beach watering holes. In addition, go-go boys perform in the garden bar Fridays, Sundays, and Mondays. No cover.

(15)

GAY MIAMI | Shopping

Shopping

Lambda Passages Bookstore 7545 Biscayne Blvd, Little Haiti ☎305/754-6900, ⊛www .lambdapassages.com. This gay and lesbian

bookstore – and unofficial community center – may be a little out-of-the-way, but it has a wide range of fiction and nonfiction, as well as a video rental library of classic films.

The Pink Palm Company 737 Lincoln Rd, South Beach ☎305/538-8373, ⒲www .pinkpalm.com. A stationery and trinkets megastore on Lincoln Road with a wide selection of gay greeting cards, as well

as a small selection of furniture and fun, kitschy gifts.

Whittal & Shon 900 Washington Ave #3, South Beach ☎305/538-2606. An orgy of feather boas and flouncing hats for boys and girls, Whittall & Shon features a smaller selection of clubbers' clothing. Great, campy fun.

Gyms and saunas

If you're going to spend any time at all on Miami's body-conscious beaches, best to stay in shape at one of the local gyms – we've listed the best known alongside the city's most popular sauna.

Club Body Center 2991 Coral Way, Little Havana ☎305/448-4357, ⒲www.clubbodycenter.com /miami. The best-known sauna/gym/sex club in town. There's super-cruisey nude sunbathing by the pool, a rough-hewn timber bar known as the KY Corral (complete with flogging stations) and plenty of social events to help encourage mingling – plus it's open 24 hours year-round.

David Barton Gym Inside the Delano Hotel, 1685 Collins Ave, South Beach ☎305/674-5757, ⒲www.davidbartongym.com. Small and lush, this gym's decorated with orchids and plenty of celebrities. It's less musclebound than most other gyms around, and has plenty of free weights, as well as yoga classes.

Idol's Gym 715 N Lincoln Lane, South Beach ☎305/532-0039. A good budget option, since a day-pass here costs only $10 – and it's open 24 hours a day during the week. The workout room, decorated with a trashy mural, is crowded with machines and looks out directly onto the street: like most gyms on the beach, Idol's is packed with super-pumped muscleboys.
Another branch is at 5556 NE 4th Court, Biscayne Corridor ☎305/751-7591.

South Beach Ironworks 1676 Alton Rd, South Beach ☎305/531-4743, ⒲www .southbeachironworks.com. Massive gym on the west side of South Beach, less sceney than others and with extensive classes available: a day-pass costs $15.

Gay beaches

There are no officially designated gay beaches in the city – however, look for the densest crowds on the South Beach seafront, and you'll find the **12th Street Beach**, a popular gay hang-out that stretches for several blocks of sand. In addition, the northern reaches (stations 27–29) of the nude beaches at Haulover Park (see p.83) are less predominantly gay but, oddly, cruisier. There are also several predominantly gay sections along the beach in Fort Lauderdale (see p.216).

Shopping

M iami provides plenty of opportunities to drop your dollars **shop-ping** for clothes, music, souvenirs, and beauty treatments – though the pickings are fairly conventional. The biggest disappointment in Miami's retail landscape is its dearth of bookstores, pitifully few for a city this size, but at least most shops generally stay open late, especially at the beach, so you can browse well into the evening – expect outlets along Lincoln Road, for instance, to be open until 10pm or later most nights.

The latest trend in Miami shopping is for New York **boutique names**, like ceramicist Jonathan Adler, drugstore Ricky's NYC, or girly clothing store Inter-mix, to open their first standalone stores outside Manhattan in Miami, in part to cater for the vast number of New Yorkers who've moved down here during the city's construction and financial boom.

Where to shop

South Beach is undeniably the place to head if you're looking for quirky, smaller boutiques, its outdoor spaces a welcome antidote to overly air-condi-tioned malls. Collins Avenue and Lincoln Road hold the largest number of browsable stores, while further north on the beach, Bal Harbour is home to the city's densest selection of designer names, albeit in an unflattering setting.

Check out **Coconut Grove** for some unusual gift stores, especially in the triangle made by Commodore Plaza, Grand Avenue, and the Main Highway; otherwise, its much-ballyhooed shopping centers are rather disappointing. **Coral Gables** has plans to reinvigorate its Miracle Mile, although at the moment most shops seem to offer older ladies' fashions with window displays that look unchanged since 1983. Around the city, a large number of suburban malls essentially replicate one another's offerings with branches of The Gap, Express, and Victoria's Secret.

In **Little Havana**, all the retail action aligns Calle Ocho: come here for cigars and Cuban knickknacks, as most of the other storefronts house mini-markets or cafés. Along **the Biscayne Corridor**, there are notable housewares stores on 40th Street in the Design District, and a burgeoning fashion scene further north closer to Little Haiti.

Finally, **Downtown Miami** is barren except for an odd assortment of a dozen or so fabric peddlers, plenty of cheap shoe stores, and numerous electronics outlets, blaring music onto the sidewalk and hooking passersby with deals that seem too good to be true – and they are.

Books

It's surprisingly hard to find a good bookstore in the city; listed below are all the major ones close to the center. Fifteenth Street Books is the only one with a sizeable selection of second-hand titles.

Barnes & Noble 152 Miracle Mile, Coral Gables ☎305/446-4152, ⓦwww.bn.com. Located in the heart of downtown Coral Gables, this is the only central branch of the book megachain – it stocks the usual wide selection of books and music, plus a large Spanish-language section of both novels and nonfiction.

Books & Books 933 Lincoln Rd, South Beach ☎305/532-3222, ⓦwww.booksandbooks.com. The city's signature bookstore, Books & Books is pleasant enough, and the café's good, too. Though smallish and filled with coffee-table books, it's the only place on the beach for reading material other than the rundown Kafka's Kafé. Another much more impressive branch – with ample stock and an appealing courtyard café – is at 265 Aragon Ave, Coral Gables ☎305/442-4408.

Borders Streets of Mayfair, Coconut Grove ☎305/447-9890, ⓦwww.borders.com. Megastore chain that offers good discounts on new hardcovers and has a strong selection of local-interest books. It also sells CDs and hosts author readings – call or drop by for schedules.

Downtown Book Center 247 SE 1st St, Downtown ☎305/377-9939. This tiny Downtown bookstore is particularly strong in popular fiction, thrillers, and romance in both Spanish and English.

Eutopia 1627 Jefferson Ave, South Beach ☎305/532-8680. This small bookstore stocks first editions and rare books – not exactly beach reading, but a joy for connoisseurs. Open Tues–Sat 2–8pm.

Fifteenth Street Books 296 Aragon Ave, Coral Gables ☎305/442-2344. While it may not be a bargain hunter's paradise, Fifteenth Street Books is well stocked with art books and old hardcovers in top condition. The knowledgeable, friendly owner was the original founder of nearby Books & Books.

Kafka's Kafé 1464 Washington Ave, South Beach ☎305/673-9669. Don't come here looking for anything specific as the filing system for this rather ratty selection of used books is erratic. The budget paperbacks are good beach throwaways, although that's all they're good for; on the plus side, there's a wide selection of magazines, and Kafka's is open until midnight.

Murder on Miami Beach 16850 Collins Ave, Sunny Isles Beach ☎305/956-7770, ⓦwww.murderonthebeach.com. Unsurprisingly, this store stocks a wide selection of murder and mystery books, both new and used, plus signed first editions and gimmicky murder-themed gifts.

Ninth Chakra 530 Lincoln Rd, South Beach ☎305/538-0671, ⓦwww.9thchakra.com. New-age bookstore and gift shop that's rather out of place in the strutting retail palace of Lincoln Road. There's a wide selection on everything from *reiki* healing to regression; though it's a pity about the disinterested staff.

Shopping categories

Clothes: new

The **high fashion** zone in Miami stretches along two blocks of Collins Avenue on South Beach, between 5th and 8th streets, and on the newly re-energised Lincoln Road nearby. On either of these stretches, elbow to elbow, you'll find many of the big-name, mid-price designer names: the upscale stuff is in the Bal Harbour shops or Village of Merrick Park. Strangely for a town as funky and fashion-conscious as Miami, there are few homegrown designers – the closest South Beach comes is with its nondescript clubwear stores, and, in fact, for local names it's better to head across the Biscayne Corridor for the likes of Ash Rana and Julian Chang.

If you need **alterations** to anything, skip the pricey in-store rates: Maria's Alteration Shop, at 1622a Alton Rd, South Beach (☎ 305/674-1552), is reliable and reasonably priced – although few of the staff speak fluent English.

Adidas 226 8th St, South Beach ☎ 305/673-8317. Boutique for the reborn sportswear brand that stocks not just its core collection of shoes, but some harder-to-find limited-editions styles, the Y-3 range produced under the direction of Yohji Yamamoto, and a few clothes.

American Apparel 720 Lincoln Rd, South Beach ☎ 305/672–1799, ⓦ www.americanapparel.net. Cruelty-free clothes churned out from the company's own factory in downtown LA: workers have full healthcare benefits and can even make or receive phone calls on the factory floor. The well-priced product's tees, sweats, and sports-inspired casual wear in sherbet colors for boys and girls.

Ash Rana 4590 NE 2nd Ave, Design District ☎ 305/572-9088. Nepalese, former drag queen Ash produces what he calls "ass with class" clothes for skinny girls with plenty of attitude: hand-printed, decal-covered stretchy clothes. There's also a small selection here of reworked vintage men's tees and shirts.

Banana Republic 1100 Lincoln Rd, South Beach ☎ 305/534-4706. The reason to come to this outlet of the national chain isn't the clothes – they're fine, if a little bland – but the building. It's an old bank, and has been sensitively converted to a clothing store using many of the original features – the fitting rooms, for instance, are in the old vault, complete with huge, swinging metal door.

Barneys Co-op 832 Collins Ave, South Beach ☎ 305/421-2010, ⓦ www.barneys.com. The younger, funkier offspring of upscale New York designer department store, Barneys, this dual-level space houses jeans. Usual suspects like Earl and Juicy are alongside lesser known, rotating names – as well as sportswear and

accessories for both men and women. Pricey, but unbeatable.

Base 939 Lincoln Rd, South Beach ☎ 305/531-4982, ⓦ www.baseworld.com. Urban clothes for men (with a few women's products thrown in), conceived by British choreographer-turned-designer Steven Giles – sexy, showy fashions from Nice Collective, Keenan Duffty, Blue Blood, and more. It's a lifestyle store, too, stocking a range of sleek homewares, plus music, books, and beauty supplies with an onsite salon at the rear.

Betsey Johnson 805 Washington Ave, South Beach ☎ 305/673-0023, ⓦ www.betseyjohnson.com. For every girl's inner Cyndi Lauper, Betsey Johnson makes clothes that are wacky, fun, and feminine. She's known for her crazy color combinations, but the real reason the clothes sell is because they're so figure-flattering.

Club Monaco 624 Collins Ave, South Beach ☎ 305/674-7446, ⓦ www.clubmonaco.com. Mostly monochromatic unisex basics from this Canadian mid-price chain now owned by Ralph Lauren. Expect preppy sweaters for guys, great white shirts, and fun accessories for women.

Earl Jean 1008 Lincoln Rd, South Beach ☎ 305/695-7301, ⓦ www.earljean.com. Countrified designer denim brand for men and women – stronger on hard-wearing, high-quality pants for around $200 than on its odd, somewhat over-priced separates.

French Connection 1026 Lincoln Rd #B, South Beach ☎ 305/673-3838. Cheeky British clothing chain known for its preppy basics for men and women, usually emblazoned with its FCUK logo – that's French Connection United Kingdom.

Hiho Batik 7030 NE 4th Court, Little Haiti ☎ 305/754-8890, ⓦ www.hihobatik.com. Local designer Julia Silver spent years knocking out tour shirts for the likes of Carlos Santana and has now launched her own label of hand-dyed, hand-painted clothes: they're much more stylish and inventive than you might expect – the prices aren't bad either.

Intermix 634 Collins Ave, South Beach ☎ 305/531-5950, ⓦ www.intermix-ny.com. This New York boutique's Miami outpost hosts the same quirky, youthful mix of women's designers alongside wardrobe staples like Earl Jeans. Great for handbags, too.

SHOPPING | Where to shop

Julian Chang 1071 NE 79th St, Little Haiti
☎ 305/571-8900, ⓦ www.julianchang.com.
The go-to gown maker for skin-baring local
socialites, Chang churns out skimpy, flashy
eveningwear and showy casual separates,
often featuring brocade. He's just launched
a capsule men's line with shirts, ties, and
pants.

Miss Sixty 845 Lincoln Rd, South Beach
☎ 305/538-3547. Cutting-edge Italian jeanswear company that's snapping at Diesel's
heels as the denim company du jour: the
pant styles are mostly flattering for the
young and skinny, while the tops and retro
accessories are a little more wearable.

Nicole Miller 656 Collins Ave, South Beach
☎ 305/535-2200. Nicole Miller's line is classy,
floaty, and just fashionable enough. Great
for glamorous clothes that don't reveal too
much skin.

Rasool Sportswear 6301 NW 7th Ave #B, Liberty
City ☎ 305/759-1250. Spectacular and bizarre
menswear bazaar crammed with zoot suits
for $200 and rack after rack of brightly
colored spats and shoes, from yellow and
mustard to baby blue, in leathers including
ostrich and gator ($120–400).

Rebel 6669 Biscayne Blvd, Little Haiti
☎ 305/758-2369. Trendy twentysomething
boutique that's the best place to pick up
a designer label for lounging by the poolside bar. Expect Juicy Couture, Rebecca
Beeson, and Jezebel as well as 1980s
revival labels like Big Star. It's still a tough
neighborhood round here, so entrance is by
buzzer only.

Rene Ruiz Couture 262 Miracle Mile, Coral
Gables ☎ 305/445-2352. One of the newest
tenants enticed here by the redevelopment,
Ruiz is a local fashion designer, known for
his lycra-packed, stretchy gowns for women
and sequined, glitzy accessories at couture
prices.

Rosa Cha by Amir Slama 830 Lincoln Rd, South
Beach ☎ 305/538-7883, ⓦ www.rosa-cha.com.
Tiny, closet-sized store stocking tiny,
skimpy beachwear and bikinis from Brazil
(plus a few men's shorts). You may have to
have a killer body to carry off these mostly
acid-colored designs, but there's nothing
hotter for the beach.

Santini Mavardi 935 Washington Ave, South
Beach ☎ 305/538-6229, ⓦ www.santinimavardi
.com. For the South Beach Cinderella, this
store stocks a small line of clothes, but is
best known for its glitzy shoes – they run

the gamut from rhinestone-studded to
super-stiletto-heeled, and custom-made.

Urban Outfitters 653 Collins Ave, South Beach
☎ 305/535-9726, ⓦ www.urbanoutf.com. While
their mothers may browse at Macy's, teens
and students can spend time at this, their
own department store: Urban carries homewares, books, vintage-inspired clothes for
guys and girls, as well as trinkets and gag
gifts.

Von Dutch 640 Collins Ave, South Beach
☎ 305/531-6550, ⓦ www.vondutch.com. Best
known for its ubiquitous trucker-inspired
hats, the Von Dutch line also includes tees,
jeans, and skater-friendly accessories,
most splattered in retro graphics, as well as
skateboards and sundries.

Clothes: vintage and thrift

There's a good selection of **vintage
shops** in South Beach, but true retro
devotees should make the pilgrimage
to Liberty City. There, you'll find half
a dozen warehouses piled high with
supercheap bargains – there's even a
strip mall housing nothing but **thrift
stores**.

Beatnix 1149 Washington Ave, South Beach
☎ 305/532-8733. Alongside the vintage
clothes, Beatnix keeps technicolor wigs,
enormous feather boas, and plenty of
rubber clubwear – half drag, half dress-up,
and definitely fun.

Consign of the Times 1635 Jefferson Ave, South
Beach ☎ 305/535-0811. Miami's obsession with
designer labels pays off here – locals offer
their Gucci cast-offs for sale, splitting the
profits with the store. Granted, there's plenty
of flashy trash, but also the occasional find if
you're prepared to sift through the racks.

Douglas Gardens Thrift Store 5713 NW 27th St,
Liberty City ☎ 305/638-1900. One of several
vast warehouses clustered together, there's
an enormous selection at rock-bottom
prices – in fact, chichi vintage stores from
New York and LA regularly arrive with vans
to scour for stock. Keep in mind that this
isn't the greatest part of town, so it's best to
visit by car or not at all.

Recycled Blues 1507 Washington Ave, South
Beach ☎ 305/538-0656. The largest thrift
store on the beach, this shop has a great
selection of cool merchandise (especially
denim). Its biggest drawback, however, is
the premium prices they charge.

Department stores and malls

Miami has a large number of **malls**, both traditional and open-air – though all tend to house the standard crop of shops and department stores. The two most noteworthy are the dueling designer meccas of old favorite Bal Harbour Shops and upstart newcomer Village of Merrick Park.

Aventura Mall 19501 Biscayne Blvd, Aventura ☎305/935-1110, ⊛www.shopaventuramall .com. North of Miami, just off I-95 (take the Miami Gardens Drive exit and follow the signposts), you'll find Aventura, the local megamall that essentially sprouted a town around it. There are several department stores here, as well as an enormous food court and the usual mall branch shops.

Bal Harbour Shops 9700 Collins Ave, Bal Harbour ☎305/886-0311, ⊛www .balharbourshops.com. The Bal Harbour Shops house every well-known designer name, plus an enormous Saks Fifth Avenue – and an oddly incongruous branch of The Gap. The mall itself is singularly unappealing, housed in a clunky concrete building, but the range and variety of stores is impressive, including upscale barber Art of Shaving, Lacoste, Vilebrequin, and Sergio Rossi.

Bayside Mall 401 N Biscayne Blvd, Downtown ☎305/577-3344, ⊛www.baysidemarketplace .com. This waterfront complex features stores much like any other: there's a large branch of the upscale jeanswear company Guess?, funky teen shoe store Skechers, and a Sharper Image.

CocoWalk 3015 Grand Ave, Coconut Grove ☎305/444-0777, ⊛www.cocowalk.com. When it opened in the early 1990s, this shopping center revitalized Coconut Grove. Now, the pleasant but unremarkable Mediterranean Revival architecture, with its covered walk-ways and plenty of eateries, houses the usual names like Victoria's Secret and The Gap.

The Falls Shopping Center 8888 SW 136th St, South Miami ☎305/255-4570, ⊛www.shop-thefalls.com. Enormous open-air shopping complex, sporting a waterscape punctuated with falls, and a funky sculpture by Romero Britto. It has more than 100 stores and is a little more upscale than most suburban malls: there's a massive Bloomingdales, plus stylish homewares from Crate & Barrel,

Pottery Barn, and Williams-Sonoma – and sexy women's wear from BCBG and Bebe.

Macy's 22 E Flagler St, Downtown ☎305/577-2410, ⊛www.macys.com. The former flagship branch of Florida's signature department store, Burdine's, has been rebranded by its current owners. The tattered Downtown branch sells homewares, clothes from the usual designer names, and plenty of perfume. The outpost at 1777 West Ave in South Beach (☎305/825-7351) is smaller and more architecturally interesting, complete with ornamental palm trees.

Shops at Sunset Place 5701 Sunset Drive, South Miami ☎305/663-0482, ⊛www.simon.com. A mammoth outdoor mall in South Miami that's notable for its large Niketown, as well as Miami's only Virgin Megastore, plus substantial branches of Barnes & Noble and Urban Outfitters.

Streets of Mayfair 2911 Grand Ave, Coconut Grove ☎305/448-1700, ⊛www.streetsofmayfair .com. Positioned as CocoWalk's posher sister, this oddly designed and unappealing mall is filled with copper statues and mosaics, but oddly empty of people; in fact, part of it's now being converted to apartments. Otherwise, there's a men's-only branch of Banana Republic, plus The Limited, Ann Taylor's Loft, United Colors of Benetton, and a huge Borders bookstore.

Village of Merrick Park Ponce de Leon and HWY-1, Coral Gables ☎305/529-0200, ⊛www .villageofmerrickpark.com. Recent upscale rival to long-established Bal Harbour Shops: amid the open-air walkways, you'll find a branch of the sumptuous Elemis Spa, as well as fashions from Burberry, Diane von Furstenberg, and Jimmy Choo.

Ethnic specialties and crafts

Stores across the city claim to sell authentic souvenirs of Miami's two dominant immigrant cultures – Cuban and Haitian – but the ones listed below offer the real thing.

Ambrosia 665 NW 62nd St, Liberty City ☎786/277-7663. Jamaican store-cum-café, selling textiles, clothing, CDs, movies, and beads – all in rasta colors of yellow, red, green, and black. There's also a small onsite take-out café selling vegetarian nibbles (sandwiches for $3) as well as doses of the intriguingly named, freshly squeezed Male Primer Juice ($5).

El Credíto Cigar Factory 1106 SW 8th St, Little Havana ☎305/858-4162. It's easy to understand why this is the best-known smokeshop in the city. Here, you'll see rows of *tabaqueros* (cigar rollers) making fat cigars by hand, using top-quality tobacco – it's generally agreed that this store's La Gloria Cubana cigar is one of the best available.

Haitian Art Factory 835 NE 79th St, Little Haiti ☎305/758-6939, ⓦwww.haitianartfactory.com. This eccentric shop, attached to a doctor's office, carries fine woodcarvings and crafts from Haiti – admittedly alongside plenty of tat. Call ahead to see if it's open, as hours can be erratic.

Halouba Botanica 101 NE 54th St, Little Haiti ☎305/751-7485. One of many *botánicas* on the *voudou* strip, this store is spacious and a little less daunting than some of the others. There's a large temple on site, which holds regular ceremonies ministered by the husband-and-wife team that runs the store.

La Casa de las Guayaberas 5840 SW 8th St, Little Havana ☎305/266-9683. This shop's specialty is the unmistakably Cuban *guayabera* shirt – cool in the tropical heat and billowy in the wind. The tailor-owner is one of the earliest Cuban-American refugees, and everything is hand-sewn by his team: he offers inexpensive options starting at $15 to $20, as well as pricey, custom-made designs starting at $250.

La Casa de las Piñatas 1756 SW 8th St, Little Havana ☎305/649-4711. Gaudy party favors bashed by guests until they'll spill their candy-stuffed guts, *piñatas* in any shape or size are sold here. Hundreds hang from the ceiling, and if your Spanish is good (and you've time and money), you can even commission custom-made shapes.

Libreri Mapou 5919 NE 2nd Ave, Little Haiti ☎305/757-9922, ⓦwww.librerimapou.com. The place to go if you want to dig deeper into Little Haiti, offering a wide selection of books on the history and politics of the Caribbean nation, as well as Haitian novels in English, French, and Kreyol, magazines, and Haitian newspapers.

Food and drink

You don't have to splurge on every meal if money's tight – there are branches of the supermarket chain Publix everywhere in the city. There are also plenty of liquor stores – although note that local ordinances limit the sale of alcohol after 10pm on the beach.

Epicure Market 1656 Alton Rd, South Beach ☎305/672-1861. A gourmet market offering high-quality – but expensive – foodstuffs like handmade biscotti, plus fresh fish and meats. There's an interesting beer selection, as well as a small, but fresh, flower stand.

Wild Oats Community Market 1020 Alton Rd, South Beach ☎305/532-1707, ⓦwww.wildoats .com. Delicious and healthy, this enormous supermarket offers more than just granola and tofu – among other things, there are freshly baked cakes, exotic juices, and organic produce. A terrific picnic lunch stop-off.

Farmers markets

A more interesting option than ploughing through Publix is checking out one of several local farmers markets held in various neighborhoods around the city; expect freshly made snacks, plants, and produce for sale, much of it organic.

Coconut Grove
Every Saturday year-round 10am–5.30pm ☎305/238-7747, junction of Grand Avenue and Margaret Street

Coral Gables
Every Saturday January–March 8am–1pm ☎305/460-5311, between Coral Gables City Hall and Merrick Park

North Beach
Every Saturday year-round 8am–8pm ☎305/531-0038, Normandy Village Fountain Plaza at 71st Street and Rue Vendome

South Beach
Every Sunday year-round 8am–8pm ☎305/531-0038, Lincoln Road between Washington and Pennsylvania avenues

Galleries

Most of the best **galleries** in town are now in Wynwood or the Design District, lured by both the aggressive marketing of the area by landlords and its low rents. Off the mainland, check out the combination studios/gallery space of the Art Center of South Florida on South Beach's Lincoln Road (see p.67).

Damien B Art Center 282 NW 36th St, Wynwood ☏ 305/573-4949, ⓦ www.damienb.com. Frenchman Damien Boisseau was one of the original pioneers in this area, and specializes in abstract and conceptual art; expect a new show every four weeks or so, rotating between local and boldfaced names like Cathy de Monchaux.

Dorsch 151 NW 24th St, Wynwood ☏ 305/576-1278, ⓦ www.dorschgallery.com. Party-boy Brook Dorsch relocated his gallery here from South Beach four years ago and in equal measure, with a mission to showcase works in every media. Not the edgiest or most exciting art perhaps, but always a hot spot.

Liquid Blue Gallery 3438 N Miami Ave, Wynwood ☏ 305/571-9123, ⓦ www.liquidbluegallery.com. Run by a team of refugee New Yorkers who fled the hipster enclave of Williamsburg when it became too mainstream, Liquid Blue's a large space with hit-and-miss multimedia shows – worth checking out if only because of the eclectic taste of the curators.

Locust Projects 105 NE 23rd St, Wynwood ☏ 305/576-8570, ⓦ www.locustprojects.org. This space is run by a charitable collective, so expect right-on shows with a political slant. The upside of this is that prices are uniformly low – a good place to dabble and actually buy a piece or two.

Rocket Projects 3440 N Miami Ave, Wynwood ☏ 305/576-6082, ⓦ www.rocket-projects.com. This sprawling gallery space in a converted furniture upholsterer's uses every area for installations – one project by local artist Cristina Lei Rodriguez was draped through the boughs of the tree in its backyard. There's a handy, browsable dresser full of pictures at the rear called the Flat File Lounge.

Snitzer 2247 NW 1st Place, Wynwood ☏ 305/448-8976, ⓦ www.snitzer.com. Fred Snitzer is one of the most famous local gallerists and his recent move from a comfy perch in Coral Gables to Wynwood was a major endorsement of the area. Snitzer specializes in 2-D contemporary art, both painting and photography.

Susane R gallery 93 NE 40th St, Design District ☏ 305/573-8483, ⓦ www.susaner.com. Gallery-cum-furniture-store that its owner calls a lifestyle boutique – much of the product's antiqued or self-consciously bohemian: not for the minimalist.

Gifts and oddities

Britto Central 818 Lincoln Rd, South Beach ☏ 305/531-8821, ⓦ www.britto.com. Local artist Romero Britto paints colorful, cartoonish images on everything from ties to handbags, available at this store/gallery. There's something sweet, trashy, and deliciously Miami about his work.

Me & Ro Inside the Shore Club, 1901 Collins Ave, South Beach ☏ 305/672-3566, ⓦ www.meandrojewelry.com. Famous as Julia Roberts' favorite jeweler, this pair of New Yorkers (Robin and Michelle – hence the name) churn out high-priced, vaguely ethnic baubles, often featuring small, bead-like clusters of semi-precious stones – big rings, jangly bracelets, and necklaces.

Pink Palm Company 737 Lincoln Rd, South Beach ☏ 305/538-8373 or 1-877/538-8373, ⓦ www.pinkpalm.com. The best card store in the city, with a wide range of greeting cards both traditional and funky, as well as an eclectic mix of candles, notebooks, and other small gifts.

Pop 1151 Washington Ave, South Beach ☏ 305/604-9604, ⓦ www.popsouthbeach.com. An eclectic mix of toys, greeting cards, and a few clothes, all chosen with the same wacky sense of style and humor, Pop is a great place for unusual gifts – check out the bootleg CDs from local circuit parties, as well as pristine 1980s memorabilia.

The Seybold Building 36 NE 1st St, Downtown ☏ 305/374-7922. Miami's diamond merchants are all housed in this one building in the heart of Downtown: here, more than 300 different jewelers, selling everything from simple gems to glitzy watches, are crammed together in one space. Not many obvious bargains, but it's well worth haggling.

Toy Town 260 Crandon Blvd, Key Biscayne ☏ 305/361-5501. Forget Toys'R'Us and F.A.O. Schwarz – this is a traditional, family-owned toy store that's the best in the city.

It sells simple, nostalgic toys like train sets, board games, and stuffed animals, perhaps as novel to today's kids as it is familiar to their parents.

Health and beauty

Brownes & Co. Apothecary 841 Lincoln Rd, South Beach ☎305/538-7544, ⓦwww .brownesbeauty.com. Stock up on sumptuous skincare lines like Fresh, as well as top-name make-up brands here. The Some Like It Hot salon (☎305/538-7544) upstairs is renowned for great, if pricey, manicures.
Kiehl's 832 Lincoln Rd, South Beach ☎305/531-0404. Brand-new Miami outpost of the once-cultish Manhattan skincare range stocking the entire range. Make sure to ask for free samples – Kiehl's is known for its generosity with testers.
Massage by Design 100 Collins Ave, South Beach ☎305/532-3112, ⓦwww.massagebydesign .com. At the tip of South Beach is a locals' favorite: this spa offers combo massages, including shiatsu and reflexology, as well as hot stone rubs, all in feng shuied surroundings. The staff is personable, and you can also arrange for manicures and waxing.
Ricky's NYC 536 Lincoln Rd ☎305/674-8150, ⓦwww.rickys-nyc.com. Saucy, sexy drug-store from New York, that stocks any and every lotion or potion possible, as well as wigs, feather boas, and drag-queen-worthy cosmetics. There's a campy salon at the rear called, naturally, The Birdcage. Upstairs, discreetly stashed behind a bead curtain, is an Adults Only room with sex toys, thongs, and a wall full of condoms.
Russian Turkish Bath Inside the Castle hotel, 5445 Collins Ave, Miami Beach ☎305/867-8313. The facilities here are a little less lush than at other spas, but it's a place utterly devoid of attitude; there's a gym, steam rooms, and a salt-water Jacuzzi. $23 for a day-pass.
Sephora 721 Collins Ave, South Beach ☎305/532-0904, ⓦwww.sephora.com. The beauty supermarket where fragrances are grouped not by fashion house but alpha-betically. There are fewer pushy sales staff and testers for every product – and it's open late: great for a pre-dinner stop if you forgot to spritz at home.

Housewares

For **housewares**, the main drag is inevitably along 40th Street in the Design District – although there you'll find as much furniture as ornaments. If you do fall in love with something large and unpackable, most stores will be happy to ship it to you anywhere in the world – at a price, of course.
Holly Hunt 3833 NE 2nd Ave, Design District ☎305/571-2012, ⓦwww.hollyhunt.com. Beyond chic, this showcase for multiple homeware lines is the last word in classic design. There's little that's daring or avant-garde (and definitely no bargains), but it's a sumptuous space with luxurious furniture – great for browsing.
Jonathan Adler 1024 Lincoln Rd, South Beach ☎305/534-5600, ⓦwww.jonathanadler.com. New York–based potter Adler is known for his chic, understated homewares – expand-ing from simple vases in muted tones like beige and cream to soft goods and rugs in geometric patterns. Pricey, but luscious.

Museum stores

There's little imaginative buying at most **museum gift shops**, but those listed below are fun enough places to browse.
Art Deco Welcome Center 1001 Ocean Drive, South Beach ☎305/672-2014, ⓦwww.mdpl.org. This lobby store is a treasure trove of offbeat trinkets, from unique embossed metal post-cards to a wide range of gifts and books on all things Deco.
Miami Art Museum Gift Shop Metro-Dade Cultural Center, 101 W Flagler St, Downtown ☎305/375-1700, ⓦwww.miamiartmuseum.org. Superb Downtown gift shop with a funky edge. Alongside the usual books and artsy cards, you'll find design-conscious house-wares at better prices than in most rarefied museum stores.

Music

For dance and club **music** in the city, there's nowhere to beat the stores on South Beach. If your taste is a little more eclectic, there are superb stores in Little Havana and Little Haiti for Caribbean and Latin American music.
Do-Re-Mi Music Center 1829 SW 8th St, Little Havana ☎305/541-3374. Come here for astonishingly wide selections of Latin music from meringue and salsa to modern pop

– a smattering of crossover types like Ricky Martin and Marc Anthony – though it's really for the encyclopedic assortment of obscure Spanish-language artists.

Grooveman Music 1543 Washington Ave, South Beach ☎305/535-6257, Ⓦwww .groovemanmusic.com. A DJ's dream, this store stocks underground house and trance – kept dark during the day and night, the place throbs with loud music and is usually packed with local club kids.

Spec's Music 501 Collins Ave, South Beach ☎305/534-3667. As Miami is sorely lacking the usual glut of Sam Goody and FYE music stores that pepper most American cities, the best local option is Spec's Music. Its beach location is good for singles and dance music, and there's an up-to-date import section – just don't look for any obscure artists.

Uncle Sam's Musiccafe 1141 Washington Ave, South Beach ☎305/532-0973, Ⓦwww .unclesamsmusic.com. Standard record store with an ample selection of popular music, as well as a secondhand section, posters for sale, and mountains of flyers and freesheets – a good place to check out what's happening music-wise in the next few weeks around the city. The weird name owes itself to an attached café that's since closed.

17

Sports, fitness, and ocean activities

Miami's climate makes it ideally suited to most outdoor **sports**, and there's plenty on offer, whether you want to stay fit by playing or just lounge around and watch. The city hosts franchises from each of the three major spectator sports – football's Miami Dolphins have been around the longest and been the most consistently successful, while the Miami Heat draw the hoops crowd and the Florida Marlins the baseball fans. College football is fanatically followed, thanks to the perennial success of the University of Miami Hurricanes; college basketball and baseball slightly less so. In addition, Miami hosts top-name tennis and golf tournaments on its numerous, quality, facilities, probably best in Key Biscayne – and most greens and courts are open to the public.

For those who don't just like to watch, biking is popular, as is rollerblading, the patron sport of South Beach. In addition, many people casually fish off the jetties at the beach; a better, though pricey, option is a charter deep-sea fishing trip. There are also plenty of shops that run diving and snorkeling outings but, other than the coral reef in Biscayne National Park, the best regional diving spots are dotted along the Keys less than two hours away.

An authentic local experience is to watch (or even attempt) a game of jai alai, a fast, frenzied sport that arrived in Miami from Spain via Cuba. Alternatively, take in a day at the greyhound track, undeniably an experience.

Baseball

The **Florida Marlins** are barely a decade old and have already managed to win two World Series (1997 and 2003). After the first one, the top stars were sold off almost immediately after and the team looked like it might be moved or even disbanded; even now there's question over their future, with an ongoing battle for a new stadium to be built near the Orange Bowl.

The season runs April to October, and ticket prices range from $4 to $55. For now, the Marlins play at Pro Player Stadium, at 2269 Dan Marino Blvd, sixteen miles northwest of Downtown Miami (information ℡1-877/MARLINS or 305/623-6100, tickets ℡305/350-5050, ⓦwww.flamarlins.com). Tickets can also be bought in person from the satellite ticket office at 3701 SW 8th Street, Coral Gables (Mon–Fri 9am–5pm).

The college team, the University of Miami **Hurricanes**, has won a number of championships, too, and produced some top pros; games are at Mark Light Stadium, 6201 San Amaro Drive in Coral Gables (tickets $6; ☎1-800/GO-CANES).

Basketball

The **Miami Heat** basketball team was for a long time defined by larger-than-life coach Pat Riley; while the team never scored a championship with him at the helm, it frequently won its division and made it to the playoffs. After he moved on to be general manager, he engineered the addition of the sport's biggest star, Shaquille O'Neal, in 2004; the team prospects were immediately improved, on the heels of a few down years, and its local profile – and the fan hysteria – raised meteorically.

To see Shaq in Black, come during the season from October to April. Ticket prices start at $10 and can reach $200–300. The Heat play at the American Airlines Arena, 601 Biscayne Blvd, Downtown – call ☎ 786/777-4328 for tickets, or visit ⓦwww.nba.com/heat/.

College basketball is also popular in Miami, and the UM **Hurricanes** attract a good following, if one less fanatical than their football team. They play in the most competitive conference in the nation, so go as much to see the opponents' skills as to root on the locals. The hoops season runs from November to March at the Convocation Center, 1245 Walsh Ave, Coral Gables (☎305/284-2263, ⓦwww.hurricanesports.com).

Beaches and swimming

Most of the notable **beaches** and **swim spots** are, of course, on Miami Beach. **Surfers** will find the best waves off South Pointe at the end of South Beach, where there's a handy pier and jetty (daily 24hr; ☎305/673-7224), but for more of a seafront scene, head to Lummus Park between 6th and 14th streets (daily 24hr; ☎305/673-7714). It's the best known of all the city's beaches, with full facilities and a **gay section** around 12th Street. Further up Miami Beach, Haulover Park – notorious as a **nudist enclave** – actually has the most appealing sands of all, not to mention full facilities and several **volleyball courts** (daily sunrise to sunset; ☎305/947-3525). Continuing north, the beaches in Sunny Isles may look lavish and wide – it's cosmetic, as much of the sand was pumped from the sea floor – but thanks to vicious undertow and currents, swimming can be tricky and dangerous here (☎305/947-3912).

For **families**, head to 3rd Street on Miami Beach, where there are lifeguards, restrooms, picnic tables, and showers. Another family-friendly spot is on Key Biscayne: Crandon Park at the northern end of the island has more than three miles of sand, but even so can be packed with people at weekends (daily 8am–sunset; $4 per car; ☎305/361-7385, ⓦwww.miamidade.gov/parks/parks/crandon_beach.asp).

The other noteworthy beach nearby is Virginia Key Beach, where blacks were banished in times of segregation and which still retains its popularity among the local African-American community (daily 8am–sunset; cars $2; ☎305/571-8230, ⓦwww.virginiakeybeach.com).

A terrific, if landlocked, option for a day in the water is, of course, the artfully landscaped Venetian Pool in Coral Gables – see p.109 for details. For a professional quality pool, head to Fort Lauderdale's International Swimming Hall of Fame (see p.214).

Biking and rollerblading

Downtown Miami is configured only for the bravest of **bikers** – there are few cycle lanes, and the slipknot of freeways that crisscross the city make it even tougher on two wheels. A bike is a good option, though, in South Beach, where car parking is both pricey and congested; even better are the cycle routes in Coconut Grove (a fourteen-mile path down to South Miami) and Key Biscayne, which is especially worthwhile: not only are the parks beautiful, but scant public transport makes getting around any other way almost impossible.

As for **rollerblading**, it's arguably Miami's signature sport: the payoff for days spent perfecting your body in the gym is a couple of hours cruising along the

△ Rollerblading on the beach

beach on a pair of blades. Don't be put off, though, even if you're a neophyte – rollerblading through South Beach's oceanfront parks is a glorious way to see the sights, well worth the occasional tumble.

Rental and repair shops

Electric Rentals 233 11th St, South Beach ☎305/532-6700, ⓦ www.electricrentals.com. They offer a brand-new, less strenuous alternative to blading: the Segway. This oddball contraption – much like a motorized pogo stick with wheels – can be rented at $39 for an obligatory 45min guided ride so that users can master its techniques, and then $50/hr after that.

Fritz's Skate, Bike & Surf 730 Lincoln Rd, South Beach ☎305/532-1954. Blades and bikes for $7.50/hr, $22/day. Daily 10am–10pm.
Mangrove Cycles 260 Crandon Blvd, in the Square Shopping Center, Key Biscayne ☎305/361-5555. Cycles at $15/day, $30/3 days. Mon–Sat 9am–6pm, Sun 10am–6pm.
Miami Beach Bicycle Center 601 5th St, South Beach ☎305/674-0150. Rates are $20/24hr. Mon–Sat 10am–7pm, Sun 10am–5pm.

Diving and snorkeling

Much is made of **diving** and **snorkeling** in Miami, and most hotels will offer some form of aquatic trips. However, locals agree that diving in Miami comes a far second to dive sites in the Keys like Looe Key or the more remote but spectacular Dry Tortugas. The one exception is the reef at Biscayne National Park near Homestead, a massive underwater park with fantastic coral formations. When booking a trip, ask whether it's better for snorkelers or scuba divers – some trips may head out to deep waters, making observation from the surface difficult. The operators below are all reliable and arrange trips at reasonable rates.

Dive operators

Bubbles Dive Center 2671 SW 27th Ave, Coconut Grove ☎305/856-0565.
South Beach Divers 850 Washington Ave, South Beach ☎305/531-6110 or 1-888/331-DIVE, ⓦ www.southbeachdivers.com.
Tarpoon Lagoon 300 Alton Rd at Miami Beach Marina, South Beach ☎305/532-1445, ⓦ www .tarpoondivecenter.com.

Fishing

Tearing into your own fresh catch for dinner is a satisfying experience, and plenty of anglers come to Miami for the **fishing** – although, as with underwater sports, the Keys are probably a better bet for variety and volume of fish. Plus, the only **public fishing pier** in the city is up in Sunny Isles at 16701 Collins Ave, next to the *Holiday Inn Crowne Plaza Hotel* ($5; ☎305/940-7905).

If you've more money or less experience, a great option is a day out on a boat **deep-sea fishing**: expect to pay around $500–600 for a half-day, and $750–1000 for a full day of private charter, including bait, supervision, and fish-gutting. For confident anglers, there are public boats, which cost $40 and up for the ride only.

Boat operators

Mark the Shark Biscayne Bay Marriott Marina, Downtown ☎305/759-5297, ⓦ www .marktheshark.com.
Reward Fishing Fleet 300 Alton Rd at Miami Beach Marina, South Beach ☎305/372-9470, ⓦ www.fishingmiami.com.
Sonny Boy Sportfishing Key Biscayne Marina ☎305/361-2217, ⓦ www.sonnyboysportfishing .com.

Football

The **Miami Dolphins** have a storied past, closely associated with (now-retired) star quarterback Dan Marino, the league's all-time leading passer, and ex-coach and local legend Don Shula, who led the team to the only perfect season in modern league history (in 1972). Unfortunately, the team has not appeared in the Super Bowl since 1985.

The season runs from September to January, and ticket prices range from $27 to $55. The Dolphins play at Pro Player stadium when the Marlins are out of season (see p.180) – call ☎305/573-8326 for tickets, or visit ⊛www.miami-dolphins.com. Tickets can also be purchased in person at Gate G onsite at the stadium (Mon–Fri 8.30am–5pm, Sat 10am–4pm).

On the collegiate level, the UM **Hurricanes** have one of the top football programs in the country, and local devotion to them is as passionate as to the Dolphins. The regular season runs September through November, and ticket prices start at $15. The 'Canes, as they're known, play at the Orange Bowl, 1400 NW 4th St, Little Havana (☎305/284-2263, ⊛www.hurricanesports.com).

Golf

Miami's large enough and warm enough to mean that there are plenty of options for **golf** in and around the city. Greens fees vary widely – anything from $15 to $250 – as does the experience. Note that some of the places below are resorts or hotels, but nonguests/nonmembers can play too, usually for a higher fee than those staying there.

Courses and greens fees

Biltmore Golf Course 1210 Anastasia Ave, Coral Gables ☎305/460-5364, ⊛www.biltmorehotel .com. Luxurious, historic course, with the prices to match, at $120 including cart.

Crandon Park 6700 Crandon Blvd, Key Biscayne ☎305/361-9129. A top-ranking public course that's the site of the Royal Caribbean Classic. A round costs from $52 to $131.

Doral Golf Resort & Spa 4400 NW 87th Ave on the mainland ☎305/592-2030, ⊛www .doralgolf.com. Lushest and best-known course (actually five courses on site), and home to the Ford Championship; $50 to $275 for 18 holes.

Normandy Shores Miami Beach, 401 Biarritz Drive at 71st St ☎305/868-6502, ⊛www .geocities.com/normandyshoresgc. Like the Biltmore, quite a venerable course, but more affordable at $35–55.

Palmetto Golf Course 9300 SW 152nd St, South Miami ☎305/238-2922. The best choice for those on a budget, but out in the suburbs a bit. Fees $13.90–22.15.

Gyms

Miami has no shortage of **gyms** for South Beach body-toning, or just general fitness; the following all offer day-pass memberships – remember to bring two forms of ID, including one with a photograph.

Crunch 1259 Washington Ave, South Beach ☎305/674-8222, ⊛www.crunch.com.
David Barton Gym at the Delano, 1685 Collins Ave, South Beach ☎305/674-5757, ⊛www .davidbartongym.com.

Downtown Athletic Club 200 S Biscayne Blvd, 15th floor, Downtown ☎305/667-0106, www .miamidac.com.
Fitness Company 2901 Florida Ave, Coconut Grove ☎305/441-8555, ⊛thefitnesscompany.com.

Jai alai

Derived from the Basque game of pelota, **jai alai** (pronounced "high-uh-lie," meaning "merry festival" in Basque) arrived in Cuba from Spain late in the nineteenth century. It quickly made the leap across the water to Miami, and there are now more jai alai frontons (or courts) in Florida than anywhere else in the world. It's a brutal, breakneck sport: a bullet-hard ball ricochets around the court at speeds up to 150mph, and players try to catch it in a cesta (basically a lacrosse basket attached to a baseball mitt). Until a star player suffered an accident in the late 1960s, helmets weren't even mandatory, and each fifteen-minute match is a thrilling, if dangerous, spectacle. The Miami Jai Alai is where the pros play: it's located at 3500 NW 37th Ave, near the airport, where you can watch matches daily except Tuesday noon to 5pm and Friday, Saturday, and Monday 7pm to midnight. General admission is $1, reserved seating $2; ⊤ 305/633-6400.

Tennis

The climate in Miami suits **tennis** as much as it does golf, and there are plenty of public courts. Most of them operate on a first-come, first-served basis and charge only nominal fees – the list below is by no means exhaustive: for other options in different neighborhoods, contact the City of Miami Parks & Recreation Department (Mon–Fri 8am–5pm; ⊤ 305/416-1308, Ⓦ www.ci.miami.fl.us) or the City of Miami Beach Parks & Recreation Department (Mon–Fri 8.30am–5pm; ⊤ 305/673-7730, Ⓦ www.ci.miami-beach.fl.us).

One of Miami's major sporting draws, the **NASDAQ-100 Open** (⊤ 305/446-2200, Ⓦ www.nasdaq100-open.com), in late March, attracts marquee players to the fifth largest tennis tournament in the world. It's held on Key Biscayne at the Crandon Park Tennis Center and tickets start at $25.

Courts and fees

Crandon Park 4000 Crandon Blvd on Key Biscayne ⊤ 305/365-2300. Wide range of surfaces: hard $3 per person/hr daytime, $5 per person/hr night, grass and clay $6 per person/hr.

Flamingo Park 1000 12th St, South Beach ⊤ 305/673-7761. $8 per person/hr.

Haulover Park Northern Miami Beach ⊤ 305/940-6719. More courts than Flamingo Park; $2.30 per person/hr.

(17)

Kids' Miami

While Florida's one of the prime family vacation destinations in the US, mostly thanks to the flawless, if soulless, mecca of Disneyworld in Orlando, if you're looking for a more cosmopolitan experience in addition to the good weather, Miami's also a smart option. Not only is there a more varied choice of attractions from art museums to animal sanctuaries, but there are also dozens of sandy and clean seaside beaches.

After its club-hopping renaissance of the late 1980s, Miami recognized its beaches were a prime family draw and worked hard for several years to market itself as a family-friendly destination. Its aggressive advertising highlighted those clean sandy stretches and modern hotels. Though the city's tourism tactics may have shifted back in the last two years or so – emphasizing once more the city's chic sexiness – Miami's still a city that caters well to kids and adults alike. Indeed, new attractions like the Children's Museum mean it's luring more families than ever. We've highlighted below the best museums and activities for kids of all ages, as well as suggested the best beaches and hotels for families.

The weather's one of the most appealing aspects, though make sure to slather little ones in **sun cream**, especially during the winter high season when the sunshine's relentless. The fact that you can walk, rather than drive, round South Beach is also appealing: kids don't have to be cooped up in the car all day to enjoy themselves, and there are plenty of cafés close to the beach for quick snack breaks. Other than the swankiest five-star eateries, most restaurants in town will either offer a children's menu or be more than happy to cater to kids.

Nevertheless, if you do want to leave the kids behind for an evening out, **babysitting** can be arranged through Nanny Poppinz Child Care Services at

Family-friendly accommodation

Most of the boutique hotels in **South Beach** are geared to young singles or couples, with few nods to families; rooms are often so small that extra beds aren't possible. Better, in fact, to stay further up in **Middle Beach**: the *Fontainebleau Hilton* (see p.134) has a huge family pool, complete with fiberglass Octopus sprawling across it, known as Cookie's World, as well as babysitting and rollaway beds. Otherwise, many families opt to stay on **Key Biscayne**. It's a smart move: the Seaquarium's close by, there are ample beaches, and most of the hotels, like the *Sonesta Resort*, can easily cater to kids (see p.135).

One caveat: don't be tempted to stay in **Sunny Isles Beach**, despite its family-friendly packages. The trip to any attraction's a long haul, and the treacherous undertows in the sea make it risky for little ones.

☎ 305/895-2486 or 1-877/263-6694, ⊛ www.nannypoppinz.com, or ask at your hotel – most of the larger ones in the city have an extensive list of qualified, on-call sitters.

Museums, aquariums, and zoos

The brand-new **Children's Museum** on Watson Island (see p.74) is the most obvious family-focused attraction: the exhibits here are jazzy and interactive, including a "design your own money" station and a play hospital. Note, though, that they're firmly geared toward pre-schoolers, and the relentless corporate branding may be offputting to some parents. Parents of older kids might prefer to head across the street to **Parrot Jungle**: it's a safe place to let them explore solo, and the ornery, idiosyncratic birds will entertain for hours. See p.73 for more info.

Elsewhere in the city, the **Museum of Science and Planetarium** in Coconut Grove is amusing, if a little old-fashioned, and better for older children; when it moves to its new Downtown site sometime in the next ten years, expect radical improvements (see p.122). The **Historical Museum of South Florida** has several interactive exhibits, including dress-up boxes with period clothes, all designed to bring the area's history to easily digestible life. Key Biscayne is home to the **Miami Seaquarium**, which showcases performing sea creatures, like Lola the acrobatic killer whale, with a thumping dance-music soundtrack. In fact, the most appealing parts of the seaquarium are its conservation efforts – kids of all ages will be captivated by the rangers' chats on the endangered manatee (see p.124).

Heading south of the city brings you to the **Miami Metrozoo** and **Monkey Jungle** (see p.202 and p.203). The zoo's well designed, with its humane enclosures and informative plaques that detail each species' survival status (those endangered are highlighted); children hoping for opportunities to feed the animals (albeit behind cage bars) will find Monkey Jungle unmissable.

Activities

If you're in town on the second Saturday of the month, head to Downtown's **Miami Art Museum** (see p.51). It boasts a stunning collection for adults, but even better, from 1 to 4pm, entrance is free for families, and the museum hosts storytellers, guides, and art programs for younger kids under 7. Older children might better enjoy the **Lowe Art Museum** in Coral Gables (see p.113): two or three times a month, there are Art Adventures, docent-led introductory tours on Saturday or Sunday at 2pm. These aren't specifically aimed at children, but they're usually immensely accessible and great fun.

Don't miss the chance to catch a performance at the **Actors' Playhouse** of its Theater for Young Audiences series ($12, $10 for kids), usually on Saturdays at 2pm: the shows range from traditional fairytales to modern work, but all are smart, engaging, and thoroughly satisfying for kids of all ages – not to mention their parents (see p.162).

The **Venetian Pool** in Coral Gables (see p.109) is a dazzling place to dawdle for an afternoon: there are full-time lifeguards, a small artificial beach-cum-sand-pit and plenty of nooks and crannies in the landscaped lagoon. The only downside is that children under 3 are not permitted.

As for **tours**, most in the city are rather heavy going for anyone with a limited attention span, children or otherwise: the best option's one of **David Brown's**

cultural tours (see p.36), which focus as much on sense of place – stopping and tasting Haitian food, for instance – as on history.

Beaches

The best place for families on **Miami Beach** is the sands around 3rd Street: there are lifeguards, restrooms, picnic tables, and showers. The beach at **Bal Harbour** provides few facilities and frankly isn't that appealing; its one draw is that its shinglier sands are packed with shells, so it's the best place to spend an afternoon looking for take-home treasures.

Over on Key Biscayne, you'll find the city's de facto family beach: **Crandon Park**. In addition to the standard amenities, there are changing facilities, outdoor grills, soccer and softball courts, and more than three miles of seafront. It can get a little busy at weekends, but during the week is an ideal place for kids (see p.125). The marina at **Matheson Hammock Park** in South Miami encloses a man-made lagoon that flushes naturally with the tides of Biscayne Bay and is popular with young children (see p.200).

Festivals

Many of Miami's high-profile events are decidedly adult affairs, but there are some that not only welcome, but cater to, the entire family.

In winter, head over to the **Coral Gables Farmers Market** (Sat 8am–1pm, Jan–March ☎305/460-5311), where, in addition to the produce on sale, there's a range of kids' activities, usually including face painting and storytelling. Then there's the **Carnaval Miami** in early March (☎305/644-8888, ⓦwww .carnavalmiami.com), when Little Havana's Calle Ocho is transformed into a riot of color, noise, and cooking smells, all celebrating Cuban heritage – it's a terrific way to introduce little ones to Miami's Latin influence.

A short drive from Miami proper, the surreal and splashy **Great Sunrise Balloon Race** in May (☎305/596-9040, ⓦwww.sunrisegroup.com) is held at Kendall-Tamiami airport. Spectators are welcome to watch dozens of hot-air balloons as they compete for charity. Bookish kids will enjoy the **Harvest Festival** on the weekend before Thanksgiving (☎305/375-1492, ⓦwww .historical-museum.org). It's overseen by the Historical Museum Downtown and celebrates South Florida's heritage – there are activities, stalls, and even historical re-enactments.

Festivals and events

M iami is always looking for an excuse to party, and plenty of **festivals and events** cater to that need throughout the year. The greatest number of events take place during peak season, from January through April; the only time when there's little, if anything, on offer is during the sticky summer months of July and August. The Orange Bowl in January whips the city into a frenzy, while the three major events that put extra strain on accommodation are the Boat Show in February, the Winter Music Conference in March, and the White Party in November.

The list below is by no means comprehensive, but includes a range of widely different activities – for detailed information, call the phone numbers listed. Otherwise, contact the Greater Miami Convention and Visitors Bureau, 701 Brickell Ave (Mon–Fri 8.30am–6pm; ☏305/539-3000, ⓦwww.gmcvb.com). Another option is to check the usual freesheets like *New Times*, for listings and events; there's also a handy, if unofficial, guide at ⓦwww.festivalsmiami.com or call the Greater Miami Festivals & Events Association at ☏305/651-9404.

January

Orange Bowl Festival January 1 ☏305/371-4600, ⓦwww.orangebowl.org. If Miami is crazy about college football, then the Orange Bowl Parade is the height of its madness. There are floats, marching bands, and even an Orange Bowl Queen. If you want to watch for free, snag a spot early on the parade route along Biscayne Boulevard; otherwise, bleacher seats start at $12. The game itself takes place at Pro Player Stadium – for ticket info, see p.184, "Sports, fitness, and ocean Activities."

Three Kings Day Parade Early January ☏305/447-1140. This celebration of the Three Wise Men is one of the biggest Latin events in the country, with crowds of up to half a million. It all takes place along Calle Ocho between 4th and 27th avenues.

Art Miami Mid-January ☏305/571-1388 or 1-866/727-7953, ⓦwww.art-miami.com. Thanks

to Miami's vibrant art scene, this massive exhibition at the Miami Beach Convention Center often showcases interesting and innovative work by local artists; entrance fee is $12.

Martin Luther King Day Parade January 16 ☏305/247-9306. This march through Liberty City commemorates the slain civil rights leader; there's a fair with music, stalls, and food in the MLK Memorial Park, at 61st and NW 32nd Court.

Art Deco Weekend Third weekend in January ☏305/672-2014, ⓦwww.artdecoweekend.com. Ocean Drive is completely taken over with booths and bands for this celebration of all things Deco. As part of the festival, the Miami Design Preservation League (ⓦwww.mdpl.prg) arranges multiple tours of the historic district.

Taste of the Grove Late January ☏305/444-7270, ⓦwww.coconutgrove.com. Coconut Grove's lively restaurants join together to

⑲

△ Fantasy Fest in Key West

stage this event in Peacock Park, each with a booth that offers samples from their menus. There's also live music.

Key Biscayne Art Festival Late January ☏305/361-0049, ⓦwww.key-biscayne.com. Crandon Boulevard hosts a small but fun party where more than 100 local artists display and sell works in every medium, from acrylic and oil to folk crafts and stained glass.

Miami International Film Festival Late January–early February ☏305/237-3456, ⓦwww.miamifilmfestival.com. Recently taken over by Florida International University, this festival includes arthouse and mainstream films from the USA and abroad, especially Cuba. Films are shown in three locations – the Colony Theater and the Regal Cinema on South Beach, and the Gusman Center in Downtown.

February

Scottish Festival and Games Early February ☎954/476-5559 or 305/871-1635, ⓦwww .sassf.org. This festival includes country dancing and an evening *ceilidh*, as well as Scottish pipe bands and Highland food. It takes place at various sites around South Florida, often in the nearby towns of Pembroke Pines or Fort Lauderdale satellite suburb Coral Springs. Entrance fee is $12.

Homestead Championship Rodeo Early February ☎305/247-3513, ⓦwww.homesteadrodeo.com. Here you can see professional rodeo cowboys competing in steer-wrestling, bull-riding, calf-roping, and bareback-riding competitions. Tickets cost $14, $12 in advance.

Miami International Boat Show Mid-February ☎954/441-3220, ⓦwww.discoverboating.com /miami. This massive luxury exhibition at the Miami Beach Convention Center showcases top-range boats for potential buyers from around the world – a great place to gawp at local million-dollar lifestyle essentials. Tickets $15–25.

Coconut Grove Arts Festival Mid-February ☎305/447-0401, ⓦwww.coconutgroveartsfest .com. Fittingly eccentric for Coconut Grove, you're as likely here to find alternative crafts – such as talking mirrors – as you are traditional painting; a lively, fun festival.

March

Toyota Indy 300 Early March ☎305/230-5000 for information or 305/230-RACE for tickets, ⓦwww.homesteadmiamispeedway.com. The season opener for the Indy Racing League, the Toyota Indy 300 – better known as the Miami Grand Prix – takes place at the Homestead track, south of Miami. Tickets cost from $25 to 45.

Carnaval Miami Early March ☎305/644-8888, ⓦwww.carnavalmiami.com. This nine-day celebration of Latin culture, held across the city, culminates in a parade at the Orange Bowl Stadium, while a Little Havana offshoot showcases Cuban arts, crafts, and cooking along Calle Ocho.

Asian Arts Festival Early March ☎305/247-5727. This festival at the Fruit and Spice Park (see p.202) features Asian crafts, cuisine, and martial arts, as well as fashion shows and acrobatic displays.

Winter Music Conference Late March ☎954/563-4444, ⓦwww.wmcon.com. Producers, managers, and promoters convene at the Miami Beach Conference Center for one of the highlights of the electronic music industry's year. Performances at South Beach clubs by scores of top-name DJs draw a huge crowd, and hotel space is often tight.

April

Miami Gay and Lesbian Film Festival Late April ☎305/534-9924, ⓦwww.mglff.com. Overseen by the director of the classic gay documentary *Beyond Stonewall*, this festival usually takes place at the Colony Theater in South Beach, and features amateur as well as professional submissions.

May

The Great Sunrise Balloon Race Early May ☎305/596-9040, ⓦwww.sunrisegroup.org. A surreal and spectacular race, where dozens of brightly colored balloons compete for charity at Kendall-Tamiami airport.

Hip-Hop Weekend Memorial Day weekend. Recent years have seen an unofficial Hip-Hop Festival held on South Beach during Memorial Day weekend – expect plenty of makeshift clubs, name DJs, and personal appearances by a handful of well-known performers.

June

Goombay Festival Early June ☎ 305/567-1399, 🌐 www.goodmbayfestival.com. This celebration of Bahamian culture takes over Peacock Park in Coconut Grove with colorful stalls and music.

International Hispanic Theater Festival Mid-June ☎ 305/445-8877, 🌐 www.teatroavante .com. Held at El Carrusel Theater in Coral Gables, this festival marks Hispanic achievement in the theater arts with performances by companies from around the world.

July

America's Birthday Bash July 4 ☎ 305/358-7550, 🌐 www.bayfrontparkmiami.com. Independence Day features fireworks and a laser show, with a three-stage music concert at Bayfront Park. The *Biltmore* hotel in Coral Gables also hosts a July 4th celebration, which is pricey but spectacular.

Tropical Agriculture Fiesta Mid-July ☎ 305/278-4185, 🌐 www.tropicalag.org. A chance to sample dozens of different varieties of mango, as well as other exotic fruits at the Fruit and Spice Park (see p.202).

August

Miami Reggae Festival First Sunday in August ☎ 305/891-2944, 🌐 www.jamaicaaware-ness.com. Jamaican Independence Day is commemorated in Bicentennial Park, with a full roster of local, national, and international musical acts.

September

International Ballet Festival of Miami Early September ☎ 305/549-7711, 🌐 www .miamihispanicballet.com. Ballet's big stars come to town for a two-week-long program that is spread among the Colony and Jackie Gleason theaters in South Beach, and the Manuel Artime Theater in Little Havana. It's overseen by the Miami Hispanic Ballet, so expect a strong Latin American slant.
Festival Miami Mid-September to mid-October ☎ 305/284-4940, 🌐 www.music.miami.edu. The University of Miami sponsors this festival, with almost four weeks of mostly classical concerts in and around Coral Gables.
Sportsman Fishing Show Late September ☎ 813/839-7696, 🌐 www.floridasportsman .com/shows/miami. Held in the Dade County Fairgrounds, this show features nearly everything to do with angling, from catnetting and fly-casting demonstrations to actual fishing seminars. Entrance fee for visitors is $7.

October

Hispanic Heritage Festival Throughout October ☎ 305/461-1014, 🌐 www.hispanicfestival.com. One of the largest events of the year, with concerts, fairs, and parades throughout Little Havana. It also features the "Discovery of America" day, and the Miss Hispanidad pageant.

Columbus Day Regatta Early October 🌐 www .columbusdayregatta.net. Held on the weekend nearest Columbus Day, this two-day race begins at Dinner Key Marina in Coconut Grove and heads out to Elliott Key in Biscayne National Park.
Lincoln Road Halloween October 31. Although there's little officially organized for Halloween

in the city, the place to see the wildest costumes (and most outrageous behavior) in Miami is along Lincoln Road on South Beach. Grab a spot at one of the outdoor cafés and watch the impromptu parade.

November

Miami Book Fair International Mid-November ☎305/237-3258, 🖢www.miamibookfair.com. Enormous fair attracting every publisher you could name to set up stalls for the weekend on the campus of Miami-Dade Community College in Downtown.

Harvest Festival Weekend before Thanksgiving ☎305/375-1492, 🖢www.historical-museum .org. Organized by the Historical Museum, this festival celebrates the agricultural traditions of South Florida. There are stalls, quilting demonstrations, and even historical re-enactments at the Dade County Fairgrounds in West Dade.

The White Party Late November ☎305/667-9296, 🖢www.whiteparty.net. Centered on South Beach, this is one of the largest HIV/AIDS fundraisers in America – a largely gay, six-day extravaganza of clubbing and cocktail parties where white clothing is *de rigeur*. It peaks with the decadent ball at Villa Vizcaya, where the white costumes are almost all elaborate, skimpy affairs. Tickets for events start at $25, while tickets for the ball start at around $100.

December

Art Basel Miami Beach Early December ☎305/674-1292, 🖢www.artbasel.com /Miami_beach. The pre-eminent modern art dealers of the world descend on Miami's Convention Center to hawk their clients – the quality's spectacular, though prices are high. There are also plenty of satellite exhibitions over in the Design District (check 🖢www.designmiami.com for more info).

Indian Arts Festival Late December ☎305/223-8380, 🖢www.miccosukeeresort.com. The Miccosukee Village in the Everglades (see p.218) plays host to Native American artists from across America who come to show and sell their work. Tickets cost $12.

King Mango Strut Late December ☎305/401-1171, 🖢www.kingmangostrut.org. Begun twenty years ago by a rejected would-be marcher in the Orange Bowl Parade, the Strut is a campy parade through Coconut Grove, whose participants take aim at topical events with their bizarre costumes.

(19)

20

Directory

Airlines Air Canada ☎1-888/247-2262, ⊛www.aircanada.ca; American Airlines ☎1-800/433-7300, ⊛www.aa.com; British Airways ☎1-800/247-9297, ⊛www.british-airways.com; Continental ☎1-800/523-3273, ⊛www.continental.com; Delta domestic ☎1-800/221-1212, international ☎1-800/241-4141, ⊛www.delta.com; JetBlue ☎1-800/JET-BLUE, ⊛www.jetblue.com; Northwest Airlines/KLM ☎1-800/225-2525, ⊛www.nwa.com; Spirit Airlines ☎1-800/772-17, ⊛www.spiritair.com; United ☎1-800/241-6522, ⊛www.ual.com; US Airways ☎1-800/428-4322, ⊛www.usair.com; Virgin Atlantic ☎1-800/862-8621, ⊛www.virgin-atlantic.com.

Airports Miami International, six miles west of Downtown Miami (☎305/876-7000, ⊛www.miami-airport.com). Take local bus #7 from Downtown Miami (around 30–45min) or local bus #J from Miami Beach (around 40–50min). There are also privately run SuperShuttle minivans (☎305/871-2000 or 1-800/874-8885). More and more travelers, especially domestic budget-airline passengers, are using Fort Lauderdale (☎954/359-1200, ⊛www.broward.org/airport/) airport as a gateway to South Florida: the best route to Miami from there is either car (see below for hire information) or SuperShuttle. More details in Basics, p.27.

American Express Main hotline (Bal Harbour) ☎1-800/325-1218. Offices around the city: in Downtown Miami, 100 N Biscayne Blvd ☎305/358-7350; in Coral Gables, 32 Miracle Mile ☎305/446-3381; in Miami Beach, at Bal Harbour Shops, 9700 Collins Ave ☎305/865-5959.

Amtrak 8303 NW 37th Ave ☎1-800/USA-RAIL, ⊛www.amtrak.com.

Area codes Miami has two prefixes – the original code (☎305), and a newer code

to accommodate demand for additional lines (☎786). Note that although numbers in the Keys share the same prefix as Miami, the call is charged as long distance, not local.

Bike rental See p.183.

Boat rental Skim over Biscayne Bay in a motorboat. Such vessels can be rented for 2–8hr – rates start at $89 for two hours – from Beach Boat Rentals, 2400 Collins Ave, Miami Beach (☎305/534-4307).

Camera repair Wolf Camera, 13120 Biscayne Blvd, North Miami ☎305/891-2120.

Coastguard ☎305/535-4472.

Consulates Canada, 200 S Biscayne Blvd, Suite 1600, Downtown Miami ☎305/579-1600; Denmark, PH 1D, 2655 Le Jeune Rd, Coral Gables ☎305/446-0020; France, 1395 Brickell Ave, Suite 1050, Downtown Miami ☎305/403-4150; Germany, Suite 2200, 100 N Biscayne Blvd, Suite 2200, Downtown Miami ☎305/358-0290; Netherlands, 701 Brickell Ave, 5th floor, Downtown Miami ☎786/866-0480; UK, 1001 Brickell Bay Drive, Suite 2800, Downtown Miami ☎305/374-1522.

Dentists To be referred to a dentist: ☎305/667-3647 or 1-800/336-8478.

Doctors To find a physician: ☎305/324-8717.

Drugs Charges for possession of under 20 grams of the widely consumed marijuana are at the discretion of the officer, though given Miami's ongoing crackdown on illicit drugs, expect a tough penalty. Being caught with more than an ounce, however, means facing a criminal charge for dealing, and a possible prison sentence. Other drugs are, of course, completely illegal and it's a much more serious offense if you're caught with any.

Electricity 110V AC.

Emergencies Dial ☎911 and ask for relevant emergency service.

Greyhound ☎1-800/231-2222, ⓦwww.greyhound.com.

Helplines Crisis Counseling Hotline ☎305/538-4357.

HIV information Care Resource ☎305/576-1234 or ⓦwww.careresource.org.

Hospitals with emergency rooms In Miami: Jackson Memorial Medical Center, 1611 NW 12th Ave ☎305/585-1111; Mercy Hospital, 3663 S Miami Ave ☎305/854-4400. In Miami Beach: Mt Sinai Medical Center, 4300 Alton Rd ☎305/674-2121; South Shore Hospital, 630 Alton Rd ☎305/672-2100.

Internet cafés Available all over Miami and South Beach in particular. Prices are generally $7–9 per hour, or $1 for five minutes. The best places to surf are at the public library (see below), which offers 45 minutes free, or the no-charge access at the Museum of Science (see p.122). Otherwise try these South Beach locations: *Kafka's Kafe*, 1464 Washington Ave (daily 8am–midnight; ☎305/673-9669), or *Cybr Caffe*, 1574 Washington Ave (daily 9am–1am; ☎305/534-0057).

Laundromats Many hotels will have some kind of laundry service, albeit a pricey one. You can also try the Wash Club of South Beach, 510 Washington Ave (8am–midnight; ☎305/534-4298), or Clean Machine, 226 12th St (open 24hr; ☎305/534-9429). If you fancy a drink while you wash, try the *Laundry Bar* (see "Gay Miami," p.169).

Library The biggest is Miami-Dade County Public Library, 101 W Flagler St (Mon–Sat 9am–6pm, Thurs until 9pm; Oct–May also Sun 1–5pm; ☎305/375-2665, ⓦwww.mdpls.org) – see p.49.

Lost and found For items lost on Metro-Dade Transit, call ☎305/375-3366 (Mon–Fri 8am–noon, 1–4pm). Otherwise contact the police (☎305/673-7960).

Parking The fine for an expired meter is $18, for parking in a residential area $23 – both increasing to $45 if not paid within thirty days. You'll find the addresses where you can pay on the back of the ticket (☎305/673-PARK).

Passport and visa office Department of State, Claude Pepper Federal Building, 51 SW 1st Ave, 2nd floor, Downtown ☎305/536-4681.

Pharmacies Usually open from 8am or 9am until 9pm or midnight. Pharmacies open 24 hours include Walgreens, 5731 Bird Rd, Coral Gables (☎305/666-0757), and 1845 Alton Rd, South Beach (☎305/531-8868).

Police Non-emergency ☎305/673-7900; emergency ☎911. If you are robbed anywhere on Miami Beach, report it at the station at 1100 Washington Ave and the report (for insurance purposes) can usually be collected within 3 to 5 days (records office Tues–Fri 8am–3pm; ☎305/673-7100).

Post offices In Miami Beach, 1300 Washington Ave (☎305/538-2708); in Downtown Miami, 500 NW 2nd Ave (☎305/373-7562); in Coral Gables, 251 Valencia Ave (☎305/443-2532); in Coconut Grove, 3191 Grand Ave (☎305/529-6700); in Homestead, 739 Washington Ave (☎305/247-1556). Most usually open Mon–Fri 8am–5pm, Sat 8.30am–1.30pm, or longer hours.

Rape crisis hotline 24hr ☎305/585-7273.

Religious services Catholics can worship at St Patrick's Church, 3716 Garden Ave on Miami Beach (☎305/531-1124), while for Episcopalians, the choice is either the picturesque but inconvenient setting of the Ancient Spanish Monastery, 16711 W Dixie Hwy, North Miami Beach (☎305/945-1461), or the All Souls Episcopal Church on Miami Beach at 4025 Pine Tree Drive (☎305/538-2244). There's a synagogue, Temple Emanu-El, at 1701 Washington Ave in South Beach (☎305/538-2503).

Road conditions ☎305/470-5277.

Rollerblading Hugely popular in Miami, especially in South Beach. Fritz Skate & Bikes, at 730 Lincoln Rd (daily 10am–10pm; ☎305/532-1954), sells and rents out rollerblades and safety gear. Rental costs around $7.50 per hour, $22 per day; bike rentals are also available at the same rates.

Tax Sales tax is 7 percent; room tax on the mainland 2 percent, anywhere on the Miami Beach sandbar 3 percent except in Surfside and Bal Harbour, where it's 4 percent.

Telegrams Western Union has numerous locations in Miami-Dade County: call ☎1-800/325-6000 or check ⓦwww.westernunion.com to find the nearest.

TicketMaster Tickets for arts and sports events, payable by credit card: ☎305/358-5885, ⓦwww.ticketmaster.com.

Time Miami and its environs are on Eastern Standard Time, five hours behind Greenwich Mean Time and three hours ahead of Pacific

Standard Time. Daylight savings takes place between the first Sunday in April and the last Sunday in October.

Tipping You really shouldn't depart a bar or restaurant without leaving a tip of *at least* 15 percent (unless the service is absolutely terrible). The whole system of service is predicated on tipping; not to do so causes a great deal of resentment, and will result in a short pay packet for the waiter or waitress at the end of the week. About the same amount should be added to taxi fares – and round them up to the nearest 50¢ or dollar. A hotel porter who has lugged your suitcases up several flights of stairs should get $1 per bag; though many people tip much more. When paying by credit or charge card, you're expected to add the tip to the total bill before filling in the amount and signing.

Weather information ☎305/229-4522.

Western Union Offices all over the city; call ☎1-800/325-6000 to find the nearest branch.

Women's resources Miami Women's Healthcenter, at North Shore Medical Center, 1100 NW 95th St (☎305/835-6165), offers education information, support, and discussion groups, physician referrals, mammograms, seminars, and workshops. Planned Parenthood of Greater Miami (ⓦwww.ppgm.org), which has branches at 681 NE 125th St, North Miami (☎305/895-7756), and 634–636 6th St, South Beach (☎305/621-6636), provides economical health care for men and women, including birth-control supplies, pregnancy testing, treatment of sexually transmitted diseases, and counseling.

South Florida

South Florida

South to Homestead

F ew visitors venture into the polished suburbs that sprawl out to the **south of Miami**, but it's here you'll sense a distinctly Floridian feel to life, a slower pace that's dominated by the land, as opposed to the breathless, cosmopolitan vibe of urban Miami. Parks and gardens abound, as well as some of the city's most idiosyncratic attractions, scattered nearby meandering Old Cutler Road and **Highway 1** – or the South Dixie Highway, as it's also known – as it carves its way down to agricultural **Homestead** and, finally, Florida City and the Keys (see p.225).

Touring this area is impractical without a car, for while there is fragmented local bus service in each town, little public transport joins the centers. It's better to **rent a car** (for rental companies, see "Basics," p.21) and shuttle between the attractions – you can easily take in most of what the region has to offer in two days or so – and then, if you're so inclined, head down to the Keys. Unless where we've suggested otherwise, along Hwy-1 it's best to **stick to the main route**, as the latticework of roads that quilts the surrounding area is poorly signposted and easy to get lost in.

South to Homestead

Moving south from Coral Gables and Coconut Grove, you arrive at the suburb now known as **South Miami**, originally dubbed Larkins in honor of the pioneer dairy farmer who first settled the area. These days, it's not milk but money that's abundant: this is one of the wealthiest suburbs in the city, filled with expansive and expensive new mansions occasionally interrupted by a golf course or two. Just past Coral Gables, Hwy-1 is mostly lined with gas stations and porn stores, and often choked with traffic, and it's far better to head down **Old Cutler Road**, a pleasant drive from Coconut Grove through a thick belt of woodland, where you'll find a series of worthy sights, beginning with the **Fairchild Tropical Garden**, with its showy collection of exotic plants; nearby, the **Charles Deering Estate** offers a dignified taste of pioneer wealth.

Further west, just a short detour over the Florida's Turnpike, the **Miami Metrozoo** is an enormous, sophisticated facility that's home to hundreds of "wild" animals. If you're a keen gardener, detour along **186th Street** south from here, off either the Turnpike or Hwy-1. It's lined with garden centers and greenhouses selling pricey tropical plants (heavily featured in the book *The Orchid Thief* and movie *Adaptation*) – many of which are open to the public, but don't expect any bargains. If you just want to browse rather than buy plants, better to stay on Hwy-1 until you reach the vast **Fruit and Spice Park**. The last sight before arriving at the agricultural hub of Homestead is **Monkey Jungle**, where the visitors are in cages and the monkeys roam free.

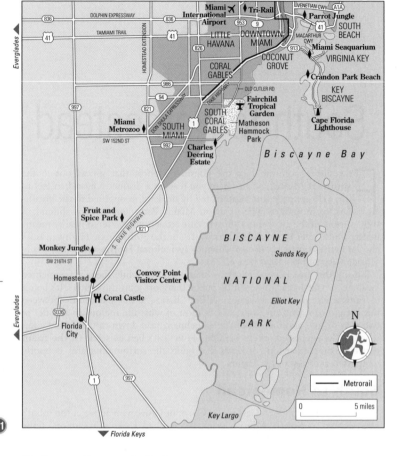

▼ *Florida Keys*

Matheson Hammock Park

On the weekends, thousands flock to **Matheson Hammock Park** (daily 6am–sunset; $4 per car; ☎305/665-5475, ⊛www.miamidade.gov/parks/parks /matheson_beach.asp), at 9601 Old Cutler Rd, to picnic, use the marina, or take a dip in the artificial lagoon. This greenspace was a coconut plantation before becoming a public park in 1930, and today, it is great for small children but has little to offer adults. The rest of the sizeable park is much less crowded, and you can easily while away a few hours strolling around the wading pond – popular with people catching crabs – or along the winding trails above the mangrove swamps.

Fairchild Tropical Garden

South from Matheson Hammock Park, at 10901 Old Cutler Rd, lies **Fairchild Tropical Garden** (daily 9.30am–4.30pm, tram tours every hour until 3pm; $10, 1st Wed of month donation suggested; ☎305/667-1651, ⊛www .fairchildgarden.org). Founded on the site of a former mango plantation by botanist David Fairchild and his palm-crazy friend Robert Montgomery in 1938, the garden was built to be a living encyclopedia of exotic plants for locals, and resident scientists still scour the world for unusual or endangered species to add to the collection. Sadly, the garden's collection was devastated by Hurricane Andrew, turning two-thirds of the plants into little more than tropical coleslaw: Disneyworld even sent cranes to help right fallen trees. Twelve years later, the scars are healing well, and there's little evidence to the casual eye of any damage aside from a few large logs.

The easiest way to take in the 83-acre garden – the largest tropical botanical garden in the continental United States – is on one of the 45-minute **tram tours**. The tour winds through the garden's different habitats, including a fine collection of rare plants from the Bahamas and the Tropical Rainforest area, specially watered by an ingenious tree-irrigation system that supplements South Florida's insufficient rainfall. As a research institution, Fairchild works with scientists all over the world to preserve the diversity of the tropical environment; many of the plant species here, such as Cape Sable Whiteweed and Alvaradoa, are extinct in their original environments, and efforts have been made to re-establish them in their places of origin. That said, it's the Windows to the Tropics hothouse that's perhaps the biggest draw, filled with beautiful bromeliads, orchids, and other sensitive plants. It also houses the garden's most famous resident, "Mr Stinky," a six-foot-high Sumatran *amorphophallus titanium* that made headlines in 1998 thanks to the rare blooming of its giant flower that's been described as smelling like "rotting elephant corpse."

The Deering Estate

Although Charles Deering's younger half-brother James was the millionaire mastermind behind Villa Vizcaya (see p.120), his own rustic **Deering Estate** (daily 10am–5pm, last admission 4pm; estate tours daily 10.30am, 11.30am, 2.30pm, 3pm, house tours daily 10.30am, 2pm; $7; ☎305/235-1668, ⊛www .deeringestate.org) at 16701 SW 72nd Ave could not be more different from Vizcaya and its opulent excess.

Both brothers, originally from the Midwest, had retired to Florida; but while James wanted fountains and formal gardens, Charles – a wealthy industrialist turned amateur botanist – set about creating an estate that would preserve the area's natural vegetation. He bought the moribund town of **Cutler**, bypassed by Flagler's railroad, and tore it down, sparing only one building, Richmond Cottage, an inn on the route from Coconut Grove to Key West. After he modernized and electrified the cottage, Deering built an adjoining stone house to hold his multi-million-dollar art collection (which included works by Toulouse-Lautrec, Gauguin, and Whistler). Both houses were tricked out in the Mediterranean Revival style, with a strong Moorish influence. The facade was built from oolitic limestone – a stone considered useful for the Revival style, since it erodes delicately in the rain and sea air, affording an artful illusion of age. The mansion's interior seems equally old: all echoing halls, dusty chandeliers, and checkerboard-tile floors, it carries a Gothic spookiness.

Deering lived here for a short time before his death in 1927, but under the terms of his will the estate remained in the family until the 1990s, when it was sold to the City of Miami and opened as a park. Unfortunately, there's little to see inside either structure, as he donated his art collection to the Art Institute of Chicago after the hurricane of 1926, while his daughters sold off much of the furniture once their mother died. Nevertheless, the estate is a tranquil respite from all the ritziness of the rest of Miami, ideal for an afternoon spent reading a book by the ocean on its sweeping front lawns.

Free **ranger-guided trips** into the woodland hammock on four-wheel-drive golf carts are fascinating, taking in Charles Deering's own avocado groves, local plants, and a 1500-year-old Tequesta burial mound where the remains of two dozen human beings, dating back 10,000 years, have been found. **Chicken Key**, just offshore from the Deering Estate, is so named because it was used as a poultry pen by Native Americans; the Deering Estate runs canoe tours out to the unspoilt landscape of the now chicken-free key for $25, including estate admission (usually Sat & Sun 8.30am, as well as occasional moonlit excursions; reservations essential – call for upcoming schedule).

The Miami Metrozoo

Just west of Florida's Turnpike, the **Miami Metrozoo**, at 12400 SW 152nd St (daily 9.30am–5.30pm, last admission 4pm; $11.50, children 3–12 $6.75, children under 3 free; tram tour $2.50; ☎305/251-0401, ⓦwww.miamimetrozoo .com), is a vast compound where hundreds of species are grouped according to their native continent: there are familiar animals, like giraffes and ostriches, alongside less commonplace creatures such as the llama-like *guanaco* and the *anoa*, which resembles a small buffalo. It's well designed, too, with humane, open enclosures – more moat-and-hill than fence-and-cage – and the frequent plaques employed to detail each species' survival status is a great educational opportunity for kids.

It's best to arrive early, as most of the animals are liveliest before the baking midday sun takes hold; visitors, though, can hop onto the air-conditioned monorail that runs through the park if the heat becomes unbearable. Whatever time you arrive, there should be a **feeding demonstration** – they're on a rolling schedule, to allow visitors a chance to talk with the animals' knowledgeable keepers; the zoo's famous group of white Bengal tigers (only one of which is actually white) is fed at 11am.

The zoo was one of the attractions worst hit by Hurricane Andrew – though the damage was mostly structural, and only 20 out of 1000 animals were killed. The birdhouse sustained the worst harm and has only just reopened as the Wings of Asia aviary. Designed like ancient ruins, it's an impressive display, leading visitors through the evolution of Asian birds from dinosaurs; the trip's set to a squawky soundtrack from today's endangered avian species.

The Fruit and Spice Park

As the name suggests, the **Fruit and Spice Park**, a few miles south from the Metrozoo at 24801 SW 187th St (daily 10am–5pm; free tours at 11am, 1.30pm, 3pm; $5; ☎305/247-5727, ⓦwww.miamidade.gov/parks/Parks/fruit_spice.asp), houses exotic fruit and spice plants – thirty acres of them in all. The different fruits and plants are grouped together by species or theme – for example, an oddball banana plantation showcases fifty different varieties, as well as a poisonous plant patch, carefully screened off from visitors. There's even a citrus quarantine to keep their specimens safe in response to the devastation wrought locally by blight.

Disappointingly, though, there are no maps available for those who'd rather walk through the grounds unaccompanied, and labeling of plants is also spotty. Unless you happen to arrive when a tour's departing, this minimally informative set-up makes the park a must-see only for avid gardeners and plant fanciers – the best part for the less interested will be the wide range of free fruit cut up ready to eat in the gift shop. For the casually curious, the Kampong in Coconut Grove (see p.118) is a much better option.

(see p.118)

Monkey Jungle

An amateur primate behaviorist first set up this park at 14805 SW 216th St to observe monkeys in the wild; when funding got tight, he began charging admission, and **Monkey Jungle** was born (daily 9.30–5pm, last admission 4pm; $17.95, children 3–9 $11.95, children under 3 free; ℡305/235-1611, ⒲www .monkeyjungle.com). Now there are thirty species living here including a roaring pack of howler monkeys and some wide-eyed red ruffed lemurs – supposedly with the twist that the monkeys roam free, while humans visit in caged walkways. It's a diverting, if not especially informative, biopark – in fact, plenty of the monkeys *are* in cages, and signage on species and habitat is frustratingly infrequent. Bring quarters to feed the animals: in a clever touch, dishes dangle from chains over the walkways, which the monkeys have learned to reel in like fishermen once a passing human has stocked a platter with seeds.

△ Orange country

Homestead and around

Decimated when the nearby airforce base closed down, **Homestead** has now been hit hard by citrus blight, and the area's definitely seen better times (see box below). One positive by-product of its agricultural economy, though, is a thriving **"pick your own"** business, where for a nominal cost per pound you can pick produce to take home – look out for the roadside signs. It's a great option if you're heading into the Everglades, where few supplies are available. In addition, the town is filled with itinerant fruitpickers, lending it a sort of bordertown transience: to take a look around – though there's not much to see – follow Krome Avenue south to reach the center of town. For accommodation or eating options in Homestead, see p.135 and p.150.

The last two places of interest before Hwy-1 curves down to the Keys are the twin delights of the eerie, magical **Coral Castle** and the mostly-underwater **Biscayne National Park**, a must-visit for any snorkel or dive enthusiast.

If you're headed south to the Keys after visiting sights in the area rather than returning to Miami, a better place to stop overnight than Homestead is in **Florida City**, just further south along Hwy-1. Things are much perkier there: in a smart move, the town's refashioned itself into a sort of **gateway to the Keys** for holidaymakers, thereby lessening its reliance on fruit farming, and bolstering the local economy, though there's little noteworthy to see in Florida City itself. One valuable amenity in Florida City is the terrific **Tropical Everglades Visitor Information Center** (Mon–Sat 8am–4.45pm, Sun varies; ☎305/245-9180 or 1-800/388-9669, ⊛www.tropicaleverglades.com), at 160 Hwy-1, close to the junction with Hwy-9336 (344th Street). It offers a wealth of information on attractions around Homestead and in the Keys, but is particularly strong (of course) on the Everglades.

The Coral Castle

The **Coral Castle**, a memorable – if tacky – stop-off at 28655 Hwy-1 (daily 7am–9pm; $9.75, children 7–12 $5, children under 6 free; ☎305/248-6345, ⊛www.coralcastle.com), is as unique and odd as the story behind it. Ed Leedskalnin, a 5-foot-tall, 100-pound immigrant, allegedly built it as a tribute to

㉑

Hurricane Andrew vs. Homestead

Homestead hit the headlines on August 24, 1992, for all the wrong reasons: it was here that **Hurricane Andrew** hit with full force. Although a comparatively compact storm, its winds reached speeds of more than 200mph – at least, that's the estimated force, as the official windspeed gauge broke at 164mph.

The three towns of Homestead, Florida City, and Naranja were puréed, and Homestead Air Force Base was also wrecked – it later closed, with a devastating effect on the local community. Once the storm passed on, heading toward Louisiana, it had left 60,000 houses destroyed, 200,000 people homeless, and damage that would cost an estimated $20 billion to repair – one of the greatest natural disasters in modern American history.

Since then, the physical scars have healed – buildings have been reconstructed in the towns and farmland has been replanted. However, the economic wound is still, with Homestead and the surrounding area still struggling to thrive, providing a gritty glimpse of Florida life.

For more on hurricanes in Florida, see p.257, Contexts: History.

the 16-year-old fiancée, Agnes Scuffs, who jilted him in his native Latvia. Heartbroken, he traveled the world, working as a stonemason, logger, and rancher, and eventually found himself in Florida in 1918 thanks to a nasty bout of TB. Buying land near Homestead a few years later, he quarried coral rock from his land and, singlehandedly, used this rock to build a simple house as well as an ornamental garden decorated with crescent moons and heart-shaped tables.

No one knows how this tiny man moved such massive blocks of stone: he worked at night, and never revealed his methodology to anyone before dying in 1951. Engineers have consistently scoffed at his feats, until trying and failing to replicate them – scientists are still baffled by the nine-ton gate, for example, which can be moved with a hefty push from a single finger.

The esoteric iconography of the Coral Castle is pegged to Leedskalnin's fascination with astronomy, astrology, and ancient Egypt. He used divining rods to check the area's alignment with ley lines, or supposed linear configurations of ancient sites, and, surprisingly, electromagnetic testing has confirmed their presence – there's a cluster of ley lines especially thick around the Moon Pond. This has made the Coral Castle an important site for local New Agers, and there have even been several Wiccan "baptisms" on the site. Whatever the explanation behind its construction, the Coral Castle is a kitschy and surreal stop-off.

Biscayne National Park

Unique among national parks, since 95 percent of it is under water, **Biscayne National Park**, at 9700 SW 328th St (daily except Christmas 7am–5.30pm, sea accessible 24 hours a day; ☎305/230-7275, ⓦwww.nps .gov/bisc), is well worth the 20-minute detour. The visitor center at Convoy Point lies at the end of a featureless road, Canal Drive or 328th Street, nine miles from Hwy-1. Technically, the Florida Keys begin here with the tiny Boca Chita Key (which special forces used to commandeer as an isolated training ground); and the **reef** in this park is the same **coral formation** that draws enthusiastic snorkelers and divers to the John Pennekamp State Park (see p.229), off Key Largo. The reef is much better preserved and more spectacular here than at the better-known dive sites further down the coast, and it's a shame so many avid divers don't make the trip here. Stop by the excellent **visitor center** (9am–5pm) for detailed information. If you're planning only one reef trip in the area, make it this one or Looe Key in the Lower Keys (see p.235).

There are several ways to see the reef, with its living coral that shelters shoals of brightly colored fish; all are run by the same concessioneer operating out of Convoy Point. The lazy way is on a ranger-guided, three-hour glass-bottomed boat trip (daily at 10am; $25.95; reservations essential ☎305/230-1100), but it is worth the effort taking the afternoon jaunt, when you can actually snorkel around the coral for the same amount of time (daily 1.30pm; $36.50 including all equipment; reservations essential). Call to check on schedules as they can vary, and trips may also be canceled due to bad weather.

The other way to enjoy Biscayne National Park is by visiting one of the barrier islands, seven miles out to sea: Elliott Key and Boca Chita Key. Overnight **camping** is permitted – there are restrooms on both islands, but Elliott Key also has showers and drinking water, as well as a station where a ranger lives year-round. Once there, there's little to do other than sunbathe or hike an easy six-mile trail round the island's forested spine. The overnight camping fee at both keys is $10. If you don't have your own boat to reach them, the

㉑

concessioneer also runs daily trips, weather permitting: Boca Chita leaves at 10am on the glass-bottomed boat ($25.95 round-trip, reservations essential) and Elliott Key at 1.30pm with the snorkel trip (each $25.95 round-trip, reservations essential). Note that the boats to the keys only run November through May; and expect mosquitoes to be fierce year-round, so bring everything you'll need (Nov–May; round-trip boat ride $25).

Fort Lauderdale

A fter a long beach-party hangover, **Fort Lauderdale**, just 40 minutes drive north from Downtown Miami, is slowly developing a distinctive, more sophisticated atmosphere. This is both thanks to its revitalized Historic District and a growing gay scene, comprised largely of refugees from South Beach – in the next few years, watch for the city to swipe some of Miami's cachet as a cool vacation destination.

It's a far cry from Fort Lauderdale's former reputation as the site of what seemed like the whole of America's college **spring break**; or indeed its origins, when the settlement began its life as a military fortification against a Seminole Indian attack (the commanding officer was a Major William Lauderdale). By the end of the nineteenth century, Lauderdale's one-time fort had grown into a thriving trading post; but it wasn't until the 1930s, when swimming teams began coming here for meets, that the town's hard-partying reputation was born. That legend was cemented by the 1960 film *Where the Boys Are*, starring Paula Prentiss and a young George Hamilton.

That movie made Fort Lauderdale synonymous with college students' spring break for more than twenty years until the mid-1980s, when numbers grew so unmanageable that the local council wrote to universities across the country expressly asking them to dissuade students from coming on vacation. This anti-student initiative, coupled with the aggressive upgrading of beach facilities, proved effective by the late 1990s and helped Fort Lauderdale slough off its somewhat tawdry image – even if some grumble that the students took some of the city's verve with them when they decamped north to Daytona Beach.

Now, as Miami grows more popular, trend-chasers and bargain-minded gays attracted by the potential of Fort Lauderdale's mid-century homes are scoping out the city. Miami restaurateurs are snapping up spaces to open new eateries like *Johnny Vs* attracted by the increasing sophistication of visitors. A further draw in comparison with Miami is Fort Lauderdale's laid-back vibe – think board shorts and flip-flops instead of heels and a thong.

Arrival, information, and getting around

Fort Lauderdale–Hollywood International Airport (FLL) is becoming an increasingly popular choice for access to both Fort Lauderdale and Miami, thanks both to the hellish disorganization at MIA and this airport's popularity with budget domestic carriers like JetBlue and Spirit Airlines (☎954/359-1200,

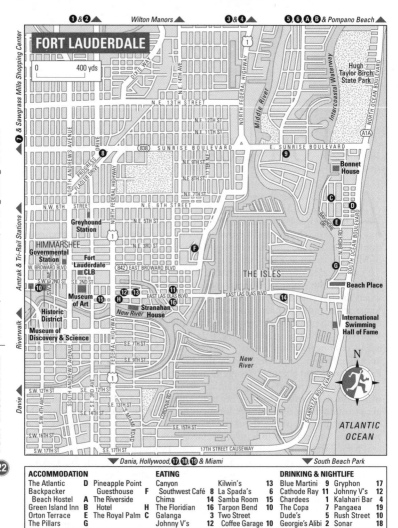

FORT LAUDERDALE

0   400 yds

❶&❷▲   Wilton Manors ▲   ❸&❹▲   ❺,❻,Ⓐ,Ⓑ & Pompano Beach ▲

DIXIE WAY
N.E. 14TH AVE
N.E. 13TH STREET
N.E. 12TH ST
N.E. 11TH ST
NORTH FEDERAL HIGHWAY
Middle River
Intercoastal Waterway
NORTH OCEAN BOULEVARD
Hugh Taylor Birch State Park

❼ & Sawgrass Mills Shopping Center

(838) SUNRISE BOULEVARD   E. SUNRISE BOULEVARD
N.E. 9TH ST
17TH TER NE
N.E. 8TH ST
N.E. 7TH ST
PROGRESSO DRIVE
FLAGLER DRIVE
NORTH ANDREWS AVENUE
❽
❾
(A1A)
Bonnet House

N.E. 6TH STREET
N W 6TH STREET
N.E. 5TH ST
N.E. 3RD ST
Ⓒ
Ⓓ
BAYSHORE DRIVE
N. BIRCH RD.
SOUTH OCEAN BOULEVARD
Ⓔ

Greyhound Station
HIMMARSHEE
Governmental Station
W. BROWARD BLVD
S.W 2ND ST
S.E. 2ND ST
Fort Lauderdale CLB
(842) EAST BROWARD BLVD
Ⓕ
THE ISLES
Ⓖ
Beach Place

Amtrak & Tri-Rail Stations
❿
⓯
⓬ ⓭
Ⓗ
EAST LAS OLAS BLVD
⓰
EAST LAS OLAS BLVD
⓮

Museum of Art
Stranahan House
New River Blvd

Historic District
Museum of Discovery & Science
International Swimming Hall of Fame

Riverwalk
NORTH FEDERAL HIGHWAY
S.E. 7TH ST
S.E. 9TH ST
New River
N
S.W. 12TH ST
S.E. 12TH ST
Davie
SOUTH ANDREWS AVENUE
S.E. 3RD AVE
S.W. 4TH AVE
S.E. 13TH ST
S.E. 14TH ST
CORDOVA RD
MAIN ROAD
S.E. 15TH ST
SEABREEZE BOULEVARD
ATLANTIC OCEAN
S.W. 16TH ST
S.W. 17TH ST
S.E. 17TH ST
17TH STREET CAUSEWAY

▼ Dania, Hollywood, ⓱, ⓲, ⓳ & Miami   ▼ South Beach Park

ACCOMMODATION		EATING				DRINKING & NIGHTLIFE			
The Atlantic	D	Canyon		Kilwin's	13	Blue Martini	9	Gryphon	17
Backpacker		Southwest Café	8	La Spada's	6	Cathode Ray	11	Johnny V's	12
Beach Hostel	A	Chima	14	Samba Room	15	Chardees	1	Kalahari Bar	4
Green Island Inn	B	The Floridian	16	Tarpon Bend	10	The Copa	7	Pangaea	19
Orton Terrace	E	Galanga	3	Two Street		Dude's	5	Rush Street	10
The Pillars	G	Johnny V's	12	Coffee Garage	10	Georgie's Alibi	2	Sonar	18
Pineapple Point									
Guesthouse	F								
The Riverside									
Hotel	H								
The Royal Palm	C								

ⓦwww.broward.org/airport/). There are ample car rental desks on site and plenty of cabs; expect to pay $12 one way to the beach.

All the long-distance public-transport terminals are in or near downtown: the Greyhound **bus station** is at 515 NE 3rd St (☎954/764-6551), while the **train** and Tri-Rail station is two miles west at 200 SW 21st Terrace (Amtrak ☎1-800/USA-RAIL, ⓦwww.amtrak.com; Tri-Rail ☎1-800-TRI-RAIL, ⓦwww.trirail .com), linked to the center by regular bus #22.

The **Convention and Visitors Bureau** has finally moved to a convenient spot that's open to the public downtown, after several years on the outskirts of the city: stop by 100 E Broward Blvd at SE 1st Ave, Suite 200 (Mon–Fri 8.30am–5pm; ☎954/765-4466 or 1-800/22-SUNNY, ⓦwww.sunny.org).

Otherwise, pick up a copy of the free *CityLink* magazine or *New Times* (available throughout the city) to find out what's going on. Also available is a free **tourism and cultural hotline** (☎954/452-0000), staffed by operators fluent in five languages.

The handiest service offered by the thorough **local bus** network (BCT ☎954/357-8400, ✆www.broward.org/bct) is the #11, which runs twice hourly along Las Olas Boulevard between downtown Fort Lauderdale and the beach; **timetables** are available from Governmental Center (at the corner of Andrews Avenue and Broward Boulevard), the bus terminal directly opposite, or from libraries and check-cashing centers. If you are using the buses, remember to buy a **Buz Pass** ($2.50), which allows unlimited travel on the buses throughout Broward County – otherwise it's $1 a journey and there are no transfers. There's also now a free, hop-on/hop-off trolley service that loops through Himmarshee every Friday and Saturday night (Fri 5–11pm, Sat noon–11pm).

More expensive than buses – but more fun – are the **water taxis** (daily 10am–midnight; ☎954/467-6677, ✆www.watertaxi.com), a series of small boats that will pick up and deliver you almost anywhere along Fort Lauderdale's many miles of waterfront, from Broward up to Seventeenth Street Causeway. These taxis are without a doubt the best way to see the city, and an all-day pass, allowing unlimited usage, costs only $5 (single tickets are $4). Though in the past locals have complained about their unreliability (and unexpected early closing), these taxis have been overhauled and are now a superb option.

If you'd rather have a structured **water tour** of the city, try the riverboat cruise-cum-cabaret show on the campy but fun *Jungle Queen Riverboat*, moored at Seabreeze Boulevard at Hwy-A1A (daily 7pm; $30.95 including dinner; ☎954/462-5596, ✆www.junglequeen.com).

△ A watertaxi on the Intracoastal Waterway

Accommodation

The Convention and Visitors Bureau leaflets and website are a superb resource for **accommodation**; even better, prices here tend to be reasonable year-round and you'll often get more for your money staying here than in Miami, especially in the motels beachside that hug the interior of the Intracoastal Waterway. There's an explosion, too, in luxury waterfront accommodation – three vast new hotels, including Florida's first *W*, are planned for the beach.

The Atlantic 601 N Fort Lauderdale Beach Blvd (A1A) at Terramar St, Beachside ☎954/567-8070, ⓦwww.theatlantichotelfortlauderdale.com. This luxury condo-hotel has large rooms, ocean-front views, and thoughtful touches – from a welcoming cocktail and warming towel at check-in to a bottle of water offered as soon as you arrive at the pool. Rooms from $249.

Backpacker Beach Hostel 2115 N Ocean Blvd at NE 21st St, Beachside ☎954/567-7275, ⓦwww.fortlauderdalehostel.com. This clean, friendly hostel has plenty of free pluses: parking, food (bread, tea, coffee, pasta, Internet access, laundry, and even pick-up from airport, bus, or train station during the day. There's also a pleasant rooftop patio and no curfew. Dorm beds $18.

Green Island Inn 3300 NE 27th St at NE 33rd Ave, Beachside ☎954/566-8951 or 1-888/505-8951, ⓦwww.greenislandinn.com. This charming, family-run inn features bright, homely rooms and kitchenettes, set around a leafy

garden. There's a small pool, and ample parking. $50 and up.

The Pillars 111 N Birch Rd at Sebastian St, Beachside ☎954/467-9639, ⓦwww.pillarshotel .com. A former private house turned upscale B&B, this beach bolthole has large, antique-crammed rooms, and a breakfast patio that overlooks the Intra-coastal Waterway. There's also a shady, tree-lined pool, and a water-taxi stop nearby. Rooms from $129.

The Riverside Hotel 620 E Las Olas Blvd at 7th St, Downtown ☎954/467-0671, ⓦwww .riversidehotel.com. The best option if you want to stay downtown, the *Riverside* is a historic inn with a 110-room modern addition. Rooms are large and filled with raffia furniture and tropical-print, Tommy Bahama–style bedspreads. The main entrance and check-in is at the rear, close to the Stranahan House, rather than on Las Olas. Rooms from $119.

The Town

The private yacht-clogged Intracoastal Waterway splits Fort Lauderdale roughly in half, between **downtown** and **beachside**. Each area has its own north–south artery: Hwy-1 (also known as the Federal Highway), which cuts through the center of the city; parallel to this along the beachfront is the drag known usually as Hwy-A1A (don't be confused by the various local designations it collects along the strip, like Fort Lauderdale Beach Boulevard or Ocean Boulevard). East–west, the handiest roads are Sunrise and Las Olas boulevards, both of which run the length of the city to the sea.

Downtown and the Historic District

Tall, anonymous, glass-fronted buildings may make an uninspiring first impression, but **downtown Fort Lauderdale** – a thin rectangle bounded by NW 7th Avenue to the west, NE 8th Avenue to the east, Broward Boulevard to the north, and Las Olas Boulevard to the south – has an outstanding modern art museum and a pleasant pedestrian area along Las Olas Boulevard where there are affordable shops and restaurants, mostly between the Federal Highway and NE 11th Avenue.

The Museum of Art

Fort Lauderdale's **Museum of Art** (Fri–Mon, Wed 11am–7pm, Thurs 11am–9pm; $6; ☎954/525-5500, ⊛www.moafl.org) is housed at 1 E Las Olas Blvd in a Postmodern building shaped like a slice of pie, and has one of the most impressive permanent collections in the state. And thanks to well-regarded new director Irvin Lippman, it's now attracting attention-grabbing temporary shows, among them art from the Vatican collection as well as commemorations of the likes of Princess Diana.

Year-round, it displays a rotating choice from its permanent collection, including household names like Andy Warhol, plus plenty more Pop Art. It's best known, though, for its exhaustive survey of work from the short-lived CoBrA movement of the early 1950s – the acronym derives from the three cities (Copenhagen, Brussels, and Amsterdam) where its artists were most active. With a desire to create without inhibitions, the CoBrA clique's Abstract Expressionism is marked by a focus on intense color, making their canvases an eye-popping, if acquired, taste; look for marquee names like Asger Jorn, Carl Henning-Pedersen, and Karel Appel.

Himmarshee

Millions were spent gussying up the oldest part of downtown into a new development known as **Riverwalk,** a shopping center and park complete with pedestrian walkways and waterfront cafés. This development brackets two different areas: one, known variously as the **Performing Arts District** or **Himmarshee** (HIM-uh-shee), boasts bars and restaurants and is humming with people most Friday and Saturday nights. It's also the site of the only road tunnel in sodden Florida, scooped under downtown in 1960 to ease traffic congestion on the Federal Highway Bridge.

At the end of the Riverwalk, at 401 SW 2nd St, you'll come to the creative, fun **Museum of Discovery and Science** (Mon–Sat 10am–5pm, Sun noon–6.30pm; $14 including admission to one IMAX film; ☎954/467-6637, ⊛www.mods.org). The interactive exhibits are engaging and educational, including "Gizmo City" on the second floor, which explains the principles of physics through everyday machines; and the "Florida EcoScapes" exhibition near the atrium, which houses native Everglades critters such as fish and turtles, plus a huge living coral reef. There's also an **IMAX theater** on site that shows a rotating schedule of 3-D films; call for showtimes and current movies (☎954/463-4629).

The Historic District

Another part of the Riverwalk renewal, Fort Lauderdale's **Historic District** (☎954/463-4431, ⊛www.oldfortlauderdale.org) comprises a small collection of buildings located around SW 2nd Street and SW 3rd Avenue. The **Hoch Heritage Center**, 219 SW 2nd Ave, is under renovation at time of writing, with plans to transform it into a sparkling visitor center and research hub; in the meantime, the three historic homes nearby can be visited individually.

The city's first tourist hotel, the 1905 **New River Inn**, 231 SW 2nd Ave (Tues–Fri 11am–5pm, Sat & Sun noon–5pm; $5), is now home to the Old Fort Lauderdale Museum of History. It showcases a varied collection of documents and artifacts on the city's history. The sports room is especially good, as is the video that shows clips from the dozens of movies – including *Porky's* and *Body Heat* – that were filmed or set locally. Next door, at 229 SW 2nd Ave, there's the **King-Cromartie House** (tours by appointment only Tues–Sun 2pm) built in 1907, and housing an unremarkable museum of early settler life. The building itself, though, is more interesting: when contractor Edwin T. King built it, this home boasted then-astonishing amenities like indoor running water. Its design – it was originally a bungalow made with termite-resistant Dade County pine and a large, airy porch – set a template for other pioneers to follow.

Unfortunately, you can't see the inside of the **Philemon Bryan House**, 227 SW 2nd Ave, as it's used as offices by the museum's administrators; the building itself was put up by King for two clients in 1905 and is notable for its unusually fancy detailing, including Classical Revival columns.

The Stranahan House

East from the Historic District stands a more complete reminder of early Fort Lauderdale life: the **Stranahan House** (Oct–May Wed–Sat 10am–3pm, Sun 1–3pm, compulsory tours begin on the hour; $6; ☎954/524-4736, ⊛www .stranahanhouse.org), at 335 SE 6th Ave. With a lovingly restored interior that belies its unprepossessing exterior, this was the home of Frank Stranahan, so-called Father of Fort Lauderdale, who set up the first trading post with the Seminoles here and accrued substantial wealth. The Florida frontier-style house gives a good idea of what life was like for wealthy early settlers, crammed as it is with antique ephemera. Frank's life – along with that of his yoga-loving, eccentric wife, Ivy – is lovingly detailed by the knowledgeable and chatty docents. The wraparound porch, raised from the ground but open on all sides much like a *chickee* (Seminole hut), is where Native Americans would spend the night during trading expeditions to the area.

Beachside

The main route to the Fort Lauderdale **beaches** is Las Olas Boulevard, lined with shops and reasonably priced restaurants; the drive leads past the swanky residences of **the Isles**, spindly finger-shaped islets that allow its rich residents to park their boats at the end of the back garden. Once across the bridge that spans the Intracoastal Waterway, you've reached **beachside** Fort Lauderdale.

It may be less brash than it was in its spring-break heyday, but there are still plenty of theme restaurants and rowdy bars, especially around the unappealing shopping center known as **Beach Place**. As for the beach itself, it's hemmed in by swaying palm trees and a swirling white wall that's one of the city's signature sights (though the broken, in-built strip of neon lighting is still awaiting funds for repair). It's usually easy to stake out a spot in the sun, and even better since the water here's been certified Blue Wave for its cleanliness and safety; if the crowds are heavy head south – the beach widens in that direction. There are facilities dotted along the stretch of sand: showers at the end of Las Olas Boulevard, and restrooms plus picnic tables a little further north at the end of Sunrise.

The Bonnet House

The **Bonnet House**, at 900 N Birch Rd (May–Nov Wed–Fri 10am–3pm, Sat 10am–4pm, Sun noon–4pm; Dec–April Wed–Sat 10am–4pm, Sun noon–4pm; obligatory tours hourly on the half hour until 90min before closing time; $10; ☎954/563-5393, ⊛www.bonnethouse.org), and its surrounding gardens are one of Fort Lauderdale's major cultural draws, a pioneer oddity nestled among the towering beachside condos. Built by trustafarian and amateur artist-collector Frederic Clay Bartlett, whose family made millions as hardware merchants in Chicago, the place is named after the yellow waterlily that grows in abundance on the estate. Bartlett snagged the land here when he married another wealthy

Midwesterner, Helen Birch, whose father Hugh had snapped up swathes of land in southern Florida in the late nineteenth century (see below); this chunk was a wedding gift. Helen died not long after, and Frederic found a second, even wealthier bride, in Evelyn Fortune Lilly – ex-wife of medicine magnate Eli. Together Frederic and Evelyn set about building their dream home.

The low-slung, pioneer-style house is set around a central courtyard, with no indoor stairways or walkways; it forms a simple backdrop to the Bartletts' vast but unexceptional trinket collection. It's a tribute more to acquisitiveness than taste, full of whimsical carved animals and menageries culled from merry-go-rounds. Bartlett was unable to resist decorating almost every surface, whether smothering woods in a cheap faux-marble finish, or with more appealing, brightly colored murals on some ceilings. The one noteworthy object is the dazzling porcelain sculpture by Lombardi in the music room; it's a virtuoso example of a mourning bust, where the artist has depicted translucent fabric of a widow's veil in china.

Evelyn donated the house to the state in 1983, with the proviso that she be able to winter here until her death – she didn't finally expire until fourteen years later, at the astonishing age of 109. Her longevity ensured that by the time the home passed into government hands, the structural problems here were clearly evident.

Visitors are free to explore the gardens alone: the paths are clearly marked and points of interest signposted. For a sweat-free, more leisurely option, pay $1 to ride the electric tram that trundles slowly through the 35 acres of greenery; it leaves from just outside the gift shop. The park itself is mostly sea grape trees and mangrove swamp, but look for several quirky buildings stashed around: most notable are the orchid house and thatched tiki-style Island Theater, a waterbound hut Bartlett built as a home moviehouse and to which he charged guests an entrance fee of two matched shells from the nearby beach.

Hugh Taylor Birch State Park

Hugh Taylor Birch was a lawyer from Chicago who handled legal work for Henry Flagler at the Standard Oil Company – and from whom he heard raves about Florida. It cost Birch only $1 an acre when he bought an enormous estate here to flee the boom in his hometown after the World's Fair of 1893; Birch's surprisingly modest house still stands. He deeded a chunk of his original holdings to son-in-law Frederic Bartlett, and then left the rest on his death to the state.

Today, that land is known as the **Hugh Taylor Birch State Park**, at 3019 East Sunrise Blvd (daily 8am–dusk, visitor center Sat & Sun 10am–5pm; $4 per vehicle

△ Sea grape trees at Hugh Taylor Birch State Park

or $1 per pedestrian; ℡954/564-4521, ⊛www.floridastateparks.org). It's packed with sea grape and tropical hardwood trees, and centered on a shady freshwater lagoon – an ideal alternative to baking on the beach. There are also picnic facilities and basic campsites – for overnight reservations, contact the visitor center.

The International Swimming Hall of Fame

The ragtag, threadbare **International Swimming Hall of Fame**, at 1 Hall of Fame Drive at Seabreeze Blvd (Mon–Fri 9am–7pm, Sat & Sun 9am–5pm; $3; ℡954/462-6536, ⊛www.ishof.org), supposedly showcases great swimmers and divers from every country across the world. Once inside, though, visitors may feel as if time stopped ten years ago; there's no mention of any Olympic Games since Seoul in 1992, or any sign of recent record-breakers like Australian Ian Thorpe. If this alone didn't render the whole place rather anachronistic, the almost creepy tribute to past titans like Johnny Weismuller and Mark Spitz are decisive, thanks to the crumbling dummies that form their centerpieces (Spitz's likeness is especially odd; while the mannequin looks at least twenty years old, its hands are brand new, donated – as noted in a large accompanying plaque – by a company that specializes in producing such prosthetics). In short, there's little here for anyone other than a dedicated swimmer with a gothic imagination.

Eating

The handiest selection of **eateries** lines Las Olas Boulevard downtown or in Himmarshee, though there are plenty of appealing options on the beach or along Wilton Drive in the largely gay district of Wilton Manors. Increasingly, the options and quality here rival that in Miami, though prices are refreshingly reasonable.

The restaurant reviews below have been **price-coded** into five categories according to per-person meals: an inexpensive place will hover at less than $15, while a moderate restaurant should cost between $15 and $30. Expensive places will run between $30 and $45 per person, while the few very expensive establishments we've listed will cost $45 and up. Bear in mind that these quotes are based on a two-course meal, not including drinks, tip, or taxes.

Cafés

Kilwin's 809 E Las Olas Blvd at 9th, Downtown ℡954/523-8338. Old-fashioned chocolate shop on the strolling drag of Las Olas downtown: wait for the smell to hit you on the sidewalk and be lured in for hunks of fudge, hand-dipped chocolate marshmallows or pecan turtles, as well as gooey ice cream. Inexpensive.

La Spada's 4349 Seagrape Drive, Lauderdale-by-the-Sea ℡954/725-0244. Yes, it's a trek, but the food at this legendary local sub shop is superb. Expect doorstop-sized sandwiches on home-made rolls for around $7; each is crammed with sliced-to-order slabs of beef, ham or turkey, plus piles of vegetables. Don't expect smiley service, but the lashings of food more than make up. Inexpensive.

Two Street Coffee Garage 209 SW 2nd Ave at SW 2nd St, Himmarshee ℡954/523-7191. Groovy, laid-back coffeehouse with art on the walls, plus plenty of comfy seating. The café's signature drink is a Thai latte flavored with plum, mango, or green tea, and served with gooey rice balls. Inexpensive.

Restaurants

Canyon Southwest Café 1818 E Sunrise Blvd at NE 18th Ave, Victoria Park ℡954/765-1950. Swanky eatery outfitted in Southwestern shades of burnished bronze, navy, and mustard tones plus crisp white tablecloths and gauzy curtains billowing round the booths. The pricey but delicious food's worth splashing out for (entrees hover around $25) – try the spicy tuna *tartare* or pork with Gorgonzola – but save room for the white chocolate and berry bread pudding. Even if you're not eating, stop in at the bar here for their signature prickly pear margarita, made in-house from fresh cactus steeped for three days in tequila. Expensive.

Chima 2400 E Las Olas Blvd at SE 25th Ave, Beachside ☎954/712-0580. Bustling outpost of an original Sao Paolo steakhouse where waiters pass through the dining room brandishing huge skewers of more than a dozen different meats, including chicken, fish, and *linguica* (Brazilian *chorizo*), from which they'll carve chunks for any diner; it's all cooked *churrascaria*-style – essentially, flame-grilled – and costs $39.60 per person. Use the casino-chip-like baton to indicate whether you're still working on appetizers (leave it orange-side up) or if you want the wait staff to serve up the meats (turn it to black). Expensive.

The Floridian 1410 E Las Olas Blvd at 14th, Downtown ☎ 954/463-4041. Old Fort Lauderdale at its finest: 1980s vintage Formica furniture, peeling autographed pictures lining the walls, and outstanding diner food at rock-bottom prices. Unpretentious and enormous, which means never having to wait for a table. Inexpensive.

Galanga 2389 Wilton Drive at NE 9th Ave, Wilton Manors ☎954/202-0000. Mixed gay/straight neighborhood favorite, worth seeking out

for its northern Thai dishes – try crab fish rools or *panang* curry, with lime leaf and peanuts. The atmosphere's casual, with low candlelight, rattan furniture, and overstuffed cushions. Moderate.

Johnny V's 625 E Las Olas Blvd at 7th, Downtown ☎954/761-7920. Swanky new eatery, all dark walnut, plush red upholstery, and backlit mirrors, owned by celebrity chef Johnny Vinczencz. The menu is his signature Floribbean, like short stacks of portobello mushroom "pancakes" and cinnamon-crusted pork tenderloin. Even if you can't manage dinner, come for a cocktail at the bar for a glimpse of Fort Lauderdale's scene. Expensive.

Samba Room 350 E Las Olas Blvd at 4th, Downtown ☎954/468-2000. Latin bar and grill, decorated with a Diego Rivera-esque mural and boasting a comfy outdoor patio equipped with squishy daybeds. It's busiest early evening when local officeworkers come for cocktails or satay tapas ($2 for chicken or beef); it serves dinner, too – try the house paella or banana-leaf-wrapped salmon for $18.95. Moderate.

Tarpon Bend 200 SW 2nd St at SW 2nd Ave, Himmarshee ☎954/523-3233. Appealing, airy sports bar that serves up flagons of beer in glasses chilled so much that it freezes solid on the sides. There are several TV screens, as well as chalkboards showcasing local and IGFA fishing records. Menus are laid out like newspapers; there are stacks of different chili sauces on each table; the American menu is comprised mostly of sandwiches and salads ($7.50– 10). Moderate.

Drinking and nightlife

Despite Fort Lauderdale's gentrification, nightlife along A1A beachside tends to revolve around chugging mixing-bowl-sized margaritas: the *Elbo Room* bar, which co-starred with Prentiss and Hamilton in *Where the Boys Are*, still stands at the corner of Las Olas Boulevard and Hwy-A1A. If this isn't your scene, head inland to the drag of drinks spots along Himmarshee: club/bar *Rush Street*, at 220 SW 2nd St at SW 3rd Ave (☎954/522-69000, ⓦwww.rushstreetbar.com), is perennially popular, especially early evenings, with a mainstream house playlist and reasonable bar prices. Otherwise, thirtysomethings can sip in more chic surroundings in some of the restaurants along Las Olas, like *Johnny V's* (see above) or at *Blue Martini* at 2432 E Sunrise Blvd in the Galleria Mall, Beachside (☎954/653-2583), which serves bar snacks and cocktails as well as offering live jazz each night. Worth a detour is the intriguingly exotic *Kalahari Bar*, 4446 NE 20th St at Floranada Rd on the north side of town (☎954/351-9371,

⊛www.kalaharibar.com), run by an expat South African couple and decked out with artifacts from their homeland; it claims to be the only such bar in the whole USA.

As for **clubbing**, head further along the coast to the satellite community of Hollywood, 20 minutes' drive south on US-1. The hippest option is *Sonar* at 2006 Hollywood Blvd at 20th, in Hollywood (☎954/920-8777, ⊛www .sonariteclub.com). It's a combo club-lounge, decorated in bright red, with futuristic furniture; programming varies night to night, but expect edgy, avant-garde music at weekends and offbeat choices, like Monday's independent film night. Otherwise, head to the Seminole Hard Rock Casino a few miles inland close to Florida's Turnpike at 1 Seminole Way (☎1-866/502-7529, ⊛www.seminolehardrockhollywood.com), where there's a choice between a new Florida outpost of long-time New York nightlife fixture, *Pangaea* (☎954/581-5454, ⊛www.pangaea-lounge.com), with its vague safari theme plus brand-name DJs, or the flashier *Gryphon* nightclub (☎954/252-1411).

Gay Fort Lauderdale

As Miami, and especially South Beach, has grown more expensive and straight in the last couple of years, Fort Lauderdale's gay and lesbian population has swelled with refugees from it as well as older "gayby boomers" looking to retire in the sun. That isn't to say that the scene here is now glitzy and hedonistic – far from it; rather it's retained a welcoming, laid-back vibe.

For up-to-date **information** on what's happening call or stop by the Gay and Lesbian Community Center of South Florida at 1717 N Andrews Ave at Sunrise (Mon–Fri 10am–10pm, Sat & Sun noon–5pm; ☎954/463-9005, ⊛www.glccftl.org), or pick up one of the flyers at the noticeboard inside the *Pride Factory* shop-café at 845 N Federal Hwy at NE 9th St (☎954/463-6600, ⊛www.pridefactory.com); reliable local **freesheets** include *Scoop, Hotspots*, and *The 411*. We've listed gay-specific accommodation and nightlife opposite. As for **gay beaches**, there are unofficial spots along A1A at Sebastian Street and the quieter, less cruisey patch at NE 18th Street.

Accommodation

There are over thirty guesthouses and B&Bs aimed at gay men in the city: there's a large cluster together on the beach around Terramar Street at the Intracoastal Waterway. Pick of the bunch is undoubtedly *The Royal Palms* at 2901 Terramar St at Orton Ave, Beachside (℗954/564-6444, ⊛www.royalpalms .com) with rooms from $179. Expect Frette linens, rainhead showers, and an ultra-private clothing-optional pool – not to mention safe-sex kits under every pillow. On the mainland, try the *Pineapple Point Guesthouse* at 315 NE 16th Terrace at NE 3rd Court, Victoria Park (℗1-888/844-7295 or 954/527-0094, ⊛www.pineapplepoint.com), with rooms from $149, tucked away in an upcoming neighborhood with a lush tropical garden, pool, and Jacuzzi, plus gloriously fluffy towels. A cheaper option, *Orton Terrace*, with simpler rooms and more basic facilities, at 606 Orton Ave at Terramar St, Beachside (℗954/566-5068 or 1-800/323-1142, ⊛www.ortonterrace.com), has rooms from $75.

Drinking and nightlife

The most popular bar at the moment is *Georgie's Alibi* at 2266 Wilton Drive at NE 22nd St, Wilton Manors (℗954/565-2526, ⊛www.georgiesalibi.com), with a few pool tables, a short bar menu, and a friendly crowd. *Chardees* at 2209 Wilton Drive at NE 22nd St, in Wilton Manors (℗954/563-1800), is a camp supper club/restaurant, with an older crowd swaying to showtunes bashed out on the piano. The handiest spot beachside is the new video bar, *Dude's*, 3720 NE 33rd St at A1A, Beachside (℗954/568-7777, ⊛www.dudesbar.com), which has go-go boys most nights.

As for **clubs**, *The Copa*, at 2800 S Federal Hwy in Port Everglades (℗954/463-1507, ⊛www.copaboy.com), is a local institution, open for more than thirty years. It's a warehouse-like space with a dancefloor, terrace, and video room – note the crowd doesn't arrive until midnight or so most nights. Downtown's *Cathode Ray*, 1307 E Las Olas Blvd at 13th (℗954/462-8611, ⊛www.cathoderayusa.com), is both cruiser and noisier, and contains a small restaurant attached – *Boulevard Café*. Since the closure of South Beach's circuit party HQ, Salvation a couple of years ago, Miamians have been driving up the coast to the *Coliseum* every weekend for A-list DJs and all-night parties at 2520 S Federal Hwy, in Port Everglades (℗954/832-0100, ⊛www .coliseumnightclub.com).

22

The Everglades

"The Everglades is a test. If we pass, we get to keep the planet."

Environmentalist Marjory Stoneman Douglas

ittle more than an hour from the condos and clubs of Miami, **Everglades National Park** is breathtakingly wild. Although the land is on the same latitude as the Sahara, more than one third of the park is made up of marine areas and underwater estuaries, and sawgrass covers nearly four million acres of swampy prairie. Both water and land teem with wildlife, from rare crocodiles and alligators to raccoons, as well as dozens of species of bird.

Despite this raw vastness, the Everglades exists in a delicate and endangered ecosystem. The area was originally formed by natural water drainage from the region around Orlando, flowing south to collect on the oolitic limestone table of Florida's swampy tip. In the last half-century, though, developers have diverted this precious water source east to cities like Miami, Fort Lauderdale, and Palm Beach, leaving the Everglades ecosystem not only thirsty but shrinking.

Coconut Grove–based environmentalist Marjory Stoneman Douglas was one of the first local lobbyists against such eco-vandalism – in fact, many say that her book *The Everglades: River of Grass* kickstarted the conservation movement in South Florida in the late 1940s (Douglas was crusading until her last breath in 1998, at the astonishing age of 108). Now, of course, there are dozens of organizations dedicated to safeguarding this unique ecosystem – though of course none could prevent the wreckage caused by Hurricane Andrew more than a decade ago, from which northern portions of the park are only now beginning to recover.

When **exploring** the Everglades, the worst thing to do is rush around. Although the speed limit on most roads is 55mph, you'll see and enjoy far more if you travel slowly and look for nature's subtleties: notice, for example, that the water everywhere is tea-brown, thanks to the tannic acid that leeches out of fallen leaves.

In the northwest region of the park, around **Everglades City**, all activities are aquatic: there's good fishing, boat tours, and canoeing. Conversely, at **Shark Valley**, in the northeastern corner of the park, there's a landbound trail too long to hike in its entirety, but accessible via bike or tram. Further south, **Flamingo** offers something for everyone: superb saltwater fishing and excellent birdwatching sites, plus boat tours, canoeing, kayaking, and hiking. As for wildlife spotting, early in the morning is the best time; during the dry season, make it a point to come during the week, as busy weekends on the waterways drive animals under cover during the day.

Note that though **airboat tours** are an image synonymous with the park, they're an iffy prospect; a reputable operator will cause no environmental

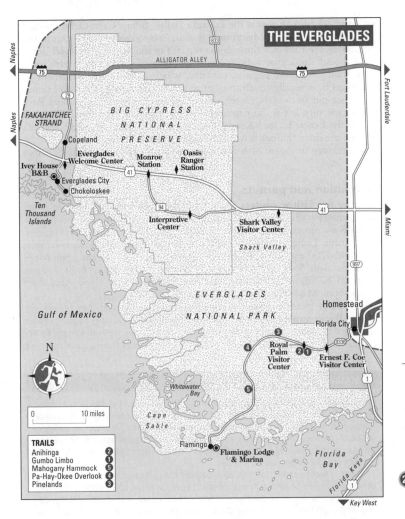

THE EVERGLADES

Naples

ALLIGATOR ALLEY

75

833

75

Naples

Fort Lauderdale

29

BIG CYPRESS

Miami

FAKAHATCHEE
STRAND

NATIONAL

Copeland

PRESERVE

Ivey House
B&B

Everglades
Welcome Center

Monroe
Station

Oasis
Ranger
Station

41

Everglades City

Chokoloskee

94

Ten
Thousand
Islands

Interpretive
Center

41

Shark Valley
Visitor Center

Shark Valley

997

EVERGLADES

Gulf of Mexico

NATIONAL PARK

Homestead

Florida City

3

9336

N

Royal
Palm
Visitor
Center

2 1

Ernest F. Coe
Visitor Center

1

0   10 miles

Whitewater
Bay

5

THE EVERGLADES

Cape
Sable

23

TRAILS
Anihinga   2
Gumbo Limbo   1
Mahogany Hammock 5
Pa-Hay-Okee Overlook 4
Pinelands   3

Flamingo

Flamingo Lodge
& Marina

Florida
Bay

Florida Keys

1

Key West

damage, but there are dozens of less scrupulous types whose gas and oil pollute the rivers and whose constant use of the same routes scars the land. If in doubt, it's much better to take a trip with one of the boat operators recommended on p.223 than to opt for an airboat.

Getting there

The park is almost impossible to reach without a **car**, as there's no public transport to or within the Everglades. The pricey day-trips offered by numerous operators in Miami are rushed and not terribly enjoyable – if you want to see the park, splash out and hire a car for a few days. See p.21 for details on car rental.

There are three **entrances** to the protected area: **Shark Valley** in the northeastern corner and **Everglades City** in the northwest are both served by the busy Hwy-41 (also known as the Tamiami Trail) – follow Calle Ocho through Little Havana and out of Miami until it morphs into this highway. Out in the countryside, the road cuts through the top half of the park and provides direct access, though don't expect much scenic beauty until you enter the park itself.

The third, and most popular, entrance, which leads to the settlement of **Flamingo** is, ironically, much tougher to reach. Drive south through Homestead; once out of the city center, either look for the poorly signposted Rte-9336 or just turn left at the ramshackle "Robert is Here" fruitstand. This road leads to the Ernest F. Coe Visitor Center at the main entrance, from which it's a 40-minute drive through a windy, two-lane road to Flamingo.

All entrances are open 24 hours a day except Shark Valley (daily 8.30am–6pm).

Information and permits

There are five **visitor centers** in the park: the **Ernest F. Coe Center** at the main entrance is the largest and most informative (daily 9am–5pm; ☎305/242-7700, ⓦwww.nps.gov/ever/), and a likely first stop-off for anyone arriving here from Miami. There are satellite offices at **Royal Palm** (daily 8am–4.15pm; ☎305/242-7700 ext 7237), **Flamingo** (Nov–April daily 7.30am–5pm; May–Oct daily 8am–5pm; ☎239/695-2945), **Shark Valley** (daily 8.30am–5pm; ☎305/221-8776), and the **Gulf Coast** near Everglades City (Nov–April daily 7.30am–5pm; May–Oct daily 8.30am–5pm; ☎239/695-3311).

A seven-day general **permit** costs $10 per vehicle and $5 per person for cyclists. **Backcountry permits** are also available from any visitor center December to April, and are $10 per permit + $10 per person for up to six people, for up to two weeks; backcountry campgrounds throughout the park

---

Everglades practicalities

Most people come during the **dry season** (Nov to April), when the park is at its most active, and the mosquitoes at their least. At this time, there are larger numbers of birds, and receding water levels leave the animals a reduced number of watering holes, thus concentrating wildlife activity; plus, there are more activities for people offered by the park and its concessionaires. The only downside, of course, is that accommodation prices will be steeper.

A visit in **wet season** (May to Oct) is only for the dedicated: the park receives at least sixty inches of rain each year, ninety percent of which falls between May and November, and insects abound – especially if the preceding winter was very dry, killing off the fish that eat bug larvae. Campsites at this time are virtually uninhabitable, and there are few birds to be spotted – so think hard before planning a trek.

As for the **shoulder season** (late April to early May or late Oct to early Nov), it's a risk: the weather may still be poor, but there will be fewer crowds.

What to bring

Whatever and whenever your plans, bring plenty of **insect repellent** and long pants. Year-round the mosquitoes are numerous, and especially ferocious during the summer wet season. If you're camping, you might also encounter sand gnats, or "no-see-ums," tiny insects that inflict painful bites. There's also little shade, so **sunblock** (plus sunglasses and hat) is essential.

For backcountry camping, bring flashlights, a compass, and water in hard containers – raccoons can (and will) tear through soft cartons. Remember that there's only one restaurant inside the park – an unremarkable café in Flamingo – so bring some **food**, too.

are little more than tended clearings, unless marked as a *chickee* (raised platform with a roof, open on all sides) on the map available from the visitor center.

Accommodation

There's only one in-park **accommodation** option, other than camping (see box, below), but it's just as feasible to use Everglades City or Florida City as bases provided you don't mind a little extra driving.

Everglades Hostel 20 SW 2nd Ave, Florida City ⓣ 305/248-1122 or 1-800/372-3874, ⓦ www .evergladeshostel.com. A clean, budget option in Florida City with the usual amenities (laundry room, kitchen, Internet access) that also runs various excursions into the park. Dorm beds $13/night or $14/night with a/c, private rooms $33, plus $3 fee for non-members.

Flamingo Lodge and Marina 1 Flamingo Lodge Hwy, Flamingo ⓣ 239/695-3101 or 1-800/600-3813, ⓦ www.flamingolodge.com. At the end of the long road through the park lies *Flamingo Lodge*, a convenient base for most Everglades activities. Rooms are standard but comfortable, plus there's a screened-in pool and a restaurant. Staff lives on site and offers friendly, knowledgeable recommendations. $95.

Ivey House Bed & Breakfast 1077 Camellia St, Everglades City ⓣ 239/695-3299, ⓦ www .iveyhouse.com. A charming B&B with reasonable rates, especially in its older building where the simple rooms share baths; the new addition has plusher rooms with private baths. Family-style dinners are also served each evening. $50 without private bath in old building, $90 with private bath in new building. Open Nov–April.

Route 9336: the road to Flamingo

Just southwest of Homestead, **Route 9336** enters the park at the main visitor center (open 24 hours; see box), leading to some of the best and most accessible sights in the Everglades, before eventually arriving at **Flamingo**, the only settlement inside the park proper. This southerly section of the park is known as Pine Island; and for a casual visitor, a few days spent here are an ideal way to glimpse all the elements that make the Everglades unique. Dotted along the 38-mile road to Flamingo are several trails, most of which are manageable for even the most inexperienced hiker; many are former roads, while others are specially constructed boardwalks.

One mile after entering the park, take a turn south toward the **Royal Palm Visitor Center**: two very different but equally intriguing brief trails start here. The **Anhinga Trail** is a half-mile concrete path through sawgrass marsh that's a dependable site for wildlife viewing. It's especially reliable for seeing alligators: remember, though, that this isn't a zoo, and the seemingly harmless and lethargic animals splayed within feet of the path can be vicious and quick if they feel threatened. The trail's named after the anhinga bird, a black and white

THE EVERGLADES

㉓

Camping

Rangers will tell you that *Long Pine Key* campground – west from the Ernest F. Coe Visitor Center and south from Rte-9336 – has the fewest bugs, but that it's worth braving the mosquitoes at **Flamingo** campground for its views and its facilities, such as hot and cold showers. The long-closed, sodden *Chekika* is unlikely to ever reopen, as it's in the center of a water-reclamation project that will leave it underwater. Camping at all sites is $14 per night, and reservations (ⓣ 1-800/365-2267 or ⓦ http://reservations.nps.gov) are recommended from November to April.

cormorant-like creature known for sunbathing on rocks after diving for fish. If you'd prefer an animal-free trek, try the **Gumbo Limbo Trail**. It's all flora not fauna, a glimpse of the Paradise Key hardwood hammock packed with strangler figs, royal palms, and, of course, the gumbo limbos with their flaky red bark.

Back on the main road, before Rte-9336 takes an unexacting turn south, the **Pa-hay-okee viewing platform** is a tall outlook, nestled in the middle of a stretch of dwarf cypress – it's worth stopping for a quick stroll from the car up a few steps to catch panoramic views across the sawgrass plain.

Heading further south, you'll come to **Paurotis Pond**. Unremarkable for much of the year, it's a stunning sight if you're here in January – the place becomes a wading-bird rookery, where egrets, woodstorks, and occasional spoonbills come to breed. Continue on until you hit **Nine Mile Pond** that is a good, manageable canoe trail choice, appropriate for amateurs. Conversely, **Hells Bay Trail**, about five miles from here, is a well-signposted adventure for more experienced canoeists – maps of these and other canoe trails are available from the visitor center.

The rest of the sights on the home stretch to Flamingo are aimed largely at the flocks of birdwatchers who make up the Everglades' most loyal tourists: try **Snake Bight Trail** (just watch out for the armies of mosquitoes) or **Mrazek Pond**, particularly appealing in February when the receding waters concentrate the fish population and draw dozens of hungry birds to feed. If you're not a birdwatcher, skip these and carry on to Flamingo, where you'll find the **Eco Pond Trail** just past the Flamingo Visitor Center. It leads to a freshwater pond, where there's a good variety of wildlife spotting, and is equipped with a proper viewing platform if you want to lurk and wait.

△ The boardwalk on the Anhinga Trail

Flamingo

The only settlement inside the park proper, **Flamingo** began as a nameless nineteenth-century pioneer village, home to a few families and plenty of renegades. It finally took a name in 1893 in order to build a post office; settlers voted for Flamingo in honor of the pink birds that were commonplace in the area. Of course, they weren't flamingoes; it's more likely they were rose-ate spoonbills. Fittingly, Flamingo has been dependent on birds throughout its history. Today, birdwatchers flock to watch them, but back then, it was hunters who clogged the town, keen to illegally harvest egret feathers for the millinery trade (indeed a game warden employed by the bird-friendly Audubon Society was famously murdered near the town in 1905 while trying to protect nests from plume hunters).

There isn't much in Flamingo other than a few houses, the *Flamingo Lodge* (see p.221), and wardens' accommodation. At the lodge, there's the moderately priced, fish-heavy *Flamingo* **restaurant** (open for breakfast, lunch, and dinner Nov–April) as well as the cheaper *Buttonwood Café* (dinner only Nov–April), which serves mostly pizza and snack foods. If you're here during the summer, the Marina Store sells sandwiches and fixings for meals, which can be cooked in the kitchenettes of each room. If you're not staying here, the lodge is still a handy departure point for boat trips, canoeing expeditions, and sports-fishing jaunts.

Boat tours run from the marina at Flamingo (☎239/695-3101); choose either the two-hour Pelican Backcountry Cruise (daily 8am, 10.30am, 1.30pm, 4pm, fewer trips out of season; $18), which journeys into Coot Bay and offers plenty of reptile spotting, or the 90-minute Bald Eagle Florida Bay Cruise (daily 10am, 12.30pm, 2.30pm, sunset, fewer trips out of season; $12), a can't-miss for bird-watchers. You can rent kayaks at the marina ($27 half-day/$43 full day), canoes ($22 half-day/$32 full day), and charter fishing skiffs (from $65 for half a day).

Shark Valley

Highway 41 enters the northeastern corner of the park near the **Shark Valley Visitor Center**: this spot's not only the best place to understand how vast the sawgrass plain truly is but also the clearest testimony of how Miami's explosive development has drained the park of water – the growing, arid patches of land here are the scars.

There's only one lengthy **trail** from here, a fourteen-mile-long loop that's off-limits to cars and a tough hike: it's paved, though, so it makes for a pleasant, if shadeless, cycling trip. Rent bikes from the Shark Valley Tram Tour Company (daily 8.30am–4pm, last rental 3pm; $4.75/hour; ☎305/221-8455) and head for the 50-foot observation tower at the trail's mid-point. A more leisurely way to see the trail is on a **tram tour** (daily 9am–4pm on the hour, fewer trips out of season; $12.75; ☎305/221-8455), where park rangers point out notable wildlife and stop regularly for viewings – alligators and turtles are plentiful, and the birdwatching is truly spectacular.

Those determined to set out on foot can enjoy two short rambles from the visitor center: the **Bobcat Boardwalk** runs through sawgrass marsh, and the rough limestone **Otter Cave trail** snakes into tropical hardwood hammock.

Everglades City

Though Flamingo is the only settlement within the preserve's boundaries, there is another town that serves the Everglades – Everglades City, just outside the

23

△ Birdlife in the Everglades

Everglades' northwestern corner. It's yet another example of a Florida pioneer's overenthusiastic optimism; the place was purchased and named in the 1920s by an advertising executive dreaming of setting up his own fiefdom. Today, the year-round population hovers around five hundred or so.

The reason to come here is to use the town and its facilities as a base for exploring the **Ten Thousand Islands**, where the park's coastline shatters into mangrove island shards that are excellent fishing sites. To reach **Everglades City**, leave Hwy-41 at Rte-29 and head three miles south. Continue through the city to the end of Rte-29 until you reach the dock at Chokoloskee Causeway, site of the official visitor center and boarding point for most **boat trips**.

Everglades National Park Boat Tours is one of the few park-sanctioned operators (daily 9.30am–5pm; ☎239/695-2591 or 1-800/445-7724), offering two trips: the 90-minute Ten Thousand Islands Tour ($16), which heads for the outer islands bordering the Gulf of Mexico, or the 2-hour Mangrove Wilderness Tour ($25), which journeys inland through the winding red mangrove waterways. Boats leave every half-hour year-round from the docks at Chokoloskee. Canoes can also be rented from the same company (daily 8.30am–5pm; $24/day).

24

The Florida Keys

The **Florida Keys** are a dash of the Caribbean in America, as distant from the US in attitude as geography. Beginning with the small islands in Biscayne National Park and ending with the Dry Tortugas, the Keys form a broken necklace of land that stretches for more than two hundred miles from Florida's southern tip. Roughly 125,000 years ago, they were a living coral reef, created when water levels rose dramatically, flooding low-lying areas. As the waters gradually receded, the upper reaches of reef were exposed, and limestone islands were formed from the dying coral. At the same time, the lower areas of the reef to the west survived, making for spectacular snorkeling and diving.

Aside from the shipping hub in Key West and a short-lived settlement on Indian Key, the islands remained sparsely populated by European settlers until well into the twentieth century, in part owing to harsh, humid summers and legions of insects. However, after Henry Flagler's railroad connected the Keys with Miami in 1912, communities grew up in clusters, supported mostly by fishing and smuggling – indeed, the narcotics trade here was endemic until well into the 1980s, as in the 1984 case of the so-called Big Pine 29, when almost thirty sheriff's deputies were arrested for drug smuggling. (Even now, it's not unusual for blocks of marijuana and cocaine to wash up along the western coast; locals call them square groupers.) Today, though, both fishing and smuggling have given way to tourism as the overwhelming local industry.

The Keys are more or less divided into three sections. The **Upper Keys**, which include the towns of Key Largo, Tavernier, and Islamorada, are used as bases for fishing and diving in the John Pennekamp State Park – though there's a definite uneasiness in the locals' relationship with tourism, and the famously laid-back local attitude is less prevalent here. Centered on the settlement of Marathon and the remarkable Seven Mile Bridge, the **Middle Keys** are more welcoming. Marathon has good amenities, plus access to clean beaches and well-stocked fishing sites nearby: for the casual traveler, this is the best base for exploring the area. South from here, the **Lower Keys**, beginning at Big Pine Key, are rewarding for landlocked wildlife-watching – most notably, the rare Key Deer.

The prime target for most visiting the Keys, of course, is fabled **Key West**. Old Town is now a feast of wooden colonial houses and winding streets, less blighted by tourism than some contend, and with much of the sleepy grace that first attracted visitors thirty years ago; it's also one of the gayest towns in America, owing to liberal local attitudes plus pure chance.

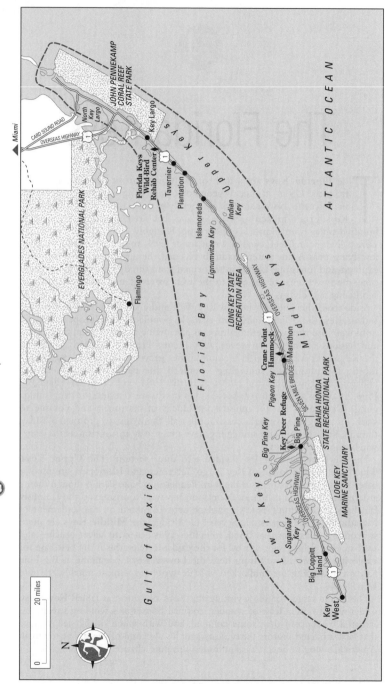

Arrival, information, and getting around

Greyhound runs a limited **bus** service connecting Miami and Key ̶
roughly five-hour trip with stops in major centers along the route ̶
one way; departures at 6.20am, 12.35pm, 3.50pm, 6.50pm; ☎1-800/231-2222,
ⓦwww.greyhound.com). Even so, since there's no local public transportation,
it's almost impossible to see or enjoy most of what the Keys have to offer

Ocean activities in the Keys

Beaches
Hands down, the best Keys beaches are all in **Bahia Honda State Recreational
Park**; otherwise, snatch some time sunbathing at **Sombrero Beach** near Marathon
and **Anne's Beach** just west of Islamorada. Around Key West, there are few options
– the best is probably the beach at **Fort Zachary Taylor Historic State Park**.

Snorkeling and diving
The **John Pennekamp State Park** (see p.229) has several notable reefs and is very
popular; however, there's livelier wildlife and more to see at **Looe Key Marine Sanctuary** (see p.235) or at **Biscayne National Park** (see p.205). **Fort Jefferson** in the
Dry Tortugas has spectacular coral formations and plenty of fish less than 100 yards
off its western shores.

    Operators include the Coral Reef Park Company at the John Pennekamp Visitor
Center (daily 8am–5pm; ☎305/451-1621, ⓦwww.pennekamppark.com), which runs
glass-bottomed-boat tours at 9.15am, 12.15pm, and 3pm for $21, or snorkel trips
at 9am, noon, and 3pm for $33.95, including equipment. Its branch in Bahia Honda
State Park runs snorkeling trips to Looe Key (daily 8am–5pm; ☎305/872-3210,
ⓦwww.bahiahondapark.com) at 9.30am, 12.30pm & 4pm (summer), and 9.30pm &
1.30pm (rest of year) for $37.95.

    In the Lower Keys, the friendly staff at Underseas, MM 30.5-Oceanside, Big Pine
Key (snorkel trips start at $30; ☎305/872-2700 or 1-800/446-5663, ⓦwww.flkeysdiv-
ing.com), run enjoyable trips out to Looe Key – a good choice for first-timers. The
leisurely alternative for coral viewing is by glass-bottomed boat: try the two-hour
trip on the *Key Largo Princess*, MM 100-Oceanside (daily 10am, 1pm, 4pm; $20;
☎305/451-4655).

    You can only visit the reef on a trip organized by one of the many diving shops
throughout the Keys; the nearest is the neighboring Looe Key Dive Center (snorkel
and diving trips start at $25 plus gear; ☎1-800/942-5397, ⓦwww.diveflkeys.com).

Fishing
A good independent bait shop is the World Class Angler, at MM 50-Bayside, Marathon (☎305/743-6139), where the staff is knowledgeable, and can make good local
fishing site recommendations. The deluxe option is to take a personal charter trip
– in Marathon, try Captain Tina Brown ($375/half-day, $475/full day; ☎305/743-7150,
ⓔtina824us@yahoo.com), who's renowned for her helpfulness with less experienced
anglers, or Captain Brian Yates (☎305/294-0281). In the Upper Keys, Robbie's, at
MM 77.5-Bayside, Islamorada, also runs larger group trips (9.30am–1.30pm and
1.45–5.45pm is $28, plus $3 rod rental; 7.30pm–12.30am is $33, plus $4 rod rental;
☎305/664-8498, ⓦwww.robbies.com.

Kayaking
Florida Keys Kayak & Ski at Robbie's Marina, MM 75.5-Bayside, Islamorada
(☎305/664-4878), runs escorted kayak tours to Indian and Lignumvitae keys, as
well as the chance to see wildlife in the mangrove swamps nearby (from $49 per
person). Kayak rentals without a guide start at $30 per half-day. In the Lower Keys,
try Sugarloaf Marina, MM 17-Bayside, Sugarloaf Key (☎305/745-3135, ⓦwww
.sugarloafmarina.com), where rental starts at $15/hr or $30/day.

without a **car** (see p.21 for rental information). Driving is easy, as the islands are joined by a single road – **Hwy-1**, also known as the **Overseas Highway**, which connects Key West with Florida City (see p.204), continuing on up the East Coast. To avoid tourist traffic, do as the locals do and branch off from Hwy-1 south of Homestead onto Card Sound Road, also known as Hwy-905A ($1 toll). It's slightly longer, but after passing through the desolate southeastern section of the Everglades, this route gives soaring views of the mangrove-dotted waters of Florida Bay (where a long wait and a lot of luck might be rewarded with the sight of a rare American crocodile) – and a glimpse of the Keys as they would all have looked long ago before commercialism took hold.

Addresses in the Keys are given using the Mile Marker (MM) system, which begins with 0 in Key West at the junction of Whitehead and Fleming streets and ends just south of Homestead. In theory, there's a sign marking each mile, but don't rely on it – keep checking progress as you drive. The only islands large enough to require street addresses in the Keys (aside from Key West) are Big Pine and Marathon. We've also followed the local convention of indicating whether buildings sit north (Bayside) or south (Oceanside) of the freeway.

There are several **visitor centers** scattered along Hwy-1. The largest is the **Florida Keys Visitor Center** at MM 106-Bayside, Key Largo (daily 9am–6pm; ℡305/451-1414 or 1-800/822-1088, ⊛www.keylargochamber .org), which provides information on the Keys in general; the Colonial-style center has piles of brochures, discount vouchers, and hotel booking information. The **Islamorada Chamber of Commerce** is unmissable in its bright red roadside caboose and good for the Upper Keys, at MM 82.5-Bayside (Mon–Sat 9am–5pm, Sun 9am–3pm; ℡305/664-4503 or 1-800/FAB-KEYS, ⊛www.islamoradachamber.com); while the **Marathon Chamber of Commerce** has ample information on the Middle Keys at MM 53.5-Bayside, Marathon (daily 9am–5pm; ℡305/743-5417 or 1-800/262-7284, ⊛www.floridakeysmarathon.com). Further along Hwy-1, there's the **Lower Keys Chamber of Commerce**, MM 31-Oceanside, Big Pine Key (Mon–Fri 9am–5pm, Sat 9am–3pm; ℡305/872-2411 or 1-800/872-3722, ⊛www .lowerkeyschamber.com).

Finally, don't forget to bring plenty of **insect repellent**: ravenous mosquitoes are plentiful whatever the time of year.

The Upper Keys

Driving south along Hwy-1, the first of the **Upper Keys'** three major communities you'll come to, **Key Largo**, is perhaps the most unappetizing of all the settlements in the Keys. There's little reason to spend much time here, though nearby is the 80-acre underwater coral reef in the **John Pennekamp State Park**, as well as the **Florida Keys Wild Bird Center** further south in Tavernier, the second major community and notable mostly as the one-time first stop on Henry Flagler's pioneering railway.

The third, **Islamorada** (pronounced eye-lah-more-RAH-dah), is actually a chain of four small islands: Plantation, Windley, and Upper and Lower Matecumbe. It's one of the larger fishing hubs in the Keys, and makes a good base for exploring both **Indian Key** and **Lignumvitae Key**. The easiest way to reach both of them is by **boat** from Robbie's Marina, located at MM 75.5-

Bayside, Islamorada (Indian Key Thurs–Mon 9am & 1pm, Lignumvitae Key Thurs–Mon 10am & 2pm; $15; ☎305/664-8498, ⊛www.robbies.com).

Key Largo

Essentially a hub of gas stations, fast-food outlets, and shopping plazas, **Key Largo** lives in the shadow of two things: the 1948 film *Key Largo* and the coral reef at **John Pennekamp State Park**. The film, starring Humphrey Bogart and Lauren Bacall, was shot entirely in Hollywood – it was so named because the title evoked the exotic tropics. So successful was its suggestiveness, in fact, that savvy locals changed their town's name in 1952 from Rock Harbor to Key Largo – *Cayo Largo*, meaning Long Island, was originally applied to the entire Keys by early Spanish explorers. For some reason, the rickety boat used by Bogie and Katharine Hepburn in *The African Queen* is moored at the *Holiday Inn* here; sadly, it's no longer used for trips but simply decoration at MM 100-Oceanside.

John Pennekamp State Park

The enormous, underwater **John Pennekamp State Park**, at MM 102.5-Oceanside, Key Largo (daily 8am–sunset; $5 per car, plus 50¢ per person, $1.50 pedestrians; ☎305/451-1202, ⊛www.floridastateparks.org/pennekamp) is, frankly, a little overrated – the beaches are far better at Bahia Honda (see

---

Swimming with the dolphins

Among marine animals, **dolphins** are by far the most intelligent, with brains similar in size to those of humans. They communicate in a **language** of clicks and whistles, and use a sonar technique called echolocation to detect food in dark waters and, perhaps, to create "sound pictures" for one another. The world's population has been reduced by several factors, including the nets of tuna fishermen; don't worry about ordering a dolphin sandwich in a local café, though – in this case, dolphin's just a colloquial term for a fish better known as *mahi mahi*.

Even so, dolphins are still a common sight around Miami and the Florida Keys, usually starring in shows at marine parks here. To truly understand why people rave about the animals (and often claim some sort of nonverbal communication with them) schedule a session to swim alongside a dolphin or two. Two of the best places to try it in the Keys are in Key Largo.

Dolphins Plus, just south of MM 100-Oceanside (daily 9am–5pm; ☎305/451-1993 or 1-866/860-7946, ⊛www.dolphinsplus.com), is a dolphin education and research facility where you can indulge in a dolphin encounter with one of twelve friendly creatures. The price of a structured half-hour swim with them is $160 (8.30am, 12.45pm, and 3pm; to observe only $10, under-15s $5), and there is also a "natural" swim with wild dolphins for $125 – though with the latter, contact is not guaranteed (9.30am & 1.30pm).

The other venue is **Dolphin Cove**, a five-acre marine environment research center at MM 102-Bayside (daily 8am–5pm; ☎305/451-4060). If you have a swimsuit, a towel, and $160, you can join sessions that run daily at 9am, 1pm, and 3.30pm (weekends only March to mid-Dec) – plan to book around four weeks in advance: the dolphins here live in a small inlet that opens directly onto the sea, so the experience is a little more authentic than swimming laps in a pool. Here, too, there's a natural swim for $125 (9.45am & 1.45pm). If you can't afford a close encounter, $20 (under-16s $15) gets you in as a non-swimming observer.

p.234), while the coral formations more spectacular in Biscayne National Park (see p.205) or the Dry Tortugas (see box, p.247).

However, for **wreck diving**, it's worth a detour away from the main banks of coral that make up the reef here: head to nearby horseshoe-shaped **Molasses Reef**. The reason it's such a good wreck-diving spot owes itself to man's destructiveness: two coastguard cutters were deliberately sunk here in 1987 since the coral was in such a bad state that authorities intervened to provide divers and tourists with other appealing sights. The best visibility for diving is a few miles northeast of Molasses at **the Elbow** – the reef closest to the cleansing Gulf Stream, which keeps the waters clear. There are a number of intriguing, barnacle-encrusted nineteenth-century specimens here.

Otherwise, head for the waters just off **Cannon Beach**, where you'll find the remains of an early Spanish shipwreck; of course, like most of the Keys' diveable wrecks, it too was deliberately brought here to bolster tourism in the Seventies, which lessens the allure somewhat and means you definitely won't find any treasure.

Arguably one of the weirdest sights in the Keys is the algae-soaked **Christ of the Deep** statue, a nine-foot bronze memorial to sailors who lost their lives at sea, which lies 20 feet down at Key Largo Dry Rocks. It was donated by an Italian industrialist and sports fisherman, and is a replica of Guido Galletti's *Christ of the Abyss*, similarly submerged off the coast of Genoa, Italy.

There are various ways to see the park's different reefs, all run by the same park concessionaire (☎305/451-6322, ⊛www.pennekamppark.com): snorkeling tours (daily 9am, noon & 3pm; 1hr 30min; $27.95, plus $6 for equipment), a guided scuba dive (daily 9.30am & 1.30pm; 1hr 30min; $41; diver's certificate required), or for the lazy, a two-and-a-half hour glass-bottomed-boat-tour (9.15am, 12.15pm & 3pm; $21)

Aside from the wrecks, there are nature trails through hardwood hammock and mangrove swamps here, as well as two man-made beaches – of the two, Far Beach close to the visitor center is better for sunbathing and paddling. It's sheltered by a well-concealed artificial seawall and there's a pavilion nearby with vending machines for snacks.

Florida Keys Wild Bird Center

Just south along Hwy-1 from the John Pennekamp State Park you'll find the **Florida Keys Wild Bird Center** at 93600 Overseas Hwy-Bayside (daily 8.30am–5.30pm; $3; ☎305/852-4486, ⊛www.fkwbc.org). Located in small, homely Tavernier, this hospital and sanctuary receives wounded birds from around the Keys; many have flown into telephone wires or choked on fishing hooks. The staff nurses most until they can be returned to the wild, while those too badly injured remain in specially constructed habitats. A visit here is a great way to get close to many of the local species like the gaggles of pelicans waddling around – an eco-friendly walkway made from recycled materials snakes through the aviary, and many long-term residents are tame enough to approach.

Islamorada

Other than a base for fishing, a terrific man-made sand strip called **Anne's Beach**, and the best local overnighting options, **Islamorada**'s known for the WPA-funded, Art Deco **Florida Keys Memorial** in the center of town at

MM 82-Oceanside. The Hurricane Monument commemorates the Labor Day storm in 1935 that swept through the Middle Keys with winds of up to 200mph and the lowest barometric reading on record. Loss of life and property was severe; the cremated remains of the 425 people who died were placed in the memorial in 1937. It's recently been spruced up after decades of disrepair – look for the sparkling mosaic showing a map of the Middle Keys and the stone relief of coconut palm trees bending ominously in the wind.

Indian Key Historic State Park

Further south along Hwy-1, past Islamorada, a trip to the wilderness of **Indian Key Historic State Park** (☎305/664-2540, ⓦwww.floridastateparks.org/indiankey) reveals the ruins of what was once the last inhabited outpost on the journey down to Key West. This is an evocative, if crumbling, reminder of early settler life in the Keys – take special note of the grassy paddock that was once the town square. Seek out the observation tower, too, which gives spectacular views across the island's lush and jumbled foliage.

Much like the vegetation here, Indian Key's history is also jumbled. In 1831, a rogue wrecker named Jacob Houseman, driven out of Key West in disgrace, bought this island to build his own fiefdom. He succeeded, racking up $30,000 and furnishing the eleven-acre island with streets, a post office, a resort hotel, and even a bowling alley; its population numbered around fifty. Houseman was frequently accused of deliberately running ships aground on the reef using misleading lanterns on the island's shore; and, eventually he did lose his license for salvaging from an anchored boat. Indian Key was eventually sold but a brutal Seminole attack in 1840 leveled the town, ending the island's habitation as quickly as it had begun.

Lignumvitae Key Botanical State Park

On the north side of Hwy-1, roughly opposite Indian Key on the south side, the **Lignumvitae Key Botanical State Park** (Thurs–Mon 8am–5pm; ☎305/664-2540, ⓦwww.floridastateparks.org/lignumvitaekey) is the best remaining example of original Florida Keys tropical hammock. It's named for the medicinal hardwood *lignumvitae* (meaning "water of life") tree, that's abundant in the Caribbean but whose habitat stretches no further north than this island.

This island was purchased for $1 by billionaire William Matheson in 1919 so that he could further his research into tropical plants. It's now primarily used as a research facility by the University of Miami and others. There's a small caretaker's house, originally built by the Mathesons in the 1930s then blown away by a hurricane in 1935 but reconstructed, though it holds little of interest inside now, other than some trinkets and ephemera.

Rather, focus on the exotic vegetation – knowledgeable rangers lead **tours** that provide thorough background on all the indigenous plants that flourish here: there are also a large number of sizeable spiders, such as the golden orb, that spin webs across the paths. Note that the island's ravaged by **mosquitoes**, so bring long sleeves and long pants plus plenty of repellent if you decide to make the trip.

Upper Keys practicalities

The best **accommodation** options for the Upper Keys are in Islamorada, though don't expect to snag a room for much less than $70, especially in high season. The popular *Holiday Isle Beach Resort*, MM 84-Oceanside (☎305/664-2321 or 1-800/327-7070, ⊛www.holidayisle.com; $130), is a psychedelic trip: vivid citrus-colored plastics and tiki huts fill this vacation village. The atmosphere is young and friendly, and the hotel itself is very comfortable. A cheaper option, the *Key Lantern/Blue Fin*, at MM 82.1-Bayside (☎305/664-4572, ⊛www.keylantern .com; $39), has basic – if a little frayed – rooms. If you have a choice, take a room in the *Blue Fin*, as these were redone more recently.

As for **eating**, try *Papa Joe's*, at MM 79-Bayside (☎305/664-8756, ⊛www .papajoesmarina.com), which serves decent seafood in a basic setting; the real reason to come here, though, is the outdoor **bar** hidden on a jetty at the back, perfect for a cheap beer and some appetizers at sunset. The *Hungry Tarpon*, at MM 77.5-Bayside, Lower Matecumbe Key (☎305/664-0535), serves superb fish from local recipes in a converted 1940s bait shop, as well as hearty breakfasts; while for high-quality, mid-priced Cuban food, head to *Manny & Isa's*, MM 81.5-Oceanside (☎305/664-5019), with its key lime tree–crammed orchard at the rear. The smartest option for budget eating, though, is back in Tavernier. Despite its dismal exterior, the *Sunshine Supermarket*, at MM 91.8-Oceanside (no phone and no English spoken), is really a hidden gem: inside, at its small café, you can get a top-notch *cafecito* for $1 and piled-high plates of Cuban food; a plate of rice and beans is only $4.

The Middle and Lower Keys

Between Islamorada and Key West lie the **Middle** and **Lower Keys**, split in half at the western end of the **Seven Mile Bridge**. The one major settle-ment in the Middle Keys is **Marathon**, an appealingly blue-collar town with ample amenities that makes a terrific base for exploring; **Bahia Honda State Recreational Park** is just twelve miles south from here.

The Lower Keys are much larger, and heavily residential: it's worth pausing here before racing on to Key West, especially on Big Pine Key for the **Key Deer Refuge**, as well as trips out to the **Looe Key Marine Sanctuary**. Aligned north–south (rather than east–west) and resting on a base of limestone (rather than a coral reef), these islands have flora and fauna that are very much their own: the reason is that this limestone erodes more easily than coral rock, leaving hollows to fill with rain water that will sustain **animals**. Species like the Key Deer, the Lower Keys Cotton Rat, and the Cudjoe Key Rice Rat – all of which are endangered – live here, though mainly tucked away miles from the Overseas Highway.

Marathon

Named after the back-breaking shifts workers endured as they raced against Henry Flagler's failing health to finish the Seven Mile Bridge, which begins just south of here, **Marathon** is the liveliest town in the Middle Keys. It wasn't always that way – by 1926, the population here was only 17 and it was thanks to the sportfishing craze of the 1950s that the town revived. Today, it's the best option for food and accommodation in the Middle Keys, and makes a terrific base for exploring. It's located on Key Vaca, so named by the Spanish because the natives they encountered here ate manatees, or sea cows, as staples in their diet.

△ A Key Deer

If you don't wish to explore the countryside here, spend the day at **Sombrero Beach** (daily 7.30am–dusk). Follow the signs for Sombrero Beach Road off the Overseas Highway near MM 50-Oceanside: at the promontory, there's a slender, well-kept strip of sand, with full facilities including showers and picnic tables, and ample shade from lush palms.

Crane Point Hammock

The tropical hardwood hammock is one of the most ecologically precious areas in the Keys, and this enormous woodland, known as Tropical Crane Point Hammock (Mon–Sat 9am–5pm, Sun noon–5pm; $7.50; ☎305/743-9100, ⓦwww.cranepoint.org), in the heart of Marathon, is a good place to see it up close. You'll find the entrance by turning right onto 55th Street at MM 50.5-Bayside (opposite the K-Mart). A free booklet gives details of the trees you'll find along the easy one-mile **nature trail**, and you'll also pass one of the last examples of Bahamian architecture in the US: **Adderley House**, built in 1903 by Bahamian immigrants, gives a vivid impression of what life was like for them, with its simple construction and bare-bones amenities. The detailed **Museum of Natural History of the Florida Keys** (Mon–Sat 9am–5pm, Sun noon–5pm; $7.50; ☎305/743-9100, ⓦwww.cranepoint.org) gives an overview of both the geological and political histories of the Keys, including the wrecking of the *HMS Looe* (see p.236), as well as a raft made of inner tubes that carried four Cuban refugees across ninety miles of ocean in the early 1990s.

The hammock's resident **mosquitoes** are a painful nuisance, so consider buying bug spray at the pharmacy directly opposite.

The Seven Mile Bridge

Connecting Marathon to the Lower Keys is the **Seven Mile Bridge**, a stunning feat of engineering when built nearly a century ago, and equally impressive now. Eschewing landfill to preserve the deep Moser Channel for commercial shipping, in 1908, Henry Flagler sought to bridge the unthinkable seven-mile gap between Key Vaca and Bahia Honda Key, thereby providing a course for extending his railroad. At one point, every US-flagged freighter on the Atlantic was hired to bring in materials while floating cranes, dredges, and scores of other craft set about a job that eventually cost the lives of 700 laborers. Using his own technicians, he oversaw the completion of the bridge in only four years (a year ahead of schedule) at a staggering cost of $22 million. Although the railway was soon wiped out by the hurricane of 1935, the bridge itself held.

By 1982, though, it was superseded by a wider, modern structure, built to better allow trucks passage back and forth along the highway; sadly, its walls are just high enough to obscure the fabulous views. Moreover, Flagler's bridge, built with imported German concrete chemically impervious to salt water seepage, is as strong as ever, while the cheaper, bigger, modern bridge is already corroding and in need of repair less than twenty years after its construction.

Pigeon Key

A flat, treeless island left to the pigeons by early European settlers (hence its name), **Pigeon Key** (daily 10am–4pm; $8.50; ☎305/289-0025, ⊛www .pigeonkey.org) was developed during the mammoth construction of Flagler's Miami–Key West railway and served as a camp from 1908 to 1935. Houses were built for the immigrant workers from the Bahamas, Cuba, and Puerto Rico who'd replaced Northeastern laborers who'd fled the heat, mosquitoes, and malaria soon after arriving. The island was bought by the University of Miami in the middle of the last century and used for scientific experiments, before being leased to a nonprofit foundation that has restored the buildings and runs residential courses for local teens to learn about marine biology.

Cars are not permitted access to Pigeon Key, which contributes to the serene atmosphere of the place. Access to Pigeon Key is via an **electric train** that leaves from close to the visitor center on Knight's Key, MM-47, that runs along Flagler's old bridge; there's a tiny museum on the island itself with pictures of former residents and revealing census data, but aside from that there's little to do other than wander around.

Bahia Honda State Recreational Park

Once you leave the soaring new Seven Mile Bridge, you've entered the Lower Keys. **Bahia Honda State Recreational Park** at MM 37-Oceanside (daily 8am–sunset; $5 per car plus 50¢ per person, $1.50 pedestrians; ☎305/872-2353, ⊛www.floridastateparks.org/bahiahonda) marks the division between the Upper and Middle Keys, comprised largely of coral rock, and the Lower Keys from here on, which are made of limestone.

Most people stop here for its **beaches**, including a glorious two-mile-long strip of white sand, one of the few natural beaches in the Keys. Closest to the park entrance, delightful Sandspur Beach has all the usual amenities and scattered plants growing in the sand, while Calusa and Loggerhead beaches at the western tip are more family-friendly, each with a specially marked swimming area and marina, though the ripe ocean smells and sea-grass debris may be off-putting to some. If you want to find a solitary spot to sunbathe, pick through the undergrowth to the two-story **Flagler Bridge**, immediately south of which lies a gloriously isolated strip of golden sand. The unusually deep waters here (Bahia Honda is Spanish for "deep bay") made this the toughest of the old railway bridges to construct, and widening it for the road proved impossible: the solution was to put the highway on a higher tier. It's actually far safer than it looks, and there's a fine view from the top of the bridge over the Bahia Honda channel toward the forest-coated Lower Keys.

Take care when swimming in the deep waters off the park's southern tip here, as currents can be strong; if you're **snorkeling**, there's a concession at the marina where you can rent equipment ($10 per person for masks, fins, and snorkels; ☎305/872-3210, ⊛www.bahiahondapark.com), which also rents kayaks and runs reef dive-trips.

Otherwise, the park's known for its rare and unusual plants, such as the endangered silver palms, and there's a pleasant nature **trail** that weaves along the coast through the tropical hardwood hammock. Self-guiding leaflets are available at the entrance, or join a ranger-led tour (Tues 11am). If you want to stay here, there's a choice of camping or one of three raised cabins on the waterfront: for these, book well ahead, as they're very popular in season – call ☎1-800/326-3521 or visit ⊛www.reserveamerica.com for reservations.

Key Deer Refuge

The 8400-acre **Key Deer Refuge**, at MM 33-Bayside (park open daily sunrise–sunset, visitor center in Big Pine Shopping Center open Mon–Fri 8am–5pm; free; ☎305/872-0774, ⊛nationalkeydeer.fws.gov), stretches across Big Pine and adjacent No Name Key and is the only home of the **Key Deer**, a rare subspecies of white-tailed deer.

The deer, no bigger than large dogs, are related to the white-tailed deer and arrived long ago when the Keys were still joined to the mainland; they provided food for sailors and Key West residents for many years, but hunting and the destruction of their natural habitat led to near-extinction by the late Forties. The **National Key Deer Refuge** was set up here in 1954 to safeguard the animals – one refuge manager went so far as to burn the cars and sink the boats of poachers – and their population has now stabilized between 250 and 300. Don't feed them (it's illegal), and be cautious when driving – signs alongside the road state the number of road-kills to date during the year.

The best time to spot them is at sunrise or sunset, when the deer take advantage of their sharp eyesight and come out to forage in safety. Don't miss the **hiking trails** here, either – Blue Hole is a large freshwater lake that's home to plenty of soft-shelled turtles and alligators, and a good place for bird spotting.

Nearby **No Name Key** is home to a few settlers, living on solar power and septic tanks. It's notable as the staging ground for the Bay of Pigs invasion; it was here that Cuban patriots practiced before their disastrous attempt to dislodge Castro and the remnants of the decaying airstrip can be made out in a clearing on the south of the Key. It's also the site of one of the quirkiest restaurants in the Keys – the *No Name Pub* (see p.236).

Looe Key Marine Sanctuary

Named after the British frigate *HMS Looe* that sank here – just off Ramrod Key – in 1744, there's no Looe Key landmass. Instead, the **Looe Key Marine**

Sanctuary (Mon–Fri 8am–5pm; ☎305/292-0311, ⊛www.fknms.nos.noaa.gov) consists of five square miles of protected coral reef that makes for some of the best and easiest snorkeling in all the Keys; if you make one dive trip along the route to Key West, make it here. The water ranges in depth from 8 to 35 feet, so it's ideal for both novices and experienced snorkelers, and like the Elbow in John Pennekamp State Park, it's cleansed by the Gulfstream, which keeps water clearer. The coral formations on the Y-shaped reef are enormous – look for showy elkhorn and star coral, not to mention deadly but shortsighted barracuda. Don't come to see a sunken ship, though: the *HMS Looe* has long since disintegrated, and all that's left are a few hard-to-spot ballast stones.

Middle and Lower Keys practicalities

In the Middle and Lower Keys, Marathon is your best bet for **accommodation**. *Banana Bay*, at MM 49.5-Bayside (☎305/743-3500 or 1-800/BANANA-1, ⊛www.bananabay.com; $95 and up) is a lush, palm-crowded resort with airy, tropical rooms and good onsite amenities, popular with holidaymaking British families. The *Flamingo Inn*, at MM 59.3-Bayside (☎305/289-1478 or 1-800/439-1478, ⊛www.theflamingoinn.com; from $62), is an old-style motel with big, clean rooms engagingly painted in lurid pinks and greens, while the *Sea Dell Motel*, at MM 50-Bayside (☎305/743-5161 or 1-800/648-3854; ⊛www.seadellmotel.com; $49 and up), features spotless, simply furnished, bright, white and turquoise rooms – and is one of the best budget options in the Keys. Midrange hotels and motels in the Lower Keys tend to be poor value; if you're determined to stay here, either splurge on a night or two at the lavish *Little Palm Island*, MM 28.5-Oceanside, Little Torch Key (☎305/872-2524 or 1-800/438-5678, ⊛www.littlepalmisland.com; no children; from $595), whose thatched cottages are set in lush gardens a few feet from the beach on the private islet.

As for **eating**, try the moderately priced *Castaway Restaurant*, at 1406 Oceanview Ave, near MM 47.5-Oceanside in Marathon (☎305/743-6247), a local place known for its tasty and unusual alligator-tail dishes – you can also bring your own fish for cooking – as well as its doughy honey-drenched buns. Nearby *Porky's BBQ*, at MM 47.5-Bayside (☎305/289-2065), is a thatched-roof shack that serves inexpensive BBQ platters. While the *Seven Mile Grill*, MM 47.5-Bayside (☎305/743-4481), may not look like much (its decoration is limited to walls covered in old beer cans), locals flock here for fine conch chowders and shrimp steamed in beer, as well as sumptuous Key Lime Pie – said to be the best outside Key West.

Further south, seek out the devilishly hard to find *No Name Pub*, MM 30-Bayside (☎305/872-9115, ⊛www.nonamepub.com). This rollicking **bar** is well worth the rather circuitous detour for a sight of the unusual wallpaper: dollar bills covering every inch of wall and ceiling inside, worth some $60,000 by the owners' account. If you fancy adding a bill or two, just ask the staff for the house staple-gun. To find the pub, turn right at the only stoplight in Big Pine (MM 30) and follow the right-hand fork when the road splits. Continue for 100 yards or so to another stop sign, and turn left; take the curving road for two miles through a residential neighborhood until the pub appears on the left, just before the bridge that leads to No Name Key. The best coffee in the Keys is at *Baby's*, MM 14.5-Oceanside, Baypoint Key (☎1-800/523-2326, ⊛www.babyscoffee .com), a roadside industrial shack where beans are roasted on site.

There isn't much nightlife in Big Pine – locals tend to drive down to Key West. Marathon's livelier: start off at *The Hurricane Grille*, MM 49.5-Bayside (☎305/743-2220), a classic roadside American bar with nightly live music on a small stage at the back. This is an early stop on the nightly pub-crawl that concludes around 4am in the *Brass Monkey*, MM 50-Oceanside in nearby K-Mart Plaza.

Key West

The southernmost point of the continental United States is in **Key West** – and it shows. An easy blend of Caribbean and American cultures, its Old Town is packed with ice-cream-colored colonial houses and unhurried locals, washed over with a sense that this could be the town at the edge of the world. It's closer to Cuba, only ninety miles to the south, than mainland America – in fact the first international long-distance telephone call from the US connected Key West to Cuba. Even now, thanks to the old cigar-makers' cottages, *café con leches*, and signs that point to Havana, Cuba's forbidden presence is strong.

Key West exudes a palpably care-free attitude; whatever happens in life, people here (known as Conchs) seem determined to remain unruffled. It's partly this supine tolerance that has allowed a huge, quietly integrated gay population to accumulate in Key West in the past twenty years. Yet as wild as it may at first appear, Key West today is far from being the misfits' paradise that it was just a decade or so ago. Much of the sleaziness has been gradually brushed away through rather cutesy restoration and revitalization; the town's soaring popularity with tourists has inflated real estate prices to an extreme where locals either can't afford to stay here, or choose to cash in a centuries-old family home for millions. The result of this exodus has been the arrival en masse of wealthy weekending Miamians – some estimates peg 40 percent of the houses here as second or holiday homes.

Some history

Key West is reportedly a corruption of the Spanish explorers' original name for the island. Native Americans here left the bones of their dead in sand dunes along the shore; these the Spaniards found, naming the place *Cayo Hueso* (meaning "Bone Island"), which was then anglicized into Key West. And though this is the westernmost of the Keys now connected by the Overseas Highway, it's not the furthest west of all the Keys – those are the Dry Tortugas (see p.247).

Although it's now a charming backwater, between 1850 and 1865 Key West was the wealthiest city per capita in the United States, its money coming from the **wrecking** business. In the treacherous Florida Straits, there were regular wrecks with precious cargoes, as well as plenty of ships in trouble that paid for rescue with one third of their booty. Inevitably, more than one local wrecker was indicted for facilitating, rather than responding to, a shipwreck. Key West played a crucial role in the **Civil War**, as, along with Fort Jefferson (see p.247), it was a Union port while the rest of Florida sided with the Confederacy. Its decision to side with the North wasn't wholly voluntary – Key West's port was being blockaded into submission, since the Union wanted to be able to liquidate the Confederate ships it captured at Key West's lucrative wreckers' auctions.

The building of reef lighthouses sounded the death knell for the wrecking business by the end of the nineteenth century, but Key West continued to prosper even so. Many **Cubans** arrived bringing cigar-making skills, and

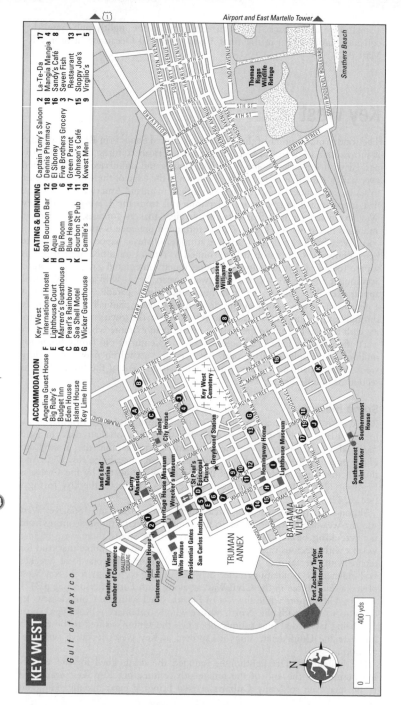

KEY WEST

Gulf of Mexico

Airport and East Martello Tower ▲

ACCOMMODATION			
Angelina Guest House	F	Key West International Hostel	D
Big Ruby's	E	Lighthouse Court	A
Budget Inn	C	Marrero's Guesthouse	C
Eden House	B	Pearl's Rainbow	B
Island House	G	Sea Shell Motel	
Key Lime Inn		Wicker Guesthouse	

EATING & DRINKING			
801 Bourbon Bar	12	Captain Tony's Saloon	2
Aqua	10	Dennis Pharmacy	18
Blu Room	6	El Siboney	16
Blue Heaven	14	Five Brothers Grocery	7
Bourbon St Pub	11	Green Parrot	15
Camille's	I	Johnson's Café	9
		Kwest Men	19
La-Te-Da	17
Mangia Mangia	4
Sandy's Café	8
Seven Fish	13
Restaurant	1
Sloppy Joe's	5
Virgilio's	

Greater Key West Chamber of Commerce

Audubon House
Customs House
Little White House
Presidential Gates
San Carlos Institute

Land's End Marina

Curry Mansion
Heritage House Museum
Wrecker's Museum
St Paul's Episcopal Church
City Hall
Island City House

Greyhound Station
Hemingway Home
Lighthouse Museum

Key West Cemetery

Tennessee Williams' House

Thomas Riggs Wildlife Refuge

Smathers Beach

Southernmost Point Marker
Southernmost House

BAHAMA VILLAGE

TRUMAN ANNEX

Fort Zachary Taylor State Historical Site

N

0   400 yds

migrant **Greeks** established a lucrative sponge enterprise (the highly absorbent sea sponges, formed from the skeletons of tiny marine creatures, were the forerunners of today's synthetic sponges). Industrial unrest and a sponge blight drove these businesses north to Tampa and Tarpon Springs, leaving Key West ill prepared to face the **Depression**, which, by the summer of 1934, had driven nearly all the Conchs into bankruptcy. The government suggested abandoning Key West entirely and moving the Conchs en masse to the mainland, but the WPA, part of Franklin Roosevelt's New Deal, was savvy enough to realize it was better to tidy up the key and ready it for tourism.

Clearly, it wasn't to be – at least then, as the **1935 Labor Day hurricane** blew away the Flagler railway, Key West's only land link to the outside world. The city settled into a sleepy easiness, and while elsewhere in postwar America, old homes were torn down for modern prefabs, there was no money for this in Key West; effectively, the city was flash frozen by its own poverty, so that the conch houses so cherished today were left untouched.

In the 1970s, Key West gained prominence as a gay mecca, although the reasons for this are foggy. Local laid-back attitudes played a part, as did the gay revolution of the 1960s, which galvanized scattered groups into a community that could act in concert, including moving to certain towns like Key West or San Francisco. Local gay historians also note that early gay residents like Tennessee Williams hosted visitors from across the country, who acted as unofficial emissaries for the town's tolerance and tropical weather when they returned home.

City transportation and tours

As the sights in Key West Old Town are virtually crammed together, the area is easily navigable on foot – though **renting a bike or scooter** is a good alternative option: try Adventure Scooter & Bicycle Rentals, at 1 Duval St (bikes $15 per day with $50 deposit, mopeds $40 per day; ☎305/293-0441) with a second branch at 3824 N Roosevelt Blvd (☎305/292-1666). If street signs appear curiously absent, you'll find them painted vertically on the base of each junction lamppost, though many are peeling off. There's also a **bus** service, with two routes that loop through town ($1 exact change; 6am–1pm; ☎305/292-8160, ⓦwww.keywestcity.com).

For information, try the useful, if unofficial, **Welcome Center** (Mon–Sat 9am–7.30pm, Sun 9am–6pm; ☎305/292-8962 or 1-800/284-4482, ⓦwww .keywestwelcomecenter.com) at 3840 N Roosevelt Blvd on the eastern edge of town as you arrive; or stop by the **Key West Chamber of Commerce**, at 402 Wall St (Mon–Fri 8.30am–6.30pm, Sat & Sun 9am–6pm; ☎305/294-2587 or 1-800/527-8539, ⓦwww.keywestchamber.org), in the heart of Old Town. Make sure to grab one of the superb free self-guided walking-tour brochures available here and written by the doyenne of local guides, Sharon Wells. She's also available for private **tours** – call ☎305/294-8380 for prices and schedules. Local ghostbuster David Sloan also runs fun "haunted" tours, which leave from the *Crowne Plaza La Concha Hotel* at 430 Duval St every night at 8pm and 9pm ($18; ☎305/294-9255, ⓦwww.hauntedtours.com). Some might bilk at hopping onto the cruise-ship-recommended 90-minute Conch Train trolley; but it's by far the best option for quick orientation – not to mention lashings of anecdotal history ($20; ☎1-800/868-7842, ⓦwww.conchtrain.com). Board either at the southern edge of Mallory Square or the so-called Flagler Station stop on Caroline Street near the port.

In addition to the daily newspaper, the *Key West Citizen* (ⓦwww.keysnews .com), a number of easily found **free publications** list current events: the monthly *Solares Hill* (ⓦwww.keysnews.com) is the most informative, but look out also for *The Conch Republic* (monthly), *Key West Citypaper* (weekly; ⓦwww.keywestcitypaper.com), as well as the various gay-centric freesheets (see p.250.)

Accommodation

Whatever the time of year, **accommodation** costs in Key West are always high: expect to pay at least $90 in high season for even the simplest motel room. But if you do decide to stay here, it's worth the extra cost to stay downtown: the hotels scattered along Hwy-1 as you approach the Old Town may be slightly cheaper, but there is little public transport and parking is nightmarish in high season.

A good lodging resource is the Key West Innkeepers Association, headquartered at 922 Caroline St (☎305/295-1334 or 1-888/KEY-INNS, ⓦwww .keywestinns.com): more than sixty guesthouses and B&Bs in Old Town are members, and the helpful staff should be able to guide you to the right accommodation for price and location.

Note that many of the restored villas operating as guesthouses in the historic district are gay- and lesbian-run, and while most welcome all adults, few accept young children. We've listed the specifically **gay-targeted accommodation** on p.250.

Angelina Guest House 302 Angela St ☎305/294-4480 or 1-888/303-4480, ⓦwww .angelinaguesthouse.com. One of the best deals in town, this charming guesthouse, with a cool, Caribbean feel, is tucked away in the back streets of the Bahama Village. Its fourteen simple rooms are decorated in pastel yellow, green, or blue, and the small pool is a great place to enjoy

the owners' cinnamon rolls at breakfast time. Shared bath from $79, private bath from $99.

Budget Inn 1031 Eaton St ☎305/294-3333, ⓦwww.budgetkeywest.com. Stashed north of the Old Town near the seaport, this is a rare find in Key West, with low prices, pleasant rooms, and good location – far from budget in feel. Onsite amenities may be minimal and the staff a little frosty, but the rooms themselves are delightful, with refrigerators and large bathrooms. $85 & up.

Eden House 1015 Fleming St ☎305/296-6868 or 1-800/533-5397, ⓦwww.edenhouse.com. Don't let the rather shabby reception put you off this place just south of the port – it's a gem. Rooms (some with private bath) are decorated in the usual pastels and pale woods, though many have large, claw-foot tubs and most overlook the pool. Best of all, there's free off-street parking and a free happy hour every night 4–5pm (plus a complimentary beer at check-in). From $130.

Key Lime Inn 725 Truman Ave ☎305/294-5229 or 1-800/549-4430, ⓦwww.keylimeinn .com. There are various different accommodations in this cluster of cottages with Key West tropical decor near the center of Old Town. A good buffet breakfast is served by the pool, and the ample onsite parking is a major plus. Splurge on one of the bungalows for the seclusion and the veranda. Rooms start at $125.

Key West International Hostel 718 South St ☎305/296-5719, ⓦwww.keywesthostel.com. The dorms here are small and grubby, but it is the only hostel on the island and as such hands down the cheapest place to stay. If the hostel's full, the adjoining *SeaShell Motel* is slightly pricier, though no more swanky. Dorms members $19.50, nonmembers $22.50; motel from $65.

Marrero's Guesthouse 410 Fleming St ☎305/294-6977 or 1-800/459-6212, ⓦwww .marreros.com. Reputed to be haunted, this fancy but friendly hotel has rooms crammed with antique furniture. Ghost-hunters should ask for Room 18, where most paranormal activity has been reported. Shared bath $125 and up, private bath $150 and up, Room 18 $180.

Wicker Guesthouse 913 Duval St ☎305/296-4275 or 1-800/880-4275, ⓦwww .wickerhousekw.com. One of the least expensive guesthouses on Key West, this complex of four restored Conch houses centers on a pool and communal Jacuzzi. The rooms are impressive given the price, splashily decorated with orange and red bedspreads and (naturally) white wicker furniture. Its biggest plus, though, is the chirpy staff. $130 and up.

The Town

Compact but not small, **Old Town** – at the western end of the island – is where most major sights can be found: it's best to rely on walking as you'll see more local color and worry less about finding parking on the cramped streets. **Mallory Square**, the old wreckers' dock, is the heart of tourist Key West, hosting the well-known sunset celebrations and featuring many museums close by; while **Duval Street**, the main drag, extends south from here.

The city's military history is clear in the **Truman Annex**, once a naval base and now an enclave of the swankiest homes in town. Close by, and very different, the Caribbean contribution to Key West's growth is evident in the old workmen's homes of the **Bahama Village**, a great place to saunter round on a hot, lazy afternoon – and the **Hemingway House**, for devoted fans of the author, is just outside the Bahamian quarter. Finally, east from the town center, you'll find **East Old Town**, home to a large wooden historic district.

Mallory Square and around

Originally the hub of Key West's wrecking industry, **Mallory Square**'s buildings were used for the storage and auction of goods salvaged from wrecked ships. Now, it's the hub of Key West's tourist trade, filled with market stalls and street performers.

Every night of the year, the **sunset celebration** sweeps over the area, when jugglers, fire-eaters, and assorted loose-screw types create a merry backdrop to the day's end. The party began with a group of hippies in the 1960s, and if it's

24

△ A street performer in Mallory Square

not quite the countercultural hang-out it once was, it's still worth a stop for the spectacular sunsets over the water and the general liveliness. The big problem these days is the cruise ships that moor here for the day, though their agreements with the local government include a guarantee to have set sail before sunset: slack passengers late to return often mean the spectacular views are blocked by the bulky monsters.

There are two small islands visible just off the northern coast of Mallory Square. To the west, one-time **Tank Key** – named after the huge fuel tanks the Navy used to stash there – is now known as Sunset Key. There's an anodyne luxury resort there, best known as the location of Oprah Winfrey's fiftieth birthday party; accessible via a free ten-minute boat ride from Mallory Square, it is hardly worth the trip. To the east, there's no public access to **Christmas Tree Island** unless you have your own skiff. This was once home to fir trees and hippie dropouts; but its owner's finally sold the spot, and its new real estate developer owners have rechristened it Wisteria Island.

Just south of Mallory Square stands the **Audubon House** at 205 Whitehead St (daily 9.30am–5pm; $9; ☎305/294-2116 or 1-877/281-BIRD, ⊛www .audubonhouse.com). When the wealthy Wolfson family purchased the place to prevent its demolition in 1958 – the site was earmarked for a gas station – they set about restoring the house to its original grandeur, using the family collection of furniture and decorative arts (see p.66). Built by Captain John Geiger, one of the most successful wreckers in Key West in the early nineteenth century, this grand house was once prime seafront property. Geiger upgraded his plans for the house after a severe hurricane passed through: as with many homes in the Old Town, it's constructed using shipbuilding techniques, making it more flexible in high winds. The house's name derives from John James Audubon, who was fascinated by Geiger's exotic-plant collection. In fact, the painter and naturalist spent little time here, as he traveled round the Keys focusing on his mammoth book of engravings, *Birds of America*. Today, the house is a superb museum, with an evocative audio tour that fully captures Key West's wrecking heyday; there's also a small onsite gallery of pricey Audubon prints for sale.

Along Duval Street

Jammed with tacky T-shirt and souvenir shops, especially at its northern end, **Duval Street** is often held up as a prime exhibit in the spoiling of Key West (who knows what today's reaction would be if a 1976 plan to turn it into a canal, complete with imported Venetian gondoliers, had been enacted). Despite appearances, though, there are some surprisingly good restaurants and bars dotted along its length, as well as Key West's most famous watering hole, **Captain Tony's Saloon**, at 428 Greene St (see p.249), where Hemingway drank back when it was called *Sloppy Joe's*. Confusingly, another bar named *Sloppy Joe's*, laden with Hemingway memorabilia, is just across the street, intended to lure ill-informed tourists to spend their money there instead.

One block east off Duval's northern tip, the exhaustively restored **Curry Mansion**, at 511 Caroline St (daily 8.30am–4.30pm; $5; ☎305/294-5349, ⊛www.currymansion.com), now a guesthouse, is an awkward hybrid of museum and hotel. The public rooms are crammed with period antiques and oddities like Henry James's piano, but there's no claim to have authentically replicated how the house looked in its prime. It was first built in 1869 as the abode of William Curry, Florida's first millionaire. The current structure dates from 1886, when Curry's son Milton rebuilt the mansion after a major fire. The real reason to stop by is the tiny lookout on the roof – known as a Captain's Walk in New England, in Key West it's called a **Widow's Walk**, since it was once used by sailors' wives to watch for their return. Now the tiny terrace gives a great view across Key West's Old Town.

Continue down Duval proper and you'll find more traditional sights, like the **Wrecker's Museum**, also known as the Oldest House Museum (daily 10am–4pm; $5; ☎305/294-9502, ⊛www.oirf.org/museums/oldesthouse). Built in 1829 when Florida was still a territory, it is located in the oldest house in town, at no. 322 (it is indeed the oldest on the street, but originally stood a few blocks away at the junction of Whitehead and Caroline streets). Hokey but entertaining, the museum presents the history of wrecking via artifacts and models, as well as the posh furniture of Captain Watlington, one of the house's first inhabitants. Three quarters of the pieces are original – look for the courting lamp in the parlor, which provided amorous couples the chance to chat as long as the oil lasted, and the lopsided cookhouse in the back garden, built separately from the main house to reduce risk of fire. There's more than a little poetic license to many of the sea dog yarns the museum recounts, and the saintliness of the selfless wreckers is unintentionally hilarious, given how often they were accused of encouraging, rather than just responding to, lucrative wrecks.

Nicknamed *La Casa Cuba*, the **San Carlos Institute** at no. 516 (Tues–Sun 11.30am–5pm; $3 suggested donation; ☎305/294-3887) was founded in 1871 by Cuban expats who wanted to celebrate the language, ideals, and culture of their people. It was here in 1892 that Cuban Revolutionary hero José Martí welded the exiles into a force that would topple the regime ten years later. The current building, which dates from 1924, was financed by a $100,000 grant from the Cuban government after a hurricane wrecked the original wooden shack. Cuban architect Francisco Centurion designed the two-story building in the Cuban Baroque style of the period, noticeable in the wrought-iron balconies and creamy facade. The soil on its grounds is from Cuba's six provinces, and a cornerstone was taken from Martí's tomb. The building has a passable permanent exhibition focusing on the revolutionary and his men, consisting mostly of old newspaper clippings and letters. You can also pick up a free map here of the **Cuban Heritage Trail**, a self-guided tour of the key sights in Key West.

Close to the southernmost point marker, the **Southernmost House**, at no. 1400 (daily 10am–6pm; $8; ☎305/296-3141, ⊛www.southernmosthouse .com), offers an experience so bad it's almost good, though the fact that admission to its "museum" includes a drink at the inviting poolside bar here should tip you off that there isn't much worth paying to see. Originally built for Florida Curry, daughter of the state's first millionaire and sister of the man behind the Curry Mansion (see p.243), in the mid-1990s, it was sadly renovated in jazzy, fruit-pastille colors, and looks more like a rickety set for a local production of *Carmen* than the jazzy 1950s Cuban nightclub it was modeled after. Exhibits are limited to celebrity autographs and a few inexplicable trinkets, which the mandatory tour-guide highlights with robot-like enthusiasm. Frankly, the best thing about the house is its lush pool, with a deck that overlooks the ocean and a loggia for the bar.

The Truman Annex

The **Truman Annex**, which encompasses much of the northwest corner of Key West, was originally part of a naval base established in 1822 to curb piracy in the area; it later became a favored place for flight training thanks to wide uninterrupted air space and clear, predictable local weather. Although the base was decommissioned in the 1970s, the charming old houses here were significantly restored when purchased by a developer in 1986. He encouraged people to amble through the chic streets by opening up the **Presidential Gates** on Caroline Street, which had previously only budged for heads of state. It's now the site of some of the most luxurious homes in Key West – pick up a free map from one of the boxes dotted throughout the complex.

The area is named after its most famous former resident, President Harry S. Truman, who first came here on doctor's orders in March 1946 to recuperate after World War II. He quickly adopted Key West as a second home and spent most of his visits in **The Little White House**, at 111 Front St (daily 9am–5pm; $10, admission only by guided tour; ☎305/294-9911, ⓦwww .trumanlittlewhitehouse.com). There's not much to see inside the museum, other than mid-twentieth-century ephemera, although the knowledge-able docents make it a worthwhile stop with an anecdote-packed account of Truman's life. The Truman Annex also provides access to Fort Zachary Taylor via a fenced roadway; close by, around its southeastern corner at the junction of Fleming and Whitehead streets, you'll find Mile Marker 0, the starting point for the Keys' idiosyncratic address system.

Fort Zachary Taylor State Historical Site

Conceived in the 1840s as part of a coastal defense system that also included Fort Jefferson (see p.247) in the Dry Tortugas, Fort Zachary Taylor's (park daily 8am–sunset, fort structure daily 8am–5pm; $1.50 pedestrians and cyclists, $3.50 for 1 person plus car, $6.00 for 2 people plus car, 50¢ each additional person; ☎305/292-6713, ⓦwww.floridastateparks.org/forttaylor) glory days came during the Civil War. As a Union stronghold, it was used to block maneuvers by the Confederate navy. Its onsite facilities were cutting edge when completed, even including a desalination plant for drinking water. Eventually, though, the fort fell into disrepair and disuse, before being turned over to the Navy as a historic site in 1947. The park offers informative guided tours (every day at noon & 2pm), where rangers provide detailed history on the fort.

For many visitors, however, the **beach** is the real reason to come here. It's the best in Key West, and there are full amenities on site, including showers. Be aware, though, that the beach has pebbles rather than sand, and the craggy sea bottom can be tough on your feet, so bring waterproof sandals.

The Bahama Village

One of the few places that still has the feel of old Key West, unrestored and untouristed, the **Bahama Village**, just southeast of the Truman Annex, sprang up in the 1820s after a law was passed making it illegal for vessels salvaged in US waters to be taken elsewhere. Many who worked in the salvage trade were Bahamian, and their temporary homes in Key West became permanent ones.

The small cottages here – formerly home to Cuban cigar-rollers – haven't yet been primped and manicured as many of the other wooden shacks in Old Town have been, and frankly, it's a refreshing contrast to the tourist-ready restored manses elsewhere. Most of the reason for coming here is to get a feel for the laid-back vibe – witness the locals relaxing out on their porches while chickens roam the streets. There may be chickens on the street everywhere in Key West, but you're likely to see the largest number here: descendants of Cuban fighting cocks, it's illegal to harm them in any way, especially as their appetite for scorpions keeps numbers down. Now-sleepy Petronia Street was once a throbbing hub for jazz clubs that boasted regular gigs by the likes of Louis Armstrong, lured to Key West since there was no racial segregation here. These days, the lone tourist sight here is eminently avoidable, the tacky Bahama Village Market, at 318 Petronia St.

The Hemingway House

Just outside the Bahama Village quarter lies the **Hemingway House**, at 907 Whitehead St (daily 9am–5pm; $10; ☎305/294-1136, ⓦwww.hemingwayhome .com). While the facts of Hemingway's life in (and love of) Key West are much disputed, his former home is one of the most enjoyable sights in town.

Hemingway came to Key West on the recommendation of fellow writer John Dos Passos, who raved about fishing here. He bought what's now the Hemingway House in 1931 with an $8000 loan from his then-wife Pauline's rich uncle. Although it had once been one of the grander homes in the town, by Hemingway's time the house had fallen into disrepair and it required substantial renovation; the swimming pool was his only major addition.

Although Hemingway's legend is inextricably linked with Key West, he lived here for only nine years, before divorcing Pauline and moving to Cuba with his fourth (and last) wife, journalist Martha Gelhorn. While in the house, though, he wrote two of his most famous novels, *For Whom the Bell Tolls* and *To Have and Have Not*, set locally during the Depression. His deer-head-dominated study is unsurprisingly compact, practical, and set apart from the rest of the house in its own smaller outbuilding. Restoration of the study and main home has taken them back to how they looked during Papa's time – although his former secretary strongly contests the authenticity of much of the furnishings.

To see inside, join one of the regular half-hour-long **tours** (every 10 minutes) led by true Key West eccentrics, who do a good job of spinning stories that play up the writer's machismo – but take everything they say with a grain of salt. One tale that's clearly more fiction than fact is that the dozens of extra-toed cats here are descendants from a feline family that lived in Hemingway's day. The large colony of inbred cats once described by Hemingway was at his home in Cuba.

East Old Town

Northeast from the Hemingway House lies Key West's **wooden historic district**, the largest of its kind in the US, bigger than better-known settlements in Savannah, Georgia, or Charleston, South Carolina. The Conch-house style here is a Colonial–Victorian fusion, and there are some excellent examples **along William Street** between Caroline and Angela streets. Shored up by a foundation of coral slabs, the houses themselves were built cheaply and quickly, fanning out from the earliest settlements around the port (now Mallory Square). The reason these houses have lasted so well is that many were put up by ship-wrights using boat-building techniques, so they sway in high winds and weather extremes of climate handily. A fine example of this early Key West architecture is the *Island City House Hotel*, at 411 William St – built in the 1880s, it's the oldest hotel in town.

On the far eastern edge of Old Town, twenty minutes' walk from the center, stands the **Tennessee Williams House**, at 1431 Duncan St, home to the Southern playwright for over thirty years. He led a quiet life in Key West and it was one of the conditions in his will under which his house in Key West was sold that it never be open to public visitors. It's still a fine Bahamian-style home, but only really worth the pilgrimage if you're a devoted fan of the *A Streetcar Named Desire* author. Note that Williams isn't buried in the cemetery here, either – against his wishes, the author's family shipped his body back to his detested home town of St Louis and interred it there.

The Key West Cemetery

On the corner of Angela and Frances streets, the **Key West Cemetery** (daily sunrise–6pm; free) was founded in 1847. Residents needed a new eternal

Dry Tortugas National Park

Almost seventy miles out from Key West lie the seven islands of **the Dry Tortugas**. They are exhilaratingly isolated and a birdwatcher's paradise; they're also the site of the ruins of Fort Jefferson, an old Union Civil War stronghold.

The islands were named by Ponce de León in 1513, who found *tortugas*, or sea turtles, plentiful here. He actually found eleven islands – since then, four have eroded completely; and their name was modified on sea charts in the 1930s to indicate that there was no freshwater on the islands – in other words, they were dry. Of the seven, **Loggerhead Key** is technically the last of the Florida Keys, almost 70 miles out from Key West: after that, the sea floor falls away sharply to 1000 feet or more.

Unfortunately, **Fort Jefferson** was militarily redundant almost from its inception in 1846: conceived as part of a coastal defense system against British naval build-up in Bermuda, much like Fort Zachary Taylor (see p.245), it was rendered useless after the invention of the rifled canon. First money and then the Civil War held up construction, as evidenced by the change in brick color half-way up the outer walls: a Union stronghold, Fort Jefferson had to switch to bricks made in the North, which have weathered far less well in southern humidity than the original, local materials.

For several years, the fort was used as a prison for Union deserters and other undesirables, most famously Dr Samuel Mudd, convicted as an accomplice in President Lincoln's assassination after setting John Wilkes Booth's broken leg the day after the shooting. (Ironically, Mudd received a pardon from President Johnson, after stepping in for the island's dead doctor and treating ailing soldiers during a virulent yellow fever outbreak.) After its period as a prison, the fort was abandoned by the army in the 1880s; it was first earmarked as a wildlife refuge before finally snagging status as an official National Park.

These days, **Bush and Long Keys** serve as sanctuaries for sooty terns and frigate birds. In addition, coral reefs here are close to the beach, especially on the western coast, making for sensational snorkeling. If you plan to stay overnight, the **camping** fee is $3 per person, but bring everything you'll need – including freshwater – as facilities are very basic. Call ☏305/242-7700 for information, or visit ⓦwww.nps.gov/drto.

The only way to make the trip here is by **boat** or plane: the *Yankee Freedom II* leaves daily from the dock at the end of Margaret St on Key West at 8am ($134 daytrip, $159 overnight; ☏305/294-7009 or 1-800/634-0939, ⓦwww.yankeefreedom.com), returning at 5pm. However, northerly winds can make for an extra-bumpy ride, so those with wobbly sea legs might prefer to spend a little extra and **fly**: try Seaplanes of Key West, at 3471 S Roosevelt Blvd ($179/half-day, $305/full day, $329/overnight; ☏305/294-0709 or 1-800/950-2FLY, ⓦwww.seaplanesofkeywest.com).

(24)

resting place after the town's original waterfront cemetery was ghoulishly churned up in a violent storm; and most of those buried in this landlocked cemetery are entombed in vaults above ground, both thanks to the hard coral rock and the high water-table. There may be a lack of celebrity stiffs here, but by wandering through this massive graveyard you'll notice the impact of immigration on Key West – the cemetery is filled with people from across the country and abroad. The sprinkling of campy epitaphs makes this a livelier graveyard than normal – look for the grave of E. Lariz, enshrined forever as "devoted fan of singer Julio Iglésias," or B.P. Roberts, who continues to carp from beyond the grave: "I told you I was sick." Use Sharon Wells' free guide (see p.240) to hit the highlights or take one of the superb tours run by the Historic Florida Keys Foundation (Tues & Thurs 9.30am; $10; ☏305/292-6718).

Eating, drinking, and nightlife

There are plenty of good **restaurants** in and around Duval Street, even if at first glance they may all seem rather tacky. It's also worth dipping into the Bahama Village for cheap, authentic Caribbean food. For Cuban coffee and sandwiches, check out the streetside lunch counters – two worth trying are *Sandy's Café* at the M&M Laundry, 1026 White St (☎305/295-0159), which also serves sloppy, filling sandwiches for $5 or so, and *Five Brothers Grocery*, at 930 Southard St (☎305/296-5205).

Every restaurant in town offers its take on **Key Lime Pie**: *Key Lime Heaven* is one of the best, topping its $4.50 slice of take-out pie with a swirl of meringue (308 Front St ☎305/294-2042) The other dish on offer everwhere is **conch fritters**; they're a local specialty, even if radical overfishing in the last hundred years depleted stocks so much that all conch is now imported from the Bahamas. Try *Bo's Fish Wagon* at 801 Caroline St (☎305/294-9272) for fritters and delicious fish sandwiches; or the conch stand on Mallory Square (daily 10.30am–6pm, no phone), where half a dozen fritters cost $6.

As for **drinking**, many hotels offer good deals on drinks during happy hour (usually 5–7pm), and there are some good rundown bars in the Old Town, many of which also showcase **live music**.

Cafés and restaurants

Blue Heaven 729 Thomas St ☎305/296-8666, ⓦ www.blueheavenkw.com. Serving outstanding food in a relaxed setting, this Bahama Village landmark has a large outdoor seating area that diners share with local chickens that wander around undisturbed. Open all day, the breakfasts are delicious (try the lobster Benedict), but lunch and dinner are even better– don't miss the shrimp with jerk seasoning or pork tenderloin with sweet potato. And of course, save room for the home-made banana bread and one of the sumptuous desserts. Expensive.

Camille's 1202 Simonton St ☎305/296-4811, ⓦ www.camilleskeywest.com. *Camille's* is known as one of the best places in town for breakfast, thanks to luxurious specials like French toast with Godiva chocolate sauce or cashew-nut waffles with coconut milk. Dinner's less exciting, though. Moderate.

Johnson's Café 801 Thomas St ☎305/292-2286. The motto at this small café is "Bust your belly" and the cheap, enormous sandwiches ($6) don't disappoint. Buy a beer from the grocery across the road and settle down on the veranda with your meal. Lunch-only Tues–Thurs, lunch and dinner Fri & Sat. Inexpensive.

Dennis Pharmacy 1229 Simonton St ☎305/294-1577. Superb *café con leche* and set breakfasts served in a real drugstore. The service is no-frills, but there's plenty of local gossip to overhear while you sip. Only open until 5pm. Inexpensive.

El Siboney 900 Catherine St ☎305/296-4184. Crammed with tables and jammed with people, this large Cuban restaurant on the eastern side of the Old Town has cheap food and vast portions; the pork tenderloin is especially tasty. Inexpensive.

Mangia Mangia 900 Southard St ☎305/294-2469. The best-value Italian restaurant on the island, with fine fresh pasta (you can watch them making it in their front window) and a large garden. The dishes are hearty and basic – marinara, soupy pesto – and each is served with hulks of crusty Cuban garlic bread. Moderate.

Seven Fish Restaurant 632 Olivia St ☎305/296-2777, ⓦ www.7fish.com. This little-known bistro, easy to miss in its tiny, white corner building, serves some of the best food in Key West – there are just over a dozen tables, so it pays to book. The cooking's simple and delicious – think shrimp scampi and meatloaf – and the crowd is a mix of straight and gay. Expensive.

Bars and nightclubs

Captain Tony's Saloon 428 Greene St ☎305/294-1838, ⓦwww.capttonyssaloon.com. This bar was the original *Sloppy Joe's* that Hemingway frequented; now, it's a grimy yellow shack where you can catch live music most nights. Not the most atmospheric place in town, but worth a quick drink.

Green Parrot 601 Whitehead St ☎ 305/294-6133, ⓦwww.greenparrot.com. Grubby pub centered on an enormous square bar that's been a landmark for more than a century. Drinks are cheap, it's full of locals, and there are antique bar games alongside the pool tables. There's often live music at weekends on its small stage.

Virgilio's Appelrouth Lane ☎305/296-8118. This ma adjoining *La Trattoria* at patio, as well as small ind stage, often occupied by l bands. Drinks are served w as each cocktail's overflow alongside your glass in a mini-carafe on ice.

Wax 422 Appelrouth Lane ☎305/296-6667. The closest Key West comes to a traditional nightclub: overstuffed red sofas and bead curtains decorate a chic, dimly lit space. Come here only if you're determined to dance, as the music's way too loud to talk.

Gay Key West

For a town deemed one of the more gay-oriented in America, the scene in Key West is surprisingly small – perhaps because the gay and straight communities are so integrated. Certainly, the wild excesses of the 1970s have been toned down – the most recent clamp-down came in the wake of a porn star's recent live performance in a local bar, which climaxed, literally, all over his audience.

Despite the new-found restraint, Key West is a place where – at least, in the Old Town – gay couples holding hands will pass unremarked upon; and almost every hotel and restaurant will be gay-friendly – we've listed below some of the best gay-targeted businesses. Stop by the **Gay and Lesbian Community Center** (☎305/292-3223, ⓦwww.glcckeywest.org) for information and leaflets on specific hotels, or try the **Key West Business Guild**, both at 513 Truman Ave (☎305/294-4603 or 1-800/535-7797, ⓦwww.gaykeywestfl.com).

The unofficial gay beach is **Higgs Memorial Beach**, at the southern end of Reynolds Street. To cruise on water rather than land, take one of the day or evening boat trips that depart from here – one of the best is the women-only

---

Fantasy Fest

In late October, Key West is taken over by **Fantasy Fest**, a week-long gay-dominated version of Mardi Gras that includes parties and events where participants don as outrageous a costume as possible. Every year there's a theme, often with a nod to Halloween: past suggestions have included "TV Jeebies," "Delirious Dreams and Hilarious Screams," and "Freaks, Geeks, and Goddesses."

One of the best-attended events is the mid-week **pet costume parade**, where animals, mostly dogs, are decked out in costumes to resemble their owners. The entire shindig's grown a little less outrageous as Key West's tourist profile's become more mainstream (there are strictly enforced rules about public nudity, for example, which emphasize that body paint does not constitute clothing). Despite the rule-tightening, it's still a huge tourist draw, and if you want a room at this time you'll need to book well in advance and expect significant rate hikes (☎305/296-1817, ⓦwww .fantasyfest.net).

e Sea, run by Sebago Watersports (Thurs $35, including unlimited and beer; ☎1–800/507-9955, ⓦwww.keywestsebago.com), which leaves ⁄pm from the dock at the end of William Street. For information on what's happening pick up a copy of the free *Southern Exposure* magazine (ⓦkwest.com) or check out *Celebrate! Key West* (ⓦwww.celebratekeywest.com), a more news-oriented, more informative freesheet.

Accommodation

Big Ruby's 409 Appelrouth Lane ☎305/296-2323 **or 1-800/477-7829,** ⓦwww.bigrubys.com. A cluster of buildings, all dotted round a lagoon pool and patio where you can lounge and listen to piped-in Motown most days. There are lots of extras, including splendid Sunday brunches (try the eggs Benedict), free drinks 6–8pm, and affable staff. Shared bath from $163, private bath from $180.

Island House 1129 Fleming St ☎305/294-6284 **or 1-800/890-6284,** ⓦwww.islandhousekeywest .com. Cruisey, men-only resort, with a sauna, video room, and large pool with sundeck (in fact, guests need only wear clothes when using the exercise

equipment in the gym). The surprisingly appealing rooms have overstuffed leather chairs, VCR, and crisp white linens. A day-pass to use the hotel's facilities is $25; make sure to bring photo ID. Shared bath $85 & up, private bath $159 & up.

Pearl's Rainbow 525 United St ☎305/292-1450 **or 1-800/749-6696,** ⓦwww.pearlsrainbow.com. The lone women-only guesthouse on the island, this attractive former cigar factory serves breakfast and has two pools and two Jacuzzis. There's also *Pearl's Patio*, a bar open year-round to nonguests (Sun–Wed noon–8pm, Thurs–Fri until 10pm, Sat until midnight). Rooms from $119.

Gay bars and clubs

801 Bourbon Bar 801 Duval St ☎305/294-4737, ⓦwww.801bourbon.com. Drag shows are held upstairs every night at 9pm & 11pm, while downstairs there's a nonde-script bar with a mixed, slightly older crowd that opens out onto the street, so you can watch passersby. The one-time backroom is now home – perhaps temporarily – to a pool table.

Aqua 711 Duval St ☎305/294-0555, ⓦwww .aquakeywest.com. Large, pumping club with a massive dancefloor; the music's main-stream house and Hi-NRG. Good happy hour specials 2–8pm daily.

Bourbon Street Pub 724 Duval St ☎305/296-1992, ⓦwww.bourbonstreetpub.com. A huge video bar with five bars, seven screens, and a pleasant garden. There are go-go boys

every night, and a happy hour until 8pm. This pub attracts both locals and tourists and, as with most bars in town, the crowd's diverse and chatty.

Kwest Men 705 Duval St ☎305/292-8500. Small, cruisey bar on the main drag where there's a daily happy hour 3–8pm with drinks specials, and go-go boys dancing to the pumping house music from 10pm nightly.

La-Te-Da 1125 Duval St ☎305/296-6706 **or 1-877/528-3320,** ⓦwww.lateda.com. The various bars and discos of this hotel complex have long been a favorite haunt of locals and visi-tors alike. The upstairs *Crystal Room* is one of the best-known showcases for drag divas in town – during season, there are shows nightly at 8pm and 10pm ($20–26).

24

Contexts

Contexts

A brief history of Miami

One of the most important cities in the United States, largely thanks to its location on the tip of Florida, **Miami** is both a gateway and a headquarters for most US companies keen to explore the exploding markets in South America. The city has managed to make itself synonymous with hedonism and a guaranteed good time, jostling with Las Vegas as the getaway spot of choice for a wicked weekend.

Though its European settlement dates back almost five hundred years, it wasn't until early in the twentieth century that the city began to prosper as a resort. The following account's intended to give an overview of Miami's history, from the Native American tribes who once lived here through the arrival of the railroad to its current role as the capital city of glitz.

Early natives and European settlement

The Miami area's earliest residents were the **Tequesta Indians**, who made their home some 10,000 years ago near what's now the Deering Estate in Cutler, just south of Miami. Likely responsible for the mysterious Miami Circle, the Tequesta lived and farmed the land alone until joined by the **Seminole Indians** in the 1400s.

A hundred years later, the **Europeans** arrived: brothers John and Sebastian Cabot in 1498 chanced upon what's now Cape Florida on Key Biscayne. However, Florida wasn't actually claimed until 1513, when **Ponce de León**, former governor of the Spanish possession of Puerto Rico, was dispatched by his king to find the fabled Fountain of Youth. Instead, five hundred years before Miami's plastic-surgery boom, he "discovered" land – what's now the Florida peninsula – during *Pascua Florida*, the Spanish Easter festival, and so named the area *La Florida*, or "Land of the Flowers."

De León continued on, sighting the Florida Keys, which he named *Los Martires* – the land fragments resembling to him the bones of Christian martyrs – and the Dry Tortugas, which he called *Las Tortugas* after the hundreds of turtles he found there.

While Florida gained in status, Miami lay dormant, having proved a troublesome place to settle. The area now known as Miami was a tough place to settle during the earliest days of European colonization. A brief attempt was made in 1567 when the **Jesuit Mission of Tequesta** built a garrison, in co-operation with the local Tequesta chief, which was home to thirty soldiers and one Brother Villareal. Unfortunately for them, the natives proved unusually resistant to evangelism; after they revolted against the Europeans, the mission was quickly abandoned. Even though communicating Christianity proved tricky for the settlers, passing on diseases did not, and in a sad and familiar story, the Tequesta were eventually wiped out, pagan to the last.

From Spanish rule to statehood

After Ponce de León's claim in 1513, Florida remained a **Spanish possession** until the late eighteenth century, while England aggressively colonized the southern seaboard of America. In the process, England seized Havana, Spain's colonial jewel, and, eager to recapture the Cuban capital, Spain was obliged to trade Florida to Britain for the return of the city in 1763.

However, after the American War of Independence was fought and won twenty years later, the 1783 Treaty of Paris – which recognized **American independence** – forced the newly formed United States to cede Florida to Spain in return for the country's support during the war.

Despite successfully snatching back this land, Spain's territorial ambitions were dealt a harsh blow with the arrival of a new, feisty group of displaced Native Americans at that time. The so-called **Seminoles** were in fact a diverse group of displaced tribes, all of whom had been driven from their homes in the state of Georgia. The Seminoles' spats with the colonists in Florida regularly turned ugly, and there were three separate **Seminole Wars** in 1818, 1835, and 1855: the second – and bloodiest – of which was caused by yet another attempt at relocation, this time to ship the Seminoles off to Oklahoma and Arkansas.

This relocation program was a US initiative – in 1822, Florida finally finished flip-flopping between powers and became American territory. The deal was simple: in return for assuming the $5 million owed in land grants to American settlers by the Spanish government, Florida was deeded to the United States. It went on to gain **full statehood on March 3, 1845**. The money, incidentally, was never repaid.

By then, there was a small settlement at the mouth of the Miami River. It was a slave plantation owned and run by **Richard Fitzpatrick** and his nephew **William English** from South Carolina; English wanted to further develop the post, beginning the first of Miami's many real-estate advertising campaigns, designed to sell plots of land to homesteaders. Other Floridian forts – Lauderdale and Pierce, for instance – were army strongholds named in honor of their commanders. Fitzpatrick's **Fort Dallas**, however, was named after a naval commander from the first Seminole War, but had no other military connection: it was just a minor trading post en route to the buzzing shipping hub of Key West.

The prospects for English's nascent city looked bright until the double blow of the third Seminole War and the Civil War. Together, these conflicts delayed any significant development in Miami, other than the building of a post office and a few other structures. It wasn't until the arrival of three visionary pioneer settlers from Ohio later that century that what we know as Miami truly began.

The birth of a city

Wealthy and fiercely private entrepreneur **William Brickell** arrived in the Fort Dallas area with his wife, Mary, in 1870; they built a grand home and set up an Indian Trading Post just south of the Miami River near what's now Downtown Miami. The next major settler was a rich widow, **Julia Tuttle**, who snapped up swathes of land along the river and shipped her family down to

Florida in 1891. Together, the Brickells and Julia Tuttle would nurse Miami through its earliest days – with a little help from the railway.

While Miami was still barely a village, there were already larger settlements in the area, **Lemon City** (an early settlement located where Little Haiti now lies) and **Cocoanut Grove** (as it was then known) in particular; even so, in 1890, the whole of Dade County, stretching down to Indian Key, held less than a thousand settlers. Of all the villages, it was the Grove that seemed most likely to flourish: the most significant pioneers included Ralph Middleton Munroe, an eccentric sea-captain-cum-architect, and his friends Charles and Isabella Peacock, business owners who came over from England and opened the first hotel in the Grove, the *Bay View House*, in 1882, prefiguring Florida's torrid affair with tourism by more than a hundred years.

The railroad arrives

Despite the inroads made by the various real estate magnates of the late 1800s, Miami still had little contact with the outside world. This would change with a deal between railroad tycoon **Henry Morrison Flagler**, who had made his fortune as a partner in John D. Rockefeller's Standard Oil Company, and Julia Tuttle. Savvy from the start, Flagler had taken full advantage of the fact that John D. and William Rockefeller could never get along. Since they wouldn't vote together on the board, he manoeuvred himself into a controlling position, and was soon unstoppable, accruing an inconceivable fortune. He used it wisely: anticipating how the railroads would transform America, he invested heavily in trains, laying the tracks of the Florida East Coast Railroad from St Augustine down to Palm Beach. A nationwide recession set in just as the final gauges were laid, and had it not been for the "**Big Freeze**," a ferociously cold winter in northern Florida in 1894, there might never have been a Miami.

The Brickells and Tuttle banded together to offer him land in exchange for extending his railroad down the coast. Then as now, citrus crops were the backbone of Florida's agricultural economy, so it was devastating when the freeze forced the yield of oranges down from 5.5m boxes in 1894 to less than 150,000 a year later. Julia Tuttle saw an opportunity for Miami in this statewide disaster and snipped fresh orange blossoms from her garden and sent them to Flagler, showing that Fort Dallas was frost-free and the climate consistently mild. Characteristic though that anecdote might be of the entrepreneurial, quick-thinking Julia, it's likely just another story cooked up by Miami's nimble marketing machine.

Whatever the reason, Flagler did come to the town and quickly realized its potential. He accepted and on that land built the magnificent **Royal Palm Hotel**, a glamorous, early greenhouse for the sprouts of Miami tourism (it stood on the northern banks of the river, just opposite the Miami Circle site today). Flagler didn't just rely on trains to encourage commerce either – he gouged out an easy shipping channel for the Port of Miami, now the waterway between South Beach and Fisher Island known as Government Cut.

Meanwhile, the **railroad** took just over a year to arrive, and in April 1896, the first passenger train entered the city, bringing with it excited refugees from elsewhere in the state. Two months later, on July 28, the city was formally incorporated; voters eventually settled on the name Miami, believing – erroneously – that it was the Tequesta word for "sweet water."

The building boom

The biggest obstacle to widespread settlement in South Florida was its swampy, low-lying land. By 1908, developers began addressing that problem head-on, systematically dredging the water-soaked inland areas in a desperate race to keep up with consumer demand. Many let their staff sell faster than they dredged, leading to reputations of offering "land by the gallon."

Despite some shady sales practices, the **building boom** in Miami was in full swing. In 1912, the department store Burdine's became the city's first "skyscraper," at five stories high, while millionaire James Deering began building the opulent Neo-Renaissance palatial estate of **Villa Vizcaya**. Mary Brickell, assisted by her husband, planned the wide vista of **Brickell Avenue** to connect Miami with Coconut Grove, and it quickly became known as **Millionaires' Row** when wealthy new residents, including presidential candidate William Jennings Bryan, built enormous mansions there. By 1920, the new city had more than 30,000 inhabitants: five years later, Miami tripled its size by annexing Coconut Grove and Lemon City.

The fuel for this expansion was largely hot air: Miami was the first American city built equally on hype and high hopes. Everest G. Sewell was one of the first masters of public relations, responsible for the relentless sloganeering and deafening marketing of the city. On its twentieth anniversary, he cooked up taglines such as "Miami: Where the Summer Spends the Winter," "Miami: the Magic City," and later, simply, "Stay through May." The local chamber of commerce funded the first press trips, bringing journalists on lavish free holidays to sample the good life in Miami – especially favored were those writing for wire services, whose stories syndicated across the country in newspapers from California to Boston. Miami Shores, Miami Springs, North Miami: confusingly named, perhaps, but deliberately so, in hopes of capitalizing on the brilliant marketing of Miami proper.

Meanwhile, in a flight of idealistic megalomania, local boy **George Merrick** began the most ambitious building project of all: **Coral Gables**. Inspired by the City Beautiful Movement (see box, p.263), he envisioned a European-style town with civic amenities and civilized settlers. By 1925, less than four years after its inception, and nourished by the local flair for publicity, Coral Gables was a viable city that had earned its founder almost $150 million.

The love affair with tourism begins

The development of Miami's mainland would soon be superseded by a piece of land that was mere swamp only decades before: **Miami Beach**. It was here that the city's love affair with tourism was ferociously consummated. Charles and Isabella Peacock's namesake inn **was** the first hotel, and Flagler's *Royal Palm* was lavish and celebrity-studded, but as the Art Deco masterpieces mushroomed in Miami Beach, a newly sun-worshipping nation was seduced by South Florida.

Of course, Miami Beach was originally planned as a plantation by the Quaker settler **John Collins**, one of the most misrepresented **men** in Miami history.

The fetid strip soon failed as farmland; so Collins – far from the meek and gentle man that history has portrayed him – turned to Plan B: a seaside resort. Impatient and energetic, he had the vision, if not the money, to transform the island into a playground for the middle classes. The only problem was that the land was in effect an offshore island, three miles east of Miami proper with nothing connecting it to the mainland. Collins set out to construct a rudimentary bridge, but ran out of money halfway through.

The extra cash came from Indianapolis-born **Carl Fisher**: Fisher was rich, middle-aged, and bored, having made millions from car headlights by the time he was 40. He saw a lucrative goldmine in Collins' island and agreed to finance the project in exchange for two hundred acres of oceanfront property. Fisher constructed Miami's first **causeway** in 1913, a more durable structure than Collins', and Miami Beach was born, incorporated into the city of Miami two years later. It wasn't long before trendy **hotels** popped up on the seafront.

A hurricane and the Great Depression

Unfortunately, nature fought back against the aggressive redevelopment: the very warm weather that had brought the railroad in the first place took its revenge. On September 17–18, 1926, a **hurricane** registering winds up to

Hurricanes in South Florida

Hurricanes have shaped South Florida's history, and are such a part of local life that the University of Miami even christened its collegiate sports teams the Hurricanes to honor the players' power. But though many locals may be sanguine about storms, recent meteorological shifts mean that Miami will have to prepare for significantly more frequent warnings and the onslaught of more hurricanes like **Andrew**, which turned the agricultural land around Homestead to coleslaw in 1992 and cost the country $25bn. Meteorologists say that in 2004, the Caribbean and its environs came out of a 25-year calm period; experts predict more frequent and more intense hurricanes in the next decade. Florida's storm season officially spans from June to November, but most storms froth up in August or September, and last around ten days; the modern coding system alternates boys' and girls' names that cycles alphabetically through three languages – French, Spanish, and English.

At the time of writing, Miami and the rest of South Florida has so far been fortunate. It escaped the wrath of the two storms that ripped through the peninsula in 2004: Charley, which made land at Punta Gorda on Florida's southwest coast, killing 27 and causing $6.8bn of damage, and the huge, lumbering Frances, which killed 32 people and landed at Fort Pierce, a few miles north along the Atlantic seaboard. Both these storms were classified as Category 4 on the **Saffir-Sampson Scale**, which is used to grade hurricanes' intensity. Strengths range from Category 1 (sustained winds 74–95mph), which usually causes little permanent damage, to the catastrophic Category 5 (sustained winds of more than 155mph), like Hurricane Camille, which tore into Mississippi's gulf in 1969 and left complete destruction that observers likened to an atomic bomb. When, or if, another storm comparable to Camille might whip up in the Atlantic, no one can know, although computer modeling to predict a storm's path, and so prepare people and property appropriately, is growing ever more sophisticated.

125mph came ashore with its eye passing directly over Miami: more than 100 people died, 5000 homes were destroyed, Downtown was flooded and Miami Beach virtually obliterated. President Machado of Cuba sent gunboats with doctors and medicines, and the city was plunged into an **economic crisis**.

In fact, the land boom was already ebbing before the storm washed it away completely, mostly thanks to the inflation rates that soared in the wake of construction, but the **Great Depression** that arrived so soon afterwards hobbled Miami's progress.

It was only the advent of commercial flying that provided any economic glimmer during those lean years to bolster the limping tourist industry. Pan-American Airlines' move its base from Key West to Coconut Grove's Dinner Key in 1928 and so connected the hub to 32 Central and South American countries.

Art Deco, World War II, and the tourism revival

With Miami in the economic throes of the Depression, Franklin Delano Roosevelt's New Deal and the Florida citrus industry saved Miami from total bankruptcy and induced the city's slow recovery. Miami Beach was actually the main beneficiary, with hundreds of hotels, residences, and other buildings erected in the mid-to-late 1930s, to keep pace with a tourist industry that was again thriving. Many of these structures were designed in the modern **Art Deco** style, led by the designs of architects L. Murray Dixon and Henry Hohauser.

World War II, when it arrived, sped the recovery process along, bringing 70,000 soldiers (including an incognito Clark Gable) to the city for training. Almost 150 hotels were used as barracks, and the *Biltmore* hotel in Coral Gables was converted into a military hospital; there was even a local Submarine Chaser School nicknamed the "Donald Duck Navy." Yet though well-known as a sailors' and soldiers' training camp, Miami's other claim to wartime fame is more chilling: Paul Tibbits, the commander of the *Enola Gay*, which dropped the first **atomic bomb** on Hiroshima, was a local boy.

After the war, these soldiers, who were said to have gotten "sand in their shoes" during training, flocked back as civilians and kickstarted another tourism boom. Capping the decade in 1949, the *Raleigh* hotel made a visionary investment in a central-air-conditioning machine. No longer would the summers be too stifling for visitors – Miami was now a year-round destination. At a national convention in the early 1950s, travel agents figured out that Miami Beach had built more hotels since the war than all other resorts worldwide put together. Soon, though, Miami's airports would be clogged not with pleasure-seekers but with refugees.

The 1950s and 1960s: racial tension and Cuban immigration

Like many other towns in the American South, Miami was a city where race was a tense issue and whose voters supported enforced **segregation.** By the time of Miami's incorporation in 1896, local blacks were sent to live in the creatively named **Coloredtown**, way out around Avenue G (now NW 2nd Avenue). This strip later became a nightlife magnet for white locals who were drawn to its top-notch music halls and movie theaters. Even after the Supreme Court ruled in favor of desegregation in 1954, economic discrimination continued. The situation did not improve in the 1960s, as the Miami local government displaced more than 20,000 residents from Coloredtown (by then, renamed **Overtown**) in order to build a massive freeway through the area. Payback came in **race riots** that ignited in Liberty City in 1968 and again in 1980, when six days of disturbances left eighteen people dead, more than 400 injured, and property damage valued at more than $200m (see box, p.58).

Miami's racial problems were exacerbated by the repercussions of the 1959 Cuban Revolution, which brought **Fidel Castro** (who was, at least at first, feted in the US) to power. Many of the immigrants who came to Miami over the next five years were members of Cuba's elite, tossed out because of the potential threat they posed. They imagined their stay would be temporary until the joint blow of the botched **Bay of Pigs** invasion in 1961 and the **Cuban Missile Crisis** – a tense standoff between the US and the USSR over Soviet nuclear-missile bases on the island – a year later effectively barred their return home. In reaction to anti-Communist outrage from Cuban expats and Americans alike, the US began so-called **Freedom Flights** in 1965. They ran for eight years, bringing more than 300,000 Cubans to Miami, including 14,000 children plucked from their parents to begin a new life in America under the aegis of the Pedro Pan program.

Many of the new Cuban immigrants settled west of Downtown in the Jewish area of Riverside, soon to be known as **Little Havana**. These doctors, lawyers, and entrepreneurs started out working menial jobs, but were soon re-establishing themselves in the professions they'd followed back home.

Still, the impact of this wave of immigration on the city was immediate and abrasive. Under the **Cuban–American Adjustment Act of 1966**, permanent residency was granted to any Cuban who'd lived in the United States for at least one year, a luxury afforded no other immigrant group before or since – and still a source of resentful friction with other ethnic minorities, like the Haitians.

Economic decline and architectural preservation

The 1970s were a quiet, if bleak, period in Miami history: as elsewhere across the nation, **economic decline** continued, and the city struggled to retain tourist dollars. In addition, during this period Dade County declared itself bilingual in 1973, in response to massive Spanish-speaking immigration. The move was highly controversial and was rescinded after the infamous Mariel Boatlift (see below).

The bright spot of the 1970s was the establishment of the **Miami Design Preservation League** by Barbara Baer Capitman, who defended the decaying Art Deco structures in Miami Beach against the wrecking ball, and kickstarted a reassessment of their architectural value (see box, "Decoding Art Deco," on p.64).

The first wave of middle-class Cuban immigrants was joined by a totally different kind of refugee thanks to the **Mariel Boatlift** in May 1980, an event which tore Miami apart. After a spat with the Peruvian government over a group seeking asylum in Havana's Peruvian embassy, Castro opened the port of Mariel and announced that anyone who wished to leave the island was free to do so. And they did: 125,000 Cubans arrived in Miami in less than three days. But Castro's seemingly capricious gesture proved a masterstroke – with a flourish, he flushed 25,000 convicted criminals out of Cuba and into America, alongside hordes of refugees who were mentally ill. The local government in Miami created a tent city under Interstate 95 and struggled to find somewhere to house the new arrivals. Many ended up in then-rundown South Beach.

The 1980s and 1990s: Miami Vices

The 1980s represented the nadir of Miami's reputation, when the city was synonymous with not just Crockett and Tubbs but also **cocaine** and **crime**. At this time it was estimated that one quarter of the cocaine that entered America arrived through Florida; and at one point, the **murder rate** in Miami was so high that the local medical examiner rented a refrigerated truck for corpses, as the 30-body capacity of the cooler in the central morgue was regularly maxing out. In addition, the now-decrepit hotels on South Beach, already filled with the old and infirm, living their last years in the warm weather (earning the area the nickname "God's Waiting Room"), added the *marielitos* to their ranks, transforming the area into a hub for local criminal activity. The bubblegum cop show *Miami Vice*, set on the beach, added an unrealistic, glossy sheen to the grubby district.

Corruption and crime continued into the 1990s, even as **South Beach** was discovered by fashion photographers and enjoying a throbbing renaissance. From 1992 to 1998, forty public officials were indicted on bribery and corruption charges, while anti-tourist violence reached its height in 1994 and 1995, prompting then-governor Lawton Chiles to create a Task Force on Tourist Safety, as well as providing special tourist-oriented police and more easily visible roadside signage for vacation-goers. To a large degree, his measures worked. Petty crime today is down, and anti-tourist violence minimal. It's been replaced with rarer but more headline-grabbing events, like the bizarre and brutal murder of designer Gianni Versace or the extensive indictment of thuggish club king (and friend of Madonna) Chris Paciello.

Miami today

Present-day Miami is still struggling to live up to the glossy reputation that it has created for itself. One major success, though, is its banking industry: after the city was grazed by **Hurricane Andrew** in 1992 (districts further south were not so lucky), the city emerged as an important banking center, with dozens of gleaming Downtown office blocks as testament to its economic vitality.

Politics and race remain contentious issues, especially with regard to Cuba. Even if the federal government's concern for the Communist regime is cooling, the ire of local exiles is boiling hotter than ever. Nowhere was that better illustrated than in the recent case of **Elián González**. After his mother was killed trying to reach America with Elián in tow on a refugee raft, the seven-year-old boy was returned – by the federal government, and by force – to his father in Cuba. Few involved in this sad mess escaped unscathed – not least President Clinton (already reviled by Cuban exiles for not being tough enough on Castro), who supported Elián's repatriation, and Florida attorney general Janet Reno, who had final say in the matter. However, Manny Diaz, the lawyer who defended Elián's right to stay in America, was elected mayor of Miami in the affair's wake.

Of course, South Florida hit the headlines in the **2000 presidential election** debacle, when the right to the White House hung on a few hard-to-read votes in Miami-Dade County. Charges of corruption still rankle: some claim that the ballots were oddly designed and confusing, and the fact that the brother of Republican George W. Bush – who was eventually awarded the presidency by the Supreme Court – was state governor only encouraged conspiracy theorists.

Economically, Miami Beach is enduring a few worries, too; though tourism remains strong, South Beach has lost a bit of luster in fashion circles, as models and photographers are air-kissing the beach goodbye to shoot catalogs in cheaper locations like South Africa and Spain. Fashionistas aside, the other group gravitating away from Miami is its long-standing gay community. The reason's simple: Miami has been a little too effective in attracting straight tourist dollars and the family-friendly vibe in South Beach has alienated many gays and lesbians there (Miami's loss is Fort Lauderdale's gain, as that group is decamping north along the coast).

Another contentious issue is nightlife. The current mayor of Miami Beach, **David Dermer**, was elected on a separatist platform: locals, tired of early-morning excesses, chose him for his promises to curb licensing laws and separate the beach from the city. Thankfully for the local economy, his hard-driving tactics have made him hugely unpopular and forced the mayor to back down on many of his more draconian promises.

In Dermer's wake, the city's scene has shifted back to the mainland. The **Biscayne Corridor**, the land along the waterfront north of the Downtown CBD, is where much of the city's attention and money is focused these days, and high-design, high-rise condos are mushrooming along the water's rim. Art galleries have thronged to old factories in **Wynwood** while the revived **Design District** is the site of showrooms and swanky homestores. The anchor of it all, and Miami's latest attempt to grab headlines, is the Cesar Pelli–designed **Performing Arts Center**, which will unite ballet, theater, and music on one huge site set to open in 2006.

Architecture

Architecture vies with warm weather and wild nightlife as the prime draw for visitors to Miami: the funky (and low-cost) modern style known variously as ZigZag, Jazz Age, Skyscraper, Streamline, or simply, Art Deco. The style grew out of the 1925 *L'Exposition des Arts Décoratifs et Industriels Modernes*, a major exhibition in Paris that showcased designs that, although inspired by the Arts and Crafts Movement of the late nineteenth century, used modern, industrial production methods. (The inspiration's ironic, given the Arts and Crafts aversion to mass marketing.) Originally called Style Moderne, or Modernistic – the term Art Deco wasn't coined until 1968, by British historian Bevis Hiller – the sleek, long-limbed designs became popular for furniture, clothing, fabrics, and, soon after, buildings, being simple to design and cheap to construct.

Art Deco's beginnings in Miami

It took the disastrous **hurricane** that swept through the city in 1926 to bring this style to Miami. As a result of the hurricane's devastation, large amounts of land were suddenly clear – especially in Miami Beach – and on much of it, buildings in the cost-efficient, popular Art Deco style were erected. For the earliest of these, the style was heavily influenced by one fabulous, spooky discovery: archeologist Howard Carter's unearthing of the Egyptian pharaoh Tutankhamen's long-buried tomb and its treasures in 1922. The opulent golden antiques from this royal time capsule were soon sent on headline-grabbing tours around the world, and fashion and design immediately incorporated the geometric, zigzagging Egyptian shapes, as did Art Deco (indeed, Deco's easy absorption of new trends into the core aesthetic of streamlined simplicity was one of its features).

During this time, Art Deco buildings were heavily decorated with ornamental panels that were often filled with symbolic images, much like the reliefs in Egyptian tombs. The difference was in subject matter: reliefs on so-called **Tropical** – or **Miami** – **Deco** buildings often featured palm trees, flamingos, pelicans, sunbursts, and other indigenous symbols. Other features, unique to buildings in the Tropical Deco style, include sun-blocking eyebrows above windows, exterior staircases, and *terrazzo* floors. These floors – essentially colored concrete laid in geometric designs like poor-man's marble – are both durable and cool, as they absorb little heat from the sun.

As the glamour of Ancient Egypt receded and the realities of the Great Depression approached, the movement splintered into factions, as Tropical Deco sloughed off its fancy panels and excessive ornamentation, resulting in two new variations. **Depression Moderne** was less decorative than its parent, in which ornamental elements were relegated to a building's interior, and **Streamline** – or **Nautical** – **Deco**, which featured rounded corners and "speed lines," intended to convey an impression of movement – and occasionally, even porthole windows and ornamental smokestacks. Later Art Deco buildings like this also feature glass blocks and banded stripes, more monolithic and less playful than the devil-may-care decorations of the Roaring Twenties.

An alternative: Mediterranean Revival

Not everything being built at this time was in the Art Deco style, though: in fact, one third of the buildings in the South Beach's Art Deco Historic District are actually **Mediterranean Revival**, a contemporary architectural refuge for those who loathed the simplicity and starkness of Deco's poured concrete. Essentially, this style is Spanish by way of California, based as it is on the Mission architecture of early West Coast settler buildings. It featured terracotta roofs that ape old-world Europe, ornate ironwork, and deliberately ramshackle facades, so that a structure would appear well-aged.

Snobs dismissed such whimsy, saying that only the *nouveau riche*, like gangsters and movie stars, would be gauche enough to prefer it to the cool intellectualism of Art Deco. Yet Miami's Latino heritage, coupled with a compatible climate, helped popularize the style. One of its biggest fans was Carl Fisher, the father of Miami Beach, who commissioned Española Way, the densest concentration of

The City Beautiful Movement

By 1910, almost one in two people in the United States lived in a city with more than 2500 inhabitants – and with this mass urbanization, problems like crime and disease germinated in the New World as they had in Europe. Benign yet patrician reformers, like Chicago's Daniel Burnham, then set about finding a way to **impose the moral order of a village** onto these growing cities and so solve such problems: their theories became known as the **City Beautiful Movement**. Though largely forgotten today, it was a powerful factor in urban planning across America in the early twentieth century and a potent inspiration to George Merrick, founder and father of Coral Gables.

Inspired by the order and harmony of Europe's new **Beaux Arts style**, as well as local successes like Frederick Law Olmstead's Central Park in Manhattan, the reformers pitched utopian cities in vaguely classical style whose beauty would inspire civic loyalty and upstanding morals in even the most impoverished resident. Cynics might argue that food and better sanitation would have been more effective salves, but the evangelical movement pressed ahead in places like St Louis and Kansas City. Burnham even outlined his blueprint for the perfect city at **Chicago's World's Fair** in 1893 – its buildings uniform, its parks enormous, the city would be crimeless, he said, from a combination of civic duty and plenty of police.

Key **features** included: wide, tree-lined avenues, monumental buildings, ample greenspace, and numerous plazas or fountains. Later additions even included proscriptions about lampposts (which should be attractive as well as functional) and straight roads (which should be broken up by winding streets whenever possible).

The City Beautiful Movement was a compelling alternative to the festering, ramshackle development of most American cities at that time, and it so inspired Merrick's utopian megalomania that he set about building **Coral Gables**. His one deviation was in the city's architectural framework: he used the Mediterranean Revival style of the 1920s, rather than insisting on a then-dated Beaux Arts aesthetic.

The controlling impact of the City Beautiful Movement is still keenly felt in Coral Gables: zoning restrictions and local ordinances are draconian and residents are rabid in their civic pride. Unfortunately, the plazas and fountains that Merrick hoped would bring people together are these days almost always empty and civic pride rarely blossoms into plain neighborliness.

the style in the city – although the City Beautiful aesthetic of George Merrick's Coral Gables owes much to Mediterranean Revival, too.

Miami Modern

After World War II, America's exuberance was refreshed in the glow of victory and economic prosperity. The wide-eyed optimism of the 1950s, which cynics today so easily dismiss, was then unstoppable; and the buildings of the time are stamped with the same sense of possibility and fun. Some have said that the **Miami Modern**, or **MiMo**, style has the same mix of **confidence and naïveté** as a 1950s bombshell screen goddess – sinuous and sexy, but utterly innocent.

More than all else, though, designers in the MiMo age were fascinated with speed. Its tail-finned cars, or sleekly patterned polyester dresses were inspired not by ocean liners or trains, but by the futuristic jets of wartime and beyond. Many MiMo buildings also feature boomerang and kidney shapes (like the shady rest areas on Lincoln Road), lending a looping sense of movement, as well as cheeky, unexpected ornamental holes, which play games with the viewer's perspective. There's great use of decorative collage, as well as architectural features like wide eaves, masonry *bris-soleils* (literally, "sunbreakers"), and jalousie windows, with louvered, overlapping glass panels, used expressly to create shade. Architects like the late, dapper **Morris Lapidus** and the still-active **Norman Giller** designed enormous, sweeping buildings, many in central Miami Beach, that dwarfed their Art Deco counterparts further south; Lapidus's philosophy, laid out clearly in the title of his autobiography, was "Too Much is Never Enough."

The preservation movement

By the 1970s, the optimism that had prompted the MiMo boom had been drained, and the city was facing all manner of urban blight, from flaring racial tensions to escalating crime; and had it not been for the efforts of an indefatigable, transplanted New Yorker, the Art Deco legacy that later helped revive the city might have succumbed to this downturn.

Barbara Baer Capitman, then editor of an interiors magazine called *The Designer*, became involved in Miami's efforts to honor America's Bicentennial in 1976. For her contribution, she seized upon the quirky, dilapidated Art Deco buildings of rundown South Beach and, along with five friends, founded the **Miami Design Preservation League**. A powerful, publicity-savvy woman who knew the value of a grand gesture, Capitman protested in person as the wrecking ball bit into the *Senator* hotel, a still-mourned Art Deco gem on Collins Avenue (the site, opposite the *Marlin Hotel*, is now a parking lot). She didn't manage to save the *Senator*, or, indeed, several other hotels nearby, but eventually, through force of persuasion and personality, she helped secure South Beach the honor of being listed on the National Register of Historic Places (though it was still some time before the area cleaned up its crime-ridden image).

Capitman didn't stop at simply conserving Art Deco: working with interior designer **Leonard Horowitz**, she then set about spiffing up the buildings she'd saved. It was Horowitz who came up with the now-familiar sherbet palette of peaches, lemons, and lavenders. Originally, most Deco buildings had been much more muted: either white or cream, with their key features picked out in navy or brown – City Hall in Coconut Grove is a rare, remaining example of this original color scheme. Horowitz's mantra was to leave the warm browns of clay, sand, and soil to the Mediterranean Revival structures and wash Art Deco buildings in the cool tones of the sky, ocean, and flowers. (The designer of the 1980s TV show *Miami Vice* has said that the key to that program's signature look was avoiding any earth tones in much the same way.) For the buildings south of Fifth Street, outside the official preservation district, he varied the palette, amping up the colors to brasher neon shades of turquoise and cerise.

Architectural preservation today

Although Capitman's crusade was at least initially successful, there are still chinks in the preservationist armor. Restorations are tweaked for modern needs: Art Deco chairs, for example, would be uncomfortable to current tastes, thanks to light padding and a seat too narrow for modern buttocks – hence most chairs are an interpretation rather than a replica of the originals. It's also expensive, and often not cost-efficient, to renovate small, dark Art Deco hotels: there are still a few that remain unloved and crumbling, even along Ocean Drive. Hopeful developers still sometimes try to sneak past regulations.

Although much loved by the local community, the late **Gianni Versace** was also responsible for an act of reckless architectural vandalism. He bought two adjoining buildings on Ocean Drive and converted one, the Mediterranean Revival **Casa Casuarina** into his home. The other, the *Revere Hotel*, was a MiMo gem; yet he still demolished it to make room for a swimming pool, just before an ordinance that could have preserved the place. That law shifted historical value from a date-based system – for example, that all conserved buildings must be at least fifty years old, which the *Revere* was not at the time – to a more flexible designation of intrinsic worth.

On a happier note, there have been several recent preservationist victories. The first involved **copyright infringement**, when two hotels on Collins Avenue were sued under the Landham Trademark Act. The *Fairmont*, which far pre-dated the litigating hotel chain, caved to pressure and changed its signage to read *Fairwind*. The *Tiffany* on the other hand, sued by its namesake jewelers, held firm: it had been an intentional pastiche when built in the 1930s since its cheeky slogan was "The Jewel on the Beach." This time, President Clinton intervened and allowed architectural elements like signs to be exempt from trademarking – in the process safeguarding other hotels from future lawsuits. In a gloriously arrogant response, the *Tiffany* retained its sign and is now known simply as *The Hotel*.

Even MiMo is starting to receive architectural TLC: the newly designated **John S. Collins Oceanfront Historic District** protects many buildings on the drag between 22nd and 44th streets, including Lapidus's masterpiece, the *Fontainebleau*. In fact, the new convention hotel on the waterfront, the *Loews*, points the way forward to a happy union between commerce and conservation: the construction project was only greenlit if its owners would renovate and run the tiny, adjoining Art Deco hotel, the *St Moritz*.

Books

Most **books** that deal with Miami revel in the one thing the city most wants to forget: crime. These hardboiled novels with hardbitten heroes – written by the likes of Elmore Leonard and Edna Buchanan, among others – are distinctive enough to form a subspecies in the thriller genre.

Unfortunately, some of the books listed below are out of print (o/p), though even these should be available at many secondhand bookstores, through online searches, or perhaps at the terrific Fifteenth Street Books in Coral Gables (see p.172).

History and society

Edward N. Akin *Flagler: Rockefeller Partner & Florida Baron*. Over-footnoted and rather overwritten, Akin's biography of the Father of Miami is crammed with detail, but readable only in short bursts. Strictly for Flagler fanatics.

T.D. Allman *Miami*. Although his endless references to *Miami Vice* soon grate on the contemporary reader, Allman's insightful observations now serve as a time capsule of late twentieth-century Miami. Worth dipping into for his sensitive analysis of what being from Miami means.

Kathryne Ashley *George E. Merrick & Coral Gables, Florida*. Brief, workmanlike account of the founding of Coral Gables that's notable for its checklist of landmarks and first-person accounts of George Merrick.

Edna Buchanan *The Corpse Had a Familiar Face* (o/p). Buchanan was a reporter covering Miami's crime scene for the *Miami Herald* in the 1970s; here, she fuses her own tough life story with the tough cases she follows. Gripping, readable, and a gory reminder of Miami's recent past.

⭐ **Mark Foster** *Castles in the Sand: Life and Times of Carl Graham Fisher*. Historian Foster tells the story of Fisher's life from its beginnings (making millions from manufacturing car headlights) to its end (in poverty after the stock-market crash of 1929). It's a gripping rags-to-riches-to-rags story, and one of the few books to provide any insight into Fisher's motives for moving to Miami.

Joan Gill Blank *Key Biscayne: A History of Miami's Tropical Island and the Cape Florida Lighthouse*. An exhaustive and readable history of one of the city's least celebrated districts. Gill Blank has a fine eye and a wry tone, managing to highlight Key Biscayne's importance in local history while retaining a critical perspective.

Howard Kleinberg *Miami Beach: A History* (o/p). This book combines text with archival photographs of Miami Beach, and is a great overview of its beginnings, with pithy, insightful commentary from Kleinberg, a former editor-in-chief of *The Miami News*.

Morris Lapidus *Too Much is Never Enough* (o/p). Lapidus's autobiography is charming, vain, and great fun – much like the man himself. The master of MiMo architecture makes his life story into a lively yarn, but it's the juicy, tangential history of mid-century Miami that really grips.

Helen Muir *The Biltmore: Beacon for Miami*. Muir's other major work is a well-rendered history of Miami's most famous hotel, the *Biltmore* in Coral Gables.

Helen Muir *Miami*. Most consider this the definitive history of the city. However, while it's strong in the early chapters, the book becomes more toothless as it approaches the modern era, where the author shies from any event too lively or controversial.

Robert Mykle *Killer 'Cane: Deadly Hurricane of 1928*. The least well known, but most deadly, of the hurricanes to devastate Florida in the early twentieth century was this Category 4 storm which ripped across Lake Okeechobee and into the Everglades, killing at least 2000 people. Mykle tells the story in human terms, via vignettes of families trying to make their lives then in the 'mucklands' who are thrown into danger – it's a sentimental but involving approach.

Maureen Ogle *Key West: History of an Island Dream*. Spicy, gossip-laden account of the island, where the author clearly relishes investigating Key West's raunchier modern times; her curious thesis that Key West is a microcosm of American history

wobbles now and then, but it's a reliable, enjoyable account.

Thelma Peters *Lemon City: Pioneering on Biscayne Bay 1850–1925* (o/p). Thorough, quirky book that focuses on the forgotten settlement of Lemon City (now Little Haiti) to the north of Downtown Miami. Readable, if a little scholarly.

★ **John Rothchild** *Up for Grabs*. Rothchild weaves his own experience of building a hippie-era house into the nasty story of South Florida's shady, postwar land boom. He dissects the pioneer psyche of Florida and its settlers while nailing the hard-sell showmanship that developers used to lure the hopeful to Miami and around.

Les Standiford *Last Train to Paradise*. Brand-new, dazzling account of Henry Flagler's epic plans to construct a railway linking Key West to the mainland, interweaving anecdotes about life in early twentieth-century Florida with stories of the difficulties in achieving Flagler's dream. Local thriller writer Standiford retains his knack for character and plot, making this a gripping historical yarn.

Fiction

Edna Buchanan *Miami, It's Murder*. The first novel by this Pulitzer Prize–winning author stars rebellious, no-nonsense crime reporter (and Cuban-American) Britt Montero. The story's entertaining enough, and zings with local detail, though it's Buchanan's ability to condense all that's good and bad about Miami into casual details that's most impressive.

Edwidge Danticat *Krik? Krak!* Danticat is the young, much-feted Haitian novelist: this set of short stories gives a luminous, brutal sense of Haitian culture. There's unfortunately little yet written by Miami's

expat community, so Danticat's spare stores are an excellent make-do in the meantime.

Stanley Elkin *Mrs Ted Bliss*. An award-winning, amusing oddity set in Miami Beach, wherein 82-year-old widow Dorothy Bliss manages to get mixed up with a drug lord and a Hebrew-speaking Native American, all by selling her late husband's car.

James W. Hall *Bones of Coral*. A standard mystery, bringing a curious big-city paramedic back to his home town of Key West to investigate his father's murder. Worth reading, though, for the cartoonish – but scary – villain Dougie Barnes.

Vicki Hendricks *Iguana Love*. This pulpy, raunchy novel is an explicit tale of a woman who leaves her husband and ends up popping steroids and chasing her younger lover. Its ripe sleepiness is signature South Florida, although Hendricks's prose can get tangled at times.

⭐ **Carl Hiaasen** Various. Local novelist Hiaasen relentlessly skewers South Florida's failings, and no one should visit Miami without having read one of his whipsmart, funny stories – try *Sick Puppy* or *Skin Tight* for starters. All the novels take breakneck tours around the area: the hero of the plastic-surgery-themed *Skin Tight*, for example, lives in a shack in Stiltsville (see p.126, "Key Biscayne and Virginia Key").

Carl Hiaasen, Edna Buchanan, and others *Naked Came the Manatee*. Thirteen of Miami's best-known novelists team up for a caper that centers on the discovery of Fidel Castro's dismembered head. It's a broad, in-jokey satire that's good, if uneven, fun – fans of local crime novels will enjoy a tale that weaves each author's signature hero together into one story.

David Leddick *My Worst Date*. The prolific gay author Leddick offers a nimble coming-of-age tale set in the model-centric world of South Beach, where smart, beautiful teenage Hugo shares a hunky lover with his unwitting mother.

⭐ **Elmore Leonard** *LaBrava* (o/p). Plenty of Leonard's stories are set in South Florida, but *LaBrava* is one of the best. In it, photographer LaBrava meets a fading Hollywood villainess, who was once his childhood idol; from there, he's drawn into a violent, balletic mess that blurs fiction and reality. Leonard's rangy prose and colloquial style clash well with the surreal world of the trance-like hero.

Theodore Pratt *The Barefoot Mailman* (o/p). Novelized account of the Barefoot Mailman service (see box, p.84): unremarkable but entertaining, and far better than the awkward film it inspired.

John Sayles *Los Gusanos*. Doorstopper novel written by the cult film director that's set in 1981, in the shadow of the Mariel Boatlift, and covers six decades of a family's life in Cuba and the United States – an intriguing, if grueling, patchwork of characters and stories.

Photography and architecture

Richard and Valerie Beaubien *Discovering South Beach Deco*. Exhaustive account of virtually every Deco masterpiece in South Beach. The authors' enthusiasm is palpable, but the prose can get bogged down with detail – worth dipping into, rather than trawling through.

Barbara Baer Capitman and Steven Brooke *Deco Delights* (o/p). The standard work on Miami's Art Deco treasures, written by the woman who championed their preservation. Glossy and fun, but insubstantial.

Laura Cerwinske and David Kaminsky *Tropical Deco: Architecture & Design of Old Miami Beach*. A brisk survey of the significant styles and buildings that make up Miami Deco; the photographs are lush, but need updating – the *Delano*, for example, is still shown and discussed in its pre-Schrager state.

Carolyn Klepser and Arva Moore Parks *Miami – Then & Now*. Two titans of local history teamed up for this picture book, which showcases antique photographs of Miami and

Miami Beach's landmarks alongside sparkling color shots from today. Hugely evocative and informative.

Aristides Millas and Ellen Uguccioni *Coral Gables: Miami Riviera.* Architect Millas and historian Uguccioni have written a readable, comprehensive guide to the Gables. It features an overview of the city as well as capsule accounts of every significant building, many with photographs.

★ **Eric Nash and Randall Robinson Jr** *MiMo: Miami Modern Revealed.* The first survey of Miami's second great architectural style is a coffeetable book, crammed with lush photographs and brightened by the sassy, chatty commentary (incorporating as much scandal and gossip as possible) from local preservationist Robinson and *New York Times* architecture critic Nash.

Bill Wisser *South Beach: America's Riviera, Miami Beach, Florida.* Glossy, glitzy pictorial history of South Beach that's strongest on the resort's origins and the building explosion that produced dozens of Art Deco hotels.

Travel and current affairs

Joan Didion *Miami.* Didion's bony prose is hard going but it's worth persevering, at least in the early chapters when her snapshot of Miami is both clear eyed and unsentimental. Unfortunately, the book rapidly loses focus and interest midway through because of her musings on the minutiae of Washington and Cuban politics.

★ **Marjory Stoneman Douglas** *The Everglades: River of Grass.* More than fifty years old, this pioneering environmentalist's book galvanized feelings against over-aggressive development, and arguably saved the Everglades. Douglas is almost too engaged with her subject (skip the more sentimental passages), but by focusing on the human history of the area she pumps life into what can seem like an innately empty place.

Susan Orlean *The Orchid Thief.* Orlean spotlights the obsessive and spat-ridden world of orchid fanciers in South Florida, following one orchid hunter into the Everglades on his illicit gathering trips. Hypnotized by the world she uncovers, Orlean tells a fascinating, if occasionally flabby, story; it was recently turned into the oddball film *Adaptation,* starring Meryl Streep as Orlean.

★ **Maureen Orth** *Vulgar Favors: Andrew Cunanan, Gianni Versace, and the Largest Failed Manhunt in US History.* A gripping account of the life of Andrew Cunanan, the man who murdered Gianni Versace, that bristles with an exhaustive and salacious eye for detail. Orth's initial incisiveness is undermined by her own obvious distaste for South Beach and its hedonistic gay culture.

David Rieff *Going to Miami: Exiles, Tourists, and Refugees in the New America.* Rieff tackles the contentious subject of immigration in Miami with pompous but maddeningly perceptive observations. Though now somewhat dated (it was published in 1988), it's still a good introduction to Cuban–American issues.

CONTEXTS | Books

C

South Florida on film

S outh Florida **on film** is much like South Florida in literature: a region of gritty crime and cynical cops. Its seedy glamour has attracted dozens of would-be noir thrillers to film there, from the classic *Scarface* to the recent *Wild Things*. It's also served as the backdrop for plenty of sunny sex comedies, including *There's Something About Mary*. That sun-soaked sinfulness has come full circle: the show, which first spotlit the city in the 1980s' *Miami Vice*, is set to be made into a movie by original helmer Michael Mann. Colin Farrell will be Crockett while Jamie Foxx steps in as Tubbs to be released some time in 2006.

What follows is a representative, but brief, list of movies set in and around Miami, with director and year given.

2 Fast 2 Furious (John Singleton, 2003). Paul Walker plays a disgraced cop assigned to infiltrate Miami's notorious street-racing subculture in this testosterone-fueled joyride. The car-chase sequences are, inevitably, astonishing, but there's little other reason to check out the movie.

Ace Ventura, Pet Detective (Tom Shadyac, 1994). The film that gave birth to Jim Carrey as a comedy phenomenon: he stars as a detective out to recover the Miami Dolphins' kidnapped mascot Snowflake, on the eve of the Superbowl.

Any Given Sunday (Oliver Stone, 1999). Al Pacino stars in this disappointing professional football movie from conspiracy master Oliver Stone. Notable for giving Cameron Diaz a rare chance to play against type as the team's fierce, determined owner.

Bad Boys II (Michael Bay, 2003). Bracing, mindless comedy-action adventure with cops Will Smith and Martin Lawrence wisecracking and shooting their way through Miami. The incomprehensible plot's apparently about drug smuggling; but the real reason to see this is watching the real multimillion-dollar mansion the producers bought be blown to smithereens onscreen.

The Bellboy (Jerry Lewis, 1960). Shot almost entirely in Miami Beach's *Fontainebleau* hotel, Jerry Lewis stars as the bellhop from Hell in this, his writer-director debut.

Big Trouble (Barry Sonnenfeld, 2002). Madcap caper based on humorist Dave Barry's novel of the same name, and featuring a top-quality comic cast including Stanley Tucci, Janeane Garofalo, and Rene Russo.

The Birdcage (Mike Nichols, 1996). Remake of the French farce *La Cage aux Folles*, this riotous, campy movie stars Robin Williams as Armand, the man behind South Beach's most successful drag club, and Nathan Lane as Albert, his lover and star. The story corkscrews when Armand's son announces his marriage to the daughter (Calista Flockhart) of ultra-conservative parents. The opening scene is a love letter to Ocean Drive, a single shot that pans in from the sea onto the riot of neon and nightlife.

Black Sunday (John Frankenheimer, 1976). A terrorist thriller, where Palestinian extremists plan to blow up Miami's Orange Bowl on Super Bowl Sunday – wiping out 80,000 football fans as well as the President. The climax of the movie offers some amazing aerial views of 1970s Miami.

Blood and Wine (Bob Rafelson, 1997). Jack Nicholson plays a wine dealer who teams up with a savvy

Cuban nanny (Jennifer Lopez) and a Brit safe-cracker (Michael Caine) in this dark, underrated thriller. The crooks plan to steal a million-dollar necklace and, when it all goes wrong, they head off in pursuit of their payoff to the Florida Keys.

The Cocoanuts (Joseph Santley & Robert Florey, 1929). Set during Florida's real-estate boom, the Marx Brothers' first film stars Groucho as an impecunious hotel proprietor attempting to keep his business afloat by auctioning off land (with the usual interference from Chico and Harpo) in Coconut Grove, "the Palm Beach of tomorrow." Groucho expounds on Florida's climate while standing in what is really a sand-filled studio lot.

Donnie Brasco (Mike Newell, 1997). Al Pacino and Johnny Depp team up for this crime movie, based on the true story of FBI Special Agent Joseph Pistone, who infiltrates the Mob. The action heads to Miami from New York as Brasco helps the Mafia expand a new nightclub operation there.

From Justin to Kelly (Robert Iscove, 2003). Quickie *American Idol*–themed movie, rushed out in the wake of the show's success, is intended as a fluffy romp in the vein of 1960s beach movies. Sadly, it's rather leaden, but location shots – taking in everywhere from the Venetian Pool in Coral Gables to the sands on South Beach – are some of the best in any recent movie.

Get Shorty (Barry Sonnenfeld, 1995). Miami makes only a cameo at the beginning of this funny, bitter movie from the novel of the same name by Elmore Leonard. John Travolta stars as Chili Palmer, a local loan shark who heads out to Los Angeles on a debt-collecting mission, but ends up making movies.

Goldfinger (Guy Hamilton, 1964). The first Bond movie to make it to Miami – the opulent *Fontainebleau* is the backdrop for the scene at the beginning where we spot Bond sunbathing. However, these scenes were shot on a set in England, and were later edited into the Miami footage.

The Heartbreak Kid (Elaine May, 1972). A neurotic Neil Simon–Elaine May gem, where Jewish New Yorker (and new husband) Charles Grodin starts regretting his marriage as soon as the honeymoon drive to Miami begins. A flirty, sexy Cybill Shepherd hitting on him on the beach while his sunburnt wife lies inside doesn't help.

Illtown (Nick Gomez, 1995). Tony Danza's a gay mob boss, joined by indie royalty like Michael Rapaport, Lili Taylor, and Kevin Corrigan, who play a supporting cast of Miami drug dealers.

Miami Blues (George Armitage, 1990). Adapted from the Charles Willeford novel, this hit-and-miss movie stars Alec Baldwin as a just-released sociopath looking to start over – crime-wise, at least – in Miami. He teams up with a college student and prostitute (Jennifer Jason Leigh), and is pursued by a burnt-out homicide detective played by Fred Ward.

Miami Rhapsody (David Frankel, 1995). Disappointing comedy of infidelity, starring Sarah Jessica Parker as Gwyn, who has to examine her commitment to a long-term boyfriend while finding out that everyone else in her family – parents included – is unable to stay faithful.

Moon Over Miami (Walter Lang, 1941). Bombshell Betty Grable comes gold-digging in Miami in this colorful, old-fashioned musical comedy. She and her on-screen sisters pose as a wealthy young woman and her two maids – a little too successfully, though, as she's soon pursued by two handsome bachelors at the same time.

Out of Time (Carl Franklin, 2003). Denzel Washington's the hunted, confused, and possibly corrupt cop in this Keys-set thriller co-starring Eva Mendes. Washington's a little too noble for his seedy role, but the bamboozling twists are great fun – a pity the pay-off's so weak.

Pledge This! (William Heins, 2005). The latest *National Lampoon* installment centers on a sorority at fictional South Beach University, and the attempts by a raft of freshmen to rush it. Notable mostly for providing celebutante Paris Hilton with her first starring film role.

Porky's (Bob Clark, 1981). The classic, revolting teenage-boy romp is set in Fort Lauderdale, and is based on a real-life strip bar there.

Scarface (Brian De Palma, 1983). A modern masterpiece set in and around Miami during the 1980 Mariel Boatlift, *Scarface* stars a young Al Pacino as a small-time Cuban thug who maneuvers his way up to control Miami's drug cartels. It was filmed all across the city, and is a brutal time capsule of Miami's darker days.

Some Like It Hot (Billy Wilder, 1959). Wilder's classic farce begins in 1920s Chicago where Tony Curtis and Jack Lemmon, witnesses to the St Valentine's Day massacre, disguise themselves in drag, and hide out in an all-girl jazz band (featuring Marilyn Monroe) headed for Miami.

The Specialist (Luis Llosa, 1994). A priapic, glossy portrait of the city (if a poor film), this stars one of Miami's former high-profile residents, Sylvester Stallone, as an ex-CIA agent hired by Sharon Stone to take revenge on the Miami mobsters who wiped out her family.

Striptease (Andrew Bergman, 1996). Wretched movie version of Carl Hiaasen's riotous novel about a single mom – played by Demi Moore – who turns to stripping to make ends meet before eventually becoming embroiled in a political scandal.

There's Something About Mary (Farrelly Brothers, 1998). This modern gross-out classic climaxes in Miami Beach, where geeky Ben Stiller – still smarting from a prom-night disaster years before – tracks down the goofy, beautiful love of his life, Mary (Cameron Diaz), and tries to win her again.

Tony Rome (Gordon Douglas, 1967). Frank Sinatra and Jill St John star in this gritty tale of pushers, strippers, and gold-diggers in 1960s Miami: worth watching as a period piece, not for the plot – there are some witty one-liners, though.

True Lies (James Cameron, 1994). Arnold Schwarzenegger plays a CIA agent with a double life, Jamie Lee Curtis co-stars as his trusting wife, and Tom Arnold wisecracks in between the explosions. Look for the scene where a portion of Henry Flagler's old railway bridge to Key West is apparently blown up; in fact, the government had already detonated that portion and producers had to repair it simply so that they could destroy it all over again.

Where the Boys Are (Henry Levin, 1960). This original spring-break movie stars a young George Hamilton and Paula Prentiss as fun-seeking, sun-worshipping teens: it's the movie that put Fort Lauderdale on the map.

Wild Things (John McNaughton, 1998). Steamy, noirish thriller with a serpentine plot that entangles sultry schoolgirls Neve Campbell and Denise Richards with their teacher Matt Dillon, as well as an upstanding local cop (Kevin Bacon).

Rough
Guides
advertiser

Rough Guides travel...

...music & reference

Africa & Middle East
Cape Town
Egypt
The Gambia
Jordan
Kenya
Marrakesh DIRECTIONS
Morocco
South Africa, Lesotho & Swaziland
Syria
Tanzania
Tunisia
West Africa
Zanzibar
Zimbabwe

Travel Theme guides
First-Time Around the World
First-Time Asia
First-Time Europe
First-Time Latin America
Skiing & Snowboarding in North America
Travel Online
Travel Health
Walks in London & SE England
Women Travel

Restaurant guides
French Hotels & Restaurants
London
New York
San Francisco

Maps
Algarve
Amsterdam
Andalucia & Costa del Sol
Argentina
Athens
Australia

Baja California
Barcelona
Berlin
Boston
Brittany
Brussels
Chicago
Crete
Croatia
Cuba
Cyprus
Czech Republic
Dominican Republic
Dubai & UAE
Dublin
Egypt
Florence & Siena
Frankfurt
Greece
Guatemala & Belize
Iceland
Ireland
Kenya
Lisbon
London
Los Angeles
Madrid
Mexico
Miami & Key West
Morocco
New York City
New Zealand
Northern Spain
Paris
Peru
Portugal
Prague
Rome
San Francisco
Sicily
South Africa
South India
Sri Lanka
Tenerife
Thailand
Toronto
Trinidad & Tobago

Tuscany
Venice
Washington DC
Yucatán Peninsula

Dictionary Phrasebooks
Czech
Dutch
Egyptian Arabic
EuropeanLanguages
(Czech, French, German, Greek, Italian, Portuguese, Spanish)
French
German
Greek
Hindi & Urdu
Hungarian
Indonesian
Italian
Japanese
Mandarin Chinese
Mexican Spanish
Polish
Portuguese
Russian
Spanish
Swahili
Thai
Turkish
Vietnamese

Music Guides
The Beatles
Bob Dylan
Cult Pop
Classical Music
Country Music
Elvis
Hip Hop
House
Irish Music
Jazz
Music USA
Opera
Reggae

Rock
Techno
World Music (2 vols)

History Guides
China
Egypt
England
France
India
Islam
Italy
Spain
USA

Reference Guides
Books for Teenagers
Children's Books, 0–5
Children's Books, 5–11
Cult Fiction
Cult Football
Cult Movies
Cult TV
Ethical Shopping
Formula 1
The iPod, iTunes & Music Online
The Internet
Internet Radio
James Bond
Kids' Movies
Lord of the Rings
Muhammed Ali
Man Utd
Personal Computers
Pregnancy & Birth
Shakespeare
Superheroes
Unexplained Phenomena
The Universe
Videogaming
Weather
Website Directory

Also! More than 120 Rough Guide music CDs are available from all good book and record stores. Listen in at www.worldmusic.net

small print and
Index

A Rough Guide to Rough Guides

In the summer of 1981, Mark Ellingham, a recent graduate from Bristol University, was traveling round Greece and couldn't find a guidebook that really met his needs. On the one hand there were the student guides, insistent on saving every last cent, and on the other the heavyweight cultural tomes whose authors seemed to have spent more time in a research library than lounging away the afternoon at a taverna or on the beach.

In a bid to avoid getting a job, Mark and a small group of writers set about creating their own guidebook. It was a guide to Greece that aimed to combine a journalistic approach to description with a thoroughly practical approach to travelers' needs – a guide that would incorporate culture, history, and contemporary insights with a critical edge, together with up-to-date, value-for-money listings. Back in London, Mark and the team finished their Rough Guide, as they called it, and talked Routledge into publishing the book.

That first *Rough Guide to Greece*, published in 1982, was a student scheme that became a publishing phenomenon. The immediate success of the book – with numerous reprints and a Thomas Cook Prize shortlisting – spawned a series that rapidly covered dozens of destinations. Rough Guides had a ready market among low-budget backpackers, but soon also acquired a much broader and older readership that relished Rough Guides' wit and inquisitiveness as much as their enthusiastic, critical approach. Everyone wants value for money, but not at any price.

Rough Guides soon began supplementing the "rougher" information about hostels and low-budget listings with the kind of detail on restaurants and quality hotels that independent-minded visitors on any budget might expect, whether on business in New York or trekking in Thailand.

These days the guides – distributed worldwide by the Penguin Group – offer recommendations from shoestring to luxury and cover more than 200 destinations around the globe, including almost every country in the Americas and Europe, more than half of Africa, and most of Asia and Australasia. Our ever-growing team of authors and photographers is spread all over the world, particularly in Europe, the USA, and Australia.

In 1994, we published the *Rough Guide to World Music* and *Rough Guide to Classical Music*, and a year later the *Rough Guide to the Internet*. All three books have become benchmark titles in their fields – which encouraged us to expand into other areas of publishing, mainly around popular culture. Rough Guides now publish:

- Travel guides to more than 200 worldwide destinations
- Dictionary phrasebooks to 22 major languages
- History guides ranging from Ireland to Islam
- Maps printed on rip-proof and waterproof Polyart™ paper
- Music guides running the gamut from Opera to Elvis
- Restaurant guides to London, New York and San Francisco
- Reference books on topics as diverse as the Weather and Shakespeare
- Sports guides from Formula 1 to Man Utd
- Pop culture books from *Lord of the Rings* to Cult TV
- World Music CDs in association with World Music Network

Visit **www.roughguides.com** to see our latest publications.

SMALL PRINT

Rough Guide credits

Text editor: Richard Koss
Layout: Amit Verma
Cartography: Ed Wright
Picture editor: Jj Luck
Proofreader: Diane Margolis
Editorial: **London** Martin Dunford, Kate Berens, Claire Saunders, Geoff Howard, Ruth Blackmore, Richard Lim, Gavin Thomas, Polly Thomas, Clifton Wilkinson, Alison Murchie, Sally Schafer, Karoline Densley, Andy Turner, Ella O'Donnell, Keith Drew, Edward Aves, Andrew Lockett, Joe Staines, Duncan Clark, Nikki Birrell, Chloë Thomson, Helen Marsden, Peter Buckley, Matthew Milton, Daniel Crewe; **New York** Andrew Rosenberg, Chris Barsanti, Steven Horak, AnneLise Sorensen, Amy Hegarty
Design & Pictures: **London** Simon Bracken, Dan May, Diana Jarvis, Mark Thomas, Harriet Mills, Chloë Roberts; **Delhi** Madhulita Mohapatra, Umesh Aggarwal, Ajay Verma, Jessica Subramanian

Production: Julia Bovis, Sophie Hewat, Katherine Owers
Cartography: **London** Maxine Repath, Katie Lloyd-Jones; **Delhi** Manish Chandra, Rajesh Chhibber, Jai Prakash Mishra, Ashutosh Bharti, Rajesh Mishra, Animesh Pathak, Jasbir Sandhu, Karobi Gogoi
Online: **New York** Jennifer Gold, Suzanne Welles; **Delhi** Manik Chauhan, Narender Kumar, Shekhar Jha, Rakesh Kumar, Lalit Sharma
Marketing & Publicity: **London** Richard Trillo, Niki Hanmer, David Wearn, Demelza Dallow; **New York** Geoff Colquitt, Megan Kennedy, Milena Perez; **Delhi** Reem Khokhar
Custom publishing and foreign rights: Philippa Hopkins
Finance: Gary Singh
Manager India: Punita Singh
Series editor: Mark Ellingham
PA to Managing Director: Megan McIntyre
Managing Director: Kevin Fitzgerald

Publishing information

This first edition published August 2005 by
Rough Guides Ltd,
80 Strand, London WC2R 0RL
345 Hudson St, 4th Floor,
New York, NY 10014, USA
14 Local Shopping Centre, Panchsheel Park,
New Delhi 110017, India.
Distributed by the Penguin Group
Penguin Books Ltd,
80 Strand, London WC2R 0RL
Penguin Putnam, Inc.,
375 Hudson St, NY 10014, USA
Penguin Group (Australia)
250 Camberwell Road, Camberwell,
Victoria 3124, Australia
Penguin Books Canada Ltd,
10 Alcorn Avenue, Toronto, ON,
M4V 1E4 Canada
Penguin Group (New Zealand),
Cnr Rosedale and Airborne Roads,
Albany, Auckland, New Zealand

Typeset in Bembo and Helvetica to an original design by Henry Iles.

Printed and bound in China

© Rough Guides Ltd, 2005

No part of this book may be reproduced in any form without permission from the publisher except for the quotation of brief passages in reviews.

288pp includes index
A catalogue record for this book is available from the British Library

ISBN 1-84353-513-0

The publishers and authors have done their best to ensure the accuracy and currency of all the information in **The Rough Guide to Miami and South Florida**, however, they can accept no responsibility for any loss, injury, or inconvenience sustained by any traveler as a result of information or advice contained in the guide.

1   3   5   7   9   8   6   4   2

SMALL PRINT

Help us update

We've gone to a lot of effort to ensure that the first edition of **The Rough Guide to Miami and South Florida** is accurate and up to date. However, things change – places get "discovered," opening hours are notoriously fickle, restaurants and rooms raise prices or lower standards. If you feel we've got it wrong or left something out, we'd like to know, and if you can remember the address, the price, the time, the phone number, so much the better.

We'll credit all contributions, and send a copy of the next edition (or any other Rough Guide if you prefer) for the best letters. Everyone who writes to us and isn't already a subscriber will receive a copy of our full-color thrice-yearly newsletter. Please mark letters: **"Rough Guide Miami and South Florida Update"** and send to: Rough Guides, 80 Strand, London WC2R 0RL, or Rough Guides, 4th Floor, 345 Hudson St, New York, NY 10014. Or send an email to **mail@roughguides.com**.

Have your questions answered and tell others about your trip at **www.roughguides.atinfopop.com**.

Acknowledgments

In Miami, thanks to Erica Freshman and Jacquelynn D. Powers, who not only always welcome me with open arms, but also cheerfully keep me posted on the Next Big Thing. For smart insights and a friendly welcome, thanks as ever to Lisa Treister, Lisa Cole, Katie Rhodes, Michelle Payer, Dindy Yokel, Linsey Harris, David Brown, as well as Tara Solomon, Nick d'Annunzio, and team. Thanks also to Michelle Revuelta at the Miami CVB for tirelessly answering my endless and relentless questions.

In Fort Lauderdale, thanks to Tracy O'Neal for her local know-how, and to Jessica Taylor at the CVB for making my visit as hassle-free as possible. In the Keys, thanks again to Josie Gullicksen and Carol Shaughnessy at Stuart Newman and Assocs for masterminding my visit and connecting me with crucial local sources; most of all, thanks to Jason for sharing his love of Key West and keeping me company there (not to mention tipping me off to a killer Key Lime Pie).

In New York and London, thanks to Richard Koss for his savvy and nuanced editing and Ed Wright for his cartographical prowess. Thanks, too, to Maureen and Ben for keeping the home fires burning.

SMALL PRINT

Photo credits

All images © Rough Guides except the
following:

Cover credits

Main front Art Deco building, South Beach
   © Getty
Small front top picture Surfing © Alamy
Small front lower picture Hibiscus © Alamy
Back top picture Lifeguard station
   © Getty
Back lower picture Raleigh Hotel pool
   © Alamy

Introduction

Looking over Biscayne Bay, the Venetian
   Causeway and towards South Beach
   © Mary Steinbacher/Alamy
Miami beach-scene © Ian Cumming/Axiom
Sunbathers at Miami Beach © James L.
   Amos/Corbis
Townhouse © Todd McPhail
Calle Ocho mural, Little Havana © Jeff
   Greenberg/Alamy
Miami hotels © Alan Schein Photography/
   Corbis

Things not to miss

02 Sky Bar at the Shore Club
   © courtesy of Morgans Hotel Group/
   www.morganshotelgroup.com
16 Beaches of Fort Lauderdale
   © Medioimages/Alamy

Black and white photos

The Atlantis Building © Patrick Ward/
   Corbis p.55
Hotels on Miami Beach © Alan Schein
   Photography/Corbis p.61
Little Havana © Jeff Greenberg/
   Alamy p.102
Park West clubbing district by night
   © DK Images p.158
Fantasy Fest © Fantasy Fest Media p.190
Trucks with oranges © Bill Bachmann/
   Alamy p.203
Anhinga Trail, Everglades National Park
   © Dave G. Houser/Corbis p.222

Photography: Angus Oborn

Index

Map entries are in color

Map symbols

Maps are listed in the full index using colored text

Interstate highway		@	Internet access
US highway			Post office
State highway		✈	International airport
Other road			Hospital
Pedestrianized street		★	Bus stop/station
Path			Golf course
River			Lighthouse
Railway			Public gardens
Metromover route & stop		♯	Castle
Metrorail route & stop		◉	Accommodation
Chapter boundary			Park/national park
Point of interest			Beach
Building			Marsh/swamp
Church			Cemetery
Information office			

GREATER MIMI

GREATER MIAMI

Fort Lauderdale

HOLLYWOOD

(822)
(820)
(820)
(858)

MIRAMAR

HALLANDALE

(95)

(823)
(820)

NORTH MIAMI BEACH

(1)

(852)

(817)

MIAMI GARDENS DRIVE

SUNNY ISLES

(A1A)

N.W. 62ND AVENUE
N.W. 57TH AVENUE
N.W. 47TH AVENUE
N.W. 37TH AVENUE

PALMETTO EXPRESSWAY
(826)

Ancient Spanish Monastery
N.E. 163RD ST.
(826)

(75)

NORTH MIAMI

(924)
(27)
(826)

N.W. 135TH ST
N.W. 27TH AVE
NORTH-SOUTH EXPWY
N.E. 6TH AVE

N.E. 135TH ST.

BAL HARBOUR

COLLINS AVENUE
BISCAYNE BOULEVARD

HIALEAH
W. 49TH STREET

(9)

(915)

SURFSIDE

FLORIDA'S TURNPIKE
OKEECHOBEE ROAD
PALMETTO EXPRESSWAY
FLAMINGO WAY
LE JEUNE ROAD
N.W. 17TH AVENUE
N.W. 7TH AVE

(955)

Amtrak Station

(441)

NORTH BEACH

(934)

E. 25TH ST

LIBERTY CITY

LITTLE HAITI
N.W. 79TH ST

A1A

Black Archives History and Research Foundation

DESIGN DISTRICT

CENTRAL MIAMI BEACH

AIRPORT EXPRESSWAY
(195)

JULIA TUTTLE CAUSEWAY

Miami International Airport

OVERTOWN

DOWNTOWN MIAMI

Parrot Jungle
VENETIAN CAUSEWAY

SOUTH BEACH

(836)
DOLPHIN EXPRESSWAY
(953)
(836)
MACARTHUR CAUSEWAY
(395)

W. FLAGLER ST
TAMIAMI TRAIL
S.W. 8TH ST

(41)
(9)

CALLE OCHO
LITTLE HAVANA

Port of Miami

Fisher Island

Virginia Key

(972)

S.W. 107TH ST
S.W. 87TH ST

CORAL GABLES
BIRD ROAD

LE JEUNE ROAD

(1)

RICKENBACKER CAUSEWAY

Virginia Beach

(826)
(976)
(973)

Miami Seaquarium

S.W. 56TH ST

COCONUT GROVE

Crandon Park

SUNSET DRIVE

S.W. 77TH ST

Biscayne Bay

Key Biscayne

(986)
(874)

SOUTH MIAMI
S.W. 88TH ST

Fairchild Tropical Gardens

DON SHULA EXPRESSWAY
KILLIAN DRIVE

Matheson Hammock Park

BILL BAGGS CAPE FLORIDA STATE PARK

OLD CUTLER ROAD
SW 57TH AVE

SW 97TH ST
SW 152ND ST
DIXIE HIGHWAY
PALMETTO ROAD
LUDLAM ROAD

Charles Deering Estate

ATLANTIC OCEAN

N

(992)

EUREKA DRIVE

OLD CUTLER ROAD

(1)

The Everglades

Metrozoo

0   5 miles

Florida City, Homestead, the Everglades, & the Florida Keys

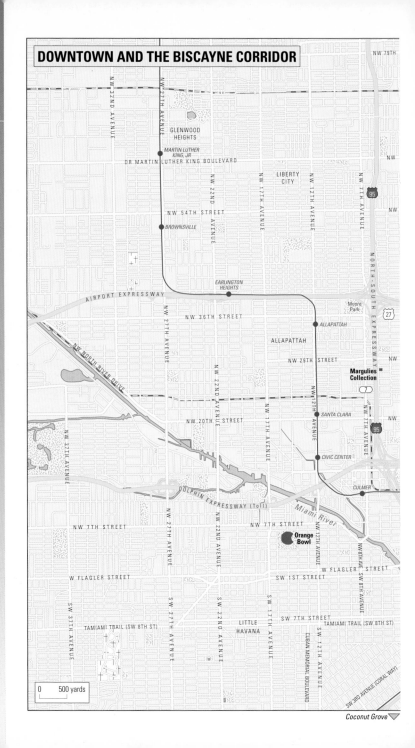

DOWNTOWN AND THE BISCAYNE CORRIDOR

NW 79TH

NW 32ND AVENUE

NW 27TH AVENUE

GLENWOOD
HEIGHTS

MARTIN LUTHER
KING, JR

DR MARTIN LUTHER KING BOULEVARD

LIBERTY
CITY

NW 22ND AVENUE

NW 17TH AVENUE

NW 12TH AVENUE

NW 7TH AVENUE

95

NW

NW

NW 54TH STREET

NW 24TH AVENUE

BROWNSVILLE

NORTH-SOUTH EXPRESSWAY

EARLINGTON
HEIGHTS

AIRPORT EXPRESSWAY

Monroe
Park

27

NW 27TH AVENUE

NW 36TH STREET

ALLAPATTAH

NW

NW NORTH RIVER DRIVE

ALLAPATTAH

NW 29TH STREET

Margulies
Collection

NW 22ND AVENUE

NW 17TH AVENUE

NW 12TH AVENUE

NW 7TH AVENUE

95

NW

NW 37TH AVENUE

NW 20TH STREET

SANTA CLARA

CIVIC CENTER

CULMER

DOLPHIN EXPRESSWAY (To I1)

Miami River

NW 7TH STREET

NW 27TH AVENUE

NW 22ND AVENUE

NW 7TH STREET

Orange
Bowl

NW 12TH AVENUE

NW 8TH AVE. SW 8TH AVENUE

W FLAGLER STREET

W FLAGLER STREET

SW 1ST STREET

SW 7TH STREET

TAMIAMI TRAIL (SW 8TH ST)

SW 37TH AVENUE

TAMIAMI TRAIL (SW 8TH ST)

SW 27TH AVENUE

SW 22ND AVENUE

LITTLE
HAVANA

SW 17TH AVENUE

SW 7TH STREET

SW 12TH AVENUE

CUBAN MEMORIAL BOULEVARD

SW 3RD AVENUE (CORAL WAY)

0   500 yards

Coconut Grove

△ Museum of Contemporary Art

NE 79TH STREET
JFK CAUSEWAY
STREET
Treasure
Island
North Bay
Island
NORTH MIAMI AVENUE
NE 2ND AVENUE
BISCAYNE BOULEVARD
BELLE
MEADE
Belle
Meade
Island
US 1
Legion
Park
Legion Park
Picnic Islands
NE 6TH AVE.
DuPuis
Building
NE 62ND ST
62ND ST
LITTLE HAITI
Caribbean
Marketplace
MORNINGSIDE
54TH ST
NE 54TH ST
Morningside
Park
Morningside
Park
Picnic
Islands
Biscayne Bay
BUENA
VISTA
DESIGN
DISTRICT
Living Room
Building
Melin
Building
Design & Architecture
Senior High School
NW 36TH ST
NE 36TH STREET
US 195
JULIA TUTTLE CAUSEWAY
BUENA
VISTA
YARD
US 1
Rubell
Collection
29TH STREET
No.1
FASHION
DISTRICT
No.2
Sunset
Islands
Pace Park
Picnic Islands
No.3
NORTH MIAMI AVENUE
NE 2ND AVENUE
BISCAYNE BOULEVARD
No.4
Bacardi Building
Di Lido
Island
20TH STREET
Margaret
Pace Park
San Marino
Island
Rivo Alto
Island
OVERTOWN
Biscayne
Island
ARTS &
ENTERTAINMENT
DISTRICT
VENETIAN CAUSEWAY
SCHOOL BOARD
M
M
OMNI
San Marco
Island
Belle Isle
US 395
NW 14TH ST
M
M
Performing Arts Center
DOLPHIN EXPRESSWAY
M
US 41
Watson
Island Park
Watson
Island
Flagler
Island
BICENTENNIAL
PARK
ELEVENTH ST
M
PARK WEST
Hibiscus
Island
OVERTOWN
ARENA
Miami
Arena
FREEDOM TOWER
ARENA-
STATE
PLAZA
M M
COLLEGE
NORTH
Palm
Island
M
M
COLLEGE
BAYSIDE
GOV'T
CENTER
M
FIRST ST
M
Star
Island
Metro-
Dade
Cultural
Center
M
MIAMI AVE.
MACARTHUR CAUSEWAY
M
BAYFRONT PARK
Dodge
Island
KNIGHT CENTER
RIVERWALK
M
FIFTH ST
Terminal
Island
M
EIGHTH ST
Claughton
Island
Lummus
Island
Causeway
Island
M
TENTH ST
Biscayne Bay
BRICKELL
M
SW 13TH ST (CORAL WAY)
SOUTH MIAMI AVENUE
BRICKELL AVENUE
US 95
M
FINANCIAL
DISTRICT
Fisher
Island
Virginia
Key

N

Central Miami Beach ▷
South Beach ▷

THE BEACHES

Sunny Isles

Atlantic Ocean

NE 131ST ST
NE 132ND ST
NE 129TH ST
WEST DIXIE HIGHWAY
NE 125TH STREET
NE 123RD ST
CYCLONE BLVD
NE 121ST ST
BISCAYNE PARK
NE 117TH ST
NE 115TH ST
NE 111TH ST
NE 110TH ST
NE 108TH ST
NE 105TH ST
NE 101ST ST
NE 96TH ST
NE 91ST TER.
NE 89TH ST
NE 83RD ST
NE 79TH ST

ARCH CREEK RD
NE 16TH AVENUE
NE 13TH AVENUE
PEACHTREE DR 10TH PLACE
SAN SOUCI BLVD
ARCH CREEK CANAL
GREENE BOULEVARD
BISCAYNE BOULEVARD
NE 6TH AVENUE
NE 4TH AVENUE
NE DIXIE DRIVE
NE 12TH AVE
NE DIXIE HIGHWAY

BROAD CAUSEWAY
KANE CONCOURSE
96TH ST
BYRON AVE
91ST ST
88TH ST

COLLINS AVENUE
BAL HARBOUR
SURFSIDE

Biscayne Island
Biscayne Bay

HARDING AVENUE
COLLINS AVENUE

NORTH BEACH

Normandy Isle
NORMANDY DRIVE
71ST STREET
JFK CAUSEWAY
Harbor Island
Treasure Island
Allison Island
La Gorce Island

North Bay Island
BELLE MEADE
Belle Meade Island

LA GORCE DRIVE
PINE TREE DRIVE
COLLINS AVENUE
ALTON ROAD

Legion Park
Legion Park Picnic Islands

Morningside Park
MORNINGSIDE
Morningside Park Picnic Islands

W 47TH ST
A. GODFREY ROAD
CHASE AVENUE
PINE TREE DRIVE
INDIAN CREEK DRIVE

Biscayne Bay

JULIA TUTTLE CAUSEWAY

Pace Park Picnic Islands

Sunset Islands No.1
No.2
No.3
No.4

Di Lido Island
San Marino Island
Rivo Alto Island

Margaret Pace Park
Biscayne Island

VENETIAN CAUSEWAY
Belle Isle

San Marco Island
OMNI
Watson Island
Watson Island Park
Hibiscus Island
Flagler Island
Palm Island
Star Island
MACARTHUR CAUSEWAY
BICENTENNIAL PARK
Dodge Island
BAYFRONT PARK
Claughton Island
Lummus Island
Terminal Island
Causeway Island

Fisher Island

17TH ST
LINCOLN RD
11TH ST
8TH ST
2ND ST
MICHIGAN AVE
PENNSYLVANIA AVE
MERIDIAN AVE
WASHINGTON AVENUE
COLLINS AVENUE
OCEAN DRIVE
MIAMI BEACH DR (5TH ST)
ALTON ROAD
DADE BOULEVARD

SOUTH BEACH
ATLANTIC OCEAN

N

0   800 yards

Art Deco Historic District

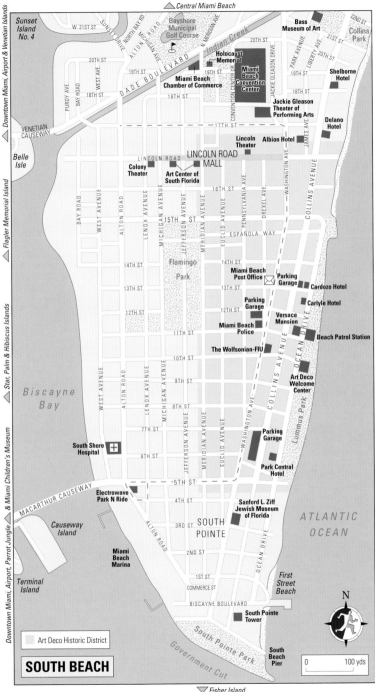

SOUTH BEACH

Art Deco Historic District

0   100 yds

N

Central Miami Beach

Sunset Island No. 4

W. 21ST ST

Bayshore Municipal Golf Course

Bass Museum of Art

22ND ST

Collins Park

21ST ST

20TH ST

Holocaust Memorial

20TH ST

LIBERTY AVE

PARK AVENUE

20TH ST

Downtown Miami, Airport & Venetian Islands

19TH ST

Miami Beach Chamber of Commerce

19TH ST

Miami Beach Convention Center

19TH ST

Shelborne Hotel

18TH ST

JACKIE GLEASON DRIVE

18TH ST

Jackie Gleason Theater of Performing Arts

Delano Hotel

VENETIAN CAUSEWAY

17TH ST

JAMES AVE

Belle Isle

Lincoln Theater

Albion Hotel

LINCOLN ROAD

LINCOLN ROAD MALL

Colony Theater

Art Center of South Florida

COLLINS AVENUE

Flagler Memorial Island

16TH ST

ESPAÑOLA WAY

BAY ROAD

WEST AVENUE

ALTON ROAD

LENOX AVENUE

MICHIGAN AVENUE

JEFFERSON AVENUE

MERIDAN AVENUE

EUCLID AVENUE

PENNSYLVANIA AVE

DREXEL AVE

WASHINGTON AVE

15TH ST

14TH ST

Flamingo Park

14TH ST

Miami Beach Post Office

Parking Garage

Cardozo Hotel

Star, Palm & Hibiscus Islands

13TH ST

13TH ST

Carlyle Hotel

12TH ST

Parking Garage

12TH ST

Versace Mansion

Miami Beach Police

Beach Patrol Station

11TH ST

The Wolfsonian-FIU

10TH ST

Biscayne Bay

9TH ST

COLLINS AVENUE

OCEAN DRIVE

Art Deco Welcome Center

Lummus Park

8TH ST

7TH ST

South Shore Hospital

WEST AVENUE

ALTON ROAD

LENOX AVENUE

MICHIGAN AVENUE

JEFFERSON AVENUE

MERIDAN AVENUE

EUCLID AVENUE

Parking Garage

6TH ST

Park Central Hotel

Downtown Miami, Airport, Parrot Jungle & Miami Children's Museum

5TH ST

Electrowave Park N Ride

4TH ST

Sanford L. Ziff Jewish Museum of Florida

ATLANTIC OCEAN

MACARTHUR CAUSEWAY

3RD ST

SOUTH POINTE

Causeway Island

2ND ST

Miami Beach Marina

ALTON ROAD

OCEAN DRIVE

1ST ST

Terminal Island

COMMERCE ST

First Street Beach

BISCAYNE BOULEVARD

South Pointe Tower

South Pointe Park

South Beach Pier

South Pointe Park

Government Cut

Fisher Island

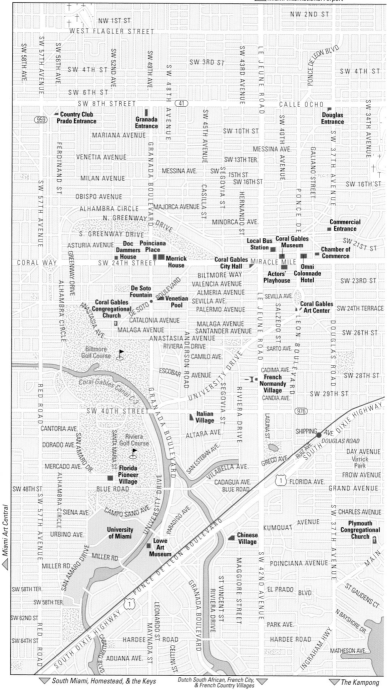

△ Miami International Airport

NW 2ND ST

NW 1ST ST
WEST FLAGLER STREET

SW 58TH AVE
SW 57TH AVENUE
SW 56TH AVE
SW 52ND AVE
SW 49TH AVE
SW 48TH AVENUE
SW 4TH ST
SW 3RD ST
SW 43RD AVENUE
LE JEUNE ROAD
PONCE DE LEON BLVD
SW 4TH ST

SW 4TH ST

SW 6TH ST

SW 8TH STREET
CALLE OCHO
SW 34TH AVENUE

(41)

(959)
● Country Club
Prado Entrance
■ Granada
Entrance
■ Douglas
Entrance

MARIANA AVENUE
SW 45TH AVENUE
SW 10TH ST
SW 40TH AVENUE
SW 37TH AVENUE
GALIANO STREET

VENETIA AVENUE
MESSINA AVE.
SW 13TH TER.

MILAN AVENUE
MESSINA AVE.
SW 15TH ST
SW 16TH ST
SW 16TH ST

OBISPO AVENUE
CASILLA ST.
HERNANDO ST.
SEGOVIA ST.

FERDINAND ST.
GRANADA BOULEVARD
ALHAMBRA CIRCLE
MAJORCA AVENUE
MINORCA AVE.

N. GREENWAY DRIVE
■ Commercial
Entrance

S. GREENWAY DRIVE
Local Bus ■ Coral Gables
Station ■ Museum
SW 21ST ST

ASTURIA AVENUE
Doc Poinciana
Dammers Place
■ Merrick
House
PONCE DE LEON BOULEVARD
■ Chamber of
Commerce

CORAL WAY
● House
Coral Gables ■
City Hall
MIRACLE MILE

GREENWAY DRIVE
SW 24TH STREET
BILTMORE WAY
Actors'
Playhouse
Omni ■
Colonnade
Hotel
SW 23RD ST

ALHAMBRA CIRCLE
De Soto
Fountain
VALENCIA AVENUE
ALMERIA AVENUE
SALZEDO ST.

Coral Gables
Congregational
Church
Venetian
Pool
SEVILLA AVE.
SEVILLA AVE.
Coral Gables ■
Art Center
SW 24TH TERRACE

CATALONIA AVENUE
PALERMO AVENUE

MALAGA AVENUE
MALAGA AVENUE
DOUGLAS ROAD
SW 26TH ST

ANASTASIA AVE.
SANTANDER AVENUE

ANDERSON ROAD
DE SOTO BOULEVARD
RIVIERA DRIVE

Biltmore
Golf Course
CAMILO AVE.

ESCOBAR AVENUE
CADIMA AVE.
SW 28TH ST

Coral Gables Canal C-3
UNIVERSITY DRIVE
French
Normandy
Village
SW 29TH ST

CANDIA AVE.

RED ROAD
SEGOVIA ST.
RIVIERA DRIVE
LAGUNA ST.
(976)
SOUTH DIXIE HIGHWAY

SW 40TH STREET
SHIPPING AVE.
DOUGLAS ROAD

CANTORIA AVE.
Italian
Village
GRECO AVE.
RIU AVE.
DAY AVENUE
Virrick
Park

DORADO AVE.
Riviera
Golf Course
ALTARA AVE.
FROW AVENUE

MERCADO AVE.
SAN AMARO DR.
SANTA MARIA ST.
SAN ESTEBAN AVE.
(1) FLORIDA AVE.
GRAND AVENUE

SW 48TH ST
■ Florida
Pioneer
Village
VILABELLA AVE.
SW 37TH AVENUE
SW CHARLES AVENUE

SIENA AVE.
BLUE ROAD
CADAGUA AVE.
KUMQUAT AVENUE
Plymouth ■
Congregational
Church

URBINO AVE.
CAMPO SANO AVE.
PARAISO AVE.
BLUE ROAD
Chinese
Village

MILLER RD.
University
of Miami
Lowe
Art
Museum
MAGGIORE STREET
POINCIANA AVENUE

MILLER RD.
PONCE DE LEON BOULEVARD
ST. VINCENT ST.
EL PRADO BLVD
MAIN

SW 58TH ST
SAN AMARO DRIVE
GRANADA BOULEVARD
ST GAUDENS CT

SW 58TH TER.
PARK AVE.
N BAYSHORE DR

SW 62ND ST
(1)
LEONARDO ST.
RIVIERA DRIVE
HARDEE ROAD

SW 64TH ST
RED ROAD
CARRILLO BLVD.
HARDEE ROAD
MATHESON AVE.

MAYNADA ST.
CELINI ST.
INGRAHAM HWY.

SOUTH DIXIE HIGHWAY
ADUANA AVE.

△ Miami Art Central

▽ South Miami, Homestead, & the Keys
▽ Dutch South African, French City,
& French Country Villages
▽ The Kampong

WEST FLAGLER STREET
WEST FLAGLER STREET
SW 1ST STREET
SW 1ST STREET
SW 3RD ST
SW 3RD STREET
SW 16TH AVE.
SW 14TH AVE.
SW 10TH AVENUE
SW 4TH STREET
22ND AVE. ROAD
SW 22ND AVENUE
SW 27TH ST
SW 6TH ST
SW 6TH ST
SW 12TH AVENUE
SW 8TH STREET
SW 8TH STREET
TAMIAMI TRAIL
41
SW 9TH ST
SW 17TH AVE.
SW 7TH STREET
LITTLE
HAVANA
SW 10TH ST
SW 11TH ST
SW 30TH AVENUE
SW 11TH ST
SW 11TH TER.
SW 13TH AVENUE
SW 14TH ST
SW 7TH AVENUE
SW 32ND AVENUE
SW 14TH ST
SW 24TH AVENUE
SW 16TH ST
SW 19TH AVENUE
SW 16TH AVENUE
SW 5TH AVENUE
SW 4TH AVENUE
SW 17TH ST
SW 19TH ST
SW 19TH ST
SW 20TH STREET
SW 27TH AVENUE
SW 22ND AVENUE
SW 22ND STREET
SW 3RD AVENUE
VIZCAYA
972 CORAL WAY
SW 22ND TERRACE
SW 23RD ST
Museum of
Science and
Space Transit
Planetarium
Villa
Vizcaya
SW 31ST AVENUE
SW 24TH ST
SW 17TH AVE.
SW 17TH DR.
SW 24TH TERRACE
BAY
HEIGHTS
9
SW 25TH ST
1
SOUTH DIXIE HIGHWAY
La Ermita
de la Caridad
del Cobre
ALATKA ST.
BAYSHORE DRIVE
SW 27TH ST
COCONUT
GROVE
SW 28TH ST
Mercy
Hospital
MICANOPY AVENUE
Grove
Key
MAIN HIGHWAY
SWANSON AVE.
TIGERTAIL AVENUE
BIRD ROAD
SHIPPING AVENUE
Fair Isle
MCDONALD STREET
BAYSHORE DRIVE
Kennedy
Park
Coco
Walk
Streets of
Mayfair
Munroe
Park
Dinner
Key
Coconut Grove
Playhouse
Coconut Grove
Exhibition Center
City
Hall
HIGHWAY
ROYAL RD.
Peacock
Park
The
Barnacle
Picnic
Island
Biscayne
Bay
Downtown
N
0   500 yds

COCONUT GROVE AND CORAL GABLES

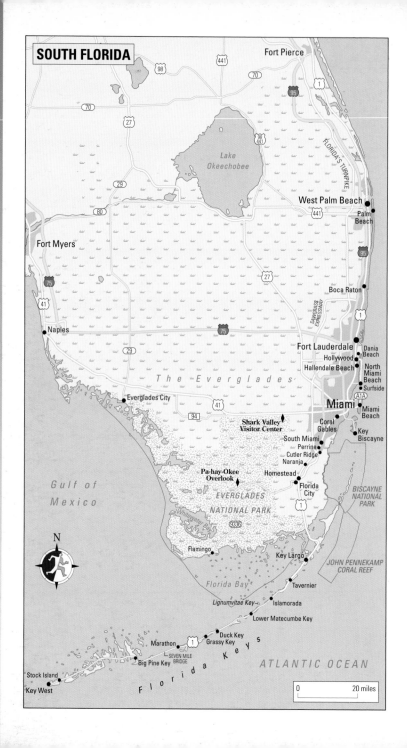